The Tragic Deception:
Marx Contra Engels

**Twentieth
Century
Series
#8**

Twentieth Century Series

Lyman H. Legters
Series Editor

German National Socialism, 1919–1945
Martin Broszat

We Survived: Fourteen Histories of the Hidden and Hunted of Nazi Germany
Eric H. Boehm

International Relations Research: Problems of Evaluation and Advancement
E. Raymond Platig

Native Fascism in the Successor States, 1918–1945
Peter F. Sugar, Editor

The Bolshevik Seizure of Power
S. P. Melgunov
S. G. Pushkarev, Editor

The Czechoslovak Reform Movement, 1968: Proceedings of a Conference Held at Reading University 12–17th July 1971
V. V. Kusin, Editor

The Tragic Deception: Marx Contra Engels
Norman Levine

The Tragic Deception: Marx Contra Engels

Norman Levine

Introduction: Lyman H. Legters

Twentieth Century Series
Lyman H. Legters, Editor

Clio Books

Oxford Santa Barbara

Library of Congress Catalog Card Number 74-14193
ISBN Clothbound Edition 0-87436-192-3
ISBN Paperbound Edition 0-87436-193-1

American Bibliographical Center—Clio Press, Inc.
2040 Alameda Padre Serra
Santa Barbara, California

European Bibliographical Center—Clio Press
Woodside House, Hinksey Hill
Oxford OX1 5BE, England

Text design by Shelly Lowenkopf
Jacket design by Scott Campbell
Composed by Datagraphics, Inc.
Printed and bound by R. R. Donnelley
and Sons Co., Crawfordsville, Ind.

To My Mother and My Father,
Alice and Max Levine

Contents

Acknowledgments/ ix
Introduction by Lyman H. Legters/ xi
Foreword/ xiii
1. The Marxian View of Nature/ 1
2. The Transcendence of Democracy/ 14
3. Toward a Philosophical Anthropology/ 29
4. Marx as a Jacobin/ 43
5. The Dialectics of Revolution in the Nineteenth Century/ 61
6. Dialectical Naturalism as a Philosophy of History/ 84
7. The Young Engels: 1839–1842/ 107
8. The Origin of Engels's Communism/ 123
9. The Foundation of Engels's Metaphysics/ 140
10. The Origins of Economic Determinism/ 157
11. Scientific Socialism as National Messianism/ 180
12. Scientific Socialism as German Ethnocentrism/ 200
13. Communism as Industrial Puritanism/ 211
14. The Dutiful Disciple and the Exploitative Master/ 228
Index/ 247

Acknowledgments

THE IDEA OF this book first came to me while I was on the faculty at De Pauw University, Greencastle, Indiana. It is a product of the student movement of the late nineteen sixties. The students at that time were eager for a knowledge of Marx and in response to their needs I organized a course on Marxism. My involvement in the study of Marx has not ceased since that time. The Vietnamese War, and its concomitant effects upon the whole of society, was a radicalizing experience.

Every writer benefits through an exchange of ideas and a sympathetic ear. I am especially indebted to Professor Clifton Phillips of De Pauw University, who listened long and patiently, oftentimes late into the night, while the major ideas of my thesis were first articulated. My thanks also to Professor Robert Calvert who also listened, not sympathetically, but critically. He was a disbeliever, but I gained much in the process of overcoming this particular negation. It would be an injustice not to mention Jim Martindale, Head Librarian at De Pauw University. Upon my request he purchased the complete works of Marx and Engels and without those books my initial research would have been impossible.

Once in open seas, other helping hands were there throughout this long journey. Professor Minna Falk, Emeritus Professor of New York University, who launched a graduate student, and convinced him that he had a debt to words; Professor A. William Salomone, The University of Rochester, who first opened a young man's mind to the "idea of history"; Professor George Iggers, State University of New York at Buffalo, a generous and talented human being who gave indispensable encouragement to the unfolding of an outlandish conception; Professor Eugene Genovese, The University of Rochester, for the example he has set of a tough-minded and unflinching Marxist scholarship. Professor Robert Tucker, Princeton University, a good friend, whose book *Philosophy and Myth in Karl Marx* opened a whole new vista for me in the perception of Marx; Professor Lyman Legters, The University of Washington, who first read an essay of mine and made me face the challenge of producing a book.

I was fortunate enough to have several summers devoted to research. I am indebted to the American Philosophical Society whose stipend allowed me to dedicate the summer of 1971 to research. I am also indebted to the University of Maryland Baltimore County Graduate Council, particularly Professor Joseph Mulligan, for supporting my research during the summer of 1972. During both these summers I was in Amsterdam at the International Institute of Social History acquainting myself with the *exzerpte* of Marx. H. P. Harstick of the Institute was singularly helpful.

The secretarial staff of the History Department at the University of Maryland Baltimore County provided invaluable assistance. Without the help of Mary Dietrich, Pat Gist, and Jo Anne Palmore this book would still be a handwritten manuscript.

Lloyd Garrison of ABC-Clio Press has produced a finished and professional text.

Of course, there was Rose. That is, there was encouragement, forbearance and laughter.

Introduction

EACH HISTORICAL ERA, including our own contemporary one, has a characteristic set of issues—events or series of events, underlying socioeconomic tendencies, and filiations of ideas—that require more than ordinary explanatory exertion. Taken together these central issues may be regarded as the problematics of an epoch; individually, however much the views of successive generations of commentators may vary, they are likely to be spoken of as pivotal or crucial elements in any coherent understanding of their era.

The Twentieth Century Series has focused largely on such pivotal events, tendencies, and ideas in its aim of making a contribution to the understanding of our own age. Accordingly, the books in this series emphasize interpretation rather than detailed account, analysis and insight rather than lengthy exposition. With few exceptions, the volumes in this series have dealt with the more puzzling problems of our time, hence on those that have evoked a large body of frequently conflicting explanation. National Socialism in Germany, Fascism, the Bolshevik Revolution, the outbreak of World War I are all challenging issues of this kind. So too, it is hardly necessary to add, is Marxism.

At first glance it might of course be supposed that Marxism, and especially the intellectual relationship obtaining between Marx and Engels, belongs properly to the nineteenth century. However, one of the defining features of ideologically informed social movements is that they seek to change as well as to explain social reality, and this necessarily entails—for those movements that survive at all—some projection into the future. Marxism happens to be *par excellence* the intellectual and social movement that has remained a live option for generations beyond the time of its original formation, a fact that is both the emblem of its success and the explanation for the wide variety of viewpoints that now, almost a century after Marx's death, claim him as their authority. It follows that any serious inquiry into ambiguities or uncertainties in the origins of Marxian teaching has a decided bearing on both intellectual and practical concerns of our own era.

Perhaps the greatest obstacle to constructive interpretation of Marxism in the United States has been the accident that we learned of Marx, so to speak, via Lenin. Marxism impinged on North American consciousness on a large scale first with the Bolshevik Revolution and then with the great power conflict that followed World War II. For most Americans this meant two things: that Marxism appeared as a threat and that alternate understandings within the Marxian tradition were overshadowed by the Soviet version. In effect we conceded the Soviet claim to Marxian orthodoxy. And it has taken us a long time to find our way back to the intellectual origins of Marxism or even to the unbroken West European tradition of critical Marxian thought and social action.

It was that European Marxian tradition that gave rise to the first serious examinations of differences between Marx and Engels. Professor Norman Levine, by relying fully on the original texts rather than on the often irrelevant layers of hostile "refutations," has in this book aligned himself with that serious variety of Marxian explication and, at the same time, continued an intellectual discussion that began with Lukács. He thus joins a company of more recent investigators of the Marx-Engels relationship that includes George Lichtheim, Eric Hobsbawm, David McLellan, and Helmut Fleischer. The point of including his study in the Twentieth Century Series is not that he and the others named would necessarily agree but that Professor Levine, besides being serious and scholarly in his analysis, propounds a viewpoint that deserves to be heard in a discussion that is far from being finished.

Lyman H. Legters, Editor
Twentieth Century Series

Seattle, Washington

Foreword

THIS BOOK IS intended to shed light on the destiny of Marxist thought in the 19th and 20th Century. It upholds the tradition of Marxism as naturalistic humanism, as negative *praxis,* against those who falsely represented Marxism as mechanistic materialism and social positivism. I propose to restate the creativity and applicability of Marxist theory. That tactic is simply stated but its execution is complex. Those elements of the Marxist tradition, many of them erroneously attributed to Marx by others, which are dogmatic, sterile—indeed distorted—must be stripped and disentangled from core Marxism. Essential Marxism must be recaptured from both the sins of history and friends.

In the contemporary world regardless of political denomination, East or West, a global society has emerged. That society is technological, bureaucratic, and centralist. It is dominated by the ethos of instrumental and functional rationality. Marxist scholarship can best respond to these unique sociohistorical conditions by jettisoning those aspects of the Marxist tradition which in the socialist and communist world directly lead to these alienating and exploitative conditions. By penetrating to the Marxism of Marx, Marxist scholarship can unearth a body of theory which is both relevant critique and a radical negation of the dehumanizing aspects of the contemporary world. It will bring to the surface a partially lost, certainly obscured, core of Marxist thought capable of reviewing radicalism and thus equipping the left with renewed philosophical and methodological viability. This book is dedicated to this task of adaptation and renewal.

The pivotally important theme in this book is the separation of Marx and Engels. The central concept is that major differences of thought existed between Marx and Engels. In effect this book argues that two divergent determinations—two divergent modalities—of a similar corpus of theory emerged. That modality which was inherent to Marx will hereafter be referred to as Marxism; and that modality which was inherent to Engels will hereafter be referred to as Engelsism.

Marx and Engels assigned different weights and densities to various aspects of a similar body of knowledge. The weights and densities assigned corresponded to the innate inclination of mind of the two men, to their inbred logical presuppositions. The cumulative effect of these different insights and densities gave rise to the divergent and unique modalities of thought represented by each. The totality of the concentrations gave rise to individual forms of perception and evaluation.

I am describing the effect and consequence of a mental filter. I am describing mechanisms similar to two chemical solutions through which an image of the world must pass—solutions composed of divergent ingredients of dissimilar concentrations. Clearly the image of the world will be presented in two different modalities as they pass through these unique solutions.

Furthermore, and as a consequence of the counterposing of Marx and Engels, I maintain that the misinterpretations of Marxism began with Engels. In spite of the admitted areas of agreement between Marx and Engels, these pages show Engels as the first revisionist to distort and misrepresent the ideas of Marx. That tradition of Marxism which became mechanistic materialism, social positivism, instrumental rationality and the morality of the Puritan work ethic and self-denial in the dress of socialist productivity, found its point of origination, its genesis, with Engels.

I have arrived at this conclusion independently yet I note that a creative generation of Marxist scholars perceived the contradiction between Marx's naturalism and Engels's mechanistic materialism during the 1920s. The published works of György Lukács, Karl Korsch, and Antonio Gramsci reveal that these men were aware that Engels distorted Marxism by applying the dialectic to nature. They all recognized that the dialectic was a methodology, not a law of nature, that history was a record of human activities within given social conditions and not a verification of positivist laws. The creative Marxism of Lukács, Korsch, and Gramsci was buried for a time under Stalin's oppressive totalitarianism and it was not revived until the 1960s. Regretfully, those men did not pursue their perceptions and insights to a logical conclusion so their work failed to alter the prevailing interpretation among their contemporaries, i.e., that Marx and Engels spoke with a single voice.

Lenin, Stalin, Trotsky—Mao in the contemporary world—all held that view and recent scholarship has generally tended to reinforce the theme of essential unanimity between Marx and Engels. The theme was articulated by Franz Mehring in *Karl Marx*, Gustav Meyer in his biography of *Friedrich Engels* and by Isaiah Berlin in his *Karl Marx, The History of Socialist Thought by* C.D.H. Cole and *To the Finland Station* by Edmund Wilson are based on the assumption of unanimity and the French school of structural Marxism (Louis Althusser) adopts that assumption as doctrine. *The Tragic Deception: Marx Contra Engels* is the only attempt to investigate an opposing view in depth.

My goal in these pages is both to extend the work of Lukács, Korsch, and Gramsci, as well as to add new and as yet unseen perspectives to the Marx-Engels problem. The new contributions made by this book arise from the attempt to explain the origins as well as the consequences of the difference between Marx and Engels concerning the philosophy of nature. It is not content to state, as Korsch, Gramsci and Lukács did, that Engels erred in applying dialectics to natural phenomena, but seek to uncover what in Engels's philosophical understanding, what in Engels's intellectual predisposition, led him to attempt this synthesis. Furthermore, once the reasons for the difference between Marx and Engels over the philosophy of nature are clarified, the implications of these differences will be traced to their divergent views of the future communist society, and of the evolutionary process of history. Lastly, I will take note of the absence of a philosophical anthropology in Engels. Unlike Marx, Engels was not influenced by Feuerbachian naturalism and consequently was not only led to define communism differently than Marx, but also the nature of the State and Bureaucracy.

We are observing the root experience of revisionism. We are audience to the process by which a disciple revises the teachings of the teacher. We are watching this irremovable subjectivity, these filters of presupposition, bring forth Marxism and Engelsism.

Engels was the first revisionist, the point of origin of the bifurcation of the world Marxist movement. To approach the history of socialism as reflecting two modalities, two centripetal forces, Marxism and Engelsism, does immediate violence to traditional forms of understanding the history of socialism. But such an approach is absolutely necessary if we are to comprehend how 20th century socialism was interpreted as social positivism, how 20th century socialism came to view the communist society as at once centralist and disciplinarian. It was the influence and prestige of Engels which predisposed the second generation of Marxists, like Kautsky and Lenin, to envision communism as a kind of factory puritanism, and history as a cosmologically determined process.

There was a clear and steady evolution from Engels to Lenin to Stalin. Lenin belonged to the great age of transmission. He was a member of the second generation of Marxists who transmitted the teachings of Marx from their 19th century setting to their 20th century environment. Lenin's pivotal figure contributed significantly to the belief that Marx-Engels composed one doctrine, one unified system of thought. Engels lived until 1895, he cast an imposing shadow, and Lenin referred to Engels as often as he did Marx. Bolshevism thus certified that Marx and Engels were of one mind, of one voice. One pillar of Bolshevism was the inherent unity of Marx and Engels.

Lenin, however, was a problematic, schizoid figure. Lenin defended communism as a centralist society, defined it as a disciplinarian society, equated communism with technological growth, at times affirmed that the laws of history necessitated the growth of capitalism throughout the world, and he wrote *Materialism and Empirico-Criticism.* In all of these actions he was a disciple of Friedrich Engels. Lenin's definition of communism was a perpetuation of the Puritan work-ethic. His concentration upon industrially modernizing Russian society and his stress upon increased productivity, enlarged consumption, and expanded acquisition all derive from Engels. Leaving aside the totalitarian aspect of Soviet Communism, which in no way derives from either Engels or Marx, the rigidity, the Calvinist repressiveness of Soviet Russia was fully foreshadowed in the writings of Engels and Lenin. Soviet communism has been basically responsible for overlooking the humanistic, creative, spontaneous aspects of Marx. It has contributed to the immediately pressing contemporary problems of technological inhumanity and puritan acquisitiveness: in short, egoistic greed.

Stalin carried this tradition of Engels and the Engelsian side of Lenin to its extreme. Stalinism was a fusion of political authoritarianism and ideological uniformity. Stalin imposed this doctrinal dogmatism as ruthlessly as his demand for political subservience. The ideas of historical inevitability and social disciplinarianism were important buttresses for Stalinist totalitarianism. Thus, the period of creative Marxism in the 1920s succumbed to Stalinist rigidity and Stalin was representative of the splintering and division of the world Marxist movement. When Marxism bifurcated, Stalin symbolized the caesarian line of this mutation. Engels was not caesaropapist. Yet it is necessary to return to the point of origination, to Engels, in order to understand Stalin as a product of history.

As indicated above, there was a Marxian side to Lenin. Lenin's *Philosophic Notebooks* was in the Marxian mode. Lenin's view of the revolutionary role of the peasants, when he pointed out the progressive, anti-imperialist role of nationalism, when he described the tactical significance of guerrilla warfare, when he stressed that a full revolution must involve the seizure of power, he emerged as a true advocate of Marx. Lenin was a genius of political strategy. At crucial points, however, Lenin deviated from the political formulas of Marx. He misunderstood what Marx meant by "the dictatorship of the proletariat," and he misunderstood what Marx felt was the relationship between the social and political aspects of a true revolution. Lenin also grossly underestimated the need to continue a policy of coalition with the non-Bolshevik left after his assumption of power. Where Lenin revised the political equations of Marx, he did so in favor of a Blanquist revolutionary elitism, a voluntarism traditional to the

Russian intelligentsia. In addition, Lenin's thinking had some dormant totalitarian features.

Nevertheless, Marx and Lenin were in basic agreement on the necessity of acquiring political power in the process of revolution. Marx did not feel that one must wait for the inevitable tides of history to produce a full-blown capitalism before indulging in insurrection. If not the communist revolution, he considered some form of progressive, socialist revolution to be possible in China, or Asiatic Russia. Furthermore, on the basis of the 1848 revolution, Marx realized that there would be times when the proletariat would not have sufficient strength to initiate insurrections. In those cases Marx surmised that the proletariat would be forced to ally with bourgeois, petit bourgeois, or peasant forces. Later on, the revolution must become permanent. That is, when the conditions were ripe the proletariat must break with these opportunistic coalitions and proceed to develop its own communist revolution. The Marxian side of Lenin was the revolutionary tradition, the side of critical political *praxis,* of negating and transcending activist behavior.

The duality of Lenin's thought returns us to a consideration of the diverse traditions of socialism, Marxism and Engelsism. My bias is apparent. I consider that Marx had the most creative, imaginative, and relevant mind. But I do not intend to set up Engels as a straw man. I want to salvage what is still relevant in Marx but I do not ascribe all that is past and outmoded to Engels. In my attempt to resurrect Marx I do not intend to crucify Engels.

Nothing in these pages is intended to deny the contribution of Engels. He made a personal commitment to Marx of immense proportions. More than anyone else, Engels sustained and nurtured the socialist movement after the death of Marx. Engels made a personal and individually unique contribution to socialist thought, and his literature played an important role in western Europe before World War I which was destined to have great historical influence, and which formed the ideological basis of scriptural Bolshevism. Engels achieved greatness. However, in judging and evaluating Engels and his contributions I conclude that his mind was of a second order when compared to that of Marx.

In truth, Engels is not disadvantaged in this comparison with Marx. Rather, Marx suffers historically from his entanglement with Engels. The search for the essential Marx is a critical function and so is the search for the essential Engels and both men gain by being seen separately. When seen in their own terms, they must be judged in their own terms. When the critical function indicates that the thoughts of Engels became the basis of Soviet ideology it is not to use Engels as a straw man, it is to state a historical fact.

Indeed, it is inexplicable to assume there was an inclusive unanimity of viewpoint between Marx and Engels, or any two human beings. That assumption would belie human subjectivity. Philosophically and psychologically no two people perceive or understand objects in exactly the same way. Thus to say that Marx and Engels disagreed is simply to assert the irreducible existential element of human subjectivity.

Both men looked at a common body of knowledge and inevitably came to differing interpretations. The thesis that there are two modalities, two gravitational fields, one Marxism and the other Engelsism, is simply a restatement of the argument and consequences of human subjectivity. This book focuses upon that domain of personal viewpoint, and explores it in depth.

One

The Marxian View of Nature

AT FIRST GLANCE it may seem strange to begin a discussion of Marx with an analysis of his concept of nature. Communist doctrine is mostly concerned with society, economics, politics, and revolution. Viewed from this perspective, Marx's idea of nature would have little to offer in penetrating to the essential principles of communism. In reality, however, an understanding of Marx's view of nature and man is central to a proper understanding of communism. Unless we instruct ourselves as to Marx's vision of man, his nature, and his place in nature we can never hope to comprehend communism in its full magnitude. We must first learn how Marx perceived human behavior and action before we can truly fathom his description of the historical process.

The understanding that Marx had of the concept of nature can be divided into four aspects: (1) the totality of nature, (2) sensate nature, (3) insensate nature, (4) sensate and insensate nature as history.[1]

(1) Nature for Marx was a totality. It included a conscious, active, sensate, modifying part—the human species—and an unconscious, inorganic, insensate, inactive part—that part of nature external to man. The two, however, could not be separated. They were both parts of an encompassing unity and process. To speak of man was by definition to speak of man's productive *praxis,* his modification and influence on insensate nature. To speak of insensate nature was by definition to reflect on how and in what fashion this passive material was altered and humanized by the activity of men. The stress was always on the active, practical activity of men, the changes wrought by them in their environment, or their attempts to extract from their surroundings objects that fulfilled their needs.

Insensate nature in Marx's writings was never discussed in isolation, never discussed as an agency that had laws and mechanisms peculiar to itself. Marx never treated the inorganic world as having a separate and distinct existence apart from man, as having an essence and metaphysics of its own. Marx did not permit himself to study chemistry, physics, or biology, or to analyze the structure of these sciences, and then proceed to describe the being of the inorganic world. The Marxian vision was always on those areas where the sensate and insensate parts of nature interchanged. Marx focused on the socioeconomic world, because it was there that the sensate and insensate commingled, mutually influenced each other, fused.[2]

Marx thus pictured an essentially complementary and interdependent relationship between man and external nature. In fact, this interdependent, interrelated relationship was exactly what Marx referred to as the "being of nature."[3] Men were compelled to express their naturalness, compelled to complete nature by the very fact that their needs could only be answered by the things with which insensate nature had surrounded them. The being of nature was a whole in which its human, i.e., conscious part must of necessity be gratified by the inorganic part in mutual complementation between sentient and insentient halves.

(2) Human nature for Marx was sensate nature, or natural being. This meant for Marx that the gratification of men's physical needs could only be gained by something outside of man. Men suffered from hunger and thirst. The gratification of this hunger and thirst could only be achieved by water and food. But the gratification of human needs was not solely answered by complementary inorganic things outside the individual. The fulfillment of human needs could also be accomplished by another human being. The needs for love, friendship, sex, cooperative social production could only be assuaged by another human subject.

In his essay "Free Human Production," Marx analyzed how two individuals mutually satisfied each other by means of the productive process. In the act of production, the individual gratified his need to objectify himself through labor and, through the thing made, fulfilled a corresponding need in another human being. Also, the individual who had produced an object of need had reconfirmed the positive relation of the other to the entire human species, and conversely reconfirmed his own social nature because he had produced for another.[4]

Another aspect of human sensate nature, according to Marx, was consciousness. On its most primitive level, consciousness simply referred to certain qualities of natural human faculties. Humans were conscious because the eye, ear, and skin had as one of their attributes the capacity to be sensuous, the ability to receive sensations, that is, to experience.[5] Consciousness for Marx, then, could be equated with sensuousness, i.e., awareness of impressions.

Marx was attempting to surmount the Hegelian and idealist reduction of life to pure consciousness.[6] If Hegel was right, then human alienation would reside in the estrangement of consciousness from itself, and human history would reflect the evolution of consciousness in time and space. Marx was affirming, on the other hand, that natural being was a precondition of consciousness, that being existed prior to thought.[7] From this perspective, Marx could proceed to argue that alienation referred to the separation of the natural being from the object of its gratification and that history was the phenomenology of human *praxis*, the forms of society brought into existence by human activity in order to satisfy and reproduce life.

Consciousness also permitted man to see that he was a species being. Men were aware that they belonged to a human species, because they became aware that all men share in common the attribute of being conscious of their activity as object. Species being, the ability of the species man to receive sensation, was then the necessary precondition for the awareness that man belonged to a species, that he belonged to a group of natural beings who were delineated by their ability to be conscious of their activity.[8]

Species being was constituted by a group of anthropological characteristics, such as the above-mentioned sensuousness and consciousness. The human species was also characterized by a system of needs. Men required water, food, and shelter to perpetuate their physical existence. They possessed feelings, passions and were thus subject to suffering. The species had an objective nature, because it could only gratify both its physical and psychological needs through objects outside itself.

For Marx, these needs formed the ground of social existence. In order to meet these needs, men had to organize or socialize their activities; that is, social existence already existed as an attribute of these needs, for it was only in society that these needs could be gratified. Need was thus a motivating force in history. Therefore, all history was in part the organizations, social and economic, that men imposed on the species in order to better answer their needs.

Lastly, activity was also an anthropological characteristic of the species. Men were active. They had to produce the conditions for their continued existence. Man's activity, i.e., his productive labor, not only modified the world external to him, but also in turn modified man. By constantly changing socioeconomic forms men also changed, not their species being, since that was a naturalistic determinant, but their social consciousness and their behavior. Species activity thus implied that the species was adaptive, that its social and cultural forms of existence were capable of endless reconstruction.

(3) Insensate nature was both the condition of human labor and the source of human affirmation. As the condition of human labor, insensate nature supplied man with materiality. It was the substance in which human objectification assumed form. Labor could only be fulfilled, could only realize itself in an object. Insensate nature was the basis of mediation, the

materiality that afforded labor the possibility to be objectified.[9] Insensate nature was the source of human affirmation, because it possessed qualities that activated and confirmed the sensuous capacities of men.[10]

In this area as well, Marx rejected Hegel. For Hegel, nature was alienated mind. The existence of consciousness in the external world was thus a *de facto* condition of self-estrangement. Nature was a force of negation, it existed in direct opposition to consciousness. On the other hand, Marx did not see the relation between sensate and insensate phases of nature as one of *de facto* alienation, but one of *de facto* reciprocation. Insensate nature was not estranged human consciousness but rather the positive affirmation of species life. Insensate nature was not negation and opposition, but rather one source of confirming human existence, one pole of the harmonious continuity between sensate and insensate phases. Natural being for Marx was not a tragic confrontation between consciousness and negation, but rather the existence of interdependence between the two modes of the being of nature.

(4) Industrial production, the change of material forms, had altered the condition of insensate nature itself. In this sense, insensate nature had become anthropological; that is, it bore the stamp of human *praxis.* The part of insensate nature that became involved in human activity and production was historicized, for it was continuously modified by human *praxis* in the course of time. External nature was humanized, for it was shaped in accordance with conscious human needs and projects.[11]

Thus, insensate nature had two sides, the historical and the nonhistorical. History for Marx was synonymous with the autogenesis of the species through its own activity. Therefore, only that part of insensate nature that was humanized could also be historicized. Laws of chemistry and physics could produce change and process, but history couldn't, because it lacked a conscious human agent or purposeful *praxis.*

Clearly, the advancement of knowledge implied the ever increasing humanization of external nature. The more men intervened in nature, assumed control of natural laws, the more nature became anthropological, and the more it was put to species purposes. Control of atomic energy, the victory of space travel meant the humanization and the historicizing of dimensions of the natural world beyond the imagination of previous generations.

Marx's view concerning the history of sensate nature led him to an ontological view of human nature: Being was process. In order to clarify this assertion, a distinction must be made between two aspects of human nature. Previous paragraphs have discussed the naturalistic substrata. The human species was constituted of passions, feelings, and sensuous needs. These were not subject to change, but formed an unchanging naturalistic substructure.

Marx believed that the human senses had been refined, "cultivated,"[12] but not created by history. The humanization of nature, e.g., the production of better musical instruments of more varied and more distinct types, had in turn improved and intensified the corresponding sensual nature of man. By objectifying himself, by making objects, man had also further humanized himself, that is, added to his enjoyment and appreciation of experience.

Only consciousness could have a history, and it was by means of consciousness that the ontological nature of man expressed itself.[13] The objects that men produced not only cultivated men's sensual existence, but also altered their mode of consciousness and thus their rational behavior. The different technologies that *praxis* brought forth, the different socio-economic structures produced by human labor, also brought forth different modes of consciousness and different forms of relating to the world. Man thus created his own consciousness, his self. Man was a being in process, a being whose nature it was to project to the future.[14]

If ontologically man was process, then history could be nothing but the manifestation of that process, the continuous self-creation of man by man. When Marx wrote that "man has his own process of genesis, history,"[15] he meant that since the essence of man was process, history itself could only be the autogenesis of man.[16]

The preceding analysis of Marx's conception of nature is based almost exclusively on the manuscripts of 1844. This does not mean, however, that Marx's conception that man was a conscious, active agent was limited to this period of his life. Throughout his life Marx adhered to the idea that human activity was the "energizing principle" of socioeconomic life. Indeed, Marx approached the problem in different ways through the different periods of his life. He emphasized different aspects, but the underlying theme of human *praxis* remained constant.

In 1841, at the age of twenty-three, Marx completed his doctoral dissertation on Democritus and Epicurus. By comparing these ancient atomists, Marx distinguished between two types of materialism. Dogmatic and absolutist, Democritus affirmed that atoms were real, objective building blocks of nature, that their joining together was pure accident, and that all human and natural processes were determined by their fortuitous cohesions. Both a sceptic and an empiricist, Epicurus looked upon atomic theory not as objectively true, but as one possible category, a model by which to interpret the world around us. A subjectivist and an experimentalist, Epicurus wished to use the notion of atoms as an abstract principle through which one could explore nature.[17]

Of the two atomists, Marx favored the Epicurean approach. He did so because Epicurus did not assert the metaphysical priority of matter, as did Democritus, but rather Epicurus looked upon atomic theory as one mode for consciousness to approach reality. The Epicurean approach was based on the idea that consciousness was the abstract universal, and made of thought the "energizing principle" of the world.[18] It is perfectly consistent, therefore, for Marx to have begun his dissertation with a note of veneration for Prometheus. "The knowledge of Prometheus . . . is his own self-awareness, his own self-consciousness as the highest godhead. There is nothing equal to him."[19] The emphasis, at this point of Marx's development, was on consciousness, on human idea. This was part of the rationalistic bias of the Hegelian left.[20]

In the 1844 manuscripts, there was both continuity and change. While the basic theme (human activity) was the same, we find Marx in a more naturalistic frame of mind. The stress in the 1844 manuscripts was not on human consciousness, in Hegelian fashion, but on man's anthropological nature in Feuerbachian fashion. Nevertheless, even though an anthropological perspective was added, Marx still pictured man as active and modifying. Man was not presented as consciously criticizing reality but as consciously and purposefully making objects and producing the conditions for his self-perpetuation.

The theme of revolutionary *praxis* was evident in the "Theses on Feuerbach." Here Marx was not referring to nature, but to society. Marx wanted to change the world.[21] It was only by changing social relationships by practical-critical activity that human changes could be brought about. The shift between the manuscripts of 1844 and the "Theses on Feuerbach" was a shift from the attempt to predicate an anthropological reciprocity between man and nature, to an assertion that revolutionary activism was necessary if man was to transcend himself. Marx moved from philosophic speculation about anthropological nature to preliminary speculations about the nature of political radicalism.

In the later writings, such as the *Grundrisse* (Foundations of a Critique of Political Economy), Marx was deeply immersed in his economic studies. Understandably, then, even though the basic theme of human activity remained persistent, it again appeared in a different form. Concerned in 1858 with how human beings provided for their existence, Marx interpreted human activity at that point as labor, that is, as the form of activity that produced the necessities of life. Labor, the making of things necessary for human subsistence, replaced the political, revolutionizing *praxis* of the "Theses on Feuerbach," as well as the activity of objectification and affirmation of the 1844 manuscripts.

Within the *Grundrisse,* the Marxian man is recognizable, but altered. His basic concern is no longer the affirmation of his species being, but the reproduction of himself and his society. A shift had taken place. The basic regard was no longer natural ontology, but rather economic productivity. "Lastly, production also is not only a particular production. Rather, it is always a certain social body, a social subject, which is active in a greater or sparser totality of branches of production."[22] Labor produced food and thus the reproduction of man. Labor produced machinery and thus reproduced the relations of society. In the later writings of Marx, human activity was seen as the instrument, i.e., labor, by which man perpetuated his personal and social existence.[23]

Not only was his concept of human activity modified but also his concept of nature. In *Kapital* nature appeared as a laboratory. Reflecting Marx's shift of emphasis from philosophical anthropology to economics, nature appeared in *Kapital* as that which offered the materials from which humans could produce food, build machinery, and experiment. Marx wrote:

> He makes use of the mechanical, physical, and chemical properties of things as means of exerting power over other things, and in order to make these other things subservient to his aims. Leaving out of consideration the gathering of ready-made means of subsistence, such as fruits, for which purpose man's own bodily organs suffice him as the instruments of labor, the object of which the worker takes direct control is not the subject matter of labor but the instrument of labor. Thus nature becomes an instrument of his activities, an instrument with which he supplements his own bodily organs adding a cubit and more to his stature, scripture notwithstanding. Just as the earth is his primitive larder so, likewise, is it his primitive tool-house.[24]

In the third volume of *Kapital,* Marx again stated, as he did throughout his work, that nature itself was never the source of value, that is, insensate nature in itself was passive. Whatever had value in the human social universe received that value from the productive modifications of man effected through his labor. In the more mature work of Marx, nature did not appear as that which affirmed the human essence. The more mature Marx was concerned with the economic reproduction of man. Thus, nature was seen as the condition of human labor. Nature was seen as a vast storehouse, an endless reservoir of dumb material upon which human labor could be expended in the process of reproducing life.

Finally, in the later Marx the notion of history was also modified to reflect his new concern with economics. By 1858 history, for Marx, had become the story of the expansion of social productive powers.[25] In 1844 Marx had seen history as the story of the humanization of nature through human *praxis;* in 1858 he saw history as the record of the various stages humanity had passed through in order to conquer economic want. In 1844 history was a reflection of human objectification; in the *Grundrisse* history was a reflection of industrial capacity.

Thus, at the end of his life Marx continued to see man as the active agent in the world, and nature as essentially passive. However, this basic theme was modified as it traversed the several periods of Marx's career. In his later work, *praxis* presented itself as labor, nature as a laboratory, and history as the escalation of productivity. Nevertheless, in *Kapital* Marx again reaffirmed the basic theme he originally expressed in 1844: "It is the independent movement of private property become conscious of itself; modern industry as Self."[26]

MARX DID NOT write at length on the philosophy of nature. What he did write on the subject, however, indicated that Marx had a clear grasp of his own place in the history of materialism. Aligning himself with the tradition of Democritus, Epicurus, and Locke, Marx referred to his philosophy of nature as "sensuous materialism." Most of what Marx wrote on the subject is found in *The Holy Family*.

Marx distinguished between two eighteenth-century materialist trends: One originated with Descartes; the other with Locke. Marx referred to Cartesianism as "mechanical materialism." Although Marx was aware that Cartesian science was a rejection of seventeenth-century metaphysics, he was also aware that Cartesian physics represented a form of materialism that he disliked.[27] Cartesian materialism did not lead to socialism or communism. Rather, in the person of Hobbes in particular, Cartesian materialism crossed with empiricism and the result was disastrous.[28]

In short, Marx was opposed to mechanical materialism. He inferred that mathematical materialism was simply a continuation of seventeenth-century metaphysics in a slightly altered form. This kind of materialism was hostile to humanity, because based on its geometrical approach to nature it drew several negative conclusions regarding man. These antihuman conclusions were: (1) Man is certain only of his own existence; (2) human feelings are merely mechanical motions; (3) man is subject to the same laws as nature; (4) what is good is simply the objects of human impulses; (5) freedom and force are the same.[29]

Clearly, Marx rejected mechanistic materialism because it was fatalistic. It tended to reduce man to an object of nature, to make man passive, something that simply reacted to larger natural forces beyond his control. In Marx's own words, this was not what he meant by "humanity." To be human for Marx obviously implied that man was not subject to mere force, but was free, that is, "through his positive power to assert his true individuality,"[30] he could shape his surroundings in accordance with his humanity.

It was the materialism of the school of Locke that led directly to socialism and communism. This tradition "developed the teaching of materialism as the teaching of real humanism and the logical basis of communism."[31] Obviously, rather than being "hostile to humanity," this kind of materialism was the essence of humanity. It was to this form of materialism that Marx adhered.

The core of Locke's materialism was its affirmation of the theme of sensuousness. The sources of all knowledge were the senses. Men were rational. Science consisted in the application of a rational method to the data provided by the senses. Any philosophy at variance with the healthy human senses and reason based on them was false. Men were not inherently evil, but rather education and environment were omnipotent in shaping their character. Marx indicated that in this kind of materialism sensuousness kept its bloom, and stated that Feuerbach's attack on Hegelian speculation was a continuation of Lockean materialism.

The critical point of transition from sensuous materialism to socialism lay in the assertion that the environment predominately shapes men's character. For if man does draw all his knowledge from environmental experience, then both common sense and morality dictate that the social world "must be arranged so that in it man experiences and gets used to what is really human and that he becomes aware of himself as man."[32]

The agent who would construct a human society so that man could be human was man himself.[33] Marx did not think of man as slavishly subject to natural or social forces beyond his control, but as the subject of history, that is, as an active agent who contributed to the evolution of human history. The construction of an anthropological society, a society whose practice corresponded with the anthropological characteristics of man, would be brought about by the creative, conscious interpenetration of man with both physical and environmental forces.

Marx's view of man as a being whose nature it was to be active tends to destroy the interpretation of Marx as an epiphenomenologist. For instance, in *The German Ideology* Marx wrote, "Life is not determined by consciousness, but consciousness by life."[34] Some have interpreted statements of this kind to mean that Marx had articulated a clear theory of knowledge. Epistemologically, these people argued, Marx held it possible to know the "thing-in-itself." They turned Marx's comments regarding consciousness into a theory of perception, maintaining that all ideas and thought derive from or are mirror reflections of external objects. This was the "copy theory" of perception. It was first expressed by Engels in "Ludwig Feuerbach and the End of Classical German Philosophy" when he wrote, "We comprehend the concepts in our heads once more materialistically—as images of real things instead of regarding the real things as images of this or that stage of the absolute concept."[35] Lenin adopted the "copy theory" approach in his *Materialism and Emperico-Criticism.* The tradition that Marx was an epiphenomenologist, that Marx held that all ideas are accurate images of the "thing-in-itself," was thereby established.

In German philosophical language of the early nineteenth century, the phrase *sinnliche Gewissheit* meant "sense-certainty," the word *Wahrnehmung* meant "perception." When Marx wrote that consciousness was derived from life, he did not use the words *sinnliche Gewissheit* or *Wahrnehmung.* In short, he was not making a statement about perception; he was not claiming that ideas reflect the "thing-in-itself." The word that Marx used was *Bewusstsein,* or "consciousness," to be understood as "to be aware of." From Kant to Hegel human consciousness was understood to be something separate from both sense-certainty and perception, and indeed, to supersede them. There is little in Marx that deals with raw epistemological problems, such as, how does one know the external object. Rather, Marx deals basically with awareness, an understanding of the world, the comprehension of the structure and relationships by which the social world functions.

It would have seemed naive to Marx to even attempt to make statements about the "thing-in-itself." Such an approach assumed that the external object could be separated, could be totally isolated from any reference outside itself, and be perceived in its own unique purity. Such an approach assumed that human perception could precede human social life. This claim would amount to a *de facto* refutation of Marxism. The essence of Marxism was that human social life was the basic precondition of all other forms of human existence. All objects, then, could only be perceived as parts of social relationships. The tools men made were social objects and therefore expressive of societal relationships. Scientific experiments were social experiments and therefore manifested social productive relations. Social life for Marx was the ground, the Gestalt, in which objects made their appearance.

In *The Holy Family* and "Theses on Feuerbach," Marx attacked both Bruno Bauer and Ludwig Feuerbach. Both men were representatives of critical philosophy. Both men argued that it was possible to change human behavior by changing the forms of consciousness, a particular mode of human thought. Criticism for Bauer and Feuerbach implied the analysis and refutation of certain concepts: Marx ridiculed such critical philosophy. He altered the meaning of criticism, changing it from a refutation of ideas to actual, real changes of social institutions and practice. Criticism in the hands of Marx became a synonym for revolution, because to criticize for Marx meant the actual "changing of circumstances."[36]

Clearly, consciousness, as understood by Marx, had an active role to play in "practical-critical activity." Societal changes could not be undertaken thoughtlessly. Consciousness would provide the format, the program. Changes could be made in terms of old form of consciousness, capitalist consciousness. Or changes could be made in terms of a new form of consciousness, the proletarian consciousness, brought into existence by the Industrial Revolution. Marx thought in terms of a coexistent relationship between activity and consciousness. Man was a being who was coevally *praxis* and consciousness, and Marx anticipated that communist consciousness would provide the program by which human activity could reconstruct the world.

IN HIS PHILOSOPHY of nature, Marx clearly tried to avoid the pitfalls of dualism.[37] He rejected all claims to the absolute priority of either mind or matter, to the radical separation of consciousness and the external world. Marx abjured the subjectivism of Fichte and Hegel, or the claim that existence was primarily determined by the self-evolution of thought. On the other hand, he rejected the objectivism of LaMettrie and Hobbes, the claim that matter determined all aspects of existence, and that thought was merely an epiphenomenon of the external world. Both the spiritual monism of Fichte and Hegel and the materialistic monism of LaMettrie and Hobbes suffered from the same logical fallacy. They were both based on the assumption of the categorical disjuncture of mind and object.

For Marx, reality could not be sundered into mind and nature. Rather, nature itself, sensate nature, was by definition conscious nature. There was no question in Marx whether mind or nature was logically anterior. Both were coexistent in sensate nature. Thus, the world, social life was a pregiven. That is, existence could only emerge because consciousness and matter interpenetrated.

Clearly Marx was a naturalist. He himself defined communism as a humanistic naturalism. But Marx's naturalism can also be described as dialectical. That is, he was not primarily interested in claims of truth or claims of goodness, neither in epistemology nor in morality. His primary concern was the production of objects for the preservation of the species. He was a dialectical naturalist because he understood the essential project of the species to be production. The program of the species was to modify the surrounding world to insure its own reproduction.[38] In so doing active man created his own world as well as himself.

Footnotes

1. For a good discussion of Marx's concept of nature, see Alfred Schmidt, *Der Begriff der Natur in der Lehre von Marx* (Frankfurt: Europäische Verlagsanstalt, 1962).
2. Karl Marx, "Alienated Labor," *Karl Marx: Early Writings,* ed. and trans. T. B. Bottomore (New York: McGraw-Hill, 1963), pp. 126–127.
3. Marx, "Critique of Hegel's Dialectic and General Philosophy," *Ibid.,* p. 207.
4. Marx, "Free Human Production," *Writings of the Young Marx on Philosophy and Society,* ed. and trans. Loyd D. Easton and Kurt H. Guddat (New York: Doubleday & Co., 1967), p. 281.
5. Marx, "Critique of Hegel's Dialectic and General Philosophy," *Karl Marx: Early Writings,* p. 208.
6. *Ibid.,* p. 204.
7. Ernst Bloch, "Weltveranderung Oder die elf Thesen von Marx Über Feuerbach," *Über Karl Marx* (Frankfurt: Suhrkamp Verlag, 1968), pp. 53–107.
8. Marx, "Alienated Labor," *Karl Marx: Early Writings,* p. 127.
9. Marx, *Grundrisse,* trans. Martin Nicolaus (New York: Vintage Press, 1973) pp. 488–493.
10. Marx, "Money," *Karl Marx: Early Writings,* p. 189.
11. Marx, "Private Property and Communism," *Ibid.,* p. 164.
12. *Ibid.,* pp. 161–162.
13. *Ibid.,* p. 166.
14. For a fuller discussion of the notion of being in Marx, see the following works: Bloch, *Über Karl Marx*; Roger Garaudy, *Marxism in the Twentieth Century,* trans. Rene Lague (New York: Charles Scribner's Sons, 1966); Jean Hyppolite, *Hegel and Marx,* trans. J. M. McNeil (New York: Pantheon Books, 1969); Henri LeFebvre, *The Sociology of Marx,* trans. Nobert Guterman (New York: Pantheon Books, 1968); Leszek Kolakowski, *Toward a Marxist Humanism,* trans. Jane Zielonko Peel (New York: Grove Press, 1969); Gajo Petrovic, *Marx in the Mid-Twentieth Century* (New York: Doubleday & Co., 1967).
15. Marx, "Critique of Hegel's Dialectic and General Philosophy," *Karl Marx: Early Writings,* p. 208.
16. Lefebvre, *Dialectical Materialism,* trans. John Sturrock (London: Jonathan

Cape, 1968). Another work that sees man as a being with a project or program is Garaudy, *From Anathema to Dialogue*, trans. Luke O'Neill (New York: Random House, 1968).

17. Marx, *Karl Marx–Friedrich Engels Historisch-Kritische Gesamtausgabe*, ed. D. Rjazanov (Frankfurt: Marx-Engels Archiv Verlags Gesellschaft, 1927), I, p. 52.
18. *Ibid.*, p. 24.
19. *Ibid.*, p. 10. For an evaluation of Marx's dissertation, see the following works: Bloch, *Über Karl Marx;* H. P. Adams, *Karl Marx in His Earlier Writings* (London: George Allen and Unwin Ltd., 1940); D. Livergood, *Marx's Philosophy of Action* (The Hague: Martinus Nimjhoff, 1967). A translation of Marx's introduction to his dissertation can be found in David McLellan, *Karl Marx: Early Texts* (New York: Barnes and Noble, 1972).
20. The literature on Marx's view of consciousness is extensive. The following list is only intended to include some of the more outstanding works in this area. August Cornu, *The Origins of Marxian Thought* (Springfield, Ill.: Charles C Thomas, 1957); Louis Dupre, *The Philosophical Foundations of Marxism* (New York: Harcourt, Brace and World, 1966); Iring Fetscher, *Karl Marx und Der Marxismus* (Munich: R. Piper, 1967); Nicholas Lobkowicz, *Theory and Practice* (Notre Dame, Indiana: University of Notre Dame Press, 1967); Karl Löwith, *Die Hegelische Linke* (Stuttgart: Friedrich Fromm Verlag, 1962); George Lukács, *Geschichte und Klassen Bewusstsein* (Berlin: Der Malik-Verlag, 1923); Nathan Rotenstreich, *Basic Problems of Marx's Philosophy* (Indianapolis: Bobbs-Merrill, 1965); Gottfried Stiehler, *Dialektik und Praxis* (Berlin: Akademie-Verlag, 1968).
21. Marx, "Theses on Feuerbach," *The German Ideology*, ed. R. Pascal (New York: International Publishers, 1947), p. 199.
22. Marx, *Grundrisse*, p. 86.
23. Marx, *Das Kapital*, trans. Eden and Cedar Paul (New York: International Publishers, 1929), I, pp. 171–172.
24. *Ibid.*, III, p. 815.
25. Marx, *Grundrisse*, pp. 649–651.
26. Marx, *Karl Marx: Early Writings*, p. 147.
27. Marx, *The Holy Family* R. Dixon, trans. (Moscow: Foreign Languages Publishing House, 1956), p. 169.
28. *Ibid.*, p. 173.
29. *Ibid.*
30. *Ibid.*, p. 176.
31. *Ibid.*, p. 177.
32. *Ibid.*, p. 176.
33. *Ibid.*
34. Marx, *The German Ideology*, p. 15.
35. Friedrich Engels, "Ludwig Feuerbach and the End of Classical German Philosophy," *Karl Marx and Friedrich Engels: Selected Works* (New York: International Publishers, 1968), p. 621.
36. Marx, "Theses on Feuerbach," *The German Ideology*, p. 198. An excellent anthology that covers the various aspects of Marxist epistemology is Schmidt (ed.), *Beiträge Zur Marxistischen Erkenntnis Theorie* (Frankfurt: Suhrkamp Verlag, 1969). In addition, for an excellent essay on the role of sensuous perception in Marx, see Herbert Marcuse, "The Foundations of Historical Materialism," in *Studies in Critical Philosophy*, trans. Joris De Bres (London: New Left Books, 1972). This essay has not received the attention it deserves,

since it was written in 1932, just after the German publication of the Paris manuscripts, and constituted a perceptive breakthrough for its time.

37. On the history of materialism, the following works have been consulted: R. G. Collingwood, *The Idea of Nature* (Oxford: Clarendon Press, 1945); G. W. F. Hegel, *The Science of Logic,* trans. U. B. Bailie (London: George Allen, 1961), II; Yervant H. Krikorian, *Naturalism and the Human Spirit* (New York: Columbia University, 1949); Frederick A. Lange, *History of Materialism* (New York: Harcourt and Co., 1925); V. I. Lenin, "Philosophical Notebooks," *Collected Works* (Moscow: Foreign Languages Publishing House, 1960), XXXVIII; John O'Connor (ed.), *Modern Materialism* (New York: Harcourt, Brace and World, 1969).
38. LeFebvre, *Dialectical Materialism.*

Two

The Transcendence of Democracy

THE FRENCH REVOLUTION not only witnessed the ascendancy of the middle classes but also laid the seeds for their eventual destruction. Bourgeois democracy triumphed in 1791, deepened into egalitarian democracy under Robespierre, and received a major challenge from the egalitarian communism of Gracchus Babeuf in 1795. The modern history of communism began with the conspiracy of the Society of Equals,[1] and thus the French Revolution was, in fact, the womb of two revolutions: the bourgeois and the proletarian. The dividing line between these two revolutions was the notion of equality. Robespierre and Babeuf, although differing on the notion of property, were in agreement in criticizing the constitution of 1791. It was apparent to them that political equality had not brought social equality. The attempt to rectify the disparity between these two forms of equality was one of the major causes for the conspiracy of 1795.

The doctrine of natural rights was at the heart of the bourgeois revolution, and natural rights theory was decidedly atomistic. Rights belonged to the person rather than collectively to the entire human species. Each person, as a particular creation of nature, was a repository of privileges. Every individual possessed the freedom, power, and will to do those things for which he was equipped by nature. The individual preceded the species. The only tie to humanity in general, the only social connectedness, was the prohibition that no person could interfere with, destroy, or retard the natural rights of another person.

Bourgeois democrats had given a political definition to equality. The common criterion they wished to apply to all men was political in nature: all men were equal before the law. Feudalism had been abolished, and with feudalism the privilege of differential justice based on estates. Those were the principles of 1791. Assuming that political equality was tantamount to total human freedom, the men of 1791 never addressed themselves to the social question. They never asked themselves whether, indeed, another common criterion of equality could be applied to man: the idea of social equality. This avenue of thought touched upon the question of property, and it was exactly at this point that bourgeois political theory stopped. Conversely, it was from this point that socialist political theory was to begin.

In a bourgeois context, the idea of equality permitted the development of enormous disparities of social wealth.[2] Bourgeois democrats ignored the extremes of luxuriant wealth counterposed to ignobling poverty, as long as rich man and poor man both had one vote. This rationalization and justification of enormous property imbalances resulted from the peculiar juncture of the notion of equality with the labor theory, not of value, but of property.[3]

The Jacobin answer to this fateful contradiction in bourgeois thought was an egalitarian response. Robespierre and Jacobinism were thoroughly grounded in natural rights theory. Nature had endowed each man with rights, and these rights belonged "to all men equally." Atomistic, emphasizing that men were anterior to society, Robespierre affirmed that society could not invade these rights but merely secure and safeguard them. In accordance with the idea of the social contract, Robespierre wrote that society and law were constituted to protect men. Property too was a natural right. As long as men did not invade or threaten "the property of other citizens," each person had the right to "enjoy and to dispose of" his property "at his pleasure."

The democratic egalitarianism of Robespierre began when he applied the idea of equality to the social, as well as the political realm. Recognizing the distinctions of talent and skill, Robespierre adamantly maintained that political and social equality were rights "whatever difference may be in their physical and moral force." No one, therefore, should be without property. Far from wishing to abolish personal property, Robespierre sought to universalize it. The doctrine of natural rights would be perfected when men were not only equal before the law, but possessed property almost equally, that is, shared in "the portion of fortune or wealth that is guaranteed to him by law."[4]

Jacobinism thus carried natural rights theory as far to the left as it was possible to reach. Even though Robespierre accepted the paternalistic responsibilities of society, accepted that "society is under obligation to provide subsistence for all its members,"[5] he never challenged the sanctity of universalized private property. The Reign of Terror illustrated the radicalism latent in the idea of equality when extended to the social question. The unresolved contradictions in the bourgeois notion of equality were explosive, and the Committee of Public Safety was proof of the unsuspected revolutionary potential of radical egalitarianism. Robespierre's faith in natural rights theory approached utopianism.[6]

Like Robespierre, Gracchus Babeuf also rejected the bourgeois notion of equality. Unlike Robespierre, Babeuf also rejected the bourgeois and Jacobin adherence to the sanctity of private possession. By accepting natural rights theory, but not the natural rights of property, Babeuf introduced egalitarian communism into modern history.[7]

Working within the natural rights framework, Babeuf maintained that equality was a law of nature applicable to all men. Where Babeuf differed from the Robespierre and bourgeois interpretation of natural rights was over the question of atomism. Men did not precede society. Labor was not simply the attribute to the individual human being. Rather, man was a social animal. Furthermore, labor was a total social product. Since men and labor were contingent upon society, the doctrine of equality necessitated the movement to "common property, or the community of goods."[8]

A precondition for the evolution of socialist or communist theory is the belief that man coexists with society. Unless man is seen as coeval with society, rather than opposed to it, it is impossible to argue the logic of community possession. When Babeuf rejected natural rights atomism, he opened the door to a discussion of man as a social being: therein lay his communism. But Babeuf retained vestiges of eighteenth-century natural rights theory, particularly the idea of equality, and thus he continued the tradition of democratic egalitarianism. Babeuf was thus a transition figure, taking with him the accomplishments of the eighteenth century into the proletarian world of the future. Prevalent in his writing was the theme of the coming socialist revolution as continuation of the bourgeois French Revolution. Just as the people had marched over the bodies of kings and priests in the past, so in the future they would destroy the new tyrants, the bourgeois capitalists.[9]

There was in Babeuf, moreover, a concept that bore tremendous relevance for the future of socialist thought. In attacking the idea of individualistic atomism Babeuf also attacked the idea and implications of private egoism.[10] Not only did Babeuf abjure egoism, but in addition the allied ideas of greed, selfishness, private acquisitiveness. He suggested that a new rationale must be sought for economic production, distribution, and enjoyment. Where property was shared in common, egoism would no longer be the basic motivation of men.[11] Since everyone would receive the same remuneration of food and shelter, some other source of human motivation must be found rather than ego gratification.

Marx's attack on natural rights theory was much broader than Babeuf's, and indeed, sprang from fundamentally different sources. Not only did Marx reject the idea of private possession, but he also rejected the philosophical notions of natural rights and equality generally. Since natural rights theory formed the basis of democracy, Marx had moved beyond democracy. Unlike Robespierre or Babeuf, Marx was forced to construct an entirely new social philosophy to correspond with his evolving theory of communism.

> None of the supposed rights of man, therefore, go beyond the egoistic man, man as he is, as a member of civil society; that is, an individual separated from the community, withdrawn into himself, wholly preoccupied with his private interest and acting in accordance with his private caprice. Man is far from being considered, in the rights of man, as a species-being, on the contrary, species-life itself—society—appears as a system which is external to the individual and as a limitation of his original independence. The only bond between men is natural necessity, need and private interest, the preservation of their property and their egoistic persons.[12]

According to Marx, natural rights theory was simply an apology for private greed. Viewing man as a self-sufficient monad, natural rights theory was merely an excuse for self-aggrandizement, both material and spiritual. Since the individual person preceded society, natural rights did not speak in terms of social cohesiveness but rather in terms of self-contained atoms. Such a world was enslaving, exploitative, and gluttonous.

In the *Critique of the Gotha Programme* Marx attacked the bourgeois notion of equality. Equal rights, in a class society like nineteenth-century bourgeois industrial society, meant unequal appropriation of wealth.[13] When placed in an unequal social context, when applied to unequal individual ability, the idea of right logically led to a disequilibrium of private possession. Right, therefore, was a poor criterion by which to structure society; it was a tool through which the bourgeoisie maintained their class domination. Labor, too, was a poor criterion. Marx's search, therefore, was to discover a new criterion for social relationships, for the control of economic forces, that categorically avoided class differentiation derived from property. Marx had to pass beyond natural rights theory, pass beyond the idea of equality, in order to discover a new social ethic, a new mode of relating to productive forces that would not create class distinction based on wealth.

Marx's surmounting of natural rights theory led him to criticize the accomplishments of the French Revolution. Even though Marx admired the persons as well as the tactics of Robespierre and Saint-Just, he was also critical of Jacobin egalitarianism. According to Marx, the failure of the French Revolution arose from the fact that it spoke for the interests of a limited, exclusive class, the bourgeoisie.[14] The ills that the French Revolution cured were thus the ills suffered by the bourgeoisie, and were thus limited, exclusive ills. No one spoke effectively for the general, universal ills of the total French society. Consequently, the general and universal sufferings were left unresolved. The triumph of the bourgeois class was thus the triumph of the ideology and interests of that class. Free competition ruled. Free trade was unchallenged. Private anarchy became the law of society. Bourgeois society witnessed the "universal struggle of man against man, individual against individual."[15] The brutal elementary forces of life were loosed from the fetters of feudal society. The modern political state had been victorious, and that state sanctified the relentless competitive struggle. The political state had dissolved the cohesiveness of the old society, and in place of a social fabric had superimposed the particularism of individual will. The French Revolution had achieved political emancipation. At best, this was only a partial triumph. The next revolution would gain full human, social emancipation.[16] Marx saw himself as the heir and perpetuator of the French revolutionary tradition, which had culminated in Babeuf.[17]

What Marx substituted for natural rights theory and the idea of equality was not a creation solely of his own mind. Many people influenced him, particularly Weitling, Hess, and Feuerbach. His own evolution toward a new social ethic was enhanced by his criticism of Proudhon and Stirner. These last two men, although differing in many areas, were the early founders of anarchism. The objections that Marx had to this form of radical individualism, indeed libertarianism, would help in an appreciation of the positive content of his new social ethic.

In *What Is Property*? Proudhon declared property to be theft. The man who took occupancy of the conditions of production, and thus deprived another of accessibility to those conditions or equal ones, did so by an arbitrary act of will. He was thus a despot, an enslaver. Proudhon, however, saved his fiercest strictures for the bourgeois economists and their advocacy of distribution in accordance with labor and exchange.[18] The problem that Proudhon set for himself was how to reconcile the idea of property, whereby each producer owned and had free access to the conditions of his labor, with the idea of equality, whereby propertied producers owned equal portions of wealth and there was no terrible imbalance of classes.

The solution to this problem lay in devising a new standard of distribution. Material rewards should be dispensed on the basis of capacity and result. Picturing a society whose task it was to fulfill human needs, Proudhon also pictured a society that contained a multitude of functions. Because modern society was so diverse, because modern society could meet and had produced a plethora of human needs, the functions to be performed by the individuals of this society were multitudinous. Consequently, individual capacities, even though obviously unequal in quality, could be utilized by society. If rewards were dispensed in terms of capacity and result and since every capacity and skill could be accommodated by society, this system insured that every producer would be the recipient of material wealth. Although there might occur differences in wealth, this new standard of distribution in terms of capacity and result overcame the extreme schism between rich and poor in bourgeois society. This system could work if each producer had free access to the means of production, that is, held the means of production as his property. In the Jacobin tradition, Proudhon did not wish to abolish private property but rather to catholicize it.[19]

Human equality still formed the essence of Proudhon's search. Total independence of judgment and will, the fact that no man would look upon another as a sovereign or master, these ideas are what Proudhon defined as sovereignty. Radical individualism, the absolute freedom of each man's conscience and volition, formed the touchstone of Proudhon's thinking. Anarchistic federalism was the societal form that best incorporated Proudhon's ideal of individual sovereignty. Such personal independence could only be guaranteed if each man were economically sovereign. Private possession, for Proudhon, formed the economic insurance for moral independence.

This attainment of such a social condition was a potentiality in the nature of man. The primary characteristic of human nature, according to Proudhon, was sociability. Anthropologically, sympathetic attraction caused men to associate in groups. Another aspect of sociability was the human tendency toward justice. Because man was sociable, he also recognized the equality between his own personality and another's. Respecting his own personality, he would also respect the personality of another person in his society. Justice, equality, and society were thus the inherent characteristics of man.[20]

Displaying a penchant for personal invective, Marx, after an initial period of friendship, later attacked Proudhon without restraint. Marx accused Proudhon of displaying a petty bourgeois mentality. The defense of property, the defense of individualism, Marx classified as a petty bourgeois mentality, the outlook of a lower middle class ambition trying to enter the mainstream.[21] In terms of knowledge of and competence with economic theory, Proudhon was no match for Marx. With his superior grasp of economic facts, his mastery of the English bourgeois economists (Ricardo, Smith, Bray), Marx easily exposed Proudhon's rather naive handling of political economy.[22] Most important, however, Marx attacked Proudhon because Proudhon assumed that economic categories were eternal. Justice, equality, and society were metaphysical entities, standing apart from society, untouched by the rush and mass of daily economic activity. For Marx, Proudhon was an idealist, a Hegelian, an economic metaphysician who failed to see that societies were constantly changing, that societies were merely organic wholes based on a peculiar interrelationship between the means and relations of production. In short, Proudhon was not a naturalist. Above all, he did not understand the dialectic of naturalism. He did not see that as the means of production evolved, they constantly called forth new economic forms. Marx was a historicist, Proudhon a Platonist.[23]

In many ways the most serious challenge to Marx's own development came from Max Stirner. At any rate, Marx himself took Stirner seriously, and he devoted the major portion of *The German Ideology* to a refutation of this adversary. The major threat that Stirner posed for Marx was his denial of a universal human essence, a being of the species. A convert to

Feuerbachian materialism and humanism, Marx had already adopted Feuerbach's notion of a human species being. In *The Ego and His Own,* Stirner launched his assaults at Feuerbach, and indirectly, therefore, at advocates of Feuerbach like Marx.

According to Stirner, men have always been enslaved to abstract, depersonalized, spiritual potencies. The individual has always lost his unique identity, always surrendered himself, always become the instrument of these supernatural powers. First, man submitted to the dark, mystical forces of nature, then to the judicial anthropomorphic God of the Old and New Testaments, and then to the universal progressive force of reason. Regardless of the name, the force external to men has always been the subject of history, men the mere predicate. Feuerbach's concept of a species being, in Stirner's terms, was nothing but a continuation of individual enslavement to an abstract, supernatural force. The concept of essence must be finally overthrown and abandoned. Essence would be transcended by ego.[24]

The abolition of the concept of essence, its substitution by the absolute "I," had ramifications for other important philosophical concepts. For instance, Stirner defined freedom as "rid of it."[25] That is, freedom was having no obligations, no commitments outside of oneself. If freedom meant the absence of external determination, will for Stirner was synonymous with power. To be powerful was to control, to have mastery over an object. To be powerful was to be an owner, that is, an absolute possessor of the world around one.[26] The definition of property for Stirner flowed naturally from his concept of power. Unlimited dominion over objects, that which was subject to the absolute law of one's will, was property for Stirner.[27] There was a predatory note to Stirner's notion of property. His vision of man was that of a conqueror, of someone who subjected the world to his own purposes. Man was the master, and anything he could enslave, anything he could make submissive to his will, was his property. Stirner hoped that man could make the world his own property.[28]

Marx's refutation of Stirner took many forms. Principally, Marx rejected Stirner's notion of the sovereign individual. The idea of an "I," personal will, existing totally apart from social conditions, self-determining, appeared to Marx to continue the Hegelian notion of consciousness. An idealist, Stirner merely empowered the "ego" with the same forces of self-generation as Hegel empowered self-consciousness. Both Stirner and Hegel referred to subjectivity as the unconditioned mover of the universe. In the same way that Marx attacked Hegel for his metaphysical obscurantism, so now he attacked Stirner. Blindly and mystically, Stirner had completely overlooked the actual social conditions in which the ego had to function. Ideas were not abstract, eternal entities, the ego was not an abstract eternal entity, and to assume so was merely to return philosophy to the alienation and dehumanization of its religious and idealist form. Real men in real social conditions formed the basis of human history, and Stirner's espousal of the doctrine of pure will was an empty apology for petty bourgeois parvenu ambitions.[29]

A more fundamental difference separated Marx from Stirner, however. Stirner's doctrine of the world, both physical and ideational, as a mere adjunct, as a property of the ego, indicated that Stirner thought of existence in terms of self-enjoyment. The "I" placed itself in the world to consume it. The ethical basis upon which Stirner was drawing was the ethic of personal pleasure. The ego should consume the world for its own self-gratification. Marx had a totally different approach to existence. Man had to objectify himself, that is, the species nature of man required him to be active, to modify. Through his activity by means of his labor, man had surrounded himself with objects that were objectifications of his own abilities, his species being. Man then created his own world, his own history, not in the sense that man was unconditioned, but in the sense that the conditions in which he worked, or upon which he worked, eventually bore the unmistakable impress of his own powers. Marx, then, talked of objectification, while Stirner talked of consumption. Marx talked of release, while Stirner talked of hoarding. Pleasure for Marx meant the use and expenditure of human ability, while for Stirner pleasure meant greed and personal acquisition. Marx wished to fill the world, to flood it; Stirner wished to denude it.

The attacks on Proudhon and Stirner reveal to us the pitfalls that Marx sought to avoid, what he was moving away from, the dangers of natural rights theory, equality, and extreme individualism. In the 1844 manuscripts, Marx acknowledged his debts to Wilhelm Weitling and Moses Hess.[30] These men primarily transmitted to Marx the principles of a new social ethic. From them he learned that the purpose of society was not material acquisition, not production, not labor (i.e., Puritanism in all its forms) but rather contentment. However, this was not the contentment of a Stirner, that is, the self-enjoyment of the predatory instinct, but rather the contentment that arose from harmony, from an equilibrium of internal needs and abilities. The Marxian social ethic was grounded in eudaemonism.

In 1842 Weitling's *Garantien der Harmonie und Freiheit* appeared. Weitling indicated that the basic illness from which mankind had suffered was inequality of possession. There could be no harmony between people, no brotherhood between people, because economic differences divided men, embittered them. Furthermore, Weitling advocated not the abolition of private property, but rather its equalization.[31] Not a communist, Weitling's voice was that of a devout Christian artisan. Weitling possessed a guild mentality, a medieval concept of a community of independent artisans living in harmony partially because all had property in the same proportion.

Weitling's breakthrough came, however, when he developed a new criterion of social value. The good society was the society that answered human needs. The fulfillment of human needs meant enjoyment, contentment. The best way to meet human needs was through the unstinted expansion of human abilities. Needs would call forth abilities; the full exercise of abilities would in turn create new needs. Weitling maintained that a good society constructed a balance between human needs and abilities. Such a harmony prevented friction, discontent, anxiety.[32]

Weitling was thus describing a society that corresponded to the anthropological condition of man. Contentment could only be achieved if the naturalistic component of human existence was fulfilled. Weitling wished for social eudaemonism. The reconstruction of the social world must be predicated on the fulfillment of the anthropological basis of human existence.[33]

Moses Hess followed a similar quest. Communism for Hess had less to do with the institutional or economic organization of society than with the creation of a unity of life. Communism was humanitarianism; that is, in a communist society man must be at one with his own nature. He must live in accordance with his anthropological being.[34] This meant, for Hess, that human activity must be its own enjoyment. It was not the rewards of human activity, but rather the activity itself that was pleasurable and, therefore, brought contentment. For Hess and for Weitling, personal happiness and well-being would be the ethical values of a new society.[35]

Work implied slavery for Hess. By the term "work," Hess understood an activity that was either under the control of another or devoted toward the acquisition of an external object. In either case, the human activity was not free. That is, the human activity was not related to itself. A free act for Hess, a communist act, was one that was self-determining. This did not mean that the act was unconditioned, unlimited. A self-determined and, therefore, free act was an act that sprang from the inner nature of the organism. When Hess said pleasure and well-being were the end of life, he meant that an organism that obeyed its own nature was happy.[36]

From this vantage point, Marx's attack upon democratic theory emerges not as a mere legalistic refutation, but as a transcendence. When Marx abjured democracy, he did so not solely because of the atomism inherent in natural rights theory, not solely because democratic individualism served as an apology for private greed, but rather because the value system, the ethical substructure of democracy appeared to him as decadent. Because Marx's flight from democracy was caused in part by his revulsion at the morality of democracy, so his evolution to communism was encouraged by the attractiveness of the morality of communism. This is not to claim that Marx was primarily a moralist. It is to claim, however, that Marx's communism cannot be described solely as a sociology of communalism, or as a philosophical overcoming of alienation, but also as an attempt to construct a morality of human well-being. In order to amplify and make specific the above assertions, Marx's attempt to create a moral system for communism will be discussed in terms of his concepts of self, freedom, power, and property.

The bourgeois concern for self, as an entity independent of society, was merely an ideological ploy for the defense of capitalism, according to Marx. Democratic theory that saw man as distinct from society, indeed, as in conflict with it not only encouraged selfish acquisitiveness, but also human isolation, the alienation of man from man. For Marx, all individualistic systems suffered from this inherent flaw. By positing an ineradicable schism between man and man, individualistic systems did violence to the interdependence of social existence, alienated man from his species, and therefore, man from his own nature. Individualism always tended to dehumanize man, that is, separate him from his species nature.[37] Individualism was a form of idealism, for it always posited a consciousness, a mentality that existed apart from the social world. Individualism was always mystification, for it completely ignored the social and naturalistic components of human life. Marx, therefore, abjured any form of individualism, be it based upon the democratic theory of natural rights, or be it based on the anarchistic theory of ego as God. To define self in these terms was to define self in terms of nonbeing.

Self for Marx was inherently social. Because man was in society, he achieved his fulfillment through society. Adopting the Feuerbachian notion of a universal human nature, Marx understood that man could only be himself when he was at the same time for other men. It was not that Marx did not think in terms of personal identity, but rather that Marx defined identity as arising only when man acted in accordance with his true nature, that is, acted socially in interdependence with other men.

The value that Marx was affirming was the value of interdependence. The world was by nature interpersonal, because social life was the ground from which individuality arose. Reference to the species was immediately reference to the self: Species affirmation was self-affirmation.[38]

If individualistic doctrines were a form of idealism, that is, if individualistic theories posit the existence of self-generating consciousness, then freedom in these doctrines must also be seen as self-produced. In other words, if freedom is to be self-produced, actions must be taken only in relation to the self-generating consciousness, and, therefore, must be entirely devoid of social conditions. Such a philosophic construct immediately sets the stage for the problem of free will versus determinism, for it is obvious that social conditions cannot be totally eliminated from human actions.

Weitling and Hess both rejected this individualistic bourgeois concept of freedom. Weitling wrote, "There is no comprehensive notion of human freedom, and there can be none, which is not grounded on the naturalistic border of this freedom namely human abilities."[39] Hess uttered similar opinions: "That being is free, which in order to live and be effective requires no force but its own nature, and thus enjoys unhindered activity."[40]

Both men rejected the approach to freedom that was predicated upon self-generating consciousness and will. Rather, they began their quest from naturalistic-anthropological presuppositions. Freedom must relate to the species nature of man. Therefore, man was immediately conditioned by his society as well as by his universal biological nature. For Hess and Weitling, freedom did not mean "riddance from," but rather "access to." Given the determination of society and species nature, if a man could act so as to affirm his own nature, act in fulfillment of his needs and abilities, he was free. If the individual could exercise his organic requirements, if it were available to the being to express its own naturalistic essence, he was free. Individualistic-bourgeois concepts of freedom talked of riddance, absence of the external, self-postulation, while communal-communist theory talked of exercise, availability, and accessibility of one's own biological substrata.

Weitling was to carry the argument a step further. Weitling did not define freedom as "performance of." Not to suffer from unfulfilled need and unexpressed talent was freedom. If the organism could escape the discomfort, anxiety, dysfunction that would arise from not being able to function as its nature dictated, it was free. Again, a eudaemonistic note appears; happiness was freedom.[41]

Marx followed along a similar line of development to Weitling and Hess. Perceptively, Marx saw that bourgeois notions of freedom as "riddance from" were merely idealist abstractions. In part, they were continuations of religious, i.e., Christian notions of freedom: to be rid of this world, to be free and at home in a self-moving God. Idealist notions of freedom, then, were imbued by a certain otherworldliness, a desire to escape this earthly society.[42]

For Marx, to live was to be conditioned. Existence did not precede essence. Rather, essence preceded existence, and the essence of man was his species being. Therefore, essence was inherently interpersonal, inherently intrasocial. Every act taken by a man was determined by his biological nature, by his society, and by the material and productive means he found before him.[43]

If essence, species being, preceded existence, then all actions were conditioned and determined by that essence.[44] Freedom for Marx, then, could only mean action in harmony with our essence. Thinking not in terms of rights, but rather of gratifying anthropological characteristics, Marx defined free activity as "the creative manifestation of life arising from the free development of all abilities."[45] Like Weitling, Marx understood that freedom was an expression of fulfilled human abilities, an expression of gratified human need, "the all-around development of the individual."[46] Marx, too, then equated freedom with human well-being. The correspondence of performance and ability, eudaemonism, was the value Marx sought to proclaim.

If freedom for the bourgeoisie meant "freedom from," then power for the bourgeoisie meant "control over." In a world of objects, in a world of private property, power was defined in an imperial sense, as dominion. It will be recalled that the bourgeois defense of private possession rested on the labor theory of property. An object became a man's property because he placed his labor in it. His labor took occupancy of the object. Since it was impossible to separate a man from his labor, it was impossible to separate the object from the man. Therefore, the object was as much his as his own labor was, and he could control it free from any external interference. He could utilize the object as he wished, consume it in any fashion he willed; it was, in fact, his own imperium, and he was imperator.

Power, for Marx, bore no such connotations. Rejecting the labor theory of property, the idea of freedom as "riddance," Marx approached the question of power from a naturalistic point of view. When Marx referred to power, he used the word *Vermögen,* which means "ability, faculty, capable."[47] In Marx's lexicon, power had nothing to do with imperium, but dealt rather with full development. A man was powerful not because he could control, not because objects or people were extensions of his sovereign will, but rather because he had developed his human abilities to their fullest extent. Powerfulness was therefore synonymous with self-development, that is, the perfection of the proper functions of men. Marx was defining power as the Greeks had defined virtue. The bourgeoisie were defining power again from a Christian perspective, as something akin to a self-contained God.

The question of property for Marx centered, obviously, not around private possession, but around accessibility to the conditions of labor. It was the nature of man to labor. He must labor, modify the world around him, if he was to continue his existence, reproduce his species. The means of production at his disposal, the conditions of his labor, were essential to his own self-reproduction. The conditions of labor, then, indispensable for his continued existence, must be accessible to his modifying activity. The conditions of labor must become generalized property; that is, the means of production must be freely available to the activity of the species. Property, for Marx, must be universal private property, for it must be universally accessible to the entire species and, therefore, belong to the entire species.[48]

In defining property as open accessibility to the means of production, Marx completely surmounted the bourgeois involvement with equality. Since the conditions of labor did not belong separately to individual men, the question of equality did not arise. Since the means of production were not possessed by private persons, the problem of distribution, in equal shares, through labor, by way of exchange of equal products, was completely transcended. Universal ownership introduced a new phase of human history, the phase of full human development. Marx was concerned not with equality, but with the perfection of human ability. The transcendence of bourgeois property was the beginning of the full productive development of the species.

Marx's search for an ethic of human well-being continued, although in altered form, in his *Grundrisse* and *Kapital.* The humanism of Marx was a constant element in his thought throughout his life. However, where the concerns of his early writing were straightforwardly anthropological, in his later writings the anthropological was seen within the context of the economic. In his later work, Marx thought a set of socioeconomic presuppositions were necessary before any new ethic would be achieved. In fact, an ethic of human well-being must be a historical product. A new morality would not be possible unless the productive powers of man created the sociological presuppositions that could call this ethic into existence.

In the *Grundrisse,* Marx continued to talk in terms of the "universal development of the individual."[49] He tried to demonstrate how full development was impossible inside capitalist society because of the barriers to full production, the inherent contradictions, of the private enterprise system. In order for the individual to achieve his full development, it was first necessary for the "full development of the forces of production" to become "the condition of production."[50] In *Kapital* he returned to the same theme. The unstinted productivity of industrial potential would mean less time devoted to necessary labor, and thus more free time to be spent on developing capacities of the individual.[51] In addition, the greater and ceaselessly expanding productive power would itself open up new areas of self-expression and self-actualization.

Thus, in his later writings, Marx continued to redefine the concepts of self, freedom, power, and property. With expanded productivity, human beings would have greater opportunity to actualize and express their inherent capacities. Since the condition of labor, the instruments of production, would belong to all, the self-expression of the individual would be indistinguishable and inseparable from the self-expression of society generally. Indeed, in the *Grundrisse,* Marx approached a definition of the idea of civilization. Because of industrial process, civilization was a society that allowed for the full expression of individual talents, abilities, skills, and that created new areas for individual and societal self-actualization. Conversely, capitalism was barbarism. Capitalism dehumanized, because it expropriated full living labor and full living time from the individual and thus left him emptied and misshapen.

A shift of emphasis had taken place in the mature Marx. In the early Marx, the emphasis was upon the anthropological precondition. In the *Grundrisse* and *Kapital,* the emphasis was upon the sociological precondition. The conquest of his new ideas of self, freedom, power, and property was contingent upon the coming into existence of the necessary sociological preconditions.

The formula that Marx expounded in the *Critique of the Gotha Programme,* "From each according to his ability, to each according to his need,"[52] was thus an attempt to formulate a new ethical criterion for social relationships. Clearly Marx was not primarily a moralist. But it is not an overstatement to assert that when Marx criticized democracy, he also criticized democratic values. On one level, Marx's humanism was a search for a transvaluation of value. He desired an anthropocentric society. He hoped for a society whose ethic was the harmonious balance of need and ability. His central concern was eudaemonism, a society in which the naturalistic components of human life were in harmony with societal existence.[53]

Footnotes

1. George Lichtheim, *The Origins of Socialism* (New York: Praeger, 1969) pp. 20–25. Also, Arthur Rosenberg, *Democracy and Socialism* (Boston: Beacon Press, 1965), pp. 33–41.
2. Lorenz von Stein, *The History of the Social Movement in France; 1789–1850,* ed. and trans. Kaethe Mengelberg (New Jersey: Bedminster Press, 1964).
3. On this question see the following works: John Locke, *Two Treaties on Government* (New York: Hafner Publishing Co., 1947); Crawford MacPherson, *The Political Theory of Possessive Individualism* (Oxford: Clarendon Press, 1962). Adam Smith, *The Wealth of Nations* (New York: Modern Library, 1937).
4. P. Buonarroti, *Babeuf's Conspiracy for Equality* (London: H. Hetherington, 1936), p. 23.
5. *Ibid.*
6. *Ibid.*, p. 22.
7. *Ibid.*, p. 314.
8. *Ibid.*, p. 315.
9. *Ibid.*
10. *Ibid.*, p. 369.
11. *Ibid.*, p. 366.
12. Karl Marx, "On the Jewish Question," *Writings of the Young Marx on Philosophy and Society,* ed. and trans. Loyd D. Easton and Kurt H. Guddat (New York: Doubleday & Co., 1967), pp. 236–237.
13. Marx, *Critique of the Gotha Programme* (New York: International Publishers, 1947), p. 86.
14. Marx, *The Holy Family,* trans. R. Dixon (Moscow: Foreign Languages Publishing House, 1956), p. 110.
15. *Ibid.*, p. 157.
16. *Ibid.*, pp. 152–158.
17. *Ibid.*, p. 161.
18. Pierre J. Proudhon, *What Is Property?* trans. Benjamin R. Tucker (London: William Reeves, 1898), pp. 134–136.
19. *Ibid.*, pp. 140–141.
20. *Ibid.*, pp. 224–225.
21. Marx to Annenkov, in Marx and Engels, *Selected Correspondence* (New York: International Publishers, 1942), pp. 5–18. Also see Marx to Schweitzer, pp. 169–176.
22. Marx, *The Poverty of Philosophy* (New York: International Publishers, 1963), pp. 112–125.
23. *Ibid.*, pp. 104–114.
24. Max Stirner, *The Ego and His Own,* trans. Steven T. Byington (New York: Benjamin R. Tucker, 1907), p. 182.
25. *Ibid.*, p. 205.
26. *Ibid.*, pp. 275–339.

27. *Ibid.*, p. 332.
28. *Ibid.*, pp. 160–169.
29. Marx, *The German Ideology,* trans. S. Ryazanskaya (Moscow: Progress Publishers, 1968), pp. 124, 133–134, 137, 164, 189, 199, 261, 333.
30. Marx, *Karl Marx: Early Writings,* ed. and trans. T. B. Bottomore (New York: McGraw-Hill, 1963), p. 64.
31. Wilhelm Weitling, *Garantien der Harmonie und Freiheit* (Hamburg: M. H. T. Christen, 1849), pp. 18–25.
32. *Ibid.*, pp. 127–129.
33. *Ibid.*, pp. 131–135.
34. Moses Hess, *Philosophische und Sozialistische Schriften,* ed. A. Cornu and W. Mönke (Berlin: Academie-Verlag, 1961), p. 200.
35. *Ibid.*, p. 204.
36. *Ibid.*, p. 360.
37. Marx, "On the Jewish Question," *Writings of the Young Marx on Philosophy and Society,* pp. 235–238.
38. Marx, "Free Human Production," *Ibid.*, pp. 277–282.
39. Weitling, *Garantien der Harmonie und Freiheit,* p. 186.
40. Hess, *Philosophische und Sozialistische Schriften,* p. 363.
41. Weitling, *Garantien der Harmonie und Freiheit,* pp. 186–187.
42. Marx, *The German Ideology,* p. 333.
43. *Ibid.*, pp. 337–338.
44. *Ibid.*, p. 321.
45. *Ibid.*, p. 246.
46. *Ibid.*, p. 322.
47. *Ibid.*, pp. 359, 412.
48. Marx, *Grundrisse,* trans. Martin Nicolaus (New York: Vintage Press, 1973), pp. 452–455.
49. *Ibid.*, p. 542.
50. *Ibid.*
51. Marx, *Das Kapital,* trans. Samuel Moore and Edward Aveling (New York: International Publishers, 1967) I., p. 512.
52. Marx, *Critique of the Gotha Programme,* p. 89.
53. Marx, *The Poverty of Philosophy,* p. 63.

Three

Toward A Philosophical Anthropology

MARX'S RELATION TO Hegel was an ambiguous one. On the one hand, Marx accepted the Hegelian notion of the dialectic, of negativity. Stripped of its idealist wrapping, the idea of negation was placed in a worldly setting by Marx, given material form, made into a social class, the proletariat, which had as its historical duty the negation and overthrow of capitalism. On the other hand, the Hegelian philosophy of culture was categorically rejected by Marx. In negating Hegel's conception of culture, Marx's intent in the "Critique of Hegel's Dialectic and General Philosophy," Marx formulated his own philosophy of culture, as well as communism.

Marxism has too often been thought of as a strategy for social revolution, as an economic system dedicated to the nationalization of property and not often enough as a philosophical anthropology. One of the major weaknesses of Marxism, it has been argued, was that it attempted no description of basic human nature. Without an analysis of the human essence, the argument concluded, it was impossible to correctly portray how the good society should be constructed. Marx, however, did indicate what he thought the human essence to be. He did speculate on anthropology, and from these speculations argued that communism was the form of society best suited to correspond to the human essence. Communism was an anthropocentric society. The attempt, therefore, to arrive at the major features of Marx's philosophical anthropology, to sketch the outline of his philosophy of culture, not only will take us into the heart of Marxism, but will illustrate most clearly how Marx envisioned a communist society.

Marx's philosophy of culture derived from four ideas. These ideas were: (1) objectification, (2) alienation, (3) reappropriation, (4) self-affirmation.

1. Objectification

Self-consciousness for Hegel was a kind of force.[1] It was compelled to express itself, to manifest itself. It had to objectify itself in the natural entities that surrounded it and to mold and shape these entities in accordance with its own laws. Objectification meant the outpouring, the release of consciousness as a modifying and reconstructing energy into the human and physical environment.

For Hegel, however, objectification was purely a spiritual process. It was mind that was the modifying instrumentality. It was mind that sculptured things, fashioned ideas, created institutions. For Hegel, man was the self-creation of consciousness, and history the museum of his myriad temporal transformations. Man could recognize the world, know the world to be, in fact, his world, because he was aware of the labor, had knowledge of the activity of his own consciousness. Knowledge, i.e., world, was self-knowledge.

In order to understand Marx's approach to the problem of objectification, and his deviation from the Hegelian format, it is first necessary to analyze what Marx meant by the objective. What was objective to Marx was human species being. Man had needs and abilities, felt hunger and pain, was passionate and sensuous. The sharing of these qualities by all of mankind was, for Marx, human species being, or human essence. The objective in Marxian philosophy was the naturalistic component of species life.

Self-consciousness did not play a part in the Marxian definition of objectification. Instead of a rational process, Marx conceived of a material, physical interchange between man and nature. Objectification for Marx meant the expression, the manifestation of human needs and abilities in the material world. Because of his essence, man had to labor. Because of his essence, man had to actively modify the physical world to satisfy his own needs. Objectification, for Marx, meant the outpouring, the release of human abilities, compelled by human need, in order to so modify the physical as to guarantee his continued existence.

The process of history, for Marx, can thus be described as the humanization of nature. Nature was not given a human form, a human visage. Rather, nature was so shaped, so altered, that it would accommodate itself to human needs. Nature was humanized because human labor forced it to affirm and support species life.

For Marx, as for Hegel, man created himself. But whereas the Hegel human self-creation was the labor of self-consciousness, for Marx, human self-creation was the labor of the naturalistic forces of the species. History was not, in the Marxian scheme, the expression of universal spirit. Man made his socioeconomic environment, and this social environment was a productive environment, which in turn determined the conditioned man's idea, thoughts, and values—determined the creator himself.

2. Alienation

The objective for Hegel, in contradistinction to Marx, was always outside of man.[2] Self-consciousness must always objectify itself. To be known, to be experienced, self-consciousness must be observed, must be seen. It can only be observed in the thing that it has fashioned, which is now external and separate from the subject. To be objective for Hegel meant that a subject must be able to contemplate its conscious activity, and this activity could only be contemplated in things external to the subject.

Alienation for Hegel was thus an existential necessity. As soon as self-consciousness fashioned a theory, an idea, it was alienated from the subject by way of the objective. Alienation was the process by which consciousness, forced by its own nature to objectify itself, and fulfilling its destiny in a thing, finds that it is no longer a part of the subject. Hegel's philosophy of culture, therefore, was a philosophy of alienation. Man lived in a cultural universe of his own making, but a universe that was estranged from him.

Hegel did not understand alienation in a totally negative sense. Because of alienation man had his cultural heritage. Because of alienation man made his history. Because of alienation man came to understand his own powers, the magnificent energies of consciousness, his self, since he could observe these energies in the objects and cultural forms with which he surrounded himself. Estrangement was the inevitable result of consciousness obeying its own necessity of objectification. It was both the power of mind and the fatality of mind.

In the Hegelian universe, man must always lose himself, in order to find himself. Some power, some force was always taken from man—lost, stolen, or surrendered. There was a tragic component to Hegel's philosophy: Man was doomed to be forever estranged in a world of his own creation. Hegel spoke of a divine discontent, of a discontent that was an essential mode of existence because alienation was an essential mode of self-consciousness. Tragic existence was Hegel's theme. The glorification of human power, self-consciousness in its activity, was at the same instant the coming into being of estrangement, heroic anxiety.

In the Marxian universe, alienation had a totally different meaning. Rather than being a necessity, alienation was a social condition. Rather than being a destiny of self-consciousness, alienation was an environmental cancer, produced by living men, in their living, conscious activity.

The expropriation of human labor, which is their life's activity, was alienation. Men spent their life's activity to sustain the species. The expenditure of their life's activity, in essence, their life, should be fully returned to them in the products and objects thereby molded. If this were not the case, if some other person or institution expropriated this life activity for his or its personal advantage, the exploited man was an alienated man.

Marx did not share Hegel's tragic discontent. Since alienation was not a fate, but a social condition to be cured, Marx dedicated himself to the overcoming of alienation. Communism was such a supersession. There was more optimism in Marx than in Hegel. The future, for Marx, could witness the beginning of a true human history. There was hope in Marx, an openness to the future. There was a project. Human rationality, understanding the class nature of past history, comprehending the condition that produced alienation, could conceive a project of revolution that would begin the age of humanized history. Rationality was a guide to action, because the construction of a de-alienated existence was fully consonant with species power.

3. Reappropriation

In the history of self-consciousness, for Hegel, alienation must be succeeded by reappropriation.[3] The thing that has been lost must be regained. Or, consciousness, as a force, sought to repossess its own creation. Alienation must be superseded, because consciousness, or desire, hungrily reached out to reoccupy the world it made and temporarily surrendered.

For Hegel, however, reappropriation takes place totally in consciousness. The thing was repossessed rationally, it was not sensuously felt. Self-consciousness made a tool, which was then alienated. Self-consciousness reappropriated the tool when it superseded it, when it could make a greater tool, a machine. Reappropriation for Hegel involved negation, the canceling of a prior moment of creation in order to absorb that moment in a continuing creation. Negation for Hegel meant transcendence.

Marx also, like Hegel, referred to reappropriation as a taking back into one's self. The objects that species activity fashioned must return to the species in an immediate, direct, sensual manner.

> The objects of his drives exist outside himself as objects independent of him, yet they are objects of his needs, essential objects which are indispensable to the exercise and confirmation of his faculties. The fact that man is an embodied, living, real, sentient, objective being with natural powers, means that he has real, sensuous objects as the objects of his being, or that he can only express his being in real sensuous objects. To be objective, natural, sentient and at the same time to have object, nature and sense outside oneself, or to be oneself object, nature and sense for a third person, is the same thing.[4]

What was made by the objective activity of the species, if not alienated from it, was also objective. If species labor produced food, the food was objective, and related immediately to the objective hunger of the species. Therefore, in an unalienated society there was an immediate reciprocity between the object made and the need it was meant to gratify. The need could not be gratified unless the object were made, and thus objective need and object coexist, and mutually complement each other. Reappropriation for Marx was thus defined as mutual complementation. It was predicated on the interdependence of man and modified nature, the harmony, balance, the sensuously pleasurable reciprocity of objective need and object. In this sense, the world for Marx should be a world of enjoyment. For if modified nature complemented need, then labor would produce its own immediate and direct pleasure. Marx was referring here to the naturalistic interconnection between man and nature, where man and nature were two modes of the same process, where the activity of one had immediately returned to it confirmation of that activity by the other.

4. Self-Affirmation

Self-affirmation, for Hegel, was a process that took place in self-consciousness.[5] It was that moment when self-consciousness was most like itself. Therefore, it was the moment of negation. Self-consciousness was most like itself when in the activity of transcendence.

The Marxian definition of self-affirmation had two forms: integration and joy. Through the production of the objective, individual man was integrated into the species. Because man's production was directly social production, man produced for the entire species and himself simultaneously. Therefore, in the act of production man reaffirmed species being in its twin modality, in its objective expression in the individual, and in its universal form throughout mankind.

Because species activity was feeling, sensuous activity, the confirmation of that activity was joyful. When a man made paint and it confirmed the sense of sight, when a man made music and it confirmed the sense of hearing, he was the recipient of joy. Communist society was to reclaim the world for man; that is, the reappropriation of human objectification was at the same time reappropriation of the human essence.

The humanism of Marx, in a modulated, economized form, was also a dominant factor in the *Grundrisse* and *Kapital.* Indeed, the crucial notion of species being was transported from the Paris manuscripts to the *Grundrisse.* In that later work, commenting upon how the economic process should enhance the interconnectedness between man and man, Marx asserted that "this proves that each of them reaches beyond his own particular need etc., as a human being, and that they relate to one another as human beings; that their common species-being (Gattungswesen) is acknowledged."[6] Further on in the same work, when discussing the evolution of man from his tribal to his communal existence, Marx wrote that "human beings become individuals only through the process of history. He appears originally as a species being (Gattungswesen), clan being herd animal—although in no way whatever as a polis creature, in the political sense."[7] Thus, in the more mature Marx, the notion of a common human essence was still present. This anthropological core, however, was understood by the economized Marx as need, as physical and psychological want, as the requirement of human self-sustenance and well-being. In addition, Marx still conceived of history as the autogenesis of man. The anthropological essence remained, but it received different forms, different modalities, was a historical product, as it moved in history through various economic and productive structures.

Nevertheless, as the later Marx speculated upon the social and economic requirements of human life, it became apparent to him that the overriding concern was the production and reproduction of subsistence. "The aim of all these communities is survival; i.e. reproduction of the individuals who compose it as proprietors ... the production, however, is at the same time necessarily new production and destruction of the old form."[8] In the *Grundrisse* and *Kapital* the central concern of Marx was the production and consumption of the necessities of life. The ideas of objectification, alienation, reappropriation, and self-affirmation were also present in these later works. But they were realized within them; they appeared from the perspective of socioeconomic contingency.

In the Marx who was concerned with the production and reproduction of life and society, objectification appeared in the form of economic labor: "All production is an objectification (Vergegenstandlichung) of the individual."[9] But this production could only correspond to the inherent talent and skills of the individual. Nature was dumb and mute, offering itself passively to the active agent man, and what was made satisfied a human need. But what was made, the modification of nature, could only be expressive of human abilities. "For the use value which he offers exists only as an ability, a capacity (Vermogen) of his bodily existence; has no existence apart from that."[10]

In order to labor, man must appropriate. What he appropriated was the materiality provided to him by nature. A vast laboratory, a storehouse of mutable objects, nature offered to man the physics upon which human powers of modification could operate. After appropriation, man must consume. The economized Marx did not talk of self-affirmation, but consumption. Human life and society were perpetuated through consumption. The human essence was not reaffirmed by consumption; rather consumption reproduced individual and societal survival.[11]

The theme of alienation was prevalent throughout the later writings of Marx. The whole structure of *Das Kapital* recounted the destiny of human labor as it was expropriated by the greed of the capitalist. Society under capitalism was alienated society *par excellence,* because the wealth in the hands of the proprietary classes was essentially the stolen labor of the masses. Part Three of Volume I of *Kapital* was devoted to a discussion of the working day. Of course, for Marx, value was created by labor. Under this formula, the working day assumed critical importance because any extension of that day, by whatever means, equaled more labor time and therefore more value. In these pages Marx described how the capitalist attempted to increase the productivity of the working day, by the use of machinery, of women, of children, by the enlargement of the population, in order to increase his profits. The length of the working day was not simply an economic problem, not merely a matter of time. Rather, it was a matter of life. By increasing that day, the capitalist, in fact, stole from the worker the time he had for his own life. The worker was then victimized, dehumanized, and the time he could expend on himself for his own enjoyments and development grew smaller and smaller.[12]

Furthermore, Part Four of Volume I of *Kapital* was devoted to a discussion of machinery. According to Marx, machinery was the best way to enlarge the working day. It did this in two ways: it improved the productivity of the laborer; and because of the better means for production and transportation, it quickened the rate of circulation. Value could be produced faster, a profit could be realized faster, and thus the circuit for the production of capital intensified and multiplied. Consequently, the introduction of machinery, factories, industrial plants was one of the major quests of capitalism. But the factory destroyed the bonds of human interconnectedness. The communal village, the familial farm passed into the wastebasket of history. In their place stepped the atomized, the barbarized factory worker. The industrial worker was thus not only alienated from his fellow worker, but also from himself. Working in unsanitary conditions, he himself was reduced to a machine. His labor was monotonous, dull, and his movements simply replicated in mindless fashion the mechanical movement of technology.[13] Alienation in *Kapital* was not primarily alienation from man's species being. It was not primarily anthropological. Alienation in *Kapital* was fundamentally socioeconomic. Human labor had made its world and within that world man was alone, dehumanized, a victim of his own creation. In a world made by the self, man was estranged.

Such were the principles of Marx's philosophical anthropology. They were derived from fundamental presuppositions regarding the nature of man. But they are not merely guidelines, mere direction. They are sources from which a radical criticism of past and existing societies can be unleashed. It is not enough to attack societies because they restrain and hinder productive forces, because they curtail economic abundance. No criticism of any society, from the Marxian perspective, can be complete unless it is shown how that society deviates from the principles of communist philosophical anthropology. In short, the human essence as conceived by Marx must always be the final criterion in judging the positive or negative features of any socioeconomic formation.

Marx's definition of communism conformed to his anthropocentric view of society. That is, in a communist society it was "impossible that anything should exist independently of individuals."[14] Marx's attack on bourgeois economic apologists, like Smith, Ricardo, and Proudhon, began from the basis that these men treated economic categories as eternal. Exchange, money, labor were seen by bourgeois economic theoreticians as adamantine categories that were present and operative in all societies at all times, in fact, determining these societies by their unchanging laws. Marx was opposed to this categorization of economic formulas, because they were there independent of man, existing above him, beyond human control, in reality determining the manner in which human beings necessarily must function.[15]

Marx's *Theories of Surplus Value* was an attack on just such an eternalization of economic categories. To begin discussing economics from the basis of exchange was at once to alienate man, because we immediately debated a mechanical process, a law of natural objects, rather than human activity. To begin discussing economics from the point of view of money was immediately to dehumanize man, because the point of discussion became the dumb, mute object money, a thing in itself without any human relationships, rather than the power of human beings to modify their environment. Thinking of economic categories as immutable, for Marx, was simply another form of Hegelianism, that is, of idealism. If things were made immutable they became in essence like the World Spirit, veritable Gods, sovereign, unchanging, all-powerful. What Marx wished to do was to historicize economics.

Communism, for Marx, was "the production of the form of intercourse itself."[16] Communism did not begin with technology, productive capacity, or systems analysis. It began by creating the forms of social intercourse through which man would have immediate accessibility to the conditions of his labor. Communism meant that man must be free to objectify himself, to reappropriate his activity, and to have his faculties reaffirmed. Communism, therefore, referred to those social relationships that would allow for objectification, reappropriation, and self-affirmation.

Marx's future society was not things; it was the self-activity of man. Proletarian society was not objects; it was "the development of the forces of the individuals themselves."[17] Proletarian society was an anthropocentric society: a mode of socioproductive existence in which man continually confirmed his essence because the natural and human environment was freely accessible to him and consequently fashioned in his image. It was a means of being humanly authenticated.

Communism was not static. It was not the final, eschatological society. It was not a given form. It was that society in which human productive forces will be at their fullest. It will therefore change—it will have a history.[18]

In a communist form of society, relationships of human authenticity, the object made confirming objective human essence, would be conquered. What would change were the productive forces, the tools by which to fashion nature. If the productive forces changed, then the social relationships built on these productive forces would also have to change. Communist society was also historical society. Presumably, however, as the relations of production change, of necessity, they would simply reexpress the central communist thesis: authenticate the human essence.[19] That is, it was entirely conceivable, in fact, necessary, to have endless forms of human social intercourse, as long as these forms of intercourse embodied the principle that the object made must affirm the objective human essence. Therefore, the form of relationship would change, but communist philosophical anthropology would always be the intent behind these relationships.

As late as 1858–1859, Marx continued to define communism as an anthropocentric society. A quotation from the *Grundrisse* is in order:

> In fact, however, when the limited bourgeois form is stripped away, what is wealth other than the universality of individual needs, capacities, pleasures, productive forces, etc., created through universal exchange? The full development of human mastery over the forces of nature, those of so-called nature as well as of humanity's own nature? The absolute working-out of his creative potentialities, with no presupposition other than the previous historic development, which makes this totality of development, i.e. the development of all human powers as such the end in itself, not as measured on a predetermined yardstick? Where he does not reproduce himself in one specificity, but produces his totality? Strives not to remain something he has become, but is in the absolute movement of becoming?[20]

From the Paris manuscripts until the *Grundrisse,* Marx's definition of communism remained substantially the same. In the economized Marx, a certain level of industrial productive capacity was a precondition. In the economized Marx, there was less emphasis on the human essence. But there remained the central idea of the release of human capacities. There remained the central idea that society must conform to and be supportive of the content of human life. Man would be not a truncated being, but a total being. Because of the productive proficiency of communism, because of the increased disposable time this productivity would leave in the hands of individuals, man would be free to enlarge all of his productive powers and his expressive abilities. "For the real wealth is the developed productive power of all individuals."[21]

In the later Marx also, communism was eudaemonistic. Happiness, for Marx, meant the freedom to be a total person, that is, the freedom to indulge all of our productive power and expressive capacities. Culture could not be separated from the realization of human abilities. The fully developed individual was the presupposition of culture. Civilization was that level of society, that degree of socioeconomic advancement, which offered the requisite conditions for the attainment of culture, the coming into being of the wealth of human power.

The preceding analysis has concerned itself with the broad principles of Marx's philosophical anthropology. Ideas like objectification, alienation, reappropriation, and self-affirmation were discussed and shown to be indispensable to his definition of the human essence. Other statements of Marx were more empirical. That is, they discussed the naturalistic basis for his philosophical anthropology. In short, Marx affirmed that the biological nature of the species substantiated the philosophical principles of his anthropology.

In *The Holy Family*, Marx juxtaposed a series of statements from Holbach:

> Man can only love himself in the objects he loves: he can have affection only for himself in the other beings of his kind. Man can never separate himself from himself for a single instant in his life, he cannot lose sight of himself. It is always our convenience, our interest that makes us hate or love things . . . but "in his own interest man must love other men, because they are necessary to his welfare . . . Moral proves to him that of all beings the most necessary to man is man."[22]

In the above paragraph, Marx affirmed that the basic nature of man was emotional, sensate. Man was a thing of passion. He felt pain and passion as well as happiness and love. He had naturalistic needs and naturalistic abilities. Rationality also inherently belonged to the species.

But the sensate nature of man was the actual condition of his sociability. Because man had needs, he had need for other people. Because man felt passion and happiness, he needed to associate himself with other people. Human sociability, human species existence, was merely the expression of the sensate character of existence.

Marx was aware of human self-interest, human selfishness. Marx was not Rousseau; he did not believe that humans basically were good. Self-interest was also a feature of species sensate existence. But self-interest could also serve as the basis of human integration, was itself the ground of the need for human relationships. "If correctly understood interest is the principle of all morality, man's private interest must be made to coincide with the interest of humanity."[23] Human rationality must devise means so that private interest can be generalized into universal interest.

In Marx's analysis of human sensate nature, he was traveling along a path similar to that of the moral philosophers Thomas Hutchinson and Adam Smith. In the eighteenth century, these men were attempting to make man's passionate nature serve as the basis of morality and society. The philosophy of emotion and empathy was replacing religious morality as the ground of brotherliness. Drawing upon English philosophy, which Marx designated as leading directly to socialism and communism, Marx felt he had found, in the sensuous substrate of species existence, the naturalistic foundation of social cooperativeness.

This sensuous substrate was also a naturalistic verification of Marx's concept of reaffirmation. Human sensate nature was by its very essence interpersonal because of its inherent need of the other. Sensate nature was by its very essence humanly interdependent, because of its quest for the other. This dependence upon the other, this fulfillment through the other, was what Marx had in mind when he talked of human and species self-affirmation.

It should be clear from the above discussion that, for Marx, human sensate nature was society itself. Social life did not derive from the passionate nature of man; rather social life had to be the passionate nature of man. Such a definition led Marx directly to his philosophy of enjoyment. Another quotation, this time from *The German Ideology,* is necessary.

> In the Middle Ages the pleasures were strictly classified; each estate had its own distinct forms of pleasure and its distinct manner of enjoying them. The nobility was the estate privileged to devote itself exclusively to pleasure while the separation of work and enjoyment already existed for the bourgeoisie and pleasure was subordinated to work . . . The present crude form of proletarian pleasure is due on the one hand to the long working hours which led to the utmost intensification of the need for recreation, and, on the other hand to the restriction—both qualitative and quantitative—of the means of pleasure accessible to the proletarian. In general, the enjoyment of all hitherto existing estates and classes had to be utter childish exhausting or crude because it was always completely divorced from the vital activity, the content of the life of the individuals, and more or less reduced to imparting an illusory content to a meaningless activity. The hitherto existing forms of enjoyment could of course, only be criticized when the contradiction between the bourgeoisie and the proletariat had developed to such an extent that the existing mode of production and intercourse could be criticized as well.[24]

In the above paragraph, Marx described the separation of species activity (work) and pleasure. In the Middle Ages pleasure was thought to be a prerogative of the aristocracy. In the age of the bourgeoisie, pleasure was subordinated to material acquisition, financial greed. A slave in the period of capitalism, the proletarian had little time for pleasure, and what little pleasure he had was debasing and degrading. The separation of *praxis* from the self-gratification of the results of that *praxis* divorced man from his own nature, for his own activity was never a source of pleasure to him.

Marx was not talking about hedonism. He was not saying that the end of life was the maximization of sensual excitement. He was not a sybarite. For Marx, the normal state of species existence was activity. The essence of man was his *praxis.* Objectification and reappropriation are aspects of his inherent *praxis.* Marx was saying that human activity in itself should be pleasurable. *Praxis* itself was enjoyment. The end of life for Marx was human well-being, based upon the naturalistic substrate of the species. Social life must correspond to the needs of species *praxis.* The forms of social intercourse and social relatedness must be species activity. Thus, at the very core of Marx's philosophical anthropology was the principle of eudaemonism. The good life was a life in which man was in harmony with his needs and abilities.[25]

Marx's philosophy of enjoyment, his definition of happiness as life in accordance with nature, also served as the basis for his definition of virtue. In *The Holy Family,* Marx attacked Eugene Sue's novel *Fleur de Marie.*

> Good and evil, in Marie's mind, are not the moral abstractions of good and evil. She is good because she has never caused suffering to anybody, she has always been human towards her inhuman surroundings. She is good because the sun and the flowers reveal to her her own sunny and blossoming nature. She is good because she is still young, full of hope and vitality. Her situation is not good because it does her unnatural violence, because it is not the expression of her human impulses, the fulfillment of her human desires; because it is full of torment and void of pleasure. She measures her situation in life by her own individuality, her natural essence, not by the ideal of good.[26]

In this passage, Marx launched an attack on Christian ethics. A morality of sin, a morality of guilt, was a complete distortion of human nature. An ethic that appealed to theological abstractions, an ethic that needed the support of institutional authority and superstitious threat, was an ethic of total self-alienation. To speak of goodness as divorced from species essence, to speak of goodness in terms of duality—the natural man evil, the spiritual man good—was to impose upon man a fateful severance from his own essence. Thus divided, thus hopelessly estranged, the creative and life-producing forces of man would die.

Marx's attack on Christianity was very similar to his attack on capitalism. In refuting capitalist economic theory, Marx was refuting the world view of the capitalist ruling class. Such an attack was absolutely necessary, because the world view of the proprietary bourgeoisie was based upon the expropriation of the human *praxis* of the laboring masses. In attacking Christianity and Christian ethics, Marx also refuted the world view of the clergy as a class. The ethics of spiritualism sundered the human personality from its naturalistic substrate. Marx was thus engaging in broad cultural criticism. He was showing that the ideological structure of capitalism and the ideological structure of Christian ethics were merely apologies for the class interests of property owners and ecclesiastics.

In the place of bourgeois and religious consciousness, Marx wished to substitute communist consciousness. The world view that Marx wished to create, the new culture Marx wished to bring into existence, was the communist culture. The proletarian ethic would not be based on sin, would not be based on material acquisition, but rather on eudaemonism, life in accordance with the nature of the species.

György Lukács, in *History and Class Consciousness,*[27] described the superstructure of society, the ideological fabric of a society, as manifestations of class interests. Private property, free enterprise, a market economy, because they served the class interests of the proprietary bourgeoisie, were concepts that were defended by that class. The ideas of the ruling class in society became the ruling ideas of that society. The proletariat as a class, because they were the enslaved, had different interests. Their interests favored the communalization of the means of production. The sociopolitical struggle of the bourgeoisie against the proletariat, class warfare, was mirrored in the struggle of the two *Weltanschauung*. If the political revolution of the proletariat were successful, the world view of the proletariat would also triumph.

Lukács thus saw the proletariat and its world view as the force of negations. Bourgeoisie and proletariat, representing two contradictory socioideological worlds, the one old and living beyond its time, the other new and the force of the future, stood in mortal dialectical opposition. The proletariat must transcend bourgeois decadence. Class-consciousness for Lukács was thus merely the expression of class interest. Cultural criticism, art, philosophy, and morality could thus only be undertaken from the point of view of class-consciousness.

Certainly the dialectic of negation was crucial to Marxian cultural consciousness. Marx spent the better part of his life demonstrating how bourgeois economic theory was merely the expression of bourgeois class interests. New classes in society, new classes spawned in the womb of an old society, will always carry with them a new ideological structure, a negation of the old. But there was more. There was the naturalistic substrate of species essence. There was that passionate and emotional basis of human existence which Marx saw as the essence of social existence. This too must be incorporated into Marxian criticism. Bourgeois society was not only decadent because it perpetuated the slavery of property. It was decadent too because it violated the species nature of man. Thus, Marxian anthropology was another tool for judging the alienation of man in society, judging whether history had indeed become true human history.

Footnotes

1. Karl Marx, "Critique of Hegel's Dialectic and General Philosophy," *Karl Marx: Early Writings*, ed. and trans. T. B. Bottomore (New York: McGraw-Hill, 1963), pp. 202–203.
2. *Ibid.*, p. 204.
3. *Ibid.*, p. 201.
4. *Ibid.*, pp. 206–207.
5. Marx, "Free Human Production," *Writings of the Young Marx on Philosophy and Society*, ed. and trans. Loyd D. Easton and Kurt H. Guddat (New York: Doubleday & Co., 1967), p. 281.
6. Marx, *Grundrisse*, trans. Martin Nicolaus (New York: Vintage Press, 1973), p. 243.
7. *Ibid.*, p. 496.
8. *Ibid.*, p. 493.
9. *Ibid.*, p. 226.

10. *Ibid.*, p. 282.
11. *Ibid.*, p. 717.
12. Marx, *Das Kapital,* trans. Samuel Moore and Edward Aveling (New York: International Publishers, 1967), I, pp. 177–303.
13. *Ibid.*, pp. 312–516.
14. Marx, *The German Ideology,* ed. R. Pascal (New York: International Publishers, 1947), p. 70.
15. Marx, *The Poverty of Philosophy* (New York: International Publishers, 1963), pp. 13–57.
16. Marx, *The German Ideology,* ed. R. Pascal, p. 70.
17. *Ibid.*, p. 72.
18. Marx, *The Poverty of Philosophy,* p. 110.
19. *Ibid.*, p. 147.
20. Marx, *Grundrisse,* p. 488.
21. *Ibid.*, p. 708.
22. Marx, *The Holy Family* trans. by R. Dixon (Moscow: Foreign Languages Publishing House, 1956), pp. 178–179.
23. *Ibid.*, p. 176.
24. Marx, *The German Ideology,* trans. S. Ryazanskaya (Moscow: Progress Publishers, 1968), pp. 470–471.
25. *Ibid.*, p. 495.
26. Marx, *The Holy Family,* pp. 226–227.
27. George Lukács, *History and Class Consciousness,* trans. Rodney Livingstone (Cambridge, Mass.: M.I.T. Press, 1971).

Four

Marx as a Jacobin

THE THREE PREVIOUS chapters discussed at some length the humanism of Marx. This humanism, however, was grounded upon the belief that the fulfillment of man was only possible through the total transformation of his social condition. For Marx, it was impossible to be a humanist without at the same time being a revolutionary, for to accept the present social environment of man was also to accept man's continued self-alienation. The presuppositions of Marx's philosophical anthropology inevitably led to political activism. The "Theses on Feuerbach" were the clearest expression of this attitude.[1]

The model that Marx had in mind when he wrote about revolution was France of 1789. Just as the bourgeoisie had overthrown feudalism and established their own class rule in 1791, so in the subsequent communist revolution the proletariat would destroy capitalism and establish its class rule. Communism would carry the development of mankind to a higher stage, onward from the conquest of political democracy to the conquest of social democracy. It was for this reason that Marx saw Babeuf as the herald of a new world order.

Revolution for Marx meant the coming into being of a different civilization. Industrialism had superseded agrarianism. Secularism had replaced the religious domination of society. A centralized representative state had replaced a decentralized aristocratic state. Equality took precedence over privilege. The class that acted as the carrier, the activating agent for this passage from one civilization to another, was a new class born in the nascent industrial-commercial society, the bourgeoisie.

When facing the problem of revolution, Marx thought in terms of basic structural alterations in society. Because of fundamental structural changes, a new style of life, a new world outlook, would also emerge. All this had occurred in the French Revolution. All this would occur in the proletarian revolution. Marx envisioned himself as the successor of Robespierre and Babeuf. Indeed, his social philosophy thoroughly differed from these two French revolutionaries. But he perpetuated their tradition because he understood, as they did, that revolution entailed the change of underlying social structures, entailed human liberation.

What Marx meant by "emancipation" was best expressed in his essay "On the Jewish Question." In this manuscript Marx dealt with the question of Jewish emancipation, but only as a particular case of the more general condition for human emancipation. In short, the conditions of freedom for the Jew were also the conditions of freedom for society as a whole.

The Jew, for Marx, was victimized because he was forced to perform certain social functions that the Christian at one time in Western society did not wish to perform. Commercial functions that the Christian abjured because of his own religious and cultural biases were allotted to the Jew. In the context of the nineteenth century, anti-Semitic persecution of the Jew for being a capitalist was to persecute the Jew for fulfilling vocations that Christian society initially impressed upon him.

Jewish emancipation could not be achieved, according to Marx, through the grant of religious toleration and civil liberties. To free the Jew one had to free the Jew from the cause of his persecution. Political and religious oppression was not the cause of his economic function; it was capitalism that was the cause of the victimization of the Jew, because it was capitalism that had created those commercial and mercantile functions that the Jew was forced to perform. To remove the cause of anti-Semitism, then, involved the destruction of capitalism, for without capitalism those functions for which the Jew was hated would no longer exist. Human emancipation, for Marx, entailed the destruction of the socioeconomic reasons for man's alienation. Political emancipation was only partial.[2]

In "Toward the Critique of Hegel's Philosophy of Law," Marx repeated the themes of "On the Jewish Question," but in a slightly different form. In the former manuscript, the idea of the proletariat was introduced for the first time in Marx's writing. The proletariat was the class to bring complete human emancipation. It could do this because the particular ills of the proletariat were at the same time the general ills of society. For instance, the wage slavery from which the proletariat suffered was merely an expression of the materialism, the greed, the rampant egoism of capitalist society in total. The cause of the enslavement of the proletariat was the wage system. It was impossible for the proletariat to free itself from wage exploitation without simultaneously freeing society in its entirety from wage exploitation, i.e., capitalism. The particular grievance of the working class was only an instance of the general disease of society, and it was therefore impossible to cure the particular ill without first abolishing the general cause of the disease.[3]

The definition that Marx gave to emancipation in "On the Jewish Question" and "Toward the Critique of Hegel's Philosophy of Law" was repeated in his *Grundrisse* (Foundations of a Critique of Political Economy). The transcendence of particular social ills was only possible through the transcendence of the general ills of a society. Complete human emancipation, therefore, could only come when society was completely free of any inclusive, structural dysfunction. For the individual to be free, society itself must be completely free from any mechanisms and institutions of oppression. This condition could only be reached by means of a revolution.

Marx believed that in order to achieve full human liberation, that is, in order to change the structural relations of society, it was necessary to use political power, force.[4] The question of power was primary. It was primary because only through the instrumentality of power, force, was it possible to compel, to bring about the desired social transformation. Thus, Marx believed that the seizure of political power was absolutely necessary in any revolution. Without the seizure of power, the bourgeoisie could not have replaced the aristocracy, industrialism could not have replaced agrarianism, because in the absence of force the old ruling class, the old mode of production would not allow itself to be displaced.

Clearly, Marx was not a Jacobin in the ideological sense. Robespierre wished to universalize private property, while Marx wished to abolish private possession. Robespierre thought in terms of individual equality, while Marx thought in terms of a collective, cooperative species being. Socially and ideologically, Jacobinism prepared the way for the final conquest of bourgeois, capitalist society.

But Marx was a Jacobin in the strategic, tactical, political sense. He never condemned Robespierre for the Terror. He never condemned Babeuf for his attemped insurrection. Even though he disagreed with Robespierre's goals, Marx accepted as necessary and justified the means by which Robespierre sought to achieve these goals. Jacobinism, even though it was not communist, was superior to the Directory, and superior to the mild liberal bourgeois victory of 1791. Marx understood that even though Robespierre had not gone far enough to the left he nevertheless had deepened the revolution, he had radicalized it. This was only possible because he conquered power and then used force and compulsion to carry the revolution further down the class hierarchy of society.[5]

The above conclusions are amply substantiated by an examination of Marx's comments on the French Revolution. In the first half of "On the Jewish Question," Marx summarized the accomplishments of the entire revolutionary epoch, from 1789 to 1815. Obviously the bourgeoisie had triumphed. The triumph of the bourgeoisie entailed the triumph of natural rights theory. In summary, then, the French Revolution was a political revolution. What it succeeded in doing was to universalize civil liberties. It did not alter society. For Marx, therefore, the French Revolution at its completion was a partial revolution, an unfinished revolution. Egoism was legalized. Greed was legalized. Property and boundless material acquisition were institutionalized. Capitalism was unleashed and alienation perpetuated. Marx's criticism of the French Revolution was a criticism of all purely political revolutions.[6]

For Marx, then, the revolution had failed. It had failed "because the most numerous part of the mass, the part most greatly differing from the bourgeoisie, did not find its real interest in the principle of the revolution."[7] The interests of the proletariat were not represented by the victorious principles of the bourgeoisie. Or, the proletariat, carrying within itself the general ills of society, did not achieve political power as a class and thus could not cleanse society of the cause of these general ills. Rather, the triumph of the bourgeoisie was a triumph of a relatively small group in society, and thus its victory was only capable of removing some particular ills, some symptoms, but not the universal conditions of distress.

Nevertheless, there were episodes in the revolution in which the masses nearly spoke. Robespierre and Saint-Just, during the Terror, were "the real representatives of the revolutionary power."[8] Notwithstanding, Marx chose not "to vindicate the mistakes of the Terrorists"[9] and was clearly of the mind that Robespierre should have moved further toward a proletarian revolution. Those who spoke for communism during the revolution were the *Enragés* Leclerc and Roux, and later Babeuf.[10]

Marx was an admirer of the Reign of Terror. In spite of ideological differences, Marx understood the Terror to be a necessary political instrument of the revolution. The Terror was the "revolution in permanence"; that is, it was the revolution as it drew closer to the mass of people. As the revolution drew closer to the mass of people, as it tried to express the wishes of the mass of people, the revolution needed political power, governmental force in order to realize some of the social hopes of the masses. The Terror was the people armed, the people acting as one, the people using coercion and murder to force structural changes upon society, to fulfill its own social dreams.

Even during the 1848 revolutions the memory of the Terror lived on in Marx. In fact, he hoped for a Jacobin solution, a Reign of Terror for Germany itself. Marx cried out against the growing counterrevolution in Germany in December 1848 by reminding the enemies of the proletariat that the "entire French terrorism was nothing else but the maturation of the plebeian style in politics, the attack on Absolutism, on Feudalism and the industrialists, all enemies of the bourgeoisie."[11] In March 1849, when Marx despaired for the revolution in Piedmont, in the hope of keeping it alive, he wrote: "But the revolt in mass, the general insurrection of the people, that is the means before which Kings will retreat in horror. Those are the means which only the republic utilized. . . . 1793 is proof of that. Those are the means, whose execution presupposes revolutionary terror, and where is a monarch who can stand before it?"[12] In May 1849, upon the suppression of the *Neue Rheinische Zeitung,* Marx called out in utter defiance of the defeat of the revolution: "... the cannibalism of the counter-revolution itself will convince the people that there is only one means by which a mortal blow can be given to the old society, and the bloody birth of the new society shortened, simplified, condensed, only one means ... revolutionary terrorism."[13]

The year 1793 epitomized the French Revolution for Marx. It was the apex of the unity between the masses and revolution, the alliance of revolutionary terror and revolutionary war. Marx referred to this year as a model, as a potential device that he hoped other revolutionaries would imitate. In the July 12, 1848, issue of the *Neue Rheinische Zeitung,* Marx asserted that German unity could only be gained through the use of war, specifically war against Russia. "Only a war with Russia is a revolutionary war for Germany, a war in which the evils of the past can be washed away. ..."[14]

In January 1849, when praising the Hungarian Revolution, Marx returned to the same theme, the same extolling of the climactic year 1793. Marx referred to Kossuth and the Hungarian Revolution as "the revolution in permanence, where we find all the characteristics of the glorious year 1793 are again utilized, organized. ..."[15] Several years later, Marx, as an editorial writer for the *New York Daily Tribune,* commented on the Crimean War. Seeing the need for the dismemberment of the Ottoman Empire, Marx saw the revolution as the best means of dissolving Turkey and simultaneously keeping reactionary Russia off the Bosporus. According to Marx there was a sixth power in Europe, the revolution, the greatest power, which would undo the plans of the conservative European powers "as it did from 1792 to 1800."[16]

This is not to say that Marx was a Blanquist.[17] For Marx, the Jacobins did not start the revolution, but were a product of it. The Jacobins did not create the revolution *ex nihilo;* their subjective will was not sufficient to bring the revolution into existence. Marx was not an exponent of voluntarism or subjectivism. He clearly understood that mass discontent, that widespread social distress, that institutional decadence, that the actual conditions for revolution were in existence and preceded the outbreak of revolution itself. Revolutions were not made, for Marx, they were products of history. But once the revolution had begun, once the laws of dialectical naturalism had produced the breakdown of the old order, then the revolution could be radicalized. Once sufficient socioeconomic conditions had given birth to the revolution, then force and compulsion could make it permanent.

Blanqui talked of a revolutionary elite. They would be the military vanguard of the revolution. Violent putschs by this elite, according to Blanqui, could in themselves create the conditions for revolution. Terror and coup d'état, Blanqui maintained, could act as galvanizing events, could serve to rouse the masses to rebellion. For Marx, Blanqui was an idealist who tended to separate social revolt from actual sociological conditions. For Marx, class warfare was the result of the clash between the means of production and the mode of production. Therefore, the sufficient conditions for revolutions were ones that slowly emerged from the objective flow of history, rather than from subjective forces. However, once the social rebellion broke out, the situation was fluid, presenting a myriad of possibilities. It was at this juncture, according to Marx, that Jacobin measures were necessary, that the seizure of power followed by the application of political force could move the revolution to the left, could ally the revolution with the masses.

Marxism, however, was a methodology, not a blueprint. The situation dictated the choice of tactical options. Marx understood quite clearly that there were historical situations in which revolutions were not called for, not needed. In his Amsterdam speech before the First International in 1872 he indicated that revolutionary policies were not needed in England or America because socialism could evolve peacefully in these countries due to their unique conditions.[18] His own political behavior inside the First International was conciliatory (except for the Bakuninists) since he recognized the need for unity as opposed to ideological purity. But Marx was opposed to a mechanical view of history. The history of society did not proceed as abstracted and extrinsic to man: the coming of a communist society would not of itself issue from the processes of history. Human action was an indispensable ingredient. Marx criticized the German Social Democrat Party because they believed that socialism would itself issue from the laws of history unattended by the midwife of human activity. When the conditions were present, revolutionary *praxis* must be applied.

Marx demonstrated his Jacobinism when he related to the political events of his time. The positions he took, the policies he advocated in relation to the German Revolution of 1848–1849, the French Revolution of 1848–1850, the First International, and the Paris Commune were all Jacobin.

As the editor of the *Neue Rheinische Zeitung,* Marx acted as the spokesman, during the 1848 revolutions, of the German communists.[19] In fact, the first issue of the *Neue Rheinische Zeitung* listed the "Demands of the Communist Party in Germany."[20] The first demand was for a unified German republic. Marx wished to see the end of feudal decentralization. He wanted Germany to become a centralized state, patterned after the unitary French state that had emerged in the course of the French Revolution. Marx was decidedly a German nationalist. He understood that the chief cause for the absence of German unity was the feudal aristocracy, feudal fragmentation. Decentralization was not only a hindrance to German national unity, but it was also a source of German weakness, allowing Germany to be victimized by the stronger powers beyond her western borders and beyond her eastern borders.

Furthermore, a republic was the form of state that corresponded to popular sovereignty. Feudal estates and feudal privileges were means by which the people were excluded from the exercise of political power. In 1848, Marx was a firm believer in the "sovereignty of the people."[21] The expression of popular will could only take place when there was direct contact between people and state, that is, when there were no intervening orders, no intervening institutions between government decision making and popular will. A republic was the political form that most closely approximated those specifications.

To achieve this goal, Marx thought it absolutely necessary for Germany to go to war against Russia. The Czarist Empire was the most conservative force on the continent. The important role that Russia had played in western and central European affairs was directly related to the weakness, the fragmentation of Germany. Obviously, Russia would not permit the growth of a unitary republican state in Germany, a state that embodied the revolutionary principle of popular sovereignty.

In addition, Marx understood that if Germany were to be unified, if the fragments of Germany were to be wedded into a whole, war was a prerequisite. Something was needed, alliance to some common national destiny, in order to supersede German particularism and cement together a German entity. Only this sense of a common purpose could compel the mass of the German population to smash the two great German monarchies and unify Germany. A war in the east, a war against the enemy of all national movements, Russia, offered the only possibility of creating such national enthusiasm.[22]

Marx wished to ally foreign war with an internal revolution. Russia would act as the political ploy by which to impassion the masses. Simultaneously, this popular enthusiasm would lead to the overthrow of the lesser and greater German states, to internal revolution. Marx's program was the program of 1793. Marx was advocating the Robespierrean formula, force to deepen the revolution, the marriage of foreign war and the leftward movement of the internal revolution.

Not only was Marx in favor of German liberation, but he also hoped for the liberation of Italians,[23] Poles, and Czechs.[24] He demanded their freedom, because he knew that the aristocracies of German Prussia and German Austria were opposed to liberating these previously oppressed people. Maintenance of Hapsburg or Hohenzollern rule in these areas entailed maintenance of the Hapsburg and Hohenzollern aristocracies. Thus, the continuity of feudal domination in Italy, Poland, or Bohemia meant the perpetuation of aristocratic conservatism not only in these regions but also inside Prussia, Austria, and Germany.

The liberation of several of the subjected nationalities of southern and eastern Europe meant the overthrow of the ruling German aristocracies. The elimination of German rule in the south and east involved the weakening of these aristocracies in the German territories themselves. Thus, Marx saw these national movements as having domestic revolutionary implications. Marx was aware of the interconnectedness between domestic structure and foreign policy. Conservative forces at home would tend to expand their influence beyond their own borders in order to strengthen their position at home. They would tend to repress revolutionary forces in foreign countries near their borders in order to strengthen their position at home. Marx felt that the proletariat should support these nationalities in their drive for freedom because this would be striking at the rear of the power of German aristocracy. Support for the subject nationalities had revolutionary possibilities.[25]

Lastly, at no time during the German Revolution of 1848 did Marx argue for a two-stage revolution. He did not feel that the German revolution should stop at the bourgeois stage. He was always critical of the ministries of Camphausen and Hansemann. He saw them as apologists for the monarchy, harbingers and executioners of the counterrevolution. He did not want the revolution to stop with Prussia in the control of the high bourgeoisie. Rather, he wanted the revolution to deepen, to move toward democracy.[26] Clearly, Marx was thinking of a permanent revolution. That is, two revolutions would be part of one process, telescoped.

Several months later, Marx in the *Neue Rheinische Zeitung* had occasion to speculate on events in Paris. In the case of France as in the case of Berlin, Marx looked upon the domination of the high bourgeoisie as an "intermezzo."[27] Indeed, it was to be a "small intermezzo," after which the revolution would deepen to the "red republic," to communism, to proletarian victory. When Marx thought of "permanent revolution," he thought of the use of force to compel the revolution to move beyond one stage onto a more radical one, a revolution that continued until it reached communism.

In situations where revolutionary conditions existed, Marx's devotion to Jacobin politics was clear. Marx affirmed that war and the support of national liberation movements were legitimate devices the revolution could use to force the revolution to move to the left. He even felt that the Jacobin policy of "revolution in permanence" was a legitimate revolutionary tool, that it was good revolutionary strategy to employ power to move the revolution beyond the bourgeois stage after a "small intermezzo." Thus, for Marx, the communist revolution could be accomplished in one revolutionary process. There need not be two revolutions. That is, it was possible to reach communism, as the end result of a revolutionary process, with the bourgeois stage only existing as a "transition step."

Marx perpetuated the tradition of Robespierre and Babeuf. His loyalties to the Terror became clear when in the face of the counterrevolution Marx refused to abandon hope, and called upon the memory of 1793 as the only palliative in the coming disaster. His message was: "Revolutionary uprising of the French working class, world war—that is the content of the year 1849."[28]

IN EXILE IN England after 1849, Marx speculated on the events of 1848–1850 in France. His *Class Struggles in France* (1850), "Address of the Central Committee to the Communist League" (1850), and *The Eighteenth Brumaire of Louis Bonaparte* (1852) were the outcome of these speculations. Marx was as much a Jacobin in 1852 as he was in 1848. The revolutionary strategies that he advocated in retrospect in 1852 were exactly parallel to the tactics he supported as editor of the *Neue Rheinische Zeitung.*

Marx was aware that conditions had been fully ripe for a proletarian revolution in France. The French proletariat was the class he had hoped would conquer power, but he recognized that they had lacked sufficient insurrectionist fervor, that economic conditions had not created in them the unyielding will to seize power. The proletarian class had compromised itself with all layers of the bourgeois class; they lacked a true revolutionary ideology and leadership, so that in the course of the events of 1848–1849 they faltered, only to be subsumed under a bourgeois dictatorship.

Even though Marx recognized the immaturity of revolutionary conditions in France, he did not offer an apology for the proletariat. There was a difference between what the working class did and the action they should have taken. For Marx, the Parisian working classes should have been bolder. The writings of the 1850–1852 period list the mistakes the proletariat made, the opportunities they missed, and it is clear that Marx would have preferred a more vehemently revolutionary behavior. By designating those tactics that Marx thought should have been followed, we will see those strategies toward which Marx was disposed, and the tradition to which he was bound. They were Jacobin.

Moreover, the writings of 1850–1852 were intended to keep alive the proletarian dream. Cognizant of the failure of the 1848 revolutions, Marx wished to prevent proletarian despair. Marx used these revolutions as learning experiences. Hopefully, the proletarians would gain in wisdom from these events, so that the next time a revolutionary situation developed they would be able to exploit it to their full advantage. The message of the writings of 1850–1852 was that a new revolutionary epoch would shortly return. This time the working classes would be prepared, prepared to avoid bourgeois treachery, prepared to impose their own class dictatorship. Marx was intending to create a proletarian legend, a proletarian heritage. Even in failure, he was intending to memorialize proletarian heroism, so that in the future revolution the working classes could draw strength and dedication from their previous history. Failure did not mean defeat, as long as one came away from the present wreckage with greater knowledge and rekindled hope for future possibilities. Marx wrote:

> On the other hand, proletarian revolutions, like those of the nineteenth century, criticize themselves constantly, interrupt themselves continually in their own course, come back to the apparently accomplished in order to begin it afresh, deride with unmerciful thoroughness the inadequacies, weaknesses and paltrineosion of their first attempts, seem to throw down their adversary only in order that he may draw new strength from the earth and rise again, more gigantic, before them, recoil ever and anon from the indefinite prodigiousness of their own arms, until a situation has been created which makes all turning back impossible, and the conditions themselves cry out:
>
> 'Here is the rose,
> here dance.'[29]

When he was in Cologne in 1848, Marx argued for a revolutionary war against Russia. Writing from London in 1850, Marx recognized the deep implications a revolutionary war could have had on events in Paris. Marx believed that the absence of a revolutionary war decidedly harmed the chances for a complete, proletariat revolution inside France.[30] Without foreign intervention in 1848, there was no need for the bourgeoisie to call to the nation. Without a call to the nation, there was no opportunity for the masses to radicalize or overthrow existing bourgeois institutions.

The theme of permanent revolution also was present in the writings of 1850 and 1852.[31] Marx had hoped that in 1848 the civil war would deepen. In fact, in *The Eighteenth Brumaire of Louis Bonaparte,* Marx contrasted the "ascending line" of the Revolution of 1789 with the "descending line" of the Revolution of 1848. In the first French Revolution control of the revolution passed from aristocracy to bourgeoisie, to petite bourgeoisie, while the proletariat as represented by Babeuf failed to achieve power in 1795. This, according to Marx, was the permanent revolution. In the second French Revolution control of the revolution passed from bourgeoisie to Bonapartists. This, according to Marx, was the counterrevolution.[32] But it was clear that Marx had hoped the second French Revolution would follow the path of the first French Revolution. Marx had wanted the 1848 civil war to move from the high bourgeoisie, to the petite bourgeoisie, and then finally to the proletariat.

Even though the "Address of the Central Committee to the Communist League" referred to the German Revolution of 1848, it was written in 1850 when Marx was in London, and thus belongs to the writings of the 1850–1852 period. In the "Address," Marx discusses the lessons of 1848 and what strategy the working class, based on the experiences of 1848, should follow in the next revolution. The working class should remain an independent organization. It should form temporary coalitions with the bourgeois parties, but only to serve the advantage of the laboring classes. That is, the coalitions should be used by the laboring classes to expose the bourgeoisie, to shatter bourgeois control, to seize the revolution for itself. The laboring classes must not relent until they have broken bourgeois power and claimed control for themselves. "Their battle cry must be: The Revolution in Permanence."[33]

The *leitmotif* of the Terror was again present in the writings of 1850–1852. Marx was proud to proclaim the communists of Paris as "the most extreme party of revolution."[34] In contrasting the communists to bourgeois liberalism he happily associated the working class with "revolutionary terrorism."[35] Lastly, the word dictatorship appeared for the first time in Marx's writing during this 1850–1852 period. Marx referred to the bourgeois victories of 1848 as initiating the bourgeois dictatorship. The proletariats only had one answer to this threat: "revolutionary dictatorship."[36] Marx quickly made revolutionary dictatorship a tactic of proletarian revolution.

There existed, then, from Marx's journalism in the *Neue Rheinische Zeitung* until the completion of *The Eighteenth Brumaire of Louis Bonaparte* a continuity of thought regarding revolutionary strategy. Marx remained in favor of using force, political compulsion in order to make social changes. Whether it involved the use of war or the use of terror, Marx felt that power could be used to make the revolution permanent, that is, to move the revolution leftward until it did become in fact a proletarian revolution.

A GREAT DIFFERENCE existed between the environment and conditions of the 1848 period and those of the eight years of the First International. Since the situations were so disparate, Marx's responses to them differed correspondingly. In the context of the revolutions of 1848, it was appropriate for Marx to appear as a Jacobin. In the context of a recently formed international organization in which political ideologies ranged over a wide spectrum, in which the continued existence of the organization was a matter of doubt, a Jacobin posture for Marx would have been entirely inappropriate.

For this reason an examination of Marx's behavior in the International does not reveal him in a radical posture. However, this was the only time in Marx's career when he was involved directly and personally in a political life. The policies that he advocated from this position thus have enormous importance for understanding his mind. They will tell us the direction in which he wanted to move the organization, as well as the political goals he hoped to reach.

It was clear that Marx had learned a great deal from the failures of the 1848 revolutions. At the end of the "Address of the Central Committee to the Communist League" (1850), Marx stressed the need of the workers to form an "independent party."[37] The working class must speak and act for itself as a political entity rather than have the bourgeoisie speak and act for it. For Marx, the founding of the International Working Men's Association in 1864 was a fulfillment of his hope of 1850. By 1864 the working class movement had revived again, and Marx saw the International as the political expression of that revival. The laboring classes would now have a political center, an organizing core, around which to coordinate their efforts, something that was so sorely lacking in 1848.

The working classes had one paramount goal: "To conquer political power has therefore become the great duty of the working classes."[38] In order to help them do this the International would seek to give a common direction to the various national working class parties. The International would not dominate or control the various national working class parties. Rather, these parties must determine their own policies. But the International could coordinate, unify, and stimulate the European working class movement.[39] "It is the business of the International Working Men's Association to combine and generalize the spontaneous movement of the working classes, but not to dictate or impose any doctrinary system whatever."[40]

As a part of this coordinated effort, the working classes must develop a common approach to foreign affairs. The proletariat must condemn the English and French for their inability to halt the advance of Czarist Russia. The proletariat must recognize that it was only their protests that kept European countries from intervening in the American Civil War. The laborers must be made aware that their fate, the success or failure of the domestic revolutionary movement, was directly related to the European diplomatic situation. "The fight for such a foreign policy forms part of the general struggle for the emancipation of the working classes."[41] Through the International, Marx wanted to politicize the laboring masses. He wanted to raise their level of political consciousness, so that they would become more effective in forcing legislation beneficial to themselves. One step toward the politicization of the workers would be the winning of the right to vote. Only through the power of the suffrage could the proletariat wrench social and economic concessions from the bourgeois state.[42]

Furthermore, Marx was an ardent trade unionist. Since "the emancipation of the working classes must be conquered by the working classes themselves,"[43] the formation of organizations composed solely of and devoted solely to the interests of the working class was an utmost necessity. The International worked diligently for the spread of the labor movement in England and on the continent. In addition, the International encouraged and supported, both morally and financially, the strike movement. Trade union militancy was thus part of the Marxist program. Marx was a vehement advocate of the eight-hour day, because a shorter work day would allow the worker more time for political activity. Through strikes and labor militancy the workers would grow aware of their self-interest. Once aware of their self-interest, they would vote at the polls to translate those interests into political legislation. The Leninist separation between labor movement and political party did not exist for Marx.

Marx's attempt to politicize the workers went beyond his demand for universal suffrage, for an eight-hour working day, and embraced the area of foreign policy. He was trying to enunciate a foreign policy that was expressive of the interests of the working class. He threw the support of the International behind the North in the American Civil War. He felt that the North, in its war against the Southern slavocracy, spoke for the working class interests, for the interests of free labor.[44] In the question of Poland and Ireland, Marx advocated liberation for both these nationalities. Irish independence would benefit the English proletariat, because the English aristocracy would be weakened by its loss of Irish possessions.[45] Polish independence would benefit the German proletariat, because a free Poland would be a buffer between Russia and Germany, thus reducing the Russian feudal conservative influence in Germany.[46]

Marx's activities in the International tried to make of it an effective political weapon in the interests of the proletariat. He understood that unless the workers organized themselves, became responsible for their own destinies, they would never become conscious of themselves as having any power—and without a consciousness of their power a proletarian revolution was out of the question. But Marx was aware that one economic struggle was not sufficient. The workers must combine their economic battles with political ones. They must always work for the political seizure of power.

THE STUDY OF Marx's responses to the Paris Commune must be seen against the backdrop of his activities in the First International. Preceding paragraphs have demonstrated how Marx tried to politicize the International. A continuity of policy existed between Marx's attitude toward the Commune and his activities in the International.[47]

In the July 23, 1870, "First Address of the General Council on the Franco-Prussian War," Marx tried to develop a foreign policy for the working classes both in Europe and America. Affirming that Louis Bonaparte was the aggressor in the war, Marx hoped that the German working classes would not allow the war to lose its defensive character and degenerate into an expansive war against the French people. Happily, Marx quoted from statements of French and German sections of the International that denounced the war as purely dynastic, and that declared the international solidarity of the working class movement. The rule of peace in the world would only come with the victory of the laboring masses. The harbinger of this new world order was the International Working Men's Association.[48] Thus, Marx used the Franco-Prussian War as an occasion to give the working class movement a foreign policy of its own. He sought to further politicize the labor movement, to deeply involve it in the interstate struggles of Europe and America.

In the September 9, 1870, "Address of the General Council," Marx categorically denounced the German annexation of Alsace-Lorraine. He saw in the annexation only seeds for a future war. He threw his support and the support of the International behind the newly proclaimed French Republic. The "Second Address" called upon all the proletarians of Europe to work for the preservation of the French Republic. Near the end of the "Address" Marx warned the workers of Paris not to rebel. It was clear to Marx that the situation, particularly with Prussian troops outside of Paris, was not favorable to insurrection. Again referring to the year 1792, Marx advised the Parisian working class that the conditions of 1870 differed from the conditions of 1792. Nevertheless, Marx had decisively committed the International to denounce annexations, and to the defense of the second French Republic. The political thrust of the International had been deepened.[49]

In the "Third Address" of May 30, 1871, three months after the outbreak of the Paris Commune, Marx defended the Commune as a symbol of proletarian heroism. "Working men's Paris, with its Commune, will be forever celebrated as the glorious harbinger of a new society. Its martyrs are enshrined in the great heart of the working class. Its exterminators history has already nailed to that eternal pillory from which all the prayers of their priest will not avail to redeem them."[50] Marx's espousal and immemorializing of the Commune was perfectly consistent with the policies he had advocated for the International since its founding. The militancy and political awareness he had worked to impart to the working classes were best served and perpetuated, even though he had warned against rebellion in the "Second Address," by defending and supporting the Commune. Since Marx had demanded a proletarian foreign policy, since Marx had attempted to politicize the laboring masses at every opportunity, for Marx to have denied the Commune once the rebellion had already broken out would have amounted to a betrayal of the principles he had worked so hard to have accepted. Furthermore, Marx saw the Commune as defending the French Republic. In the beginning of the "Third Address," Marx recounts the maneuvers of Thiers to destroy the republic. Versailles represented the forces of counterrevolution. The Parisian Revolution, then, was a rebellion for the republic. Since Marx had committed the International to the republic, he could not have disavowed the Commune.

This is not to say that Marx thought all the members of the Commune were proletarian.[51] Nor is it to claim that all the legislation passed by the Commune was socialistic. In his letter to F. Domila-Nieumenhuis of February 22, 1881, Marx indicated that "the majority of the Commune was in no wise socialist, nor could it be."[52] It is to say, however, that Marx was again the political Jacobin. He accepted the need to use force and violence to make social changes. He saw the need of the revolution in Paris to protect the republic.

In fact, Marx criticized the Commune because it was not bold enough. The Communards had made two mistakes. First, they had not declared the civil war immediately, not marched immediately on Versailles. This delay had given Thiers and the Versailles provisional government the needed time to mobilize their forces. Second, the Central Committee of the National Guard in Paris had surrendered power too quickly, too quickly stepped aside for the coming of the Commune government. Marx would have preferred the centralization of power during the prosecution of civil war.[53] Even though Marx had warned against the outbreak of the Commune, once the rebellion was a fact Marx thought bold, violent action a necessity. The Commune should have declared the civil war, attempted to capture Versailles and by the use of force and power destroyed the counterrevolution, and thus changed the political and social nature of France. More forceful Jacobin measures would not have produced a communist France, but they might have produced a true republican France.

More importantly, for the duration of the Commune, force had brought positive accomplishments. In Part Three of the "Third Address," Marx briefly summarized the history of the bourgeois state in Europe. The empire of Louis Bonaparte had been an expression of that state form, a bourgeois dictatorship. The Paris Commune had demonstrated the need to break "the modern state power."[54] In *The Eighteenth Brumaire of Louis Bonaparte,* Marx had talked of the need of the proletariat to "smash the state."[55] Nineteen years later Marx reaffirmed that need and saw in the violence and war of the Commune an attempt to achieve that goal. In addition, the Commune had experimented with sociopolitical forms that could serve as the basis for a future communist society. The Commune had been a social laboratory, had found a substitute for the bourgeois state, had created social forms for a proletarian society.

Lastly, Marx wished to enshrine the Commune as a proletarian myth. In his letter to Kugelmann of April 17, 1871, Marx wrote that the Commune had been doomed from the start, but necessary. Faced with a choice of surrender or struggle, the Commune correctly chose struggle. Surrender would have led to the demoralization of the working class. Even though the immediate outcome was and could be foreseen as a failure, a proletarian example of heroism had been established and "a new point of departure of worldwide importance has been gained."[56] Later, in August 1872, in a report to the General Council of the Amsterdam Congress of the International, Marx again memorialized the Commune as a heroic saga of the working class movement of all lands.[57]

THE CONTINUITY OF Marx's thought on the question of revolution has been established. From his early writings in 1844 until the Paris Commune of 1871, Marx demonstrated a consistency of thought on the nature of radical social change. Structural changes in society, total transformations of social relationships were impossible without the use of political violence. Ruling classes did not voluntarily surrender their power. Moral persuasion has never been an effective instrument of change. Force was an indispensable tool in producing new social forms.

Nothing in this chapter was meant to imply that Marx was a voluntarist. Nor was it intended to interpret Marx as a Blanquist. Marx was well aware that thought itself, that desire itself did not make revolutions. Conditions must be ripe. The existence of capitalism was necessary before a proletariat could be produced. Revolution came from the dialectical opposition of the means and mode of production. Such were the inescapable principles of dialectical naturalism. Nor did Marx believe that all nineteenth-century revolutions were necessarily proletarian. Some would be bourgeois. Some would move further to the left and become democratic egalitarian revolutions. In the last analysis, historical conditions would be determinate.

Nevertheless, Marx did not think the human subject should quiescently wait while social forces themselves produced communism. The human subject must act. Options existed for him. True, the human subject did not create conditions, but he nevertheless could exploit those in which he found himself. The active agent, the agent who was to exercise options and exploit conditions through violence was the practical-critical human being.

Marx's Jacobinism was intimately related to his humanism. For Marx, the human potential was realizable. That is, the full human potential already was present in the human being. The human being possessed inherently all the attributes necessary for his complete emancipation and humanization. Human perfection need not be created, as it was already latent in the species. What was necessary was to unleash these latent powers. What was necessary was to bring about those social conditions in which the latent powers of the species could be expressed and thus realized. If man possessed the powers of his perfection, so he also possessed the power to bring forth those social conditions in which his perfection could be expressed. But those social conditions could only be brought about through a complete transformation of existing society. Thus, Marx's humanism was inherently revolutionary, because in asserting that human perfection was realizable Marx also asserted the obligation to realize that potential. In positing the latent presence in the species of full human emancipation, Marx also posited the ability of the species to fulfill that presence. Social revolution, then, was the exercise of human power to make human perfection a historical datum. Or, revolution was only the process by which human emancipation became permanent—a mode, a moment of human perfection itself. Man was most like himself when he was becoming most like himself. The doctrine of *praxis* was at the center of Marx's philosophy. His theories of social revolution and political violence are extensions of his doctrine of *praxis*.

Footnotes

1. Karl Marx, "Theses on Feuerbach," *Writings of the Young Marx on Philosophy and Society*, ed. and trans. Loyd D. Easton and Kurt H. Guddat (New York: Doubleday & Co., 1967), pp. 400–402. See particularly the eleventh thesis. The author is particularly indebted to five works that focused his attention on the importance of *praxis* and activity in Marx: Ernst Bloch, "Weltveranderung oder die elf thesen von Marx über Feuerbach," *Über Karl Marx* (Frankfurt: Suhrkamp Verlag, 1968); Karl Löwith, *Die Hegelische Linke* (Stuttgart: Friedrich Fromm Verlag, 1962), pp. 53–107; Gajo Petrovic, *Marx in the Mid-Twentieth Century* (New York: Doubleday & Co., 1967); Nathan Rotenstreich, *Basic Problems of Marx's Philosophy* (Indianapolis: Bobbs-Merrill, 1965); Gottfried Stiehler, *Dialektik und Praxis* (Berlin: Akademie-Verlag, 1968).
2. Marx, "On the Jewish Question," *Karl Marx: Early Writings*, ed. and trans. T. B. Bottomore (New York: McGraw-Hill, 1963), pp. 3–40.
3. Marx, "Toward the Critique of Hegel's Philosophy of Law: Introduction," *Writings of the Young Marx on Philosophy and Society*, pp. 249–264.
4. Marx, "The King of Prussia and Social Reform," *Ibid.*, p. 357.

5. Marx's relation to the Jacobins has been the subject of debate. However, none of the discussions explore in depth or accurately the extent and meaning of this relationship. Two books, although generally hostile to Marx, do see Marx as influenced by the state centralization of the Jacobins: John Plamenetz, *German Marxism and Russian Communism* (New York: Harper & Row, 1965), pp. 159–160; Bertram D. Wolfe, *Marxism: 100 Years in the Life of a Doctrine* (New York: Dial Press, 1965), p. 20. Shlomo Avineri's *The Social and Political Thought of Karl Marx* (London: Cambridge University Press, 1968) generally misinterprets Marx and Jacobinism. Avineri sees Marx rejecting in total the Jacobin tradition. More insightful is George Lichtheim's *Marxism: An Historical and Critical Study* (New York: Praeger, 1962). Lichtheim sees Marx as continuing the spirit of Jacobinism. The view contained within these pages is in line with Lichtheim.
6. Marx, "On the Jewish Question," *Karl Marx: Early Writings,* p. 29.
7. Marx, *The Holy Family* trans. R. Dixon (Moscow: Foreign Languages Publishing House, 1956), p. 110.
8. Marx, *The German Ideology,* trans. S. Ryazanskaya (Moscow: Progress Publishers, 1968), p. 192.
9. Marx, *The Holy Family,* p. 165.
10. *Ibid.,* p. 161.
11. *Marx-Engels Werke* (Berlin: Dietz Verlag, 1968), VI, p. 107.
12. *Ibid.,* VI, pp. 388–389.
13. *Ibid.,* VI, p. 505.
14. *Ibid.,* V, p. 202.
15. *Ibid.,* VI, p. 166.
16. Marx, *The Eastern Question,* ed. Eleanor Marx Aveling and Edward Aveling (New York: Augustus M. Kelly, 1969), p. 221.
17. Marx's opposition to Blanquism is well documented. The core of Marx's opposition to Blanquism was exposed by Franz Mehring who understood Marx's rejection of "small, useless *putsches.*" See Mehring, *Karl Marx,* trans. Edward Fitzgerald (Ann Arbor: University of Michigan Press, 1962), p. 83. A similar argument has been developed in David McLellan's *Marx Before Marxism* (New York: Harper & Row, 1970), pp. 180–185. In a slightly different vein, Isaiah Berlin, although cognizant of the difference between Marx and Blanqui, correctly draws attention to the openly revolutionary intention of Marx's thought and to the organizational awareness of Marx. See Berlin, "Comments on a Paper by Richard Pipes," *Revolutionary Russia* (New York: Doubleday & Co., 1960), pp. 66–76. The reader himself will be struck by the differences between Marx and Blanqui by reading first hand the work of Blanqui. The best anthology of Blanqui's work is Auguste Blanqui, *Instruktionen für den Aufstand* (Frankfurt: Europäische Verlagsanstalt, 1971).
18. *Marx-Engels Werke,* XVII, pp. 159–161.
19. Oscar Hammen's *The Red '48ers* (New York: Charles Scribner's Sons, 1969) is probably the best description of the political activities of Marx and Engels during the 1848 revolutions. Hammen is correct in his assessment of Marx as being a radical revolutionary during this period.
20. *Marx-Engels Werke,* V, p. 3.
21. *Ibid.,* V, p. 14.
22. *Ibid.,* V, p. 105.
23. *Ibid.,* VI, p. 389.
24. For specific reference to the Czechs see *Ibid.,* V, pp. 202–205.
25. *Ibid.,* V, pp. 81, 202.
26. *Ibid.,* V, p. 65.

27. *Ibid.*, VI, p. 211.
28. *Ibid.*, p. 506.
29. Marx, *The Eighteenth Brumaire of Louis Bonaparte*, (New York: International Publishers, 1963) p. 19.
30. Marx, *The Class Struggles in France, 1848–1850* (New York: International Publishers, 1964), pp. 45–46.
31. *Ibid.*, p. 126.
32. Marx, *The Eighteenth Brumaire of Louis Bonaparte*, p. 42.
33. Marx, "Address of the Central Committee to the Communist League," in Marx-Engels, *Selected Works* (Moscow: Foreign Languages Publishing House, 1955), I, p. 117.
34. Marx, *The Class Struggles in France, 1848–1850*, p. 124.
35. *Ibid.*
36. *Ibid*, p. 92.
37. Marx, "Address of the Central Committee to the Communist League," in Marx-Engels, *Selected Works*, I, p. 117.
38. Marx, "Inaugural Address," *The General Council of the First International* (Moscow: Progress Publishers, 1965), I, p. 286.
39. Marx, "Provisional Rules of the Association," *Ibid.*, I, pp. 290–292.
40. Marx, "Instructions for Delegates of Provisional Council," *Ibid.*, I, p. 346.
41. Marx, "Inaugural Address," *Ibid.*, I, p. 287.
42. Marx, "Minutes of the General Council, July 9, 1867," *Ibid.*, II, p. 137.
43. Marx, "Provisional Rules of the Association," *Ibid.*, I, p. 288.
44. Marx, "To Abraham Lincoln, President of the United States of America," *Ibid.*, I, pp. 51–53.
45. Marx, "Notes for an Undelivered Speech on Ireland," *Ibid.*, II, p. 253.
46. Marx, "Poland," *Ibid.*, II, pp. 277–279.
47. The views offered in this discussion of the Paris Commune contradict the opinion held by Shlomo Avineri in his *The Social and Political Thought of Karl Marx.* Avineri feels that Marx repudiated the Paris Commune. The author feels that Marx determinedly supported the Commune. Bertram Wolfe, in *Marxism: 100 Years in the Life of a Doctrine*, does not feel that Marx repudiated the Commune, but rather that Marx falsified its meaning. According to Wolfe the Commune was not socialist, but rather Proudhonist and Blanquist. Wolfe is right on this point, but this does not detract from the thesis presented here, that Marx supported the Commune because of its political and revolutionary potentials.
48. Marx, *The Civil War in France* (New York: International Publishers, 1940), pp. 25–27.
49. *Ibid.*, pp. 33–35.
50. *Ibid.*, pp. 81–82.
51. Marx and Engels, *Writings on the Paris Commune*, ed. Hal Draper (New York: Monthly Review Press, 1970), p. 223.
52. *Ibid.*, p. 233. Avineri and Wolfe particularly stress this passage.
53. Marx to Dr. Kugelmann, April 12, 1871, *Ibid.*, p. 221.
54. Marx, *The Civil War in France*, p. 59.
55. Marx, *The Eighteenth Brumaire of Louis Bonaparte*, p. 101.
56. Marx to Dr. Kugelmann, April 17, 1871, *Writings on the Paris Commune*, p. 222.
57. *Marx-Engels Werke*, XVIII, pp. 129–137.

Five

The Dialectics of Revolution in the Nineteenth Century

FROM MARX'S PERSPECTIVE, two great powers contended with each other during the nineteenth century in Europe: the revolution and conservatism. Marx showed an acute grasp of the struggle for power between the five great European states, but felt nevertheless that the fate of Europe would ultimately be decided in the clash between the revolution and the status quo. For Marx, interstate conflicts were symptoms rather than causes. They were symptoms because they merely reflected the more fundamental class structure of each state. Marx defined the state as the legalization of the domination of one class over society. Thus, interstate conflicts were really conflicts between one national ruling class and another national ruling class. In discussing foreign policy, Marx's vision was always focused on the domestic structure of states, and he saw foreign policy as an expression of that domestic class arrangement.

When Marx used the term "the Revolution," he had in mind four types of revolution: the bourgeois, the proletarian, the peasant, and the national. When Marx used the term "conservative," he had in mind two different types of defenders of the status quo: either the bourgeois capitalist conservatives of France or England or the feudal aristocratic conservatives of Prussia, Russia, Austria, and Turkey. By "the Revolution," Marx meant a continuing process that would destroy feudalism or capitalism, destroy one type of civilization to replace it by another as a step toward communism. In the context of France in 1789, "the Revolution" had been bourgeois and antifeudal. In England "the Revolution" must be proletarian, must overthrow capitalism. However, in Marx's Amsterdam speech of 1872, he recognized that England might progress peacefully to socialism. In the context of central and eastern Europe, "the Revolution" must be national, must free several of the subject Slavonic nationalities there and thus lead to the dismemberment of the outmoded feudal empires of Russia, Austria, and Turkey. In the case of Russia, Marx thought it possible for communism to be won there without a transition stage of capitalism. As a continuing movement toward communism, as a process of social transformation begun in 1789, "the Revolution" could manifest itself either in its French form as bourgeois, in its English form as proletarian, in its central or east European form as national, or in its Russian form of building communism without an intervening capitalist period.

The vision that Marx had of the European state system penetrated into the decadence of that system. In the mid-nineteenth century, the European balance of power was held by the three feudal conservative powers of the East, Russia, Austria, and Prussia. Even though these powers clashed over certain diplomatic aims, their overriding common interest was the preservation of the feudal aristocratic order. This common interest made them implicit allies. Marx believed that internal concerns of the state always took precedence over diplomatic concerns of the state. But Marx also believed that these aristocratic conservative states, those who held the European balance of power, were also the most vulnerable states on the continent. The forces of nationalism were eroding their strength. Thus, the apparent stability of Europe was really a myth. The European system of the nineteenth century was decadent, because the states upon which that system rested were decadent.

Thus, nationalism in this context was a progressive force, indeed, was a phase of the deeper revolutionary process. Feudal conservatism was the bulwark of European reaction, the chief antagonist of "the Revolution" on the continent. National liberation was the best way to destroy these reactionary powers. Hopefully, the national liberation movements of the East, by the destruction of these autocratic powers, would unleash a more fundamental proletarian revolution in the West, in France and in England. In a word, only "the Revolution" was capable of annihilating the decadent state system of Europe and thus allowing more progressive forces, be they national or be they proletarian, to come to the surface.

For Marx, then, nationalism could be a progressive force. Not the nationalism of the Czar, for in that context, nationalism was allied with social conservatism. Rather, the nationalism of the Germans in 1848, for in that context, nationalism was allied with the forces of social reform. Two elements, then, were necessary from Marx's viewpoint before a national movement could be considered progressive. First, the national movement must seek to liberate the nationality from feudal or foreign imperial control, and second, the nationality must seek to make either liberal or proletarian social reform a part of that liberation movement.[1] This is not to argue that Marx believed in a two-stage revolution, that it was necessary to have a bourgeois revolution before having a proletarian revolution. It is simply a statement that Marx believed that the proletarian revolution could only take place within a national unit. A simultaneous transcontinental proletarian revolution for Marx was an impossibility. Rather, the proletariat must first come to power within a state. After the seizure of national power, the proletariat would have political and military power. They could then join hands with the proletariats of other states. They could then declare war against the conservative states and thereby liberate the oppressed classes in those countries. Russia was a national unit although it had not experienced a bourgeois revolution, and according to Marx, Russia could become a communist society. Germany until 1871 was not a national unit, had not experienced a successful bourgeois revolution, but Marx thought it possible for the German proletariat to lead the national revolution. What was crucial for Marx was not the bourgeois revolution, but the national state.[2]

Marx's awareness that the proletarian revolution must take place within national units was first expressed in his "Toward the Critique of Hegel's Philosophy of Law."[3] In 1844, Germany was a politically and culturally backward area of Europe. Politically, the institutional arrangements of Germany were the institutional arrangements of the Ancien Régime. German philosophy and thought were sterile, because the Germans substituted speculation for practice; that is, they substituted and escaped into metaphysics rather than deal constructively with the actual politico-social problems of Germany. The problems of Germany were thus compounded. Not only were they political, but they were also cultural and economic. The German middle classes had completely failed to surmount any of these problems.

For Germany to be emancipated at all it must be emancipated totally. Since German life generally existed at the stage of the eighteenth century, for German life to be brought into the nineteenth century emancipation must be general and inclusive.[4] Since Marx was attacking feudalism, since Marx was attacking the Ancien Régime, the only means to gain freedom from these archaic political forms was in the national state. Thus, a unitary German state was a precondition for total German emancipation. Marx was to continue this plea in the 1848 revolution. In the program of the Communist Party of Germany in the first issue of the *Neue Rheinische Zeitung,* he called for a unified German state, a unitary social republic.

Marx assigned the role of carrying through the national revolution not to the German bourgeoisie, but to the German proletariat. Marx did not think that all national revolutions had to be categorically bourgeois revolutions. The proletariat was the most radical class in Germany, the class suffering from all the general ills of society. Thus, the proletariat must carry through the national revolution and the communist revolution. Marx talked of a one-stage revolution for Germany, or of a permanent revolution for Germany. The proletariat would fulfill all the historic tasks fulfilled earlier by the French bourgeoisie in their country. Thus, in the context of Germany, it was the historic mission of the proletariat to conquer the nation-state, to overthrow the aristocracy and monarchy (tasks formerly performed by the French and English bourgeoisie), and to march on resolutely to communism.

The idea that a national unit was an indispensable framework in which a proletarian revolution must take place remained throughout Marx's life a dominant theoretical principle. After the debacle of the 1848 revolutions, Marx in 1850 advised the Communist League:

> While the democratic petty bourgeois wish to bring the revolution to a conclusion as quickly as possible, and with the achievement, at most, of the above demand, it is our interest and our task to make the revolution permanent, until all more or less possessing classes have been forced out of their position of dominance, until the proletariat has conquered state power and the association of proletarians, not only in one country but in all the dominant countries of the world, has advanced so far that competition among the proletarians of these countries has ceased and that at least the decisive productive forces are concentrated in the hands of the proletarians.[5]

A few pages later in his "Address to the Communist League," Marx said:

> The workers, in opposition to this plan, must not only strive for a single and indivisible German republic, but also within this republic for the most determined centralization of power in the hands of state authority.—As in France in 1793 so today in Germany it is the task of the really revolutionary party to carry through the strictest centralization.[6]

There could be no communist revolution without the seizure of state power, and there could be no seizure of power without the prior existence of the state. Therefore, the proletariat must either conquer power within a state that already existed, or they must create a state in the process of their coming to power. This latter course was the one that Marx prescribed for the German working classes in 1844, 1848, and 1850. Furthermore, the proletariat must come to power "not only in one country but in all the dominant countries of the world." That is, national proletarian parties must seize control of their respective national entities. When Marx at the end of the *Communist Manifesto* wrote "Workers of the World Unite," he did not envision a simultaneous global proletarian revolution. Rather, Marx's blueprint for the eventual global victory of communism was based on the presupposition that individual countries would singularly and successively become communist, and that only after these communist parties were in power could "competition among the proletarians" cease, cooperation begin, unity between these various communist nations commence, and the worldwide epoch of communist society be inaugurated.[7]

When Marx wrote the constitution of the International Working Men's Association, he incorporated in it the principle of national proletarian parties.[8] For Marx, the First International was to be a federation of national proletarian parties. The function of the International was to coordinate efforts among these national proletarian parties, to conduct research, to disseminate information, to designate the best policies to be followed, but never to dominate, never to obliterate national autonomy. Consistent with his theory, Marx, in fact, did in actuality support national revolutions. During the course of his life he backed the national liberation movements on the part of Poland, Ireland, Italy, Hungary, Germany, Spain, the Balkan nationalities, and the North in the American Civil War. Poland, however, was the revolutionary barometer for the rest of the European continent.[9]

The restoration of Polish sovereignty was crucial for Europe. Poland must be reestablished within the borders of 1772.[10] Marx favored the reconstruction of a large Poland. Marx did not feel that every nationality in Europe warranted its own nation-state, because he found it perfectly acceptable for non-Polish people to remain in a re-created Poland as long as they were guaranteed complete civil, legal, and religious equality.[11] Polish independence for Marx must be allied to democracy and republicanism. Furthermore, a reconstituted large Poland would push reactionary Russia out of Europe and far to the east. A democratic Poland would end the influence of Russian conservatism in Europe generally and thus release the repressed democratic forces within Europe.[12] Germany would be the first to feel the change. Without an independent Poland, Prussia and Russia would continue their partition of Poland, continue their mutual dependence, and therefore Prussia must remain conservative. With an independent Poland, Prussian conservatism would be stripped of its support from Russia, and thus Prussia and the remainder of Germany would be democratized.[13] The restoration of Poland was vital to the European revolutionary movement.

If an independent Poland was crucial to the spread of the revolutionary movement in Europe, an independent Ireland, in Marx's eyes, was almost equally important. From 1848 until his death, Marx continuously advocated the national independence of Ireland. In February 1848, Marx identified "the national cause with that of democracy and the liberation of the oppressed class" and went on to affirm that the "correctness of [this] principle is borne out by the situation in Ireland."[14] Marx repeatedly threw the support of the International Working Men's Association behind the cause of Irish independence.[15] Furthermore, he supported the Fenian movement. Unlike prior Irish independence movements that were composed of Catholic churchmen and aristocracy, the Fenians, Marx found, were radically and refreshingly different because this movement "took root (and is still really rooted) only in the masses of the people, the lower orders."[16]

Irish national independence was important, because it struck at the foundation of British landlordism. The position of the English aristocracy at home was buttressed by the expropriated land they held in Ireland. "Ireland is therefore the great means by which the English aristocracy maintains its domination in England herself."[17] Irish national independence was thus a thrust at the rear of the English aristocracy and a necessary prelude to social revolution in England. "And it is the special task of the Central Council in London to awaken a consciousness in the English workers that for them the national emancipation of Ireland is no question of abstract justice or humanitarian sentiment, but the first condition of their own social emancipation."[18] Therefore, not only the International, but the working classes in general should support Irish autonomy. Obviously a revolution in England, the center of world capitalism, would have pivotal consequences for revolutionary prospects on the continent and throughout the world. "To accelerate the social development in Europe, you must push on the catastrophe of official England—attack her in Ireland—her weakest point—[for till] Ireland lost, the British 'Empire' is gone, and the class war in England til now somnolent and chronic will assume acute form—England is the metropolis of landlordism and capitalism all over the world."[19]

The paradigm with which Marx interpreted events in Ireland was the same paradigm he used to interpret events in Germany, Russia, Austria, Hungary, and the Ottoman Empire. As the English landed aristocracy fattened upon the land of Ireland, the German and Russian aristocracy fattened on Polish land, the Austrian on Slavic land, and the Ottoman also on Slavic land. As in Ireland, nationalism in Poland and the Balkans was an antiaristocratic, anti-imperial weapon. The weakening of conservative forces, be they landed aristocrats or industrial capitalists, was, according to Marx, a progressive as well as revolutionary advance.

Similarly, Marx supported the movement for Italian independence. This does not mean, however, that Marx supported either Cavour or Victor Emmanuel. In Marx's eyes, both these men were instruments of Napoleon III. According to Marx, Napoleon III was not only a fraud, but a representative of the financial bourgeoisie in France. Thus, any movement toward national independence in Italy that passed from Louis Napoleon to Victor Emmanuel to Cavour was not really a revolution, but merely a movement that would insure the control and domination of the bourgeoisie in Italy.[20] Furthermore, Marx was not a supporter of Mazzini. Marx thought Mazzini an enemy of the Italian proletariat.[21] Mazzini was a liberal whose basic mistake was to draw his support from the urban nobility and bourgeoisie.[22] The man who really carried the national revolutionary mission of the Italian people was Garibaldi. Marx followed Garibaldi's campaign with close attention. In fact, a good friend of Marx, J. P. Becker, was with Garibaldi in Caprera and wrote letters to Marx informing Marx of the details and travails of the campaign.[23] In 1864 Marx even wrote to his uncle Lion Philips of his hope to visit with Garibaldi in Caprera.[24] The superiority of Garibaldi to Cavour and Mazzini lay in the fact that Garibaldi fought a true revolutionary war; that is, he allied himself with the masses. Thus, Italian national independence accomplished along the lines of Garibaldi would free Italy not only from Napoleon III, but from Austro-Hungary as well. Nationalism would triumph in Italy, while delivering a setback to conservative capitalism in France, and manorial conservatism in the Hapsburg Empire. On September 15, 1860, Marx wrote to Ferdinand

Lassalle that "our (here in England) support of nationalism, appears to me as a tactic—judged from internal considerations—to be correct."[25]

Likewise, Marx was a lifetime advocate of Hungarian independence. In 1848, Marx was a champion of Louis Kossuth. However, after Kossuth's exile from Hungary, he involved himself in the circle around Louis Napoleon. For Marx, this amounted to a denial of the true revolutionary cause in Hungary.[26] But Marx's devotion to Hungarian independence did not wane. He threw his support to another representative of Hungarian independence, Bertalan Szemere. According to Marx, Szemere had not capitulated to the western capitalists and thus was the best spokesman for Hungarian autonomy.[27] Marx's support of Hungary was in line with his anti-imperial policy, which was based, in part, on the hope of the destruction of both Hapsburg and Hohenzollern empires. On April 6, 1866, he wrote to Ludwig Kugelman that "without a revolution, which destroyed both Hapsburg and Hohenzollern, there must finally be another Thirty Years' War and a new partition of Germany."[28] Clearly, Marx was an advocate of self-determination. Marx wrote as much to Herman Jung on November 20, 1865, when discussing the policies of the International. Marx talked of "the necessity to counteract the influence of Russia in Europe through the development of the right of the nations to self-determination, and the reconstruction of Poland on democratic and socialist foundations."[29]

In addition, Marx supported the North during the American Civil War. Marx saw the war as a struggle between two ruling classes, the Southern slavocracy and the Northern bourgeois capitalists. He thought the South the aggressor, since the South had controlled the government of the United States and largely dictated its policies. Marx supported Northern nationalism, because it was allied to the cause of free labor.[30] A victory for Lincoln would not only destroy a reactionary feudal class in the South, but it would also abolish the slave system. The destruction of slavery was a victory for free labor since the laborer would not have to compete against a slave system and have his wages forced to a minimum. Lincoln's victory would thus be a victory for the worldwide proletarian movement. Marx proudly claimed that it was only the opposition of the English working classes that kept the English government from intervening in the war on the side of the South.[31]

Even in the case of Bismarckian Prussia, Marx favored the cause of German unification. The failure of the 1848 revolutions meant that Germany would not be unified on a democratic basis. Marx had no illusions about Prussia, arguing as late as 1863 that this "State of Prussia must be demolished."[32] It only continued to exist due to the support of Russia, and its dynasty, the Hohenzollern, had a record of indecisiveness and vacillation.

Nevertheless, Marx thought Bismarck's victory in 1871 a progressive step for Germany generally and the German labor movement specifically.

Prussia's victory meant the centralization of Germany, and the centralization of Germany meant the centralization of the German labor movement. The predominance of this new Germany on the continent would shift the center of gravity of the European labor movement from western Europe to Germany. This was in the best interests of the European labor movement, for the German proletariat was the most advanced and most militant on the continent. It also meant the victory of Marx's doctrine over that of Proudhon, since the German movement was essentially Marxist.[33]

The war of 1870–1871 had been a conservative one. It had created Germany, a centralized German labor movement, but preserved the feudal nature of Prussia. But it was the best that Germany could expect in the circumstances. A war in the east, a war against Russia, would be a truly revolutionary war. A German war against Russia would "act as the midwife to the inevitable social revolution in Russia."[34] Or, a war to the east would itself revolutionize Germany, ending Prussia's hold over Germany.[35] The ultimate democratization of central Europe would only come after Russia herself had been revolutionized. The fate of German nationalism was tied to the fate of the social revolution.

Just as Marx favored the national sovereignty of Poland, Ireland, Italy, Hungary, the United States, and Germany, so he favored the national sovereignty of several of the peoples of eastern Europe and the Balkans.[36] It was clear to Marx that the Ottoman Empire had lost its capacity to rule the Balkan peoples. The Empire was decadent, ruled by a religious elite, and ready for dismemberment. Indeed, far from bringing civilization to the Balkans, Marx recognized "that the presence of the Turks in Europe is a real obstacle to the development of the resources of the Thraco-Illyrian Peninsula."[37] The only issue involved in the "Eastern Question," according to Marx, related to what nation would replace Turkish rule.

Prompted by the Crimean War, Marx quickly acquainted himself with the native populations of the Balkans. He concluded that three nationalities in that region, the Wallachians, the Greeks, the Slavonians, had the vitality to replace their Turkish masters. The Greeks and Slavonians were the trading classes in all the large towns. They were that part of the population constantly rising in wealth and influence. Serbians in particular among the Slavonian nationalities had been active in bringing newer ideas into the Balkans.[38] The Wallachians had displayed a virile and courageous spirit during the 1848 revolutions, and Marx believed they "may yet play an important part in the ultimate disposal of the territories in question."[39] However, because the Greeks and Slavonians formed the bulwark of progress in the area, Marx believed that the Ottoman Empire should be replaced by either "the establishment of a Greek Empire, or of a Federal Republic of Slavonic States."[40]

Furthermore, a Greek empire or a Slavonic confederation would not only drive the Ottomans out of Europe, not only revolutionize the Thraco-Illyrian Peninsula, but also serve to contain the imperial ambitions of

Russia. National liberation in the Balkans would be like national liberation in Poland.[41] In both cases, Czarist penetration into Europe would be halted. "There is no doubt that, should the Greco-Slavonian population ever obtain the mastery in the land which it inhabits, and where it forms three-fourths of the whole population (seven millions) the same necessities would by-and-by give birth to an anti-Russian Progressive Party. . . ."[42]

Both preceding and during the Crimean War, Marx hoped that England and France would follow a revolutionary policy in the Balkans. That is, Marx wanted England and France to destroy the Ottoman Empire, to contain Russia and Austria, and to support Slavonic nationalism. At the very least, British diplomatic and commercial interests could not allow Czarist despotism to entrench itself on the Bosporus. "In this instance the interests of the revolutionary Democracy and of England go hand in hand."[43] Knowing that a victory for nationalism in the Balkans would be a progressive step, knowing that a weakening of the three eastern autocracies, Russia, Turkey, and Austria, would be a victory for the revolutionary movement in general, Marx longed for "the generals of 1792–1800."[44] In the course of the Crimean War, it became clear to Marx that England and France were not to pursue such a policy. Marx then thought the Crimean War a sham, a masquerade. The war had not been fought to dismember the Ottoman Empire but rather to preserve the Empire as a buffer against Russia. The war had not been fought to dismember Russia but rather to preserve Russia at the expense of all the Slavic nationalities. The war had been a conservative war fought for limited ends, the maintenance of Constantinople in the power of the Sultan. In allowing the three eastern dynasties to perpetuate themselves, the English had allowed aristocratic conservatism to perpetuate itself throughout eastern and central Europe.

As the conservative nature of the war revealed itself to Marx, he became increasingly desperate. He was aware that it was "the Greek and Slavonic middle-class in all the towns and trading posts who are the real support of whatever civilization is affectively imported into the country."[45] He lamented the fact that the timidity of the English and French forbade "the Sultan to emancipate himself from the Czar and the Slavonians to emancipate themselves from the Sultan."[46] More and more he longed for an alliance of all repressed nationalities to a climactic struggle against the forces of reaction. He hoped for "something like the grand wars of Napoleon."[47] He wished to see "the battles of the European peoples against the now victorious and severe European despots."[48] The revolution was indeed the sixth great power in Europe. He dreamed that "Germans, Hungarians, Poles, Italians, Croats, are loosened from the forced bond which ties them together [Hapsburg Empire], and instead of the undetermined and haphazard alliances and antagonisms of today, Europe will again be divided into two great camps with distinct banners and issues—between the Democratic Revolution on the one side and the Monarchical counter-revolution on the other."[49]

Indeed, Marx was aware of the debility of the Hapsburg Empire. He was sensitive to and supportive of the revolutionary potential of Slavic nationalism in relation to the Hapsburg Empire. Formerly, Marx wrote, the "great points of weakness in Austria are usually supposed to be her bankrupt treasury and the revolutionary elements of Italy and Hungary."[50] Marx recognized and explicitly stated that the "German, Hungarian, and Italian movements were decidedly progressive and revolutionary."[51] He further stated that Austria hoped "to restore the ancient Hungarian Constitution thus aiming to blot Hungary out of the map of revolutionary Europe."[52] In addition to Germany, Italy, and Hungary, Marx recognized that the Austrian Slavonians were "seeking their reunion either among each other, or with the main body of their separate nationalities."[53] He recognized too that the Slavonians sought "to create a political party with the unmistakable aim of upsetting Austria, and instituting a vast Slavonian empire in its place."[54] Marx welcomed Austrian Slavonian nationalism and was appreciative of its revolutionary vitality.

> Austrian Pan-Slavism possesses, perhaps, at this moment a greater latent force than ever ... [it was] the only element in Austria which was not broken down in the late revolutionary struggle [1848] ... Italians, the Hungarians, the Germans even, all, came debilitated and discouraged out of that vehement convulsion ... the Slavonians alone put themselves unconquered and unreduced.[55]

Thus, Marx not only favored the dismemberment of the Ottoman Empire, the Muscovite Empire, but also of the Hapsburg Empire. Slavonian nationalism would be the chief force in the destruction of Hapsburg aristocratic landlordism. Marx, however, did not wish to see the unity of Austrian Slavonians with Russian Slavonians. Such a denouement would be a victory for Russian Pan-Slavism, which Marx identified as the most reactionary force in Europe. Slavonian nationalism yes, but the Slavonians of the Danube must remain independent, and as such act as a check to the imperial ambitions of Russia, the Ottomans, and the Hapsburg Germans. In this fashion, Slavonian nationalism would abet the revolutionary forces of Europe, it would join the camp of the "Democratic Revolution on the one side and the Monarchical counter-revolution on the other."

Nevertheless, as England and France increasingly displayed their intention to fight a conservative war in the Crimea, Marx accused England and Russia of duplicity. Marx was bitterly disappointed in England, Lord Palmerston in particular, because he had betrayed the cause of democracy and nationalism, i.e., the revolution, in the Balkans. *The Secret Diplomatic History of the Eighteenth Century* was written by Marx to document the existence of a tacit alliance between Britain and Russia.[56] The substance of this alliance was the containment by Czarist conservatism and capitalist conservatism of the European revolution, and it found its origins back in the eighteenth century. The secret complicity of England and Russia was evidenced again in the conservative conduct of the Crimean War, and Marx was bitterly critical of British activity in the Caucasus. In that region, Marx asserted, the British in essence acquiesced in an extension, at the expense of the Ottomans, of Muscovite territory in the region of Kars.[57] Marx even went so far as to call Palmerston an agent in the pay of the Russians.[58]

As late as the Russo-Turkish War of 1876, Marx continued to see the revolutionary potential of the "Eastern Question." At this time, however, the Danubian nationalities remained generally quiescent, so the revolutionary center did not spring from Slavonic self-determination. Rather, the revolutionary movement would ignite from the defeat of Russia by Turkey. As the continued bastion of conservatism in Europe, the chief enemy was Czarist Russia. As an old man, Marx hoped for a Turkish victory. A Czarist defeat would fire the revolution in Russia and perhaps be the first stage as the revolution would move to the west.[59]

Marx's espousal of movements of national self-determination when allied to progressive social principles was an antifeudal, anti-imperial tactic. In the achievement of these ends, Marx was well aware of the revolutionary potential of the peasantry.[60] Marx's Jacobinism is again manifest in his relation to the peasantry. In the achievement of the revolution, in the achievement of a socially progressive national sovereignty, Marx welcomed the alliance of any class in society that was willing to work for such a revolution, including the peasantry.

Some students of Marx maintain that he held a basically hostile attitude to the peasants, that he saw them as inherently passive and inherently conservative.[61] Such a view is defensible up to the 1848–1849 period. Marx did believe that one of the major reasons for the failure of the 1848 revolutions was the alliance between the peasants and the conservative classes throughout Europe. In the post-1848 period, however, Marx's attitude changed radically. It was because he recognized the crucial role the peasantry could play in any revolutionary movement that after 1848 he was willing to accept a proletarian-peasant alliance, where one was possible, as a justifiable revolutionary strategy. This is not to say that Marx ever surrendered his belief that the land must be nationalized. Land nationalization remained throughout his life an unshakeable tenet of communism.[62] It is to say, nevertheless, that Marx was aware of the vitality of the peasantry, the importance of the peasantry, an importance that could not be overlooked, because under certain conditions the peasantry had been and could be a revolutionary force.

One model that Marx hoped to use to exploit the revolutionary potential of the peasantry was a peasant-worker alliance. The strategy of a proletarian-peasant alliance was first advocated by Marx in 1850, in his "Address of the Central Committee to the Communist League." Based upon the experiences of 1848, Marx recognized that the "democratic petty bourgeois"[63] party would seek to give private property to the peasants. The petty bourgeoisie would confiscate the property of the aristocracy and distribute it among the peasantry, thus forming "a petty bourgeois peasant class"[64] and also strengthening the principle of private property generally. To counter this petty bourgeois tactic, Marx saw that the proletarian party must seek allies amongst the peasantry. Confiscated aristocratic property must be nationalized and cultivated by the rural proletariat by means of large-scale farming procedures. The class war must be brought into the countryside. The rural proletariat must be made to see that its chief class enemy was the rural petty bourgeoisie. "Just as the democrats combine with the peasants so must the workers combine with the rural proletariat."[65]

Another model Marx devised to harness the peasantry to the revolution was a peasant-national revolution. In a letter Marx sent to Georg Weydemeyer in 1851 commenting on Mazzini and the Italian movement toward unification, Marx criticized Mazzini for not allying himself with the Italian peasant class. By neglecting the peasantry, Mazzini had simply allowed them to be courted and absorbed by the counterrevolution. With great acidity, Marx said of Mazzini:

> Mr. Mazzini only knows the towns with their liberal aristocracy and enlightened citizens. The material needs of the agricultural population of Italy —who like the Irish are sucked dry and systematically exhausted and stupefied —are of course too low for the heaven-in-words of his cosmopolitan-no-catholic-ideological manifesto. But it would certainly have required some courage to have informed the bourgeoisie and aristocracy that the first steps toward the independence of Italy is the complete emancipation of the peasants and the transformation of their system of semitenancy into free bourgeois property.[66]

Within the Italian context, a peasant revolution would further the cause of Italian self-determination. Communism would not be the outcome of an Italian peasant rebellion. Rather, the Italian peasants would confiscate property and become petit bourgeois peasants. The Italian revolution then would not be a national communist revolution, but a national democratic revolution.

The model of a national revolution supported by a rebellious peasantry that Marx applied to Italy, he also applied to Ireland. In 1867 he wrote to Engels that what "the Irish need is: (1) self-government and independence from England; (2) an agrarian revolution."[67] On December 10, 1869, Marx again wrote to Engels that what distinguished the "present Irish movement" was "the coming out of the agricultural labouring class."[68] The movement of the peasant masses, as encouraged by the Fenians, was a bright new development for Irish independence.

In the case of the Spanish Revolution of 1808–1809 against Napoleonic imperialism, Marx felt that whatever success the Spanish national movement had was due to the support the movement received from the peasantry. In relation to the 1808 Iberian national liberation movement, Marx wrote:

> There was no measure of social reform transferring property and influence from the Church and the aristocracy to the middle class and the peasants which the cause of defending the common country could not have enabled them to carry. They had the same good luck as the French *Comité du salut public*—that the convulsion within was backed by the necessities of defense against aggressions from without—.[69]

The national rebellion of Spain was to fail. But Marx, again recalling, again using the Jacobin period of 1792–1793 as a revolutionary paradigm, thought that it could have had greater success. The cause of defending Spain against Napoleonic imperialism could have been used to internally transform Spain. The exigencies of foreign wars worked to stimulate internal social progress. Aristocratic and ecclesiastical lands could have been expropriated and distributed amongst the peasantry. The Spanish did not respond in a Jacobin fashion to the Jacobin circumstances of 1808. They did not use the fervor of national defense to create a peasant bourgeoisie, and gain the loyalty and fervor of this new peasant proprietorship for the national war. "Exclusively under the reign of the Central Junta, it was possible to blend with the actualities and exigencies of national defense the transformation of Spanish society. . . ."[70] Thus the Spanish Revolution failed. "The Central Junta failed in the defense of their country because they failed in their revolutionary mission."[71] In other words, the nationalism of Spain never succeeded in allying itself to a rebellious peasantry, to the forces of social progressivism.

On other historic occasions, Marx saw the need to return to the model of a worker-peasant alliance. While speculating on the future of German nationalism in 1856, Marx wrote to Engels: "The whole thing in Germany will depend on the possibility of covering the rear of the proletarian revolution by a second edition of the Peasants War."[72] Six years later, as he pondered the beginnings of the American Civil War, Marx wrote to Engels: "The long and short of the business seems to me to be that a war of this kind must be conducted on revolutionary lines, while the Yankees have so far been trying to conduct it constitutionally."[73] Marx wanted Lincoln to arm the Southern blacks, and through the alliance of Union Armies and insurrectionary black forces in the South the Confederate aristocracy would be doomed. Or, the forces of free labor in the North would join an agrarian slave class in the South for the final overthrow of cotton feudalism. Therefore, when the circumstances were propitious, the proletariat could find a revolutionary ally in the peasantry, or in an agrarian slave class. In fact, Marx thought that the Paris Commune had enormous advantages to offer to the French peasants. One reason for the failure of the Commune, Marx lamented, was the failure of the French peasants to join the Commune. They failed to appreciate the advantages the Parisian proletariat held open to them.[74]

Furthermore, peasants could become proletarianized. Marx's economic studies and predictions in *Das Kapital* were to confirm what he had surmised in his early writings—the capitalization of agriculture would turn the landless peasant into a rural proletarian. The transformation of the peasant into a proletarian would take place when the peasant faced the identical nature and mechanism of exploitation as the industrial worker. Marx held this opinion as early as 1844. In one of his early manuscripts, entitled "Rent of Land," Marx wrote:

> Consequently, the agricultural workers are soon reduced to the minimum level of subsistence, and the former class establishes the power of industry and capital within landed property. Through competition with foreign countries the rent of land ceases, in the main, to constitute an independent source of income. A large section of the landowners is obliged to take the place of the tenant farmers who sink in this way into the proletariat.[75]

The theme of the proletarianization of the farmer was more fully developed in the third volume of *Das Kapital.* Capitalism, the profit motive, the hunger for surplus value, had become the ruling relations of production in the European countryside.

> We assume, then, that agriculture is dominated by the capitalist mode of production, just as manufacture is; in other words, that agriculture is carried on by capitalists who differ from other capitalists primarily in the manner in which their capital, and the wage-labor set in motion by this capital, are invested. So far as we are concerned, the farmer produces wheat, etc., in much the same way as the manufacturer produces yarn or machines. . . . Just as the capitalist mode of production in general is based on the expropriation of the conditions of labor from the laborers, so does it in agriculture presuppose the expropriation of the rural laborers from the land and their subordination to a capitalist, who carries on agriculture for the sake of profit.[76]

Dehumanized, abandoned to the profit system, the peasant would suffer the same impoverishment as the proletariat. The once independent peasant, unable to compete with the large capitalist landowning aristocracy, would gradually lose his land, his autonomy, and become a totally dependent wage-laborer.[77]

Peasants could develop a communist consciousness. Because they faced social conditions in which their labor was expropriated, they would become aware that only the common ownership of the means of production would prevent further exploitation of their productive *praxis.* Peasant and industrial laborers worked in different environments. One labored in rural areas, the other in the factory system. Even though their laboring environments differed, their social conditions were the same. Their social conditions were alienating and exploitative. The communist consciousness of both the proletarianized peasant and the proletarianized industrial laborer stemmed from the commonality of social conditions each faced.

The preceding paragraphs have shown that peasants could help in the making of a national revolution. They could also ally themselves with the bourgeoisie in the making of an antifeudal revolution or perhaps with the proletariat in the overthrow of the bourgeoisie. Peasants could also form the phalanx of a communist revolution. Furthermore, peasants could conduct a guerrilla warfare. The example of the Spanish resistance to French domination after the collapse of the regular Spanish armies did not escape Marx's attention. It was a heroic exploit on the part of the Spanish masses, and made Marx aware of the uses to which guerrilla warfare could be put.[78] The appeal to mass popular armies was a tactic that Marx had advocated as early as the 1848 revolutions.[79]

The attitude that Marx held toward nationalism in Europe corresponded exactly with his attitude toward nationalism in Asia. Marx's life spanned events that carried great historical significance for the development of India and China. Marx lived through the First and Second Opium Wars (1839–1842), the Taiping Rebellion (1850–1865) in China, the Sepoy Mutiny (1857) in India, and the British wars in Persia and Afghanistan. He was acquainted with the Asian imperialism of the British as well as the Asian imperialism of Russia. Marx thus had ample opportunity to reflect on the mechanism and nature of European overseas imperialism, and the nascent nationalism of India and China. His articles on these matters for the *New York Daily Tribune* are extensive enough to offer precise insight into his opinions on these matters.

Capitalism, for Marx, was a self-expansive system. The desire for profit, the endless acquisitiveness of the system, impelled the capitalist economy to expand around the world. In fact, it was the historical destiny of the capitalist mode of production to create a world market, to make the world an economic whole. The unification of the world would be a result of the capitalist epoch of human development.

The arrival of the European as master in Asia was thus not an accident, but rather the fulfillment of the inherent logic of the capitalist mode of production. The society that he found there when he came as conqueror was vastly different from his own. The Asiatic mode of production formed the substructure of Far Eastern society generally. Out of this meeting of East and West, out of this confrontation between the Asiatic mode of production and the capitalist mode of production, profound changes must result.

The Asiatic mode of production was characterized by a public works system built and administered by the central government. Water was an indispensable element to a predominantly agricultural society. Thus, artificial irrigation and drainage came to form the basis of Oriental agriculture. Because village life was so isolated, because the reaches of Asia were too vast to facilitate voluntary village association, the responsibility of constructing and maintaining these irrigation systems fell to the despot. The Asiatic mode of production was thus a hydraulic form of society; that is, it was sustained through the ability of the despot to maintain a constant supply of water for all the isolated villages.[80]

Furthermore, the constituent unit of this hydraulic society was the local village. Although the land belonged to the Asiatic potentate, the management of the land was left to each of the villages. Normally the land was cultivated on a communal basis. Basically, manufacture was of the handicraft variety, the spinning and weaving of cotton goods in peasant huts being the most prevalent form. Economically, the villages were self-sufficient, thus making for a great deal of decentralization and localism. Even though the Oriental despot retained absolute political authority, in practice the village particularism of Asiatic society produced a disunited and fragmented state structure. Thus, India could not defend herself and was left exposed to numerous foreign invasions and conquests. Although labor practices in the villages were collective, although the common ownership of land was the basic mode of production, Marx did not confuse this unchanged, stagnant, ancient communalism with his western, dynamic image of communism.[81]

Marx referred to India as the Ireland of the East. Just as Ireland was an island of woe, so India under British rule was a subcontinent of woe. British imperialism came to India as it came to Ireland, for plunder. The British occupation of India increased the wealth not of the English masses, but of the capitalists of the East India Company, and afforded the English aristocracy an opportunity to enlarge its ranks and enhance its prestige.

It was a self-contradiction to Marx to hope for the emancipation of labor in the mother country, while at the same time supporting the expropriation of labor in the colonized territory. The strengthening of the capitalist class in either area would mean the strengthening of the capitalist class in both areas. Conversely, the weakening of the capitalist class in either area would mean the weakening of the capitalist class in both areas. Because capitalism had created a world market, a global political interrelationship, it had also synthesized eastern and western revolutions.

British plunder in India centered on the destruction of the independent communal agrarian villages. The *zemindar* gathered taxes from the communal villages. He worked for the East India Company, turning over nine-tenths of the taxes he collected to the company, and keeping one-tenth for himself. Under the pressure of a rising tax burden, the people lost their hereditary claim to the soil, and the land itself defaulted into the possession of the *zemindar.* The *zemindar* was later to be replaced by larger mercantile land speculators. Of interest here, however, was the fact that under the auspices of British imperialism the ancient communal Indian village lost control over its land. Using the *zemindar* as its agent, the East India Company was causing an agricultural revolution in the Indian countryside. Agrarian capitalism had replaced agrarian collectivism. The Indian village was now subject to the unmerciful laws of the capitalist marketplace.[82]

The *ryot* was a former independent landowner who had lost his land and had been reduced to the level of a serf. The *ryot* had had no hereditary or permanent title to his land. He had been forced to divide his produce with the state, and yet the state had no obligation toward him, either in terms of securing him from destitution or supplying him with advanced funds for planting. In 1853 Marx calculated that eleven-twelfths of the whole Indian population were *ryots*, that is, "wretchedly pauperized"[83] and had just about "sunk as low as the Irish cottiers."[84] In short, even the independent landed class of India had been ruined by capitalism and turned into proletarianized peasants.

The imposition of capitalist relations of production upon the Indian countryside was not the only way to revolutionize an ancient social structure. The introduction of western technology was another. Railroads were a powerful dissolvent of the Asiatic mode of production. Railroads would destroy the isolation of the Indian villages and thus also their self-sufficient inertia. These disconnected atoms with their stereotyped forms of social organization would find themselves engulfed and overwhelmed by the full range of industrial modernization brought in the wake of the railroad.

> You cannot maintain a net of railways over an immense country without introducing all those industrial processes necessary to meet the immediate and current wants of railway locomotion, and out of which there must grow the application of machinery to those branches of industry not immediately connected with railways. The railway system will therefore become, in India, truly the forerunner of modern industry.[85]

In this confrontation between East and West, the Orient must succumb. The triumph of the capitalist mode of production in the countryside meant the expropriation of the villages and the Indian landowning classes by the agricultural capitalist practices of the East India Company. The introduction of western technology in the form of the railroad entailed the introduction into this basically agrarian country of the full complement of industrial machinery, to the detriment of the village handicraft industries. Either in terms of sheer industrial power or in terms of capitalist social relations, the victory of the West was assured. Asiatic society was to be revolutionized from the ground up. The situation in India was complicated by the fact that the country that was bringing about the revolution was also the country that dominated India. In short, the revolution was being carried through in the interests of the British imperium.

The Indian response to the British imperium was a national revolution. At least, Marx interpreted the Sepoy Mutiny as a national revolution. Marx understood that the principle of destroying native princes, of disturbing the settlement of property, and of tampering with religion added up to the "principle of destroying nationality."[86] Thus, the Indian people had reacted, and the sepoys did not simply instigate a military mutiny, "but a national revolt of which the sepoys are the acting instruments only."[87]

Marx noted how the common hatred of the British had brought Hindu and Moslem together.[88] He noted that the rebellion was not limited to a few provinces, but was in fact widespread and reached down to the mass of the people. He drew analogies between the British position in India and the French position in Spain in 1808.[89] He hoped that the outnumbered British would be surrounded and overpowered by the Indian masses. He understood the major characteristics of a national anticolonial revolution. He understood too that all Asia was aflame with revolution.[90]

Marx's attitude toward imperialism was ambivalent. On the level of immediacy, from the perspective of the mid-nineteenth century, he felt its horrors and its exploitation. He saw the essential cruelty of a capitalistic system that came to foreign lands solely for the sake of plunder. On the level of the future, from the perspective of the general movement of historical forces, Marx thought imperialism was ultimately a progressive force. It was destroying an outmoded Asiatic economy. It was bringing the advances of western science and technology to the Orient. Ultimately, Western industry and imperialism were the wave of the future, and their introduction into Asiatic society was for the good.[91]

Imperialism was thus a revolutionizing force in the Orient. But this did not mean that the Asian revolution must follow the path of the West, that Asia must pass from the Oriental mode of production, to capitalism and the proletariat, to communism. A revolution was coming to Asia, but Marx never fully delineated the full dimensions of the revolution. Marx definitely thought it would be national, but he never indicated the relations of production that would emerge from the revolution, never stated they must be capitalist relations of production. The only thing he categorically stated was that imperialism was laying "the material foundations of Western society in Asia."[92] But "the material foundations" were not social foundations, not a specific mode of production, not inevitably capitalism. Thus, Marx's view of imperialism does not suggest that he was a macrocosmic determinist, that he believed in a unilinear view of history, that he believed Asia must follow the path of Western evolution. The only conclusion Marx's writing on imperialism permits is that Western colonialism was a revolutionizing force, that as a reaction to and consequence of Western colonialism a national revolution was brewing in Asia. The Asian revolution need not be capitalist. It might be capitalist, but then again it also might assume a different form.

Marx was consistent in applying his ideas on nationalism to Asia. China, Persia, India, must each experience their own national revolutions; although all Asia was aflame with rebellion, the rebellion could only manifest itself successfully within national units. Secondly, Marx supported the national revolutions of the Orient because they were allied with socially progressive forces. They were simultaneously anti-imperial and antifeudal. As such, they could not fail to bring a more advanced form of society to Asia. These were the same principles by which he judged the national revolutions of Europe.

Chinese society was also a manifestation of the Asiatic mode of production, according to Marx. Like the Indian, the Chinese economy was characterized by small-scale agriculture and domestic industry. Basically composed of isolated villages, Chinese society had stagnated at the level of minute husbandry and household manufacture. Chinese society had until the mid-nineteenth century withstood and checked the domination of western wares. China was unlike India in this respect. The difference arose from the fact that in India the British were the supreme landlords, and thus they could "forcibly convert part of the Hindu self-sustaining communities into mere farms producing opium, cotton, indigo, hemp and other raw materials, in exchange for British stuffs."[93] In China, the British were not the supreme landlords. Consequently, the self-sufficient village communities had not as yet been overwhelmed by English power and economic wares.

Furthermore, Marx ridiculed those who expected England to reap vast profits from its Chinese trade. The advanced factory system of England could not undersell the cloth produced by the primitive looms of China. The cost of manufacturing cloth in Manchester, even with the aid of machinery, and shipping it to the East, was greater than the cost of cloth manufactured in the Asiatic mode of production, characterized by family artisans.[94] Nevertheless, parallel to the Indian experience, England was a revolutionizing force in China. Western material civilization would bring about a social revolution in the celestial empire. "Yet it is a gratifying fact that the bales of calico of the English bourgeoisie have in eight years brought the oldest and most imperturbable empire on earth to the threshold of a social upheaval, one that will in any case hold most significant consequences for civilization."[95] The coming revolution in China was "a gratifying fact" because it would destroy the Asiatic mode of production as well as perhaps sparking a revolution in Europe.

The Opium Wars were examples of a Chinese national revolution. Ostensibly resisting the opium trade, the Chinese were more fundamentally resisting English imperialism and reasserting their national sovereignty.[96] The need to defend their civilization required the Chinese to defend their national independence.

> It is almost needless to observe that, in the same measure in which opium has obtained the sovereignty over the Chinese, the Emperor and his staff of pedantic mandarins have become dispossessed of their own sovereignty. It would seem as though history had first to make this whole people drunk before it could rouse them out of their hereditary stupidity.[97]

The negation of colonialism was national revolution.

Marx was aware that bourgeois society had created an economically and politically interdependent world. He doubted that a revolution could succeed in Europe if bourgeois society were ascendant in Asia.[98] He doubted that a revolution could succeed in Asia if bourgeois society were ascendant in Europe. The global dimensions of capitalism meant that the anticapitalist revolution must be global. The European and Asian revolutions were interdependent, because the preservation of Asian and European capitalism was interdependent.[99]

Marxism was a philosophy of world revolution.[100] At issue here is not the question of whether revolutions everywhere would be communist. Under discussion here is the point that Marx saw a basic and inherent continuity in the global revolutionary forces when these revolutions combined nationalism and social progressivism. The connecting link was capitalism and capitalist imperialism. The common enemy of all revolutionary forces, either in Europe or in Asia or in the Near East, was the capitalist mode of production. If all these national, socially progressive revolutions succeeded on a worldwide basis, capitalism would cease to exist on a worldwide basis. Whether Asia would immediately become communist is an issue that will be discussed in the next chapter. But even on this point, the Asian revolution, whatever anticapitalist form it assumed, was seen by Marx as both inherently good and crucial for the West, because it would allow the Western communist revolution to maintain itself.

Footnotes

1. Norman Levine, "Karl Marx and the Arab-Israeli Conflict," *Judaism,* Vol. 19, No. 2 (Spring 1970), pp. 145–157.
2. Marx's willingness to use nationalism as a revolutionary device has been misinterpreted by many students of Marx. Richard Pipes commented that "Marx and Engels left their followers little guidance in matters of nationalism" (*The Formation of The Soviet Union* [New York: Atheneum Press, 1968], p. 21). Robert Tucker, in his *The Marxian Revolutionary Idea* (New York: W. W. Norton, 1969), postulated an essential difference between what he calls "classical Marxism" and nationalism. In his book, *The Social and Political Thought of Karl Marx* (London: Cambridge University Press, 1968), Shlomo Avineri neglected to comment at all on the national problem in Marx. More insightful on this question, and closer to the intent and spirit of Marx was George Lichtheim's *Marxism: An Historical and Critical Study* (New York: Praeger, 1962).
3. Karl Marx, "Toward the Critique of Hegel's Philosophy of Law," *Writings of the Young Marx on Philosophy and Society,* ed. and trans. Loyd D. Easton and Kurt H. Guddat (New York: Doubleday & Co., 1967), p. 264.
4. *Ibid.,* p. 264.
5. Marx, "Address of The Central Committee to the Communist League," in Karl Marx–Friedrich Engels, *Selected Works* (Moscow: Foreign Languages Publishing House, 1955), I, p. 110.
6. *Ibid.,* p. 115.
7. The opinion expressed here is different from the interpretation offered by Avineri in *The Social and Political Thought of Karl Marx.* In this book Avineri maintained "that any particularistic, national communism is doomed to failure" (p. 167). Avineri appears to have overlooked Marx's extensive writing on national liberation movements.

8. *The General Council of the First International Minutes* (Moscow: Progress Publishers, 1952), I, pp. 290–291.
9. Marx to Engels, December 2, 1856, in Marx and Engels, *Selected Correspondence* trans. Dona Torr (New York: International Publishers, 1942), p. 95.
10. *The General Council of the First International Minutes,* II, p. 279.
11. *Ibid.,* pp. 277–278.
12. *Ibid.,* p. 350.
13. Marx to Engels, March 24, 1863, in Marx and Engels, trans. S. Ryazanskaya *Selected Correspondence,* p. 145.
14. Marx, *Ireland and the Irish Question* trans. S. Ryazanskaya (Moscow: Progress Publishers, 1971), p. 51.
15. *Ibid.,* pp. 150–165.
16. *Ibid.,* p. 126.
17. *Ibid.,* p. 292.
18. *Ibid.,* p. 294.
19. *Ibid.,* p. 290.
20. *Marx-Engels Werke* (Berlin: Dietz Verlag, 1964), XXX, p. 568. Also see XXXI, p. 504.
21. *Ibid.,* XXXI, 1965 p. 473.
22. *Ibid.,* XXVII, 1965 p. 580.
23. *Ibid.,* XXX, 1964 p. 578.
24. *Ibid.,* XXX, p. 667.
25. *Ibid.,* XXX, pp. 564–565.
26. *Ibid.,* XXVIII, 1963 pp. 567–569.
27. *Ibid.,* XXVIII, 1963 pp. 521–522. See also XXX, p. 550. Letters to Bertalan Szemere are scattered throughout the correspondence of Marx.
28. *Ibid.,* XXXI, p. 514.
29. *Ibid., p. 486.*
30. *The General Council of the First International Minutes,* I, pp. 51–53.
31. Marx, *The Civil War in the United States* (New York: International Publishers, 1937), p. 128.
32. Marx to Engels, March 24, 1863, in Marx and Engels, *Selected Correspondence,* p. 146.
33. Marx to Engels, July 27, 1866, *Ibid.,* pp. 212–213. See also Marx to Engels, July 20, 1870, pp. 292–293. Marx was also opposed to the annexation of Alsace-Lorraine, feeling that such a German move would simply lay the seeds for a future war. On this point, see Marx to Engels, August 17, 1870, pp. 298–299.
34. Marx to Sorge, September 1, 1870, *Ibid.,* p. 301.
35. Marx to Engels, May 18, 1854, *Ibid.,* p. 122.
36. *Marx-Engels Werke,* VI, pp. 149–150.
37. Marx, *The Eastern Question,* ed. Eleanor Marx Aveling and Edward Aveling (New York: Augustus M. Kelley, 1969), p. 5.
38. *Ibid.,* pp. 25–26.
39. *Ibid.,* p. 7.
40. *Ibid.,* p. 75.
41. On this point see Bertram D. Wolfe, *Marxism: 100 Years In The Life Of A Doctrine* (New York: Dial Press, 1965), pp. 3–42. Wolfe correctly points out that Engels had no respect for the South Slav people. Wolfe overlooks the fact that Marx and Engels disagreed on this point. Marx did not share the same anti-Slav bias that possessed Engels.
42. Marx, *The Eastern Question,* p. 9. Marx's attitude toward Russia is perhaps most clearly expressed in his *The Secret Diplomatic History of the Eighteenth Century,* ed. Lester Hutchinson (New York: International Publishers, 1969).

43. Avineri, *Karl Marx on Colonialism and Modernization* (New York; Doubleday & Co., 1969), p. 63.
44. Marx and Engels, *The Russian Menace to Europe,* ed. Paul W. Blackstock and Bert F. Hoselitz (Glencoe, Ill.: Free Press, 1952), p. 183.
45. Marx, *The Eastern Question,* p. 26.
46. *Ibid.*, p. 75.
47. *Ibid.*, p. 491.
48. *Ibid.*
49. *Ibid.*, pp. 524–525.
50. *Ibid.*, p. 545.
51. *Ibid.*, p. 549.
52. *Ibid.*, p. 505.
53. *Ibid.*, p. 547.
54. *Ibid.*, p. 548.
55. *Ibid.*, p. 550.
56. See note 42.
57. *Marx-Engels Werke,* XI, pp. 603–635, 573–576.
58. *Ibid.*, XXIX, pp. 584, 598.
59. *Ibid.*, XXXIV, pp. 296–297, 317–319, 320–324.
60. Marx's appreciation of the peasantry has not as yet been adequately evaluated. David Mitrany, *Marx Against the Peasant* (New York: Collier Books, 1961) is totally deceiving. Mitrany holds that Marx was simply bent on destroying the peasantry, a view that simply does not stand against the test of evidence. Avineri in *The Social and Political Thought of Karl Marx* does not even discuss the question of the peasantry, and Tucker in *The Marxian Revolutionary Idea* implies that peasant revolutions in the twentieth century were un-Marxian. A good start toward a reevaluation of the role of the peasantry in Marx and Engels is Oscar Hammen's "Marx and The Agrarian Question," *The American Historical Review,* Vol. 77, No. 3 (June 1972), pp. 679–704. Marx's concern on this question was shown in his letter, Marx to Engels, January 11, 1860, in Marx and Engels, *Selected Correspondence,* p. 124.
61. On this point see Mitrany, *Marx Against the Peasant.* Standard interpretations of Lenin see Lenin as revising Marx on the problem of the peasant. Bertram D. Wolfe in *Three Who Made a Revolution* (New York: Praeger, 1951) and Alfred G. Meyer in *Leninism* (Ann Arbor: University of Michigan Press, 1960) see Marx as primarily concerned with the proletariat while indicating that it was Lenin who discovered the revolutionary potential of the peasants.
62. Marx-Engels, "Über Die Nationalisierung des Grund' Und Boden," *Marx-Engels Werke,* XVIII, pp. 59–62.
63. Marx, "Address of the Central Committee to the Communist League," in Marx-Engels, *Selected Works,* I, p. 111.
64. *Ibid.*, p. 114.
65. *Ibid.*, pp. 114–115.
66. *Marx-Engels Werke,* XXVII, p. 580.
67. Marx to Engels, November 30, 1867, *Ibid.*, p. 229.
68. Marx, *Ireland and the Irish Question,* p. 285.
69. Marx, *Revolution in Spain* (New York: International Publishers, 1939), p. 48.
70. *Ibid.*, p. 49.
71. *Ibid.*, p. 50.
72. Marx to Engels, April 16, 1856, in Marx and Engels, *Selected Correspondence,* p. 87.
73. Marx to Engels, August 7, 1862, *Ibid.*, p. 135.
74. Marx, *The Civil War in France* (New York: International Publishers, 1962), p. 64.

75. Marx, *Karl Marx: Early Writings,* ed. and trans. T. B. Bottomore (New York: McGraw-Hill, 1963), p. 118.
76. Marx, *Das Kapital,* trans. Samuel Moore and Edward Aveling (New York: International Publishers, 1967), III, pp. 614–615.
77. *Ibid.*, p. 650. For the theme of alienation and the peasant, see also p. 677.
78. Marx, *Revolution in Spain,* pp. 52–57.
79. *Marx-Engels Werke,* VI, pp. 386–319.
80. On the Asiatic mode of production, see Kart Wittfogel, *Oriental Despotism* (New Haven, Conn.: Yale University Press, 1965). Also see the "*Introduction*" by Avineri to his book *Karl Marx on Colonialism and Modernization.* The author has relied heavily upon Wittfogel.
81. Marx, "The British Rule in India," *Karl Marx on Colonialism and Modernization,* pp. 92–93.
82. Marx, "Indian Affairs," *Ibid.*, p. 129.
83. *Ibid.*, p. 130.
84. *Ibid.*
85. Marx, "The Future Results of British Rule In India," *Ibid.*, p. 136.
86. Marx, "The Indian Question," *Ibid.*, p. 201.
87. *Ibid.*, p. 204.
88. Marx, "The Revolt in the Indian Army," *Ibid.*, p. 192.
89. Marx, "The Revolt in India," *Ibid.*, p. 197.
90. Marx, "The Revolt in the Indian Army," *Ibid.*, p. 192.
91. Marx, "The Future Results of British Rule in India," *Ibid.*, pp. 132–139.
92. *Ibid.*, p. 133.
93. Marx, "Trade with China," *Marx on China,* ed. Dona Torr (London: Lawrence & Wishart, 1951), pp. 91–92.
94. *Ibid.*, p. 87–90.
95. Marx, "Chinese Socialism," *On Colonialism* (Moscow: Foreign Languages Publishing House, 1949), p. 14.
96. Marx, "Revolution in China and in Europe," *Karl Marx on Colonialism and Modernization,* p. 67.
97. *Ibid.*, p. 68.
98. Marx to Engels, October 8, 1858, in Marx and Engels, *Selected Correspondence,* p. 118.
99. Marx, "Revolution in China and in Europe," *Karl Marx on Colonialism and Modernization,* pp. 67–75.
100. See Franz Marek, *Philosophy of World Revolution* (New York: International Publishers, 1969).

Six

Dialectical Naturalism as a Philosophy of History

PREVIOUS CHAPTERS OF this book explored the principles of Marx's philosophical anthropology. In Chapter Two, Marx's view of nature was discussed, with particular attention to the notion of *praxis,* the activity of the species as it modified the physical world in order to produce its sustenance. Chapter Four analyzed the naturalistic basis of Marx's humanism, his understanding that the state conform to the anthropological nature of man.

Marx's thought changed during his lifetime. The Marx of *Das Kapital* was not the same man who wrote the 1844 manuscripts. On the other hand, the young humanist philosopher of 1844 was still clearly visible within the profusely scholarly pages of *Kapital* and the *Grundrisse.* There was an unbroken continuity in Marx's thinking. The naturalistic foundations of his thought were always present. In his middle period, Marx was in search of revolution, and his humanism was obscured by his passionate quest for a politics of the seizure of power. In his mature period, Marx committed to paper his years of study of economics, and his naturalism was heavily overlaid with his formulas for the behavioral regularity of the capitalist system. There is only one Marx, however, even though he could assume several distinct postures. This book is not concerned with the modalities of his career, with the periods of his life. It is concerned with establishing the unity and continuity of his thought, in uncovering and illuminating those ideas and presuppositions that were constant and permanently present throughout the phases of an extraordinarily productive life.

The notions of *praxis,* of history as the autogenesis of man, of species being, of society as a totality, of relational structures, were ever present in Marx's work. This chapter will demonstrate the unity and continuity of Marx's thought by showing how the principles of his philosophical anthropology were present in his writing on political economy. It will illustrate how Marx's understanding of economics and history was erected upon the foundation of his naturalistic humanism.

Social systems in the Marxian schema were always totalities.[1] They were composites of relational structures. That is, a given society adopted a certain mode of relating to the means of production. The means of production could be privately owned, communally owned, or despotically owned. This mode of relating to the means of production was the dominant, the prevailing mode of relationship within a given societal structure and pervaded all other relational structures within that society.[2] This did not mean that all societies were based on the same relational mode. In fact, Marx distinguished four major types of relational modes in the history of the world: the Asiatic (or despotic), the Greco-Roman (or polis-community), the Germanic (or geographical communities), the capitalistic (or private property).[3] In addition, within these four major types of relational modes there were numerous gradations and subdivisions. For instance, the German village communities were different from the Slavic village communities, and both differed from the ancient village communities of India. Therefore, although it is possible to speak of four categories of relational modes, according to Marx it is also important to recall the individuality and uniqueness of the societies being described.

Marx believed that every society manifested behavioral regularities. Each society functioned in a particular way, and the pattern of its functioning conformed to its dominant relational mode, establishing patterns of behavior which that society statistically followed. Although it is true that Marx maintained that all societies functioned in accordance with behavioral regularities, it is not true that Marx believed that all societies functioned in accordance with identical laws. Rather, different societies operated according to different regularities, regularities unique and indigenous to it. Therefore, the developmental patterns of societies would differ; they would grow and behave uniquely and individually. Because the laws of a society were indigenous to that society and none other, the behavioral and developmental patterns of separate societies would be separate. Marx was not a positivist. He was not a macrocosmic determinist. He did not believe in the existence of a universal law of development that was applicable to all societies and that compelled all societies to evolve in a uniform and unilinear fashion. The historical process was not monolinear and nondevelopmental, but rather multilinear and multidevelopmental.

Marx was a structural historicist.[4] In his sociological and economic studies, he was concerned with change and process. Dialectical naturalism was a formula for, and was most applicable when accounting for social change and process. Marx wished to describe the variety of socioeconomic formations that had come into existence within historical time. Every socioeconomic totality passed away: that was the essence of dialectical naturalism. In its place there arose another socioeconomic totality.

Marx's theory of development was not primarily concerned with temporal succession or mechanical causality. Basically, Marx's method of sociological analysis was comparative. He sought to examine the manner in which similar functions—like circulation, consumption, wages—changed their essential meaning as they were encapsulated in different economic epochs. Marx was seeking the diachronic and the synchronic.[5] By such a comparison, Marx hoped to penetrate to the uniqueness of a historical era, its immanent relationship, its law. Marx's theory of development was not focused upon chronological order or historical inevitability, but rather upon transformation and metamorphosis.

In *Kapital,* Marx's chapter on "The So-Called Primitive Accumulation" describes the early beginnings of capitalist society in the West. Clearly, Marx understood that one historic age, period, era, epoch must follow another. Tribalism has succumbed to agrarian communalism, and in the modern world the tendency was for capitalism to sublate agrarian communalism. But this did not mean that the process was either inevitable or macrocosmic. The immanent structure of different societies would respond differently to the forces of the era. For instance, in that same chapter Marx wrote that in "England alone which we take as our example, has it the classic form."[6] Marx meant that the process he was describing in *Kapital* was unique to England and need not be replicated in its exact form in other parts of the globe. His awareness of differential or multilinear development was demonstrated when he compared Italian evolution in the early capitalist period to that of England. In Italy, the coming of the trade expansion of the fifteenth century forced the laborers of the towns back into the country, to a renewed serfdom. Antithetically, the trade expansion was one of the major reasons for the destruction not only of serfdom, but of the yeoman in England.[7] Societal transformation was contingent upon the immanent structure of any given economic totality. "The history of this expropriation, in different countries, assumes different aspects, and runs through its various phases in different orders of succession, and at different periods."[8]

Marx wished to describe the form, the mode, the presuppositions of a social totality or historical epoch. The *Grundrisse* began with an analysis of production. He quickly indicated that production was not an unchanging, eternal economic datum, but rather that "all production is appropriation of nature on the part of an individual within and through a specific form of society."[9] It was Marx's sociological and historical method to select the diachronic and synchronic within each society, and then penetrate to the essential relational mode of any society. Again in the *Grundrisse,* Marx wrote,

> . . . whenever we speak of production, then, what is meant is always production of a definite stage of social development; in order to talk about production at all we must either pursue the process of historic development

through its different phases, or declare beforehand that we are dealing with a specific historic epoch such as e.g. modern bourgeois production, which is indeed our particular theme.[10]

History, for Marx, was then the appearance and disappearance of specific economic modes, forms, categories. The process itself had to be temporal, but his focus was never on the temporal. Rather, Marx was concerned with an analysis of the form, of the structure, of the totality, into its relational manifestations.

In the *Grundrisse,* Marx wrote that "human anatomy contains a key to the anatomy of the ape ... [and] the intimations of higher development among the subordinate animal species, however, can be understood only after the higher development is already known. . . ."[11] Thus, only by understanding the uniqueness of the present was it possible for us to understand the uniqueness of the past. Similar organs could be present in capitalist society as were present in classical society, but these organs would have different meanings, different functions, because they would exist as parts in different anatomical totalities. The whole colored and shaped the part. Marx assumed progressive development, but within that progressive development, he was primarily concerned with the continuity or discontinuity, the mutations, of previous structures of social organisms. He was concerned with "the succession of economic categories."[12]

Marx's theory of development was centered around the ideas of transformation and metamorphosis. Of course, capitalism had superseded agrarianism in the West. Because of its inherent laws, Western capitalism had a catastrophic impact upon the non-Western areas of the globe. But such a belief, which Marx held, did not entail the adoption of a theory of historical necessity, of inevitable chronological order, of unilinearism. Change must come. But change for Marx came from the inherent contradiction within a social structure, as that structure related to its historical environment. There were internal as well as external forces of decomposition. Changes were a result of the interplay of the internal and external laws of decomposition. The important point was that both the internal structure of a society and the external historical environment were always unique, and thus the evolution of history was always multilinear and multidevelopmental. Again in the *Grundrisse,* Marx wrote that the "exact development of the concept of capital (is) necessary, since it [is] the fundamental concept of modern economics, just as capital itself, whose abstract, reflected image (is) its concept (is) the foundation of bourgeois society."[13] The vital element for Marx was the exact concept, the immanence of a society. For it was only with this immanence that a society and its functioning in time could be comprehended and described.

In order to best understand the structural historicist basis of Marx's socioeconomic thought, an analysis of his concept of labor would be helpful. Marx divided labor into two parts. The source of all energy in the social universe was labor power. This was the hydraulic pump, the unending supply of human activity, without which life could not be sustained. Labor power was the source of the generative activity of the species. Labor power was the ground from which all creative and modified *praxis* of the species originated.

The concrete form of labor power, the form that produced objects society needed, Marx termed useful labor. It was useful labor, a specific form of labor power, that was directed to produce food, tools, and all objects beneficial to men. While labor power was constant, the ground of existence, useful labor was made to assume different forms dependent upon the relational structure that directed it. In short, useful labor produced, not exchange-value, but use-value.[14] It was useful labor that manifested Marx's historicism, because it was the mode of useful labor that was constantly being modified as it traversed differing social totalities.[15]

Marx maintained that useful labor was "a product of historical conditions."[16] He also understood that all production, all industry, was production "within and through a definite form of society."[17] Furthermore, he believed that there were no universal or general laws of production, but rather that "the so-called general conditions of all production are nothing but abstract conceptions which do not go to make up any real stage in the history of production."[18] Marx repeated this thought innumerable times. Useful labor, the creator of use-value, had thus undergone several transformations in the economic-social history of mankind. It was not and could never be an ontological category.

For instance, during the early history of mankind labor was carried on in its primitive natural form, in a communal setting. The very nature of a communal system made labor appear as a function of the entire social organism. The labor of the individual, then, did not manifest itself in a communal environment as private labor, nor did the product of labor appear as a private product. Labor, in a communal setting, where the individual had no existence apart from the collective, showed itself as universal labor or labor power. For these reasons, there was no production of exchange-value in communal societies.[19] Conversely, slave labor was totally different from labor in the primitive collective. The slave was an individual, but did not belong to a group. The slave, together with his labor power, was sold to his owner. The slave himself was a commodity, not the labor power of the slave. Thus, the person of the slave could be transferred from one owner to the next, and his labor power would follow him as an appendage. Nevertheless, as a private person, apart from a group, the slave could manifest his labor power as useful labor. He could produce use-value and exchange-value.[20]

The labor of the serf was also unique. Medieval society was characterized by an undeveloped system of exchange, and therefore personal relations, relations of personal dependence, were widespread.[21] The serf himself was not a commodity, and only a part of the serf's useful labor was given to the lord as a tribute. No wages passed between lord and serf, and thus the useful labor of the serf could not be looked upon as a commodity. Rather, since the serf belonged to the soil and the lord owned the soil, the serf gave a part of his useful labor as tribute to the lord for the use of his land and for protection.[22] On the other hand, the position of the free laborer in a capitalist society was totally different from any of the above-mentioned modes of labor. Capitalist society perfected exchange relationships, and thus all personal ties and links of the feudal society were dissolved. The wage system was universalized, and so useful labor itself became a commodity, something to be bought and sold on the marketplace like any other useful commodity. The free laborer of the capitalist society was required to auction eight, ten, or fifteen hours a day to the highest bidder in order to live.[23] In the 1844 manuscripts, Marx wrote that "Engels is right, therefore, in calling Adam Smith the Luther of the political economy."[24] Marx meant that before the advent of capitalism wealth was considered as something apart from man, as a thing external to him. Capitalism had made man himself wealth, that is, the source of wealth. Consequently, if one wished to acquire wealth, one must acquire men; the hoarding of money entailed the expropriation of useful labor.

The historicist basis of Marx's socioeconomic thought is additionally confirmed through a study of his definition of value. In *Theories of Surplus Value,* Marx took the Physiocrats to task because their "method of exposition is, of course, necessarily governed by their general view of the nature of value, which to them is not a definite social mode of existence of human activity (labor), but consists of material things—land, nature and the various modifications of these material things."[25] For Marx, then, value had to be "a definite social mode of existence of human activity." A similar idea was expressed in the *Grundrisse,* where Marx referred to value as a "realized relationship," or a "value realized as capital and living labor as mere use value opposed to capital."[26] In his analysis of value in *Das Kapital* Marx persisted in identifying value as a social relationship. It is clear, Marx wrote in this work, "that the value of commodities has a purely social reality."[27] Therefore, Marx concluded, "it follows as a matter of course that value can only manifest itself in the social relation of commodity to commodity."[28]

Value for Marx was the realization of social relationship. It was the concretization, the objectification of a social relationship. In different societies with different modes of relationship, value would undergo the same kinds of societal transformation as useful labor had manifested. But this was the exact meaning of Marx's socioeconomic historicism. Value was not an eternal, abstract, economic category. An object, a commodity, had value only insofar as it itself was an expression of a productive relationship.

Within capitalistic society, for example, value most concretely revealed itself as exchange-value. This was the case, according to Marx, because the dominant relational mode of capitalist society was exchange for profit. Marx algebraically symbolized the essence of capitalist relationship by his formula M-C-M' (money–commodity–money augmented), or C-M-C' (commodity–money–commodity augmented). In other words, the purpose, the intent, of all productive relationships in capitalist society was profit; therefore, any successful exchange relationship could only end with an augmentation of either money or commodities.[29] Since profit was the intent of capitalist relationship, value had to appear in capitalist society as an expression of that intent. Therefore, within the bourgeois system value assumed the mode, assumed the form of exchange-value.[30]

There was an inherent connection between Marx's historicism and his philosophical anthropology. The Marxian view of the world was predicated upon the idea of human *praxis.* Man was the subject in the study of man, and society was the subject in the study of history. Man and society were the generative forces in the autogenesis of mankind. The universal source of energy in the Marxian world was human labor power. This was the ground of all existence, the source of human *praxis* itself, the activating principle and force in the construction of social totalities.[31]

Marx's economic writing can best be described as an attempt to reconstruct that dismal science on the basis of a naturalistic anthropology. Marx had made the same attempt in his early life in relation to religion and the state. Here again, the essential continuity of Marx's thought becomes apparent. In his early writings Marx attacked religion from the basis of Feuerbachian naturalism: religion was simply the alienation of the anthropological essence of man. In his "On the Jewish Question" and "Toward the Critique of Hegel's Philosophy of Law," Marx similarly attacked the idea of the state. The state, too, was simply the alienated anthropological essence of man. The anthropological being of man had been fragmented because of the existence of social classes, and the state was merely an invention to impose or maintain those fractures with a minimum of violence. Classical economy had deified things. Classical economy had made religious and eternal categories out of labor, exchange, and profit. The theories of Smith, Ricardo, and Malthus were apologies for economic alienation. By treating economic categories as supernatural and unchanging fetishes, the classical economists as bourgeois apologists could argue that the capitalist system was justified and justifiable because it derived from these totemistic categories. Marx's economic writing must be seen not only as a refutation of bourgeois, capitalist economics, but as a theoretic attempt to construct a scientific and methodologically sound economics from a naturalistic basis and thus to overcome economic alienation.[32]

Marx's multilinear approach to historical development was most clearly evidenced in his writing on Asiatic and Russian societies. In these portions of his literature, Marx said that not only had Oriental society in the past followed a different line of development than western Europe, but that Russian society in the future could pursue a separate line of development from the West. In short, when Marx wrote about Asia and Russia, he did so as a multilinearist, as someone who assumed that Asia and Russia would evolve along a different path from the West, and along different paths from each other.

During the later half of his life, Marx became increasingly interested in the study of anthropology. A voluminous reader, Marx also took extensive notes on the material he was studying. Marx's *exzerpte,* his notebooks, clearly document that beginning in the 1850s he had become deeply involved in the study of primitive, communal forms of life, in their Indian, Slavic, or Germanic varieties.[33]

The initial sign that Marx was reading in Asian history appeared in the notebooks of 1853. He read eight books on Indian history and society during that year, including such works as J. F. Royle's *Essay on the Productive Resources of India* and *An Inquiry into the Causes of the Long Continued Stationary Condition of India;* Thomas St. Raffle's *The History of Java;* Robert Patton's *The Principles of Asiatic Monarchies.* Furthermore, there were eleven titles on Russian history for the same year.

Marx's acquaintance with the anthropological work of G. L. von Maurer began in 1868. He read, in that year, Maurer's *Enleitung zur Geschichte der Mark, Hof, Dorf und Stadtverfassung.* In 1876 he returned to von Maurer again, reading at this time *Geschichte der Markenverfassung, Geschichte der Fronhofe,* and the *Geschichte der Dorfverfassung in Deutschland.* Ancient Slavic institutions also preoccupied Marx during the years of 1876 and 1878. He read M. Utiesenovic's *Die Hauskommuninen der Sudslaven* in 1876, and completed Haxthausen's *Die Landlicheverfassung Russlands* in 1878.

Marx continued his study of ancient institutions in 1881 and 1882. L. H. Morgan's *Ancient Society,* J. W. B. Money's *Java, How To Manage a Colony,* V. Phear's *The Aryan Village in India and Ceylon,* and H. J. S. Maine's *Lectures on the Early History of Institutions* were all read in 1881. J. Lubbock's *The Origin of Civilization and the Primitive Condition of Man,* a *Chronologische Aufzeichmungen über die Aufhebung die Leibeigenschaft in Russland,* and D. M. Wallace's *Russia* were finished one year later.

The above list is not exhaustive. It does show that in the later half of his life he was seriously studying the unique and indigenous social structures of German, Slavic, and Indian communal existence. Having studied the emergence of capitalism in western Europe, he was now familiarizing himself with the dominant relational modes of ancient, village societies. Initially a student of capitalism, the fundamental contrast between Occident and Orient was apparent to him. He saw the world divided between a young, dynamic European economy based on private property and a primitive Asiatic society based on village communalism. Marx's *exzerpte* on anthropology show that there existed in his mind an outline, a tentative structure for a comparative study of the destruction of communal life and its supersession by a different form of society. He was studying how one layer of human history had been destroyed by a new layer of human history, that is, how societies with different social structures based on communal property were replaced by societies with different structures based on private property.

Marx concluded, then, that Occidental civilization had taken a different path of development from Oriental civilization. At the end of 1880 Marx read H. J. S. Maine's *Lectures on the Early History of Institutions.* The major thrust of Maine's book was to trace the different forms of landed proprietorship that evolved in Europe, Brittany, England, and Ireland. While dealing basically with western Europe, Maine could not help but be aware that other races (Oriental) had pursued a path of development different from the Germanic. Marx copied the following from Maine's monograph: " . . . modern research conveys a stronger impression than ever of the separation between the Aryan races and races of other stocks."[34] For Maine, the breakdown of tribal communalism stemmed from two factors: (1) the disentanglement of individual rights from the collective rights of the tribe, (2) the "transmutation of sovereignty of the tribal chief."[35] It was evident to Maine that the feudal decentralization of western Europe was a stark contrast to the hydraulic despotism of the Orient, which proved that different historical evolutions had led to a "separation between the Aryan races and races of other stocks." Marx found in Maine's research confirmation of his own belief that Asia and Europe had pursued separate paths of development.

Earlier writings of Marx show conclusively that from the 1850s Marx was dedicated to the multilinear view of history. In the *Critique of Political Economy,* Marx affirmed a multilinear view of historical development, for he argued that "from the different forms of primitive communism different forms of its dissolution have been developed."[36] In Marx's eyes, when tracing the history of ancient communal societies, one should begin with the "various forms of Indian communism." India, then, was the great mother, the original source of all later communal forms of life. From this common base, various lines of historical evolution had emerged. Specifically, the type of private property known as Roman and Teuton "can be traced back to various forms of Indian communism." Marx therefore affirmed two complementary theses: (1) Within the spectrum of communal societies generally, different communal societies had evolved along different lines; (2) Marx agreed with H. J. S. Maine that Western and Eastern societies had broken off into separate lines of evolution.

Marx's conviction that communal societies could assume unique shapes and acquire histories was more definitively expressed in his *Grundrisse.* It was in *Grundrisse,* written during the years 1857–1859, that Marx incorporated much of his research on primitive societies. The first form of communal society described in the *Grundrisse* was the Asiatic form.[37] In this socioeconomic totality, the Oriental despot was the sole proprietor of the land. Although the elemental component of the Asiatic form of society was the isolated village, in fact the village was both powerless and propertyless, because the land belonged to the despot who formed therein an all-embracing unity. The specific manner in which the Asiatic despot exercised his social control, as well as his social usefulness, was through his maintenance of public works. Village communities in arid regions needed water to carry on their agriculture, and the Asiatic lord had as his primary social duty the construction and preservation of irrigation canals. Consequently, the local community was absorbed in the encompassing unity of the peasant commune.

Marx was quick to point out that the Oriental social organism could develop along distinctly different lines. First, Asiatic societies, in order to defray the costs of the community as such, for war, for religious worship, could make a certain amount of labor communal property. Where this line of development was taken, serfdom emerged. The domination of an aristocracy evolved from this path, as shown in the ancient Slavonic and Rumanian communities. Secondly, Asiatic societies could turn all labor into communal labor. Where this line of development was taken, absolute state capitalism emerged. In other words, the despot became the sole proprietor of all labor and therefore of all value, and thus became the universal capitalist. This line of development had been taken in Mexico, in Peru, and among the ancient Celts.[38]

The second form of communal society described in the *Grundrisse* was the Greco-Roman.[39] In this form, the basis of the community was not the land, but the political unit of the city. A precondition for ownership of land was membership in the polis: the political bond was primary. The great common labor of the city-commune was war. Therefore, the polis-community was expansive. Private property could more readily evolve from the Greco-Roman form than from the Asiatic.[40] In the Asiatic form, property belonged first to the community, but ultimately to the despot. In the Greco-Roman form, private property was not inconsistent with membership in the polis-community. Because the political bond was primary, a member of the polis-community could contribute to the common labor through service in war or religious worship, and not in the least abrogate the politico-communal basis of the city-state because of private possession of land. Marx's inference was obvious here. The development of a capitalist system in the West had definite historic antecedents; that is, the existence of economic private property in the classical world introduced into Western history not only the toleration of, but the tendency toward a complete system of private ownership. This was not true of the Orient. The absorption of property into the local community and the despot distinctly blocked any movement to private ownership.

The third form of ancient communal life, according to Marx, was the Germanic.[41] Greco-Roman history was the history of cities; Asian history was the history of small villages; while in the Middle Ages German history was the history of the countryside. Because of the nature of settlement during the invasion, because of the long distances that separated one tribe from another, the German community was less a natural political or economic union than a voluntary association based upon tribal descent, language, common past and history. In the German form, if the community was to exercise a real existence, it must hold an assembly, seek, in short, a tangible form. In Greece, Rome, and India, the community existed apart from such assemblies, in the common territory of the city or village itself. In the Germanic form, as distinct from the Greco-Roman, the economic took precedence over the political. The Germanic knew no private property. Property belonged to the tribal community; the individual was merely a possessor, really an agent of the community in the cultivation of the land.

This discussion of Marx's writing on anthropology and ancient societies can be summarized on two different levels; as method, and as content. Methodologically, Marx was looking for the forms, the total structures of ancient and communal societies. He distinguished among Greco-Roman, German, capitalist, and Asian societies in terms of their dominant relational modes. Marx's method of scientific procedure, the manner in which he conceptualized data, reveals that he was not seeking unilinear laws of historical growth. The empirical procedure under which Marx chose to operate was calculated to depict the uniqueness of societies, the differences between societies, and their different paths of historical evolution.

From the point of view of content, Marx had demonstrated three cases in which societies had developed along separate paths of development: (1) Asia and western Europe had developed differently; (2) within the Oriental form, communal societies could either develop in a Slavo-Rumanian aristocratic fashion, or else in a Peruvian-Mexican state capitalist fashion; (3) because of the unique structure of the Greco-Roman forms, private property already existed in these economies. Since, in the classical world, community was defined in political terms, thus allowing for private property economically, the Greco-Roman polis-community would develop differently from either Asian or Germanic forms. Thus, both in terms of method and in terms of specific content, Marx denied that all societies were compelled by some universal law to develop along uniform and fixed lines. He was not a universal determinist.

Beginning in the 1870s, Marx was forced to deal with the problem of the future historical development of Russia. The emancipation of the serfs, the rise of a revolutionary spirit among the Russian intelligentsia made the question of the possibility of a communist revolution in Russia an immediate one. In dealing with the problem of Russian development, Marx displayed the same attitude, the same method and content of thought, that he exercised when dealing with ancient and communal societies. Marx stressed two points. One, that the laws and predictions of *Das Kapital* were intended to be descriptive only of Western, capitalist society. Marx did not intend *Das Kapital* to be a universal deterministic scheme of historical development. *Das Kapital*, therefore, was not necessarily applicable to Russia. Two, that Russian society could evolve in a manner totally different from the West. The Russian *mir* was a social unit which could act as the force to drive Russian society as a whole in a unique, communal direction.

In 1877 Marx wrote a letter to the editor of the Russian journal *Otyecestvenniye Zapisky* indicating that *Das Kapital* only tried to trace the path along which one area of the globe, western Europe, had evolved. Any attempt, Marx said, to make his "historical sketch of the genesis of capitalism in Western Europe into a historicophilosophic theory of the *marche générale* (general path) imposed by fate upon every people, whatever the historic circumstances in which it finds itself," was in error.[42] In the preface to the second German edition of *Das Kapital,* Marx alluded to a Russian review of his book, with which he agreed, that paralleled Marx's evolutionary history to the domain of biology. Unlike earlier economists, the reviewer stated, Marx had not compared his economic theories to the laws of physics and chemistry. Rather, Marx had demonstrated "that social organisms differ from one another as fundamentally as do vegetable and animal organisms."[43] Indeed, the same event is subject to quite different conditions in terms of the unique organism in which it is found. The internal constitutions of economic organisms differ, as well as their individual organs, because these organs function under a wide variety of conditions.

In the correspondence that Marx had with Vera Zasoulich, he reiterated his conviction that *Das Kapital* only analyzed, and therefore was only applicable to western Europe. On March 8, 1881, he wrote to Zasoulich:

> At the bottom of the capitalist is, therefore, the radical separation of the producer from the means of production. ... The basis of this whole evolution is the expropriation of the peasants. ... It has been accomplished in a final form only in England ... but all the other countries of Western Europe are going through the same movement. The "historical necessity" of this movement is thus explicitly restricted to the countries of Western Europe.. . .[44]

In the same letter, Marx commented on the utter futility of any attempt to find universally deterministic laws of social evolution. He said:

> By studying each one of these evolutions separately ... the key to these phenomena can easily be found, but one will never succeed with the open sesame of an historic-philosophical theory of which the supreme virtue consists in its being supra-historical (i.e., beyond the pole of history).[45]

It was in his writings on the *mir* that Marx most clearly expressed his view that Russia could evolve in a manner totally different from the West. Marx addressed himself to the question of the *mir* when Vera Zasoulich wrote to him asking whether or not the *mir* might act as the transition point to communism. Zasoulich wanted to know whether in order to attain a communist society Russia must pass through capitalism (imitate the western path of development: Menshevism) or whether it was possible for Russia to skip capitalism and build communism upon the communal nature of the *mir.* In replying to Zasoulich, Marx wrote three drafts of the letter.

These drafts to Zasoulich will be discussed under three separate questions: Could Russian society develop along a different path from western Europe? Could the Russian *mir* act in itself as a transition point to communism? What was Marx's opinion about the idea of historical inevitability?

In the past, Russian development and western development had differed. Western Europe had gone through "a long period of incubation"[46] before reaching the industrial capitalism of the nineteenth century. Europe had first to develop steamships, railroads, machine technology, as well as banks, institutions of credit, and the entire mechanism of exchange. It had taken Europe centuries to develop the technological and institutional basis for the type of capitalism that existed in the nineteenth century. Russia had not undergone any similar development. Thus, when trying to speculate on the future course of Russian history, one must take into account that the past history of Russia and Europe differed, and that in terms of the nineteenth century these two areas of the globe began with entirely different social structures.

It was true that the ancient communal village had been destroyed in India and western Europe. But this was no reason to conclude that the communal village was also inevitably doomed in Russia as well. The Russian situation differed from both the Indian and European examples. In India, the communal village was destroyed under the pressure of British imperialism. But Russia was an independent country. No foreign power because of military supremacy had unilaterally intervened into its domestic affairs to wantonly eradicate a native social system.[47]

The Russian village community and the western Germanic village community shared a common historical lineage. They both were offshoots of the archaic Indian type. But there the similarity ended. They had experienced radically different histories. Even though vestiges of the Germanic community still lingered, basically it had been destroyed during the Middle Ages and the early modern period. The Germanic conquests of Roman territory had laid the foundations for feudalism. As new land was taken, a Germanic aristocracy was formed. The village community still existed, but alongside it there had developed private property in land in the possession of new Germanic nobility. Also, the Germanic community, like the Russian, was composed of families; i.e., kinship relationships were primary. Given the existence of a private propertied feudality, gradually the German community began to dissolve as each family acquired private possession for itself. Thus, the historical environment in which the German community was placed accentuated the forces of dissolution; that is, the political and social forces surrounding the German community were such as to extinguish its community basis, and to replace it with a private property basis. Nothing like this had happened to the Russian *mir.* Enjoying a different history, the *mir* had survived until the nineteenth century, which testified both to its strength and to its uniqueness. Even though it faced enormous difficulties, there was no inherent reason, according to Marx, for the *mir* to be dissolved.[48]

The village community disappeared in western Europe because its economic development was blocked and cut short by the development of capitalism. Village communalism and capitalism had been contradictory forces in western Europe.[49] In nineteenth-century Russia, on the other hand, Marx felt that capitalism and the *mir* could complement each other. Peasant property sharing continued to be an accepted part of Russian society. The *mir* need not be destroyed by industrialism, but rather could incorporate and utilize in its own interest the advances of industrialism. For instance, the world market created by industrialism had opened up new markets for agricultural products, and thus the *mir* could find new outlets for its products. In addition, recent technological advances in agriculture, like plows and fertilizing equipment of all kinds, could be incorporated in the *mir* structure and increase the output of the *mir*. Thus, the progress brought by capitalism and industrialism during the nineteenth century need not impede or obstruct the survival of the *mir*. There existed the possibility, even if small, that capitalism and industrialism could create the conditions, in terms of markets and increased productivity, that would sustain and enhance the very existence of the *mir*.[50]

The political situation favored the survival of the *mir*. The workers' movement in Europe and America was anticapitalist. The masses of both continents were seeking alternatives to the private property system. The *mir* was clearly one such alternative. From the political standpoint of the dissenting masses, the preservation of the *mir* was something to be desired. The socialist revolution would overthrow capitalism, but it would be self-defeating to overthrow any form of already existing agrarian collectivism.

Because of the different histories of Russia and the West, if the Russian countryside were to be capitalized this development would be accomplished in a vastly different fashion from that of the West. In Europe, private property was already in existence under feudalism. This form of private property was landed private property. In Europe, under capitalism private property was extended to the industrial and commercial means of production. The line of development for the Occident, thus, went from one form of private property to another form of private property. The line of development for Russia if it were to be completely capitalized would have to be totally different, according to Marx. In the countryside, communalism existed. Thus, Russia would have to move from communalism to private property. This was not only a different path of development from the West, but was a process that would require a different set of circumstances and factors than had operated in the West.[51]

The three drafts of Marx's letter to Vera Zasoulich clearly document two sets of conclusions at which he had arrived: The past history of Russia and the West had been different; the conditions within Russian society were such that the future development of Russia and Europe could remain different—i.e., the *mir* could survive and act as the basis of a collective society generally.

Concerning the question of whether the *mir* in itself could act as a transition point to communism, Marx saw in the *mir* certain elements which were superior to other industrial forms that were completely dominated by the capitalist system. Even in the form in which it existed in the mid-nineteenth century, the collective nature of the *mir* made it a more desirable social form than capitalism.

It was not necessary for either Russia or the *mir* to pass through capitalism. It was possible for the *mir* to incorporate "all the positive accomplishments that have been created by the capitalist system without having to pass through all the horror of that system."[53] In short, all the productive capacities of the modern industrial system could be grafted onto the collective social structure of the *mir*. Modern machinery could be immediately owned communally.

Marx believed that it would be an avoidable misfortune for Russia to pass through capitalism. To do so would be to throw away one of the best historical opportunities to bypass the horrors of the system.[54]

There existed a chance that the *mir* could regenerate Russian society. The *mir* could be "the direct point of transition to that economic system toward which modern society tends; it could open a new way of life without beginning with its own self-destruction."[55] In other words, it was possible to build a socialist society, without passing through capitalism, on the collective foundation of the *mir*.

In order for Russia to make this transition, it was necessary for the country to have a political revolution.[56] Marx believed that the policies of the Czar favored the strengthening of capitalism and therefore the destruction of the *mir*. Consequently, if the *mir* were to survive the Czar must be overthrown.

However, if a Russian revolution were to succeed, it was necessary for the revolution in Russia to be supported by a revolution in western Europe. On this point, Marx wrote:

> If the Russian revolution sounds the signal for a proletarian revolt in the west, the decomposition of the communal ownership of land in Russia can be evaded, so that each complements the other, the prevailing form of communal ownership of land in Russia may form a starting-point for a communist course of development.[57]

Marx's strategy for a successful communist revolution in Russia had the following ingredients: the political seizure of power in Russia by those who wished to build socialism; a proletarian revolution in western Europe, which would prevent a capitalist western Europe from intervening in Russia and destroying the revolution there; with the *mir* preserved, the use of the collectivist nature of the *mir* as an immediate foundation for the building of a communal society.

Concerning the question of historical inevitability, in the letters to Vera Zasoulich, Marx specifically rejected the possibility of historical determinism. When discussing the collapse of the communal village in western Europe, Marx posed himself the rhetorical question, whether the Russian *mir* also must be destroyed. In his first draft to Vera Zasoulich, Marx answered the question in the following way: "Does that mean that under all conditions the development of the peasant commune must take the same path? Not by any means."[58] In the third draft to Zasoulich Marx repeated the same idea: "But does that mean that the historical course of the peasant community must inevitably lead to the same result? Not by any means."[59] In the second draft of the letter Marx addressed himself to a slightly different self-imposed question. Marx asked what were the real forces that menaced the *mir* and answered that what threatened the *mir* "was neither historic inevitably nor a theory."[60]

The idea that it was not necessary to pass through capitalism to arrive at communism (that there were no indispensable stages of historical evolution) and that the development of different societies could vary, was not expressed by Marx for the first time in his writing on Russia. The earliest indication of such beliefs are found in Marx's "Toward a Critique of Hegel's Philosophy of Law." In that essay, written in 1843, Marx clearly pointed out how Germany's development had differed from French and English development. Marx also believed that it was possible to have a radical, a communist revolution in Germany. In fact, Marx maintained that the only real revolution that was possible in Germany was a radical, proletarian, communist revolution. Thus, Germany need not pass through capitalism before starting to build socialism. Furthermore, the proletarian revolution in Germany was the counterpart of the liberal bourgeois revolution in France, and so the development of France and Germany would continue to differ. "Toward a Critique of Hegel's Philosophy of Law" was the first statement of Marx's belief, which was to remain unchanged throughout his life, that it was possible to move directly from a basically feudal society to communism, by a one-stage revolutionary process.[61]

Marx's writing on the *mir* not only demonstrates his multilinear approach to history, but also clarifies the methodology of dialectical naturalism. When Marx analyzed a society, he concentrated upon the social relationships of that society; he tried to isolate the dominant relational mode of that society. Societal meaning, value, was an expression of that dominant relational mode. Marx was not primarily concerned with materiality, with thingness. Economics for Marx did not mean the study of objects, of instruments, of tools and money. What made a society unique were not the material objects that helped compose it, but rather the social relations that were its essential structure. Dialectical naturalism postulated that society was determined by the basic material need to reproduce life, but that in the reproduction of life—the creation of human sustenance—social relationships, not material objectivity, were the dominant forces.

Dialectical naturalism was a tool of social analysis rather than a predictive device. Dialectical naturalism allowed Marx to see into the dualism, the inherent contradictions of the *mir*, so that he could better understand the options and possibilities of its development. He could not absolutely predict the history of the *mir*; he could, however, see its potentials.

Marx looked upon the *mir* as a unique social structure. It was a totality, but at the same time it was composed of contradictory elements. The dominant relational mode was communal; however, there existed in it the potential to move in the direction of private property. The *mir*, like any other social structure, according to Marx, was a totality superimposed upon the conflict of form and content.

The dominant relational mode of the Russian peasant commune was collective: Land belonged to clans and was worked cooperatively by the kinship group. Its form, therefore, was cooperative. However, because land belonged to families, it was possible for the totality of the *mir* to dissolve and fragment into kinship groups who held property. Its content, consequently, was potentially bourgeois. Like any other social structure, Marx maintained, the *mir* was a totality that incorporated mutually contradictory elements.[62] In the case of the *mir*, the decision whether it was to remain communal or dissolve into private property would be made by the external forces surrounding this structure. The political and social environment in which the *mir* found itself, the forces in operation around the *mir*, would reinforce either the communal potential or the private property potential and therefore determine the developmental option of the *mir*. For instance, if there were no Russian Revolution, and the Czar remained on the throne, he would support the development of capitalism in Russia. Capitalism would be the dominant force surrounding the *mir*; therefore the potential inside the *mir* for private property would be made dominant, and the *mir* would be destroyed. Or, if there were a Russian Revolution, if the Czar were overthrown and socialists came to power, they would preserve any collectivist entity. Communalism would be the dominant force surrounding the *mir*, the potential inside the *mir* for cooperative ownership would be made dominant, and the *mir* would survive.

Marx looked upon societies as total social structures that contained inherent oppositions. He was concerned with social mutation, fissions, mutual contradiction. Dialectical naturalism was intended as an analytic tool to measure the oppositional tensions within a total social structure, the internal contradiction of form and content. Marx was not concerned with historical inevitability. Dialectical naturalism was not meant to be a macrocosmic law of unilinear social development.

Furthermore, dialectical naturalism was not meant to be eschatological.[63] Communism was not equivalent to the Kingdom of God, to the salvation of man after his fall into original sin, i.e., capitalism. The proletariat was not a secular version of the Messiah who came to redeem man from his fallen state, nor was communist society a paradisiacal state, one in which pain, suffering, mutability were entirely absent. Communism entailed the abolition of the state, of social classes. With the destruction of state and social classes, a new epoch of human history would begin: the conquest of human freedom. But Marx was not an impossibilist; he did not believe it possible to have a human condition without pain, without individual suffering, without historical process and individual mutability. He did believe it possible to create a society that was anthropocentric, that is, a society that fully coincided with man's natural being. Such a condition was eudaemonistic, but that was not the same as a total absence of mortality.

Footnotes

1. Alfred Schmidt, *Der Begriff der Natur in der Lehre von Marx* (Frankfurt: Europ-
äische Verlagsanstalt, 1962); for an excellent discussion of the question of totality in the work of Marx see Theodor Adorno and Jurgen Habermas, *Der Positivismusstreit in Der Deutschen Soziologie* (Berlin: Herman Luchterhand, 1970).
2. Karl Marx, "Preface to a Contribution to the Critique of Political Economy," in Karl Marx–Friedrich Engels, *Selected Works,* I (Moscow: Foreign Languages Publishing House, 1955), pp. 361–365.
3. Marx, *Grundrisse,* trans. Martin Nicolaus (New York: Vintage Press, 1973), pp. 472–488.
4. There were and are many commentators who have attacked the positivist interpretation of Marx as an economic determinist, or a unilinearist. Antonio Gramsci, Karl Korsch, and George Lukács in the 1920s pioneered the attempt to reinterpret Marx and overcome vulgar determinism. Karl Korsch, *Marxismus und Philosophie* (Frankfurt: Europäische Verlagsanstalt, 1966), and George Lukács, *History and Class Consciousness,* trans. Rodney Livingstone (Cambridge, Mass.: M.I.T. Press, 1971) did not, however, see Marx as a historicist. It was Antonio Gramsci, *Selections from the Prison Notebooks,* ed. and trans. by Quintin Hoare and Geoffrey Nowell Smith (New York: International Publishers, 1971), who pointed to and examined the historicist inclinations of Marx's thought.
5. Claude Levi-Strauss, *Structural Anthropology,* trans. Claire Jacobson (New York: Doubleday & Co., 1963), pp. 1–26. Also see Emmanuel Terray, *Marxism and "Primitive Societies,"* trans. Mary Klopper (New York: Monthly Review Press, 1972).
6. Marx, *Das Kapital,* trans. Samuel Moore and Edward Aveling (New York: International Publishers, 1967), I, p. 716.
7. *Ibid.*
8. *Ibid.*
9. Marx, *Grundrisse,* p. 87.
10. *Ibid.,* p. 85.
11. *Ibid.,* p. 105.
12. *Ibid.,* p. 106.

13. *Ibid.*, p. 331.
14. Marx, *Das Kapital,* trans. Samuel Moore and Edward Aveling, I, pp. 41–45.
15. *Ibid.*, p. 46.
16. Marx, *Grundrisse,* p. 286.
17. *Ibid.*, p. 274.
18. *Ibid.*, p. 275.
19. Marx, *Critique of Political Economy* (New York: International Publishers, 1971), p. 29.
20. Marx, *Wage-Labour and Capital* (New York: International Publishers, 1933), pp. 19–20.
21. Marx, *Grundrisse,* p. 480.
22. Marx, *Wage-Labour and Capital,* p. 20.
23. *Ibid.*
24. Marx, "Private Property and Labour," *Karl Marx: Early Writings;* trans. T. B. Bottomore (New York: McGraw-Hill, 1963), p. 147.
25. Marx, *Theories of Surplus Value* (London: Lawrence & Wishart, 1969), p. 46.
26. Marx, *Grundrisse,* p. 108.
27. Marx, *Das Kapital,* trans. Samuel Moore and Edward Aveling, I, p. 47.
28. *Ibid.*
29. Marx, *Das Kapital,* trans. Samuel Moore and Edward Aveling, II, pp. 23–62.
30. In the twentieth century, George Lukács, Karl Korsch, Antonio Gramsci, and Louis Althusser have debated the problem of historicism in Marx. All begin on the assumption that Marx was not an economic determinist, that he was not a positivist. In his book, *History and Class Consciousness,* Lukács used the term "vulgar Marxism" to refer to all those who interpreted historical materialism as a universal law applicable to the development of all societies. Lukács was one of the first to protest the philosophical and historical rigidities of Stalinist orthodoxy. But Lukács did not think Marx a historicist. Lukács recognized that all socioeconomic systems were historical phenomena, that they changed in time. Nevertheless, Lukács's major concern was the fusion of theoretical Marxism to the proletarian class struggle. Therefore, Lukács believed that the major concern of historical materialism was the criticism of capitalist society. He also believed that historical materialism should be used by the proletariat to strengthen its own self-knowledge, to enhance its own potential as a revolutionary force. Consequently, even though Lukács understood the historical nature of the economic process in Marx's thought, the direction of Lukács's comments was aimed at making historical materialism a politically efficacious theory in the revolutionary class struggle of the 1920s rather than at viewing historical materialism as a philosophy of history.

    Karl Korsch, a German contemporary of Lukács, joined Lukács in rejecting the absurdities of Stalinist mechanistic materialism. In his book, *Karl Marx* (New York: Russell and Russell, 1963), Korsch used the phrase "historical specification" in trying to describe Marx's dialectical naturalism. Korsch, by the use of this phrase, tried to indicate that Marx believed each socioeconomic society was specific to its age. That is, each society was a specific and unique historical product, with behavioral regularities peculiar to it, but in no way subsumed under a universal law. For Korsch, the liberation of historical materialism from its positivistic distortion had immediate political implications as well, because it meant that the proletariat was to undogmatically adjust its tactics to conform to the political realities of a given historical period. Korsch, however, never used the term "historicism" to refer to Marx, and seemed more concerned, like Lukács, with immediately combating both capitalism and Stalinism than with making statements about Marx's philosophy of history.

Gramsci's *Prison Notebooks* did directly refer to Marxism as historicism. For Gramsci, Marxism was above all a philosophy of *praxis.* Marxism was primarily about human activity. Since human activity was constant, the changes it would introduce into socioeconomic formation were constant. When Gramsci referred to Marxism as historicism, he meant that it embodied a "realist immanence," i.e., the generative force of history existed in history itself, as man.

Most recently, the French Communist Louis Althusser has attacked Luk ács, Korsch, and particularly, of course, Gramsci. Althusser's *On Reading Capital,* (trans. Ben Brewster, London: New Left Books, 1970), adamantly maintained that "Marxism is not a historicism." This does not mean that Althusser was returning to the positivism and the absolutist materialism of the Stalinist era. He has much too incisive a mind to fall into that confinement. Althusser wanted to defend the truth claim of Marxism, he wanted to show that Marx had indeed penetrated to the essence of the capitalistic system. Distinguishing between epistemology and the philosophy of history, Althusser wished to validate the epistemological correctness of Marxism. Aware that socioeconomic structures and their laws change in time, Althusser believed it possible to grasp the essential concept of each socioeconomic formation, to grasp its truth. In other words, Althusser did not want a historicist philosophy of history to co-opt epistemology. He did not want to state that because societies change in time truth changes in time. He wanted to say that although it was granted that societies change in time, it was also granted that the human mind had the ability to grasp the essential concept of every society, to discover its truth, and that this truth would not change. Whereas Gramsci saw historical materialism arising from a philosophy of *praxis,* Althusser saw historical materialism as a methodological tool of social analysis. Lukács and Korsch saw historical materialism in its relation to the political warfare of the laboring classes. Leaving aside the epistemological question, the center of gravity of this present chapter is upon Marxism as a philosophy of history. Within this context, there can be little doubt that Marx was a structural historicist. This means that Marx opposed any imputation of eternal categories in human history. There were no laws in general, only regularities unique to each social totality. There were no ideas in general, only ideas unique to each social totality. There were no production relations in general, only relations of production indigenous to each social organism. Since human *praxis* was at the center of Marx's philosophy of man, so process was at the center of his philosophy of history. Social totalities had changed in the past; there had been four—ancient, classical, feudal, and bourgeois. The system was open-ended, and transformations would continue to occur in the future.

31. Schmidt, *Der Begriff der Natur in der Lehre von Marx.*
32. The thesis that Marx was a unilinearist was essentially a product of Engels, Kautsky, and Stalin. Because of the political and ideological need to make Soviet Russia appear as the vanguard of the world communist revolution, Soviet scholars interpreted Marx as an economic determinist. They interpreted dialectical materialism as a sociological formula, as a cosmically valid pattern of development for all societies which required that they move through three necessary stages: feudalism, capitalism, and communism. If this three-stage pattern were true, and since Soviet Russia was already building toward communism, then it logically followed that Stalinist Russia was lead-

ing the world revolution. Economic determinism was not only a perversion of Marx, but served as a political platform. It not only justified the Bolshevik Revolution of 1917, not only made the Soviet Union the leader of Marxist revolutions, but also strengthened Stalin's personal position inside the Kremlin because it could be used to substantiate his policies.

As we have seen, several scholars of central and western Europe rebelled against the rigidities and absurdities of Stalinist orthodoxy. Opposed to Stalinism as a political system, they were also opposed to Stalinism in its theoretical forms. Lukács, Korsch, and Gramsci, who almost simultaneously rediscovered the notion of *praxis* in Marx, were also unanimous in rejecting the Stalinist interpretation of Marx as economic determinism. They referred to Stalinism as "vulgar Marxism" and maintained that it was an utter distortion of Marx's theory to see it as a macrocosmic law of historical development.

The debate concerning Marx and determinism continues to the present day. Many scholars maintain an essentially Stalinist picture of Marx, without, of course, the political intent and purposes of Stalinism. John Plamenatz, in his book *German Marxism and Russian Communism* (New York: Harper & Row, 1965), not only referred to Marx as an "economic determinist," but also found that Marx "invented a law which he believed must apply to the whole of history." There was no discussion in the Plamenatz book concerning the idea of *praxis* in Marx. Furthermore, Plamenatz failed to take into account the manuscripts of 1844, or the *Grundrisse.* Zbigniew A. Jordan, in his penetrating book *The Evolution of Dialectical Materialism* (New York: St. Martins Press, 1967), basically defended the thesis that Marx ended his life as a social determinist. In discussing Marx's philosophy of history, Jordan insightfully distinguished between two periods of Marx's thought. During Marx's early period, Jordan concluded that Marx thought of dialectical naturalism as a method of social analysis rather than a metaphysical assumption regarding the cause of history. However, Jordan affirmed that in the second period of his career Marx conceived of dialectical naturalism as a "metaphysical theory as well," and that in its second formulation the materialist conception of history had been "transformed from a hypothesis concerning the genesis of social and historical events to a theory of historical causation, supposed to be based upon a study of historical causes and historical effects." In *The Open Society and Its Enemies* (New York: Harper and Row, 1963), Karl R. Popper not only misinterpreted the word "historicism," but also distorted Marx. In Popper's eyes Marx was a social "prophet," to be classed with Plato and Hegel. Within the pages of Popper's book Marxism was defined as "sociological determinism" whose sole aim was to predict "the future course of economic and power-political developments and especially of revolution." A similar note was struck by Isaiah Berlin, particularly in his book *Historical Inevitability* (London: Oxford University Press, 1954), the title of which describes in essence Berlin's own reading of Marx. Those who still defend the view of Marx as a positivist can be classified as the contemporary apologists of "vulgar Marxism."

A growing literature that rejects the interpretation of Marx as a universal determinist has been forthcoming within the past two decades, basically from European scholars. Two notable exceptions to this rule, however, are Karl Wittfogel and Irving M. Zeitlin. In *Oriental Despotism* (New Haven, Conn.: Yale University Press, 1964), Wittfogel discussed for perhaps the first time Marx's concept of Asiatic society. Wittfogel showed that Marx held Oriental society to be unique, to be distinct from Western capitalist society and to possess its own pattern of development. Wittfogel concluded then that Marx did not believe in a necessary three-stage development for all societies, from feudalism to communism. In a small book, *Marxism: A Re-examination* (Princeton, New Jersey: D. Van Nostrand, 1967), which has not received the attention it deserves, Zeitlin interpreted dialectical naturalism as a method of social analysis. Zeitlin correctly maintained that it was possible for dialectical naturalism as a method of analysis to be correct and yet not commit itself to statements about the metaphysical nature of history. Dialectical naturalism was an analytical tool, not a predictive device. On the European side, it is not a distortion to say that all the intellectual leaders of French Marxism have categorically rejected the positivist view of Marx. See Henri Le Febvre, *Dialectical Materialism,* trans. John Sturrock (London: Jonathan Cape, 1968); Le Febvre, *The Sociology of Marx,* trans. Norbert Guterman (New York: Pantheon Books, 1968); Lucien Goldman, *The Human Sciences and Philosophy* (London: Jonathan Cape, 1968); August Cornu, *The Origins of Marxian Thought* (Springfield, Ill.: Charles C Thomas, 1957); Jean Paul Sartre, *Critique de la raison dialectique* (Paris: Gallinard, 1960). For a fuller analysis of Cornu's interpretation of Marx, see his *Karl Marx et Friedrich Engels,* 3 vols. (Paris: Presses Universitaires de France, 1955–1962). Two books by Louis Althusser are important in this respect. We have already mentioned *On Reading Capital.* See also *For Marx,* trans. Ben Brewster (New York: Random House, 1970). All of these writers credit Marx with a multilinear view of history. For West Germany, where the tradition of Korsch still lives, see Schmidt, *Der Begriff der Natur in der Lehre von Marx;* Schmidt, *Beitrage zur Marxistischen Erkenntnisbedrie* (Frankfurt: Suhrkamp Verlag, 1969); Irving Fetscher *Karl Marx und der Marxismus* (Munich: R. Poper, 1967); and works from the Frankfurt School of Marxism. The two outstanding figures of the Frankfurt School of Marxism are Theodor Adorno and Jurgen Habermas. The views of both these men are contained in the anthology *Der Positivismusstreit in der deutschen Soziologie* (Berlin: Hermann Luchterhand, 1970). Also see Horkheimer, *Critical Theory,* trans. Matthew J. O'Connell (New York: Herder & Herder, 1972). A few of the more meritorious articles on Marx to be found in the pages of *Marxismusstudien* are: Ludwig Landgrebe, "Das Problem der Dialektik," *Marxismusstudien* (Tubingen: J. C. B. Mohr, 1960), pp. 1–65; Landgrebe, "Hegel und Marx," *Ibid.,* 1954, pp. 39–53; Erwin Metzke, "Mensch und Geschichte im ursprunglichen ansatz des Marxinterpretation," *Ibid.,* p. 954, pp. 1–38. These authors are in basic agreement with the French, upholding dialectical materialism as a methodology and again placing human *praxis* in the center of Marx's thought.

33. The entire corpus of Marx's notebooks is in the archives of the International Institute of Social Research in Amsterdam. The author would like to acknowledge the generous support of the American Philosophical Society, which allowed him during the summer of 1971 to read all of Marx's anthropological *exzerpte.*
34. Marx, *Exzerpte* on H. J. S. Maine, *Lectures on the Early History of Institution;* Vol. B. 162, p. 164.
35. *Ibid.*, p. 166.
36. Marx, *Critique of Political Economy,* p. 29.
37. Marx, *Grundrisse,* p. 480.
38. *Ibid.*, p. 482.
39. *Ibid.*, p. 484.
40. *Ibid.*, p. 485.
41. *Ibid.*, p. 486.

42. Karl Marx–Friedrich Engels, *Selected Correspondence,* trans. Dona Torr (New York: International Publishers, 1954), p. 354.
43. Marx, *Das Kapital,* trans. Samuel Moore and Edward Aveling, I, pp. 872–873.
44. Marx and Engels, *The Russian Menace to Europe,* ed. Paul W. Blackstock and Bert F. Hoselitz (Glencoe, Ill.: Free Press, 1952), p. 278.
45. *Ibid.,* p. 279.
46. Marx, "Entwurfe einer antwort auf den brief von. V.I. Zassulitsch," *Marx-Engels Werke* (Berlin: Dietz Verlag, 1969), XIX, p. 385.
47. *Ibid.,* p. 389.
48. "Dritter Entwurf," *Ibid.,* pp. 402–404.
49. "Erster Entwurf," *Ibid.,* p. 386.
50. "Zweiter Entwurf," *Ibid.,* p. 398.
51. "Erster Entwurf," p. 384; "Zweiter Entwurf," p. 396; "Dritter Entwurf," p. 401; *Ibid.*
52. "Erster Entwurf," *Ibid.,* p. 385.
53. "Erster Entwurf," *Ibid.,* p. 389.
54. "Erster Entwurf," *Ibid.,* p. 391.
55. "Dritter Entwurf," *Ibid.,* p. 405.
56. "Erster Entwurf," *Ibid.,* p. 395.
57. Marx, "Letter on the Russian Village Community," in Marx and Engels, *The Russian Menace to Europe,* p. 228.
58. "Erster Entwurf," *Werke, Marx-Engels* XIX, p. 388.
59. "Dritter Entwurf," *Ibid.,* p. 404.
60. "Zweiter Entwurf," *Ibid.,* p. 400.
61. Marx, "Toward a Critique of Hegel's Philosophy of Law," *Writings of the Young Marx on Philosophy and Society,* ed. and trans. Loyd D. Easton and Kurt H. Guddat (New York: Doubleday & Co., 1967), pp. 249–264.
62. Marx, "Erster Entwurf," *Marx-Engels, Werke,* XIX, pp. 384–395.
63. See my article "Humanism without Eschatology," *Journal of the History of Ideas,* Vol. 33, No. 2 (April–June 1972), pp. 281–298. For a view that Marxism is eschatological, see among others Martin Buber, *Paths in Utopia* (Boston: Beacon Press, 1959); and Robert Tucker, *Philosophy and Myth in Karl Marx* (New York: Norton Press, 1964)

Seven

The Young Engels

THE RELATIONSHIP BETWEEN Marx and Engels was a complex one.[1] In evaluating this relationship, greater clarity will be brought to the problem by separating the areas in which they were in agreement from the areas in which they were in disagreement. In this way, those points in which harmony of viewpoint existed can be distinguished from those points where disparity was apparent. When a balance sheet has been struck, when the areas of agreement have been contrasted with the areas of disagreement, it will be possible to ascertain whether there was unanimity of viewpoint between the two men, or whether in fact major differences separated them.

The areas of agreement were undeniably ample. They were lifelong friends and intellectual companions. Marx was a contentious and arrogant person, but Engels was one of the few people with whom Marx did not experience a personal rupture. Engels always accepted Marx's intellectual superiority, Marx's genius. Engels made a personal sacrifice for this genius, since he worked for many years, years lost to his own career, in his family's firm in Manchester, England, in order to financially support Marx. During the early years of their friendship, they collaborated on books together, and their correspondence is noticeably lacking in pettiness or feuding.

In the intellectual sphere, both, of course, were communists. Both thought that capitalism would destroy itself, and that the proletariat had the mission to initiate that destruction. Both felt that the proper subject of history was the social life of man, the manner in which men gained their sustenance, and they each ridiculed all philosophies and historiographies that were based on God, Spirit, or any form of idealism. Each participated in the 1848 revolutions, and each saw Russian Czarism as the final bastion of reaction in Europe. Marx and Engels supported German nationalism, Italian nationalism, Irish nationalism. Each was an enemy of European overseas imperialism, and each felt that when the means of production were held in common by an association of the nation the productive capacities of industry and men would expand enormously. Marx and Engels disliked Napoleon III, thought the unification of Germany under Bismarck the only viable outcome for Germany, supported the North in the American Civil War, and were violently opposed to Bakunin and anarchism. The list of agreements could be broadened.

Equally striking, however, is the fact that the areas of disagreement between the two men were extensive. There were differences over the philosophy of nature. Marx saw man as basically a being of *praxis,* a being who through his activity modified the natural world, humanized that world, that is, exploited it for human purposes, thus imparting to it a human character. Engels was a metaphysical materialist. The elemental forces in the universe, for Engels, were matter and motion, and from these two forces Engels thought it possible to derive the remainder of the natural world as well as human history. Marx did not look upon history as a necessary and inevitable process. He did not think the course of history was unilinear, driven in one direction by macrocosmic forces. Engels did see history as a unilinear process. Engels did believe that macrocosmic forces determined the inevitable path of history. Marx interpreted communism as the end of human alienation, the end of dehumanization, the beginning of free human history, when man would be one with his *praxis.* Communism, for Marx, was that stage of human history when man could live harmoniously and in accordance with his naturalistic essence. From his perspective, Engels envisioned communist society as an enormous factory. It would be regimented, highly supervised, devoted to the work ethic, but highly productive of the necessities and luxuries of life. Although favoring German unification, Marx did not believe that Germany had to lead the European socialist movement, nor Europe lead and direct the world movement toward socialism. Conversely, Engels was a strong German nationalist. He possessed a blatant dislike, except of the Poles, of Slavic peoples. German socialism, according to Engels, must lead the European movement. Only Europe had reached the necessary historic stage to achieve communism. The remainder of the globe must wait and traverse the same historic stages as Europe before being ready to advance to communism. Europe, like Germany, must lead.

The questions that must be answered in the following chapters relate to the dimensions of this catalogue of differences. Before these questions can be answered, however, it is necessary to analyze in depth the full horizons of Engels's own thought patterns. In order to do this fully, we must first observe the origins of these thought patterns in his youth. Only in this way will his mature speculations be understood completely.

The perimeters of Engels's later life style, the thrust and direction of his creative energies, were already shaped as a consequence of his youthful rebellion against his parents and their value system. Engels came into manhood, seized his own meaning and purposefulness, by first categorically rejecting the philistinism and religious fundamentalism of his familial home. His parents were devout Pietists and wanted their son to enter the family business. In "Letters from Wuppertal,"[2] Engels ridiculed the social insensitivity and religious hypocrisy of his birthplace, Barmen. The town was an industrial area, and the local bourgeoisie remained totally callous to the suffering of the working class. The religion of the town was Pietist, and instead of relief from poverty, the local clergy offered the promise of peace in the afterlife. In 1839 Engels implied what was later affirmatively stated in *Communist Manifesto,* that "religion was the opiate of the people."

Social poverty was something that Engels knew from his immediate life experiences. His father had grown rich from expropriated labor. Social conscience arose in Engels from the direct, visceral contact with economic poverty. Practical, empirical, Engels saw the need to relieve the daily distress of the worker and so rebelled against the major contributors of that impoverishment, bourgeois conservatism and religious obscurantism. Family relations toward the prodigal son were severely strained, of course. In early 1845, Engels had returned to his home to complete work on his book, *The Situation of the Working Class in England.* On March 17, 1845, he wrote to Marx about the uncomfortable atmosphere in the home, his parents' disbelief at his politically radical affiliations, and the incessant and irritating reminders of his lost religious fundamentalism.[3]

Engels's rebellion was against what he called "bourgeois fanaticism."[4] This path took him to a youthful career in journalism. From 1841 until 1842 Engels fulfilled his military service in the Prussian army as an artillery officer stationed in Berlin. During this same period, he began writing literary criticism for various German journals under the name of Friedrich Oswald. The young artillery officer with a gift for lucid prose found the bohemian life of the great capital an exciting contrast to the drabness and conformity of his parental environment. To his sister, Marie, he wrote of long nights of conversation with literary friends during which bourgeois idols were destroyed with irreverent gusto. He drew pictures caricaturing the pompousness, snobbery, and vanity of bourgeois life.[5]

The youthful coefficients of Engels's search for identity, his personal predisposition of thought, the horizons of his early movement to social conscience and humanitarianism were clearly manifested during the years 1840–1842. There was a touch of dilettantism. He possessed an agile mind, one that was restless rather than a mind that preferred not to roam broadly but penetrate deeply into a subject. He was a commentator, rather than an originator. He was a popularizer, rather than a seminal mind. He fled the sterility of his parental traditions. The world of art provided the stimulation and new vision that he desired. Literary work was the first step he was to take on the path to political and social commitment, and thus, was really a brief halfway house.

Above all, Engels did not practice self-deception. He was honest, even to the point of self-effacement, and had a realistic grasp of the limitations of his own abilities. On July 26, 1842, Engels wrote to Arnold Ruge:

> I have reached the decision to give up for a time all literary activity in order to devote more time to study. The reasons for the decision are the following. I am young and self-taught in philosophy. I have learned enough in order to form a connection and to defend it if need be. But not enough to be able to work with it with success and effectiveness. I have not, through the acquisition of a doctoral degree earned the right to philosophize; so if one places demands on me I must confess that I am now only a "major philosophical sieve." Later, I hope I can, after a period of study when I again am ready to write, and then under my own name, satisfy these more exacting demands. And for that purpose it is best that I do not now divide my time between study and writing since it will shortly again be claimed by mercantile work. Until now my literary activity has been confined to journalism, and I have had to learn from that activity whether my natural talents have had a fruitful effectiveness on the progress, have formed a living contribution to the progressive movements of this century. So far I am satisfied with my contribution, and hold it to be my duty now, through study, which I will carry on with intense ambition, to make myself acquire by hard work talents that were not naturally inborn.[6]

As a literary commentator, as one trying to familiarize the popular mind with the latest movements in literary thought, Engels became an adherent of, and a spokesman for, the Young German movement. Rebelling against bourgeois conservatism and Pietist fundamentalism, Engels found in Young German art the requisite antidotes of nationalism, liberalism, and rationalism. Engels wished to participate in the more progressive movements of his time. In a series of articles called "Retrograde Zeichen der Zeit," which he wrote for the *Telegraph für Deutschland* in early 1840, Engels described the attempt of outmoded thought patterns as well as decadent political forms to retain their hold in postrevolutionary Europe. "The feudalism of the Middle Ages and the absolutism of Louis XIV, the hierarchy of Rome and the Pietism of the previous century join together around the principle of repressing and destroying free thought."[7] Furthermore, "the colossal reactions in church and political life conform with unobserved tendencies in painting and literature, to unconsciously return to earlier centuries,"[8] and it was against this continuation of the past that Engels fought. Young Germany was attempting to bring the "ideas of the time" to fruition, to see that contemporary consciousness was given its opportunity to refashion the archaic present. Engels wished to contribute in this endeavor, to be a part of history.

Young Germany was nationalistic. "We do not change our demands: no estates, but a large, unified nation of citizens sharing equal rights."[9] The doctrine of natural rights was crucial to Young Germany and Engels, and equally dear were the ideas of citizen participation in the administration of the state, constitutionalism, further emancipation of the Jews, and destruction of all religious privileges. Engels wanted to destroy the alliance of Throne and Altar.[10] He also wanted to destroy the nobility, bulwarks of German particularism, but not the Prussian monarch, probable center of German unification.[11]

The voice of Engels in 1840–1842 was the voice of the liberalism and nationalism of the "Wars of Liberation." Foreign intervention and domination of German soil, particularly by the French, must be ended. Prophetically, Engels predicted that "without doubt a war will come between us and France which itself will decide who is worthy of the left bank of the Rhine."[12] The fragmentation of Germany, the political impotence of Germany made any hope of civil liberties, constitutionalism, and freedom of the press a "pious wish."[13] But Engels wanted more than political unification. He wanted a cleansed national German culture. He wanted to rid Germany of all "infamous foreign custom and modes, all superfluous foreign expression."[14]

It was to Prussia that Engels looked to lead the unification of Germany. South German liberalism had made valuable contributions to German history. Parliamentarian life had been awakened in the South, and the South had added immeasurably to the political sophistication of all Germans. But South German liberalism was too theoretical; it lacked a needed sense of practicality, of realism. North German liberalism, as represented by Prussia, possessed the proper balance between theory and practice. Even though Prussia was admittedly a conservative state, it still possessed the necessary national character, the necessary power base to act as the source of German unification. Above all it was in Prussia, the heart of Germany, that the greatest accomplishment of German genius came to fruition, modern German philosophy as epitomized by Hegel and Kant. Thus, Prussia contained both a national culture and a statist base, the dream of the patriots of the Befreiungskrieg, and, according to Engels, the indispensable elements for any national liberation movement.[15]

Ludwig Börne was the brightest flame of the Young German movement, the writer whom Engels most admired. It was Börne who ridiculed the cosmopolitanism of earlier German history, who brought a more penetrating political realism to the questions of German national life. It was Börne who recognized the need for power in the German national movement, who understood that force was necessary to break the French hold on Germany. Complementing the rationalism of Hegel, Börne had taught the Young German of his day that it was not thought, not ideas, but rather action, deeds, that could bring freedom to any sphere of life.[16]

Börne's literary work was also written from an activist, political perspective. Art was a mirror of society. Not only must art reflect its society, it must criticize and expose it. Art had a social function, the improvement of the condition of the German masses. The only art that would live, according to Börne, was "that which demands universal equality, constitutionalism, independence for citizens."[17] Engels learned from Börne. He learned the need for practical action. He learned that art was an expression of social classes and social forces. He learned that art had the social mission to awaken in the peasant, the laborer, the apprentice, the desire for freedom, liberty, to make him conscious of his power.[18]

Unlike Marx, Engels's movement toward political radicalism did not spring from a philosophical radicalism. In his doctoral dissertation, Marx explained how it was the function of philosophy to expose the real to the merciless criticism of the rational. Mind must have as its task the illumination of the irrationality of the real. Marx was a part of the Hegelian left; indeed, Marx helped to construct it. Engels, on the other hand, approached his radicalism from the perspective of literary protest. Engels was a dissenter, and his radicalism sprang from moral and artistic indignation. The "Letters from Wuppertal" were patterned after the socially critical style of Heine and Börne.[19] Thus, Engels from the first lacked a deep philosophical knowledge and ability. Nevertheless, he wished to partake in the movement toward German unification and social freedom.

Politically, Engels in his early years emerged as a liberal nationalist. Philosophically, Engels moved from boyhood Pietism to Hegelian pantheism. The two movements were syncopated. His movement toward philosophic rationalism was paralleled by his movement toward liberal nationalism. It was within this framework, pantheism and patriotism, that Engels acted out the drama of his years of becoming.

The drama of Engels's youthful spiritual journey unfolded in the letters to his close friend, Friedrich Graeber. Three steps, three distinct philosophical positions, reveal themselves in these letters. The evolution of his *Weltanschauung,* the formation of the basic patterns, the central concepts of Engels's intellectual approach to reality were illustrated in these letters, and other of his writings from the same period.

On April 8/9, 1839, Engels wrote to Graeber: "No, I have never been a Pietist; for a short time I was a mystic, but that was a passing phase."[20] Engels's rejection of mysticism, his utter disdain of Pietism, stemmed from the fact that neither of these doctrines was capable of explaining the world in rational terms. In later letters to Graeber, Engels ridiculed any religious fundamentalism that could not accommodate reason and science. How can we trust, Engels asked, the divinity and authority of the Bible when it was composed by many authors, none of whom claimed to be divinely inspired? How is it possible to believe that only one flood occurred in the ancient history of man when geology has proved the existence of many such floods at various times and various places? Did the Bible really teach that men like Kant, Börne, Spinoza, who wished to perfect the best in mankind, would be eternally damned simply because they did not believe in God?[21]

The direction in which Engels was moving was clearly portrayed in his redefinition of the idea of sin. Original sin was an absurd Christian belief. Under the influence of the "new theology,"[22] Engels had come to define sin as the inability of mankind to completely fulfill the Idea. If man were to perfect, to realize the idea of humanity, he would be as God. Sin, then, was not an inherent quality in man's nature, but a failure of performance, man's lack of capacity to perfect the idea of humanity. Mankind had its godly origins in consciousness, for it was in consciousness that the power to rule nature and achieve human freedom was imbedded.[23] Consciousness possessed the potentiality of human perfection, but in actuality, the realization of this potentiality had never come into being. Nevertheless, Engels still believed that "Humanity which is born free, is free."[24]

The mystic phase of Engels's religious involvement ended under the impact of critical rationalism. However, this did not mean that Engels became at once a devotee of Strauss and Hegel. That would come later. First there was a second stage, a temporary commitment to the liberal Christianity of Schleiermacher. Engels still felt the need for a spiritual, nonrational component to human life. Engels still recognized man as a being who felt, who had spiritual needs that could not be answered by reason alone.

At the end of July 1839, Engels referred to himself as believing in "liberal Supernaturalism."[25] "That is Schleiermacher's doctrine, and I believe in it."[26] Schleiermacher indicated that religion was an affair of the heart. A person was compassionate, could identify with the suffering of others, could become pious. Liberal supernaturalism as Engels defined it in the later summer of 1839 complemented his rationalism, for it allowed him to believe that there was a realm of value, a realm of ethics that sprang from sources more constant and unchanging than the human mind.

By October 8, he wrote to Graeber, "I am now a dedicated Straussianer."[27] Later in the letter he challenged his friend: "If you could disprove Strauss, then I will again become a Pietist."[28] A month later Engels had moved beyond Strauss to Hegel. On November 20, 1839, Engels wrote to his friend: "I am at the point of becoming an Hegelian."[29] The complete conversion to Hegelianism was made between December 1839 and February 1840. On December 21, Engels wrote: "I have now passed through Strauss on the exacting path toward Hegelianism."[30] Engels had come to rest temporarily in "the modern pantheism, that is, Hegel."[31]

Engels had moved from mysticism to rationalistic humanism. He had developed from one who deified an unseen spirit, to one who saw reason, not mankind, as deity. The content of his Hegelianism will be examined in the coming pages. But the passage of Engels from mysticism to rationalistic humanism occurred in less than a year. This was too quick. For an individual to pass through three major philosophical positions in less than a year indicated that none of these positions was even clearly analyzed in depth. In the letters that Engels wrote to Graeber describing his intellectual journey, he repeatedly referred to each stage with words or phrases like "temporary," "awhile," "I am now," "I am still." This was an impressionable mind, a little dilettantish. It was a sensitive mind, quickly responsive to new ideas, but it was far from systematic. Even though Engels was young when he wrote these letters, about twenty years old, and thus at an impressionable age, there was nothing in the tone, in the quality, to suggest a disciplined, rigorously analytic approach to the realm of ideas. But Engels was already involved in a career of journalism and could not spare the time for serious study or even scholarship. "I hope to experience a radical change in the religious consciousness of the world; I should make it clear to myself first. That should come if I had the time to peacefully and undisturbed develop my ideas."[32] There is much the same resonance and complaint in the lines quoted above as in the letter Engels wrote to Arnold Ruge in 1842. In both letters, Engels admitted that he was not a specialist, did not have mastery of one particular field, and needed time to study. But the decision for mastery, for absolute competence in one area of knowledge, was never made by Engels. This was not how he defined himself. His contribution was in the popularization of ideas. In this way he would participate in the great social movements of the nineteenth century.

Engels wrote to Graeber at the beginning of 1840 that he read Hegel's *History of Philosophy* "every evening."[33] Earlier he had indicated to Graeber that he was a convert to the "Hegelian idea of God."[34] Interestingly, Engels gave a right-wing interpretation to Hegel. That is, he denied that Hegel equated God and humanity. There was no absolute unity between the particular and the universal, and thus mankind itself could not be divinity. Engels felt this "because Hegel separated the whole very sharply from the imperfect individual."[35] Thus, Engels stressed the objective side of Hegel. He stressed the universal, the general, the potency of absolute reason as opposed to the subjective and the individual. "The Hegelian idea of God" meant for Engels the inclusive Absolute Spirit, existing separate and apart from the individual, and moving imperviously in time. As we have seen, Engels never categorically rejected the idea of God, but rather sought more rational substitutes for that belief. In 1840, he found that substitute in the Hegelian notion of Objective Spirit.

In the discussion of Hegel contained in his essay "Schelling und die Offenbarung," Engels clearly manifested his conservative, right-wing interpretation of Hegel. The active agent in the universe, the causal factor, was Objective Spirit. Man was merely a passive factor, an element activated entirely by forces outside himself rather than the activating agent itself.

> All the fundamental principles of Christianity, even those that one generally refers to as religion, retreat before the unembittered criticism of reason; the absolute idea makes the claim to be the fundamental principle of the era. The great transformation, of which French philosophy of the previous century was only the precursor, has accomplished its self-creation, has its

> completion in the kingdom of thought. The philosophy of Protestantism beginning with Descartes is completed; a new period is commencing, and it is the holy duty of all who attend to the self-development of spirit to convey the magnificent results to the consciousness of the nation and to raise them to the life principles of Germany.[36]

The causal agent in the above paragraph was "the absolute idea." It was Objective Spirit, which had postulated itself as the central principle of the era of the 1840s. French eighteenth-century philosophy was a forerunner to the perfection of Objective Spirit, was Objective Spirit in its infancy. By the early nineteenth century, however, Objective Spirit, through its own self-creation, had reached its ultimate fulfillment as "absolute idea," that is, idea or thought as absolute self-determination. Engels reiterated this same idea in later pages of "Schelling und die Offenbarung."

> The Hegelian dialectic, this powerful, never resting energy of thought, is nothing else than the consciousness of humanity in pure thought, the consciousness of the universal, Hegel's consciousness of God. Where, as with Hegel, everything is derived from itself, is a godly personality entirely superficial?[37]

Hegel, according to Engels, maintained that the activating principle in the universe was Idea. The prime mover was thought, which existed separate from man, above man, as God. Man was acted upon by thought, man received his impetus to activity from absolute idea and was therefore himself not a causal agent. Man, who did not himself initiate action, but only reflected "the never resting energy of thought," also reacted and responded to self-created and self-generating powers of the dialectic. The generative power of the universe resided in universal consciousness, and it was this dynamic that propelled the movement of history. It was Objective Spirit that predicated and man who was predicated.

For Engels, in his Hegelian stage, reason meant necessity.[38] What was reasonable for Engels was also necessary. Engels made the correlation between reason, or logic, and orderly sequence. That is, the test of reason was the obligation or need to pass through successive stages. Or, reason was predictability. If it could be shown that a given process had to pass through a fixed series, then it was logical. Engels understood logic or reason to mean the fixed stages, the necessary sequence, through which a given process must pass.

Engels was basically a metaphysician. There was a need in him to discover some absolute, some power dwelling outside of man, from which the entire universe could be logically and reasonably derived. Engels was a man in search of a substitute God. Engels never rid himself of the idea of God. He only sought God in different forms. In his Hegelian stage, reason had replaced religion. But reason had been deified. That is, reason now was self-generative, the omnipotent energizing principle, separate from man in its self-containment and self-perpetuation. Engels was on the Hegelian right. Man was still alienated.[39]

The stages of Engels's youthful development took him from Pietism to Supernaturalism to the pantheism of reason. The God of his youth was to be transmitted into the Idea, which permeated the entire universe. The God of his youth that moved the world was to become Reason that moved the world as necessary sequential process. The tendency to think in metaphysical terms persisted as a characteristic of his thought throughout his life. The basic structures of his thought had been formed by 1842.

In the 1880s, particularly in the *Dialectics of Nature* and *Anti-Dühring*, Engels came to grips with the problems of natural science. The structures of thought he had developed in his youth were applied to the questions of the physical universe. Engels approached the physical cosmos as a metaphysician. The answers that he gave, his formulation of scientific data were metaphysical. Engels emerged in later life as a metaphysical materialist. He reduced the physical cosmos to one elemental force, motion. From the laws of motion, Engels believed it possible to derive all other components of that cosmos. Here again, in his philosophy of science, Engels was seeking the single origin of things. Here again, he postulated the existence of one pivotal cause of the universe, which existed apart from man, which was eternal and self-generating.

The physical world was rational because it manifested necessary sequence; that is, there existed a necessary succession of stages from motion to matter, to inorganic life, to conscious organic life. Since rationality meant for Engels necessary sequence, his interpretation of the cosmos was deterministic. That is, the processes of the universe could not unfold but in fixed stages, absolutely conditioned series, in the pattern of mechanistic determinism. A continuity of thought, the repetition of a basic pattern of thought, was demonstrated in all of Engels's deliberations. His conception of Reason was the same as his conception of God, and his conception of Nature was the same as his conception of Reason. Just as Reason has been a substitute for God, so Nature was to be a substitute for Reason.

Engels's inability to understand abstract speculative thought was manifested not only in his treatment of Hegel but also in his treatment of Feuerbach. Engels's lack of academic training in philosophy impaired his ability to comprehend subtle philosophic arguments. There existed a void in Engels's intellectual equipment through which gross misconceptions and naive oversimplifications were to enter into his literature. His interpretation of Feuerbach was entirely erroneous because it lacked any reference to or knowledge of the role "species being" played in Feuerbach's thought.

Engels wrote two letters to Marx in which he discussed Feuerbach. These letters date from 1846, the period when Marx and Engels were collaborating on *The German Ideology*. Although outside the formal period covered by the chapter, Engels's views on Feuerbach will be included here, because they substantiate Engels's lack of philosophic sophistication. Engels was opposed to including an analysis of Feuerbach in *The German Ideology,* and even referred to Feuerbach's work as "Dreck" (excrement).[40]

Engels was critical because he thought Feuerbach was attempting to account for the evolution of religion totally on the basis of external nature.[41] Men invented gods because they needed to explain the cycle of seasons, the fact of death, natural disasters like storms and hurricanes. Engels thought Feuerbach superficial, of no interest either to himself or Marx, because he interpreted Feuerbach as trying to describe religious consciousness as merely the personification of natural phenomena. Such an undertaking Engels felt was quite traditional.

Engels was critical of what he considered to be Feuerbach's lack of realism. To account for the rise of religion without including political factors, without including the history of religion, from Engels's point of view was a gross oversight.

> Supernaturalism, the creation *ex nihilo,* derived from the rule of reason and will cover the world, and monotheism itself was explained from the "unity of human consciousness. Feuerbach completely overlooked the fact that the one god was not capable of organizing the plurality of natural appearances into a unity, was not capable of fusing the contradictory natural forces into an omage of the one god, without a true political king, without a real oriental despot bringing order to conflicting and self-seeking individuals."[42]

Engels misunderstood Feuerbach. He did not understand that when Feuerbach talked of nature he meant external nature as well as the internal nature of the species man. Engels did not understand the naturalistic humanism of Feuerbach. He did not understand what Feuerbach meant by "species being." Thus, for Engels, the attempt to derive religion from nature was the attempt to derive religion from external natural phenomena. Religion in this sense came to be the symbolic illustration of natural events. In reality, however, Feuerbach attempted to derive religion from human nature, from the alienated naturalistic essence of humanity. Thus, God was not the personification of thunder, but the alienation of human generative powers. Love was not the attribute of Deity, but the naturalistic ontology of man, his sociability and empathy for other men. Engels could not understand Feuerbach because he continued to make the distinction between man and nature. As we have seen, Engels understood nature as something separated and divorced from man. He never came to see, as Feuerbach and Marx had, that nature was a whole, a unity, in which man as one moment of that unity was an active agent who interrelated with the other, unconscious modes.

A similar weakness in Engels's intellectual equipment was demonstrated in Engels's evaluation of Fourier. "The fellow is truly insane," Engels said of Fourier.[43] He ridiculed Fourier's attempt to construct a unitary social science, and was equally unconvinced by Fourier's theory of attraction. He did not even think Fourier essentially in agreement with the communist movement.[44]

What is of interest here is not whether Fourier could be classified as a communist or not. What is of interest is that Engels had no appreciation of the naturalistic humanism of Fourier's theory of attraction. Regardless of the eccentricities of Fourier, he was attempting to construct a society that conformed to human biological needs as he understood them. In this sense, Fourier's intellectual endeavor ran parallel to Feuerbach. A good society for Fourier and Feuerbach was one in which man was happy because his environment was in total conformity with his essence. Engels did not understand this about Fourier, because there did not exist in Engels's intellectual makeup an appreciation of naturalistic humanism.

This discussion of Engels's early intellectual development has revealed the existence of definite structures of thought. By 1842, the clear outlines of his *Weltanschauung* were beginning to emerge. What has also become apparent are those structures of thought, those ideas that Engels did not possess. It is equally important in order to understand Engels fully to grasp the absence of concepts, that is, those ideas that he would never use in comprehending the world. To understand the absence of concepts is to understand the ways in which Engels was never to perceive the world.

Engels was never familiar with the ideas of alienation and objectification. His failure to appropriate fully the philosophy of Hegel meant that these Hegelian notions were never absorbed by him. Engels was able, even though superficially, to deal with ideas like Necessity, Reason, Idea, but he did not see that side of Hegel which concerned objectification and alienation. Furthermore, as we have just seen in the preceding paragraphs, Engels did not understand Feuerbachian materialism. The true dimension, the vast implications of the idea of "species being" were never grasped by him. Engels did not see that the social universe was an anthropocentric universe, that is, that man in his universal essence stood at the center of creation.

Without the notion of "species being," without the notions of "alienation" and "objectification," Engles could not criticize religion in the sense of Marx's criticism. Without understanding that the world was an objectification of human powers, Engels could not see religion as a means of separating, of divorcing the individual from his own powers. Since Engels did not begin from the assumption that man was the generative force of the universe, that it was human powers that had modified and altered the natural world, then he could not see religion as the expropriation of these powers, as hyperbolically, the universal capitalist.

In addition, Engels could not understand the state in Marx's fashion. Lacking the presuppositions of Feuerbachian naturalism, Engels could not see the state as an instrument of dehumanization. Lacking the Hegelian notion of objectification, Engels could not recognize the state as selfishly appropriating human powers for its own interest. In short, without recognizing the world as the objectification of human essence, Engels did not interpret the world as the play of powers, forces and institutions, attempting to rob that human essence. Nowhere in *The Origin of the Family, Private Property and the State* does Engels refer to the state as a product of alienation. Basically, he defines the state as an instrument of class oppression. Marx also was aware of the state as force, but he in addition recognized the state as expropriated species power.

Furthermore, Engels did not have the same definition of society as Marx possessed. Society, for Marx, was the species being of man, behavior in accordance with his anthropological core. Society, for Engels, was the division of labor. The end of the state for Marx meant that man's social life, his actual species practice, would at the same time be his political life. The end of the state for Engels meant the abolition of the division of labor. Without understanding the notion of species being, without understanding the notion of human essence, Engels could not have understood what Marx meant by society, nor could Engels understand the differences between society and state as Marx grasped them. For Marx, there could be no true society that was distinct from species being. For Engels, since society was basically division of labor and social productivity, there could be a society in distinction from the human anthropological core.

The contrast between society and state, for Marx, was the opposition between human anthropology and alienated species being. The contrast between society and state, for Engels, was the contrast between the social division of labor and class domination.

Also, Engels's definition of communism was to be different from the Marxian definition. For Marx, communism was to be the end of human alienation. Communism was to be the absolute correspondence of social life, species essence, with political life. Communism was basically a form of naturalistic humanism. Engels could not have defined communism in this manner, because he did not understand the concept of alienation, did not appreciate the difference between society (species life) and state (alienated human essence), and did not have a deep understanding of the philosophic basis of naturalistic humanism.

Missing the Hegelian notion of objectification, missing what Hegel included as the subjective element in the dialectic, Engels never acquired the idea of *praxis.* Engels never understood that human activity interpenetrated with the world, that human *praxis* intermingled with the world to modify it in accordance with human essence. He had no idea of *praxis* because he had no idea of objectification and negation. For Engels, the dialectical process was the self-contained movement of Idea. The dialectical process was reducible to the necessity of Idea, the inevitability that Idea would find its completion at the end of a given sequence of events. Engels, unlike Marx, did not understand the dialectic, or negation. He did not see that movement, that change came from destruction, that negation was one potential feature of human *praxis.* The dialectic was not self-contained and self-perpetuating, but rather the dialectic was the expression of *praxis* that destroyed and transcended. Unlike Marx, Engels failed to grasp this side of Hegel, the side of Hegel that made of human activity the transcending force of negation.

Furthermore, Marx saw the role of philosophy as a fundamental criticism of all that existed. Marx was aware that Hegel had completed philosophy. He saw his own role as using the tools bequeathed by Hegel to radically criticize the universe. That is what, in a sense, Epicurus and Democritus had done in terms of Greek philosophy. The systems of Plato and Aristotle were sovereign and magisterial. Greek philosophy after the Age of Pericles must turn to a criticism of the existing, and Epicurus and Democritus were to use materialism as an instrument of criticism. Thus, Marx saw philosophy as criticism, as negation. Philosophy, for Marx, was an active agent, the negative mode of the dialectic, which transformed actual existence through the destruction of existing life. At the end of Hegel's *Phenomenology of Mind,* one of the more radical of Hegel's works, philosophy returned to the world. Armed by its journey through the world of science, culture, and history, Mind when it returned to the world, returned as a force of critical activity. Marx saw philosophy and himself as fulfilling this role of critical negation of the existent. He and philosophy were active, change-producing agents.

Engels did not conceive the role of philosophy to be critical *praxis.* In the *Philosophy of History,* one of the more conservative of Hegel's works, Hegel described the course of human history as the necessary conquest of Freedom. It was not the human agent who acted, but rather Absolute Spirit. Engels did not see philosophy as a critical activity, but rather the description of the sequence and successive stages in the evolution of Idea to Freedom. The triumph of Idea, the realization of Freedom was inevitable and lay in the self-generating powers of Freedom and Idea themselves.

Footnotes

1. For books dealing with the relationship between Marx and Engels see the following: Iring Fetscher, *Karl Marx und der Marxismus* (Munich: R. Piper, 1967); Zbigniew Jordan, *The Evolution of Dialectical Materialism* (New York: St. Martins Press, 1967); Karl Korsch, *Marxismus und Philosophie* (Frankfurt: Europäische Verlagsanstalt, 1966); Georg Lichtheim, *Marxism* (New York: Praeger, 1961); George Lukács, *History and Class Consciousness,* trans. Rodney Livingstone (Cambridge, Mass.: M.I.T. Press, 1968); Franz Mehring, *Karl Marx,* trans. Edward Fitzgerald (Ann Arbor: University of Michigan Press, 1962); Gustav Meyer, *Friedrich Engels* (The Hague: Mouton Verlag, 1934); Alfred Schmidt, *Der Begriff der Natur in der Lehre von Marx* (Frankfurt: Beitrage zur Soziologie, 1962); A. Walicki, *The Controversy over Capitalism* (Oxford: Clarendon Press, 1969). For articles dealing with the relationship

between Marx and Engels, see the following essays: Herman Bellnow, "Engels Auffassung von Revolution und Entwicklung in Seinem 'Grundsatzen des Kommunismus (1847),' " *Marxismusstudien* (Tubingen: V. C. B. Mohr, 1954), pp. 77–144; Ludwig Landgrebe, "Das Problem der Dialektik," *Ibid.*, 1960, pp. 1–65; Erhard Lucas, "Marx und Engels Auseinandersetzung mit Darwin," *Ibid.*, 1964, pp. 433–469; Thilo Ramm, "Die Kunftige Gesellschafts orDnung Nach der Theorie von Marx and Engels," *Ibid.*, 1957, pp. 77–119; Erich Thier, "Etappen der Marx Interpretation," *Ibid.*, 1954, pp. 1–38.

2. Friedrich Engels, "Briefe aus dem Wuppertal," *Marx-Engels Werke* (Berlin: Dietz Verlag, 1970), I, pp. 413–432.
3. Engels an Marx 17 März 1854, *Ibid.*, XXVII, p. 27.
4. *Ibid.*, p. 26.
5. For the letters of Engels to his sister Marie, see *Marx-Engels Werke, Erganzungsband*, II. These letters offer a colorful portrait of Engels's life in Berlin.
6. Engels an Arnold Ruge 26 Juli 1942, *Marx-Engels Werke, XXVII, p. 408.*
7. Engels, "Retrograde Zeichen der Zeit," *Marx-Engels Werke, Erganzungsband*, II, p. 28.
8. *Ibid.*
9. Engels, "Ernst Moritz Arndt," *Ibid.*, p. 127.
10. Engels an Friedrich Graeber 8/9 April 1839, *Ibid.*, p. 366.
11. Engels, "Requiem für die deutsche Adelszeitung," *Ibid.*, p. 64.
12. Engels, "Ernst Moritz Arndt," *Ibid.*, p. 131.
13. *Ibid.*
14. *Ibid.*
15. On Engels's attitude toward Prussia and North German liberalism see the following two of his essays: "Nord-und Suddeutscher Liberalismus," *Ibid.*, pp. 246–248; and "Tagebuch Eines Hospitantem," *Ibid.*, pp. 249–254.
16. Engels, "Ernst Moritz Arndt," *Ibid.*, pp. 123–124.
17. Peter Demetz, *Marx, Engels and the Poets* (Chicago: University of Chicago Press, 1967), p. 18.
18. *Ibid.*
19. *Ibid.*, pp. 18–19.
20. Engels an Friedrich Graeber 8/9 April 1839, *Marx-Engels Werke, Erganzungsband*, II, p. 368.
21. Engels an Friedrich Graeber 15 Juni 1839, *Ibid.*, p. 401.
22. Engels an Friedrich Graeber 12–27 Juli 1839, *Ibid.*, p. 405.
23. *Ibid.*, p. 404.
24. Engels an Friedrich Graeber 15 Juni 1839, *Ibid.*, p. 402.
25. Engels an Friedrich Graeber 30 Juli 1839, *Ibid.*, p. 413.
26. Engels an Friedrich Graeber 12–27 Juli 1839, *Ibid.*, p. 409.
27. Engels an Wilhelm Graeber 8 Oktober 1839, *Ibid.*, p. 419.
28. *Ibid.*
29. Engels an Wilhelm Graeber 13–20 November 1839, *Ibid.*, p. 435.
30. Engels an Friedrich Graeber 9 Dezember–5 Februar 1840, *Ibid.*, p. 438.
31. *Ibid.*, p. 439.
32. Engels an Friedrich Graeber 15 Juni 1839, *Ibid.*, p. 402.
33. Engels an Friedrich Graeber 9 Dezember–5 Februar 1840, *Ibid.*, p. 440.
34. *Ibid.*, p. 438.
35. *Ibid.*, p. 440.
36. Engels, "Schelling und die Offenbarung," *Ibid.*, p. 177.
37. *Ibid.*, p. 217.
38. *Ibid.*, p. 180.

39. *Ibid.*, p. 220.
40. Engels an Marx 18 Oktober 1846, *Marx-Engels Werke,* XXVII, p. 55.
41. Engels an Marx 19 August 1846, *Ibid.*, p. 33.
42. *Ibid.*, p. 57.
43. Here again Engels's writings on Fourier lie outside the time bands of this chapter, but are included because they did shed important light on the content being discussed. Engels, "An das Kommunistische Koorrspondenz-Komitee in Brüssel", *Ibid.*, p. 37.
44. Engels, "Die Times' über den deutschen Kommunismus," *Marx-Engels Werke, Erganzungsband,* II, p. 320.

Eight

The Origins of Engels's Communism

WHEN ENGELS LEFT the continent to journey to England in November 1842, he was already a communist. In actuality, Engels's transition to communism occurred during the first half of 1842. In March of that year, he began to write for Marx's *Neue Rheinische Zeitung,* and in June also for Arnold Ruge's Young Hegelian periodical the *Deutsche Jahrbücher.* In his 1841 letter to Ruge, Engels had indicated that he wished to suspend his career in journalism in order to devote an extended period to the study of philosophy. In less than a year Engels had again returned to journalism. He did not give himself the prolonged and concentrated period of study that would lead to mastery of the subject. From the point of view of his avocation, however, Engels's residence in Berlin during 1841, the year of his military service as an artillery officer, brought great dividends to him. Through the friendships he made in Berlin with the Young Hegelian luminaries, Engels had gained entrance into fashionable intellectual circles. By 1842, Engels was writing for the more sophisticated radical journals.

Engels's decision for communism stemmed from the experiences and associations he gained from his work with the *Neue Rheinische Zeitung.* In this respect, the figure of Moses Hess was crucial. With Hess as the primary influence, Engels changed from a liberal nationalist to a revolutionary communist. Engels's former expectation that a national revolution would bring in its stead political liberalism was now replaced by the hope that a social revolution would bring political unification. By the fall of 1842, the social question had assumed paramount importance in Engels's list of priorities. There was no mention of revolution, no mention of the nationalization of property in any of Engels's writing up to 1842. It was only when Engels became a communist that he also became a revolutionary.

> Already in August 1842, some in the party fought for their view that political changes would be insufficient and explained that according to their opinion a social revolution on the foundation of the common ownership of property should be the basic societal condition, which they fitted with their abstract principles. However, even the leaders of the party, for example Dr. Bruno Bauer, Dr. Feuerbach, and Dr. Ruge, were at that time not ready for this decisive step. The political organ of the party, the *Rheinische Zeitung*, published some essays, essays that advocated communism, but not with the expected success. Nevertheless, communism was such a necessary consequence of neo-Hegelian philosophy that no opposition was able to repress it, and in the course of the year the founders had the satisfaction to see one republican after another join their ranks. In addition to Dr. Hess, one of the editors of the now repressed *Rheinische Zeitung*, who in fact was the first communist in the party, there were also many others, as Dr. Ruge, publisher of the *Deutsche Jahrbücher*, the scientific periodical of the Young Hegelians, which was repressed by the decision of the German Reichstag, Dr. Marx, also an editor of the *Rheinische Zeitung*, Georg Herwegh, the poet, whose letters to the King of Prussia have been translated during the past winter in most English newspapers, and many others, and we hoped that the remainder of the republican party would gradually come over to us.[1]

Engels basically learned his communism from Moses Hess. It was Hess who made Engels aware that modern society was polarized between "pauperism" and "the aristocracy of gold."[2] In short, Hess acquainted Engels with the fact that property defined class lines in the nineteenth-century society and that the struggle for possession of property was the basis for class conflict in that century. Only the destruction of private property could relieve the economic slavery of the pauper.

Hess saw England as the classic example of social polarization, the confrontation between rich and poor. English capitalism had concentrated both production and commerce in the hands of a propertied aristocracy, thus occasioning the extreme suffering of the poor. Impressed by the Chartists, Hess believed England on the verge of a revolution. Political reforms could not answer the needs of the English proletariat. The revolution must be social in nature, that is, fundamentally alter property relations.[3]

Sensitive to national differences, Hess felt that communism was a product of German, French, and English cultural traditions. Speculative and introspective, the Germans had given communism its philosophical foundation. Having a revolutionary tradition, the French had imparted to communism its political attributes. Practical, the land of the industrial revolution, the English had contributed to communism its economic dimensions. The rebirth of European culture and society on the basis of communism, on the destruction of private property, would be achieved through the unity, through the consolidation of these three unique national traditions.[4] Pure egoism and its corollary, private property, would be abolished in the next stage, the communist stage, of European development.

Heinrich Heine and Wilhelm Weitling had influenced Hess. In his *Religion and Philosophy in Germany*, Heine was one of the first to call for the unity of German metaphysics, French radicalism, and English empiricism. Heine felt that such a cultural synthesis had revolutionary implications for European society.[5] In his book *Garantieen der Harmonie und Freiheit,* Weitling had argued that the origin of inequality between men lay in the unequal apportionment of wealth. Engels himself was to call Weitling "the founder of German communism."[6] Furthermore, it was Weitling who saw in the laboring classes the force that would eventually destroy the differences between rich and poor by abolishing property.[7] Thus Engels through his association with Hess was exposed to the wider currents of European radicalism. Above all, Engels had learned that it was the poor who were going to act as the destroyers of private property.

If Engels acquired his belief in the poor as a revolutionary force from Hess, he learned his egalitarianism from Gracchus Babeuf. It was Babeuf who termed equality the basis of all just societies. Therefore, Babeuf maintained, every person should partake of equal shares of labor, equal shares of enjoyment, and have an equal amount of goods distributed to him.[8] Babeuf was an economic egalitarian. Communism, for Babeuf, meant pure equality. Engels's brand of communism was decidedly Babouvist. In "Fortschritte der Sozialreform auf dem Kontinent," Engels was to write that "pure freedom and pure equality was communism."[9] For Engels, communism would always imply equal distribution to the entire population of things was produced by the industrial machine. Economic egalitarianism, the distribution of equal shares to all, was a paramount feature of what Engels defined as communism.

The third major influence on Engels at this period of his life was Saint-Simon. It was Saint-Simon who was the prophet of industrial society. It was Saint-Simon who felt that poverty could be eradicated through industrial productivity.[10] The creation of a technocracy, the placing of the limitless power of modern industry into the hands of professional managers, would bring forth such a plethora of goods that poverty, the existence of the poor, would be finally ended.[11] Technological growth formed the core of Saint-Simon's social theory. There was a latent positivism in Saint-Simon's thought. The age of agriculture was to be superseded by the age of industrial modernization.

Technological growth was a pervasive feature of Engels's definition of communism. In fact, communism, for Engels, could not be attained unless the productive industrial forces of society had reached a high stage of development. Thus, technology itself, for Engels, as for Saint-Simon, would be the ultimate reason for the overcoming of poverty and consequently the transcendence of class. There was a latent positivism in Engels's thought pattern. Capitalism had necessarily superseded the age of agriculture. But capitalism was distinguished as an age of industrial scarcity. Communism was merely a product of technological growth, and in a communist society there would be a change from capitalistic scarcity to industrial abundance and, as a consequence, equal distribution or economic egalitarianism.

Engels's communism then was an amalgam of Saint-Simonean technocracy, Babouvist economic egalitarianism, and Hessian belief that the poor would seize the means of production. It was in terms of this structure, in terms of this group of core ideas that Engels was to interpret English society and history when he was residing in that country. Moreover, this amalgam of technocracy, economic egalitarianism, and pauper revolutionism was to remain throughout his life the major feature of Engelsian communism. A product of his own history and style, Engelsian communism was a unique personal expression.

When Engels arrived in England, he again acted as a part-time reporter. While working for Erman and Engels, his family's cotton factory in Manchester, Engels wrote articles for continental periodicals describing social conditions in England. Instead of commenting on literature, philosophy, and religion, Engels was now commenting on the Chartists, the Corn Laws, the English Constitution. Although his function remained the same, that of publicist, the content of his reporting had drastically changed. He was not interested in Schelling or Börne, but rather in the environmental conditions of the land of the industrial revolution. Engels began writing economics and sociology rather than philosophic-cultural essays.

Like Hess, Engels was fully cognizant of the different national traditions of the three western European powers. The French, perpetuating the spirit of Greco-Roman materialism, had executed the revolution in a political fashion. The Germans, a Christian-spiritualist people, had experienced the revolution in its philosophic form. The English, however, combining both French and German elements, were the only Western people to have lived through a social revolution.[12]

Throughout his first residence, Engels was convinced that England was on the verge of revolution. In fact, the revolution had been in progress for two hundred years. The beginning of industry, the creation of the proletariat, had brought far-reaching changes to England and pitted proletariat against bourgeoisie. The denouement of their class conflict was not too far off.[13] The English Revolution, in contrast to the French, had been and would be social rather than political. The change from an agricultural economy to an industrial economy, the change from agrarian labor to industrial wage-labor, had all taken place outside the boundaries of the state. A new society had come into being in England, and this new society was now pushing against the institutions of an older political structure. Thus, Engels was describing the dysfunction between political forms and actual social content. But this new awareness on the part of Engels of the importance of the social did not mean that Engels understood society as Marx. Engels did not conceive of the state as a form of alienated human essence, because he did not conceive of society as representing the species being of man. For Engels, the state was a mechanism of repression in the hands of those who possessed property, just as society was practice dictated to people by the necessities of industrial property. Society, for Engels, was not human essence, but rather custom imposed by the techniques (tools, instruments) of production. In 1842 Engels became a materialist, because only materialism could supply answers to the problems of social distress and pauperism.

The awareness that Engels gained in 1842 of the struggle between rich and poor predisposed him to see England as a class society. Political parties, politics in general, were simply an expression of social class.[14] In Engels's lexicon, however, class itself was defined by possession of property.[15] The possession or lack of possession of wealth placed one either in the middle classes or in the poorer classes. Class, according to Engels, also defined politics. Engels described English society as composed of three great classes. The Tories had their wealth in land, the Whigs had their wealth in industry and commerce, and the proletariat had no wealth at all.[16] Even though the Whigs and the Tories received their wealth from different sources, they were wealthy in equal proportion and thus composed the middle classes. England was then a tyranny of the middle class.

The activity of possession, the sociopolitical influence of possession, was clearly manifested in the struggle over the Corn Law. "The nobility knew that its power, outside the constitutional framework of the House of Lords, derived chiefly from its wealth,"[17] and were therefore opposed to a repeal of the corn tariff. The nobility were afraid that a reduction of the corn tariff would lead to a reduction of ground rents. Since loss of rents would mean loss of wealth, and the loss of wealth would mean loss of social power, the Tories fought politically to retain the corn tariff. The manufacturing classes, on the other hand, wished to increase their wealth by paying less wages. Repeal of the corn tariff meant that the price of bread would fall, giving the manufacturer an excuse not to increase, or even to lower his wages. The incentive for greater wealth encouraged the Whigs to vote for repeal. The poor, of course, wanted prices to be as low as possible, and so Radicals and Chartists advocated total free trade.[18]

Engels saw the Chartists as representing the English proletariat.[19] As a proletarian movement, however, the Chartists had gained little support among English intellectuals.[20] Chartism, furthermore, was not a socialist movement. Rather, it was a "radical-democratic"[21] movement. Socialists in England did not as yet form a political party. Wherever adherents of socialism existed, they could be found in the lower middle classes and among small segments of the proletariat.[22] Furthermore, the Chartists were not basically a revolutionary movement. The Chartists talked of achieving power legally, of a "legal revolution." Engels called this an "impossibility," and indicated that a revolutionary movement whose aim was the overthrow of the aristocracy, the smashing of the old establishment, could only accomplish this aim through violence. Unless the Chartists were prepared to use violence, and they were not, their expectations of seizing power were a chimera.[23]

On the other hand, the social revolution was a certainty for England. Chartism, although it would not affect the revolution, was a good preparation. The proletariat had learned through the Chartist movement. The proletariat was now radical-democratic, and bound to a stultifying sense of legality. However, with increasing periods of depression, when bread was scarce and hunger plentiful, the proletariat would be further radicalized. With starvation before him, the proletarian would learn in the future that his own best interests were served through the seizure of property and through the use of violence to accomplish the expropriation of the means of production.[24]

Whether the Chartists drew their support from a true proletariat, industrial workers, does not concern us. Of more importance was the way Engels described the coming into being of what he considered the proletariat. The first step in this process was the rise of religious individualism during the Reformation. The religious principles of inwardness, of subjectivity, triumphed during the Reformation. Later the principle of subjectivity, when applied to the social world, was translated into the doctrine of pure self-interest. "For the interest is essentially subjective, egoistic, individual interest and as such is the epitome of the German-Christian subjective and individualization principle."[25] Modern egoism was thus the completion and perfection of Christianity. But modern egoism had led to the isolation and atomization of man in society. This fragmentation of the social universe into isolated persons was again the last consequence of the Christian doctrine of subjectivity. Private property was simply another expression of this modern egoism. Consequently, men had become slaves to property. Since property ruled the world, men now bowed before the new God, money.[26]

The second step in the rise of capitalism in England was the scientific revolution of the seventeenth century. Man had begun his mastery over nature. Philosophically, man's conquest of nature resulted in the triumph of materialism. Practically, man's mastery of the natural was manifest in the technological advances of the eighteenth century. The English were a practical, empirical people. The interconnection of abstract science and its practical application formed the basis of the technological revolution of the eighteenth century. Furthermore, technological changes brought forth social changes. "We have seen that the introduction of mechanical devices and general scientific principles were the engines of progress."[27] In other words, technology was the primary causal factor in social history.[28]

The third step in the evolution of capitalism in England was the creation of the proletariat. Here again, the revolution in industrial technique brought forth the proleteriat, the entire reorganization of English social classes. As a result of the coming of the machine, England divided into three classes: "the aristocracy of land, the aristocracy of money, and the working democracy."[29] It was this "working democracy" that was being prepared by the Chartist movement to eventually seize the means of production. The proletariat must cease being radical democrats in the Chartist sense and become socialists. Only socialism could cure the problems of England; because the problems that confronted England were not political, but decidedly social.

A more insightful glimpse into Engels's socioeconomic understanding at this stage of his life can be gotten by dividing his thinking on this matter into categories. Engels's account of the evolution of capitalism in England will take on greater significance once we have a clearer comprehension of each of the following conceptual categories: (1) property, (2) competition, (3) industrial growth, (4) value, (5) the proletariat, (6) the theory of cataclysm and revolution, and (7) communism.

1. Property

Private property was the creation of industry.[30] Private property had not always existed. At the end of the Middle Ages, the development of machine manufacture required a new form of property relationship. The property relationships of the Middle Ages could not accommodate machine manufacture. The property relationship that could accommodate industry was private property. Thus, every change in society, the creation of new property relationships, was brought into existence by an initial change in the forces of production. It divided the natural conditions of production from the human activity of production. The soil and tools upon which and with which men labored were separated from the human force of labor. Property, by removing the natural conditions of production from the free access of all men, separated the natural and human aspects of production.[31]

Furthermore, property divided labor itself in two. Labor was at once activity and wages. The product of labor, i.e., wages, confronted the laborer, who was inherently free activity. Property separated labor from its own satisfactions. In short, property separated capital and labor.[32]

By dividing labor, and by dividing production, property tended to isolate individuals and create conflicts. Laborer was opposed to capitalist, capitalist was opposed to landowner, and laborer confronted laborer. Because it divided men, property led to discord. Because it divided men, property led to class conflict. Property, as we have seen above, formed the basis of social classes; it was the ground for the distinction between rich and poor.

Trade was also an outgrowth of property. "The immediate consequence of private property is trade—exchange of reciprocal demand—buying and selling."[33] Competition too was an outgrowth of property.[34] In the course of trade, a buyer and a seller faced each other. The object of the duel between the buyer and the seller was profit for the seller. He must sell as dearly as possible. Property occasioned trade, and the contest of trade was carried on for profit.

The destruction of private property then meant the disappearance of the division in production and the divisions in labor. It meant the end of the artificial isolation of man from man. It meant the abolition of profit and the termination of competition. It meant the overthrow of classes. With the destruction of property, the unity of the natural side of production with the human side would be achieved, and a man's labor would become truly his self-rewarding activity. Property, then, was the basic cause of human atomization; it was the cause of the war of all against all.[35]

2. Competition

In his "Outline of a Critique of Political Economy," Engels defined competition as the rule that "each must seek to sell as dear as possible and buy as cheap as possible."[36] Competition then could be understood as economic self-interest. Competition, which was an expression of private property, meant that the desire for economic gain would compel the owner of property to increase the value of that property.

The rise of the proletariat was a function of competition. Economic self-interest compelled the peasant to surrender the livelihood of the land to seek the higher wages of a weaver. The desire for economic gain also meant that peasants would drift into the towns in search of higher wages. Conversely, competition not only created the proletariat, but also the capitalist. The economic self-aggrandizement of the large property owner drove the lesser property owner out of business and thus proleterianized former members of the lower middle classes. Thus, modern class structure was an expression of competition.

Industrial wages too were functions of competition.[37] The centralization of the means of production into the hands of a few capitalists was immanent in the laws of competition. By pitting capitalist against capitalist, landowner against landowner, competition turned economic life into the condition of a jungle. The stronger would survive, the weaker were destroyed. Engels referred to this process as the "law of the centralization of private property."[38] Business cycles, recurrent depressions were functions of competition. Inherent in "the law of competition"[39] was the striving of supply and demand to balance each other. However, they never succeeded. Under capitalism, then, built on the permanent dysfunction of supply and demand, economic life was characterized by perpetual fluctuation of boom followed by bust. But as long as competition determined economic life, as long as there was no plan to production, capitalist society was prone to successive crises. Gradually, due to these recurrent depressions, larger and larger sections of society would be pauperized. Eventually in this polarized society, the pauperized workers would one day rebel to overthrow the private property system in a revolutionary cataclysm.

Economic self-interest, economic gain, was merely the "expression of that war of all against all which dominates modern middle class society."[40] Social atomization, the isolation of individuals, was thus the logical outcome of the Christian principle of pure inwardness, of spiritual subjectivity. Egoism was the ruling principle of social life during the industrial revolution, and economic self-aggrandizement was the social expression of this egoism. Society was now a jungle, and the brute law of the stronger ruled. Social chaos and ultimate cataclysm were necessary consequences of rule by force.

3. Industrial Growth

Industrial growth had brought the proletariat into existence. As we have seen, industrial growth had also created private property.[41] In fact, industry was the basis of all modern English relationships, "the driving force of the entire social movement."[42] Thus, industry was the ground upon which all social structures and all social relationships were built. It was the most important causal agent in the social universe.

By industry, Engels really meant machines. By machines, Engels really meant inventions. The industrial revolution itself was "precipitated by the discovery of the steam engine, various spinning machines, the mechanical loom, and a whole series of other mechanical devices."[43] Thus, industrial society for Engels was reducible to technology. He saw mechanics, then, engineering, as the innovating force within any society.

Abstract science itself was a productive force. Scientific knowledge would improve engineering, would improve mechanism, and thus would improve the power and effectiveness of technology. Engels asked rhetorically: "And what is impossible to science?"[44] Science obviously had no limits, and so technology had no limits, and so the productive horizons of industry were also limitless. The natural inventiveness of science was an inherent component of the boundless productivity of modern industry. Engels rejected Malthus and the fear of overproduction on this basis: there could be no fear of overpopulation as long as scientific knowledge itself increased in "geometrical progression."[45]

Technology would produce economic abundance, but technology would also create social distress. First, in the contest between men and machines, men would lose. Unemployment was destined to increase, because machines would gradually replace laborers. Secondly, the machine was the cause of dehumanization. Factory work allowed no opportunity for physical exercise or muscular activity. Excessive boredom was the prevailing mood in the factory. Work itself became tedious and wearisome, while physical and mental powers atrophied in an industrial environment.[46]

4. Value

Value was derivative. In other words, for Engels, there was no essence of value, no unchanging substance of value.[47] Rather, value was a function of production costs and utility, or of competition. Value was not essence, but something produced out of utility or competition. Utility and competition were primary. The use of an object, the desire for economic self-aggrandizement, determined value.

Production costs were composed of three elements: (1) the rent of land required to produce the raw materials, (2) capital, (3) the wages of labor. For instance, the value of a piece of land was to be determined by the relation of its productivity to its competitive stance on the marketplace. The productivity of the land was to be measured by the production costs entailed for the land to produce objects. Thus, the value of a piece of land was determined by its productivity, i.e., costs of production for producing objects and its utility or competitive market position. Value again was derivative, a function essentially of competition or utility.

Even though competition and utility determined value, Engels assigned costs of production a high priority status. In doing this, he remained close to the English classical economists. Rent, capital, and labor assumed just as important a position in Engels's economic theory as they did in Smith's and Ricardo's. In describing capitalist society, Engels assumed that rent, capital, and labor were constant components of value. Engels's definition of value then approximated that of the British classical economists. Within a capitalist framework, capital, rent, and labor were unchanged elements in value, that is, necessary parts of value. The sufficient part of value was competition and utility.

5. The Proletariat

The Industrial Revolution created the proletarian. This industrial proletarian suffered from the worst form of economic enslavement in the history of Western civilization. The perpetuation of his own existence was completely removed from his own control, and was placed at the disposal of blind market forces. Not so much a slave, the proletarian was a mere economic contingency.[48]

English society has been polarized between proletarian and capitalist. Indeed, modern industrial society was the scene of a social, civil war. The decisive struggle was between the impoverished and pauperized workers and the exploitative bourgeoisie. Although the English proletariat was not yet prepared for revolution, an actual uprising would come in the not too distant future. Strikes, although not the revolution itself, were a preparation for the decisive struggle.

Trade unions were a source of strength for the proletariat. Competition amongst themselves weakened the workers, placed them at the mercy of the capitalist. The formation of unions, indicating a cooperative and unified spirit, meant that the workers would no longer allow themselves to be bought and sold at the cheapest price. The trade union movement would destroy all forms of competition, and thereby insure that the laborer would receive a just share of the fruits of his labor. Hopefully, the working class movement would become socialist. When Engels wrote *The Condition of the Working Class in England*, the laboring classes were not of such a temperament. English socialism was too intellectual and too metaphysical. English socialist leaders came basically from the middle classes. For these two reasons, then, the socialist movement and the trade union movement had remained separate and distinct. However, the English proletarians supported the Chartist movement.

Engels tended to romanticize the proletariat. In particular, he saw the industrial proletariat as the most rigorous, intelligent, radical wing of the labor movement. These were not the people to be destroyed by the unemployment foisted upon society by the capitalists. A "reserve of unemployed workers"[49] was an economic requirement of capitalism. Such a reserve kept wages down. The labor union, by destroying competition, also destroyed the conditions that made a "reserve of unemployed" a possibility.

6. The Theory of Cataclysm and Revolution

Because of the polarization of society, revolution was inevitable. The law of centralization meant that property must be concentrated in fewer hands. The law of competition meant that the poor must always increase geometrically. Cyclic trade crises drove the worker to desperation, and thus capitalism would end in a cataclysmic fashion.

Industrial growth had united all sections of the globe. Industrial growth had created a world market, eradicating sectional and national differences. The social development of all bourgeois countries was thereby coordinated, since the social war between bourgeois and proletariat was endemic to all of them. The communist revolution, then, could not be simply national in scope, but must spread to all the countries of the Western world. Because of the different rate of industrial growth in France, Germany, England, and America, the revolution would strike first in England, the most highly modernized, last in Germany, industrially the most backward. Subsequently the revolution would spread to Asia. The world market, imperialism, had forced Asian countries out of their isolation. A new mechanical invention in England was capable of depriving Chinese workers of their livelihood. Lower prices for industrial goods occasioned the collapse of ancient Oriental hand and village manufacture. Thus, India was experiencing a thorough revolution, and China was on the verge of being revolutionized. In the nineteenth century, revolution would occur on a worldwide basis.[50]

7. Communism

The chaos of the capitalistic system had proven the inefficiency of the private ownership system. The alternation of boom and depression had underscored the inability of industry in private hands to supply sufficient goods for the entire population. Under communism, the industrial machine would be run in accordance with a plan. This plan would bring order and efficiency, and the productive capacity of society would be raised considerably.

In fact, communism could not be fully achieved until productivity had reached a certain level. Communism was therefore dependent upon productivity. "In all probability, the proletarian revolution, will transform existing society gradually and will be able to abolish private property only when the means of production are available in sufficient quantity."[51] In other words, only when the productive capacity had matured enough to meet the basic needs of all members of society would it be possible to construct a communist society. For only when their basic needs were fulfilled, would individuals transcend their inherent selfishness and consent to the cooperative management of industry.

Under communism, then, an economic plan, sufficient productive power, would mean that social output would meet the basic needs of the entire population. People would share equally. Engels's economic egalitarianism was an attempt to overcome human selfishness and isolation. If all people possessed equally, there would be no need for jealousy, no need for one person to envy another. Such was the message of Wilhelm Weitling and such was the message of Gracchus Babeuf. Economic egalitarianism, by imposing equality, meant the end of human divisiveness; it meant harmony.[52]

Communism for Engels also meant the end of classes, and the end of the social division of labor. People would not be impressed into one job, into one specialization. Rather, in the course of a lifetime they could work at many occupations. Thus, a more rounded, self-developed personality would emerge from a communist society. Because a person was not locked into one occupational caste, he would be able to experience himself in different functions, and thus experience his personality in its most complete form.

THIS ANALYSIS OF the core ideas of Engels socioeconomic thinking has revealed some fundamental conceptual differences between Marx and Engels. For instance, for Engels, the most important moderating force in all societies in all times was technology. Engels affirmed repeatedly that all social changes, alterations in class relations, alterations in property relations, were brought about by technological advances. The rigid socioeconomic determinism of his thought becomes apparent.

The reductive tendencies of Engels's thinking were manifested in his approach to industry. By the middle of 1842, Engels was a materialist; he had begun to study the human environment rather than religious or artistic ideas. In Engels's grasp of historical movement, he reduced the most important cause of that movement to technology. In the same way, when Engels was in his Hegelian period, he reduced the movement of world history to the unfolding of Logic, or Idea. In his Hegelian period, the inclusive, ontological agent was Reason, and in his materialist period, the inclusive agent was machinery. Later, in his writings on physics and chemistry, matter would become motion. Repeatedly, Engels was to place the causative agent, the source of motion and energy, in something outside of man. Man himself, for Engels, was never the source of energy for the social universe. The origination of social energy lay in a source distinct and separate from man.

Furthermore, Engels did not reject British classical economics. He openly borrowed their economic categories, their economic definitions. Industry, property, competition, and costs of production shared one (but not only one) common denominator. They were all forces outside of man (even recognizing the exception that human labor was a production cost). Essentially, what he had in common with the English economists was the common belief that capitalism could be explained in terms of forces, of laws external to man. In short, the determinants of value lay outside of man. The tragedy of man under capitalism, for Engels, was the tragedy of a traveler who found himself in an environment that controlled him, exploited him for its own interests.

To compare Engels's economics with Marx's, taking 1844 as our point of departure, immediately exposes the fundamental differences between the two men. Marx applied the theme of alienation to economics. Labor was an alienated force. Value was totally constituted of alienated labor. In short, Marx's economics was an attempt to derive social value entirely from human activity. Marx did overthrow English classical economics, and did seek to create a new theoretical economics. He rejected any attempt to locate the determinants of value in sources external to man. The new economics Marx was attempting to create made man the subject of economic value, the creator of all value. To do this Marx had to apply his theory of alienation to economics. He had to show that capitalism was the tragedy of man who allowed his creative *praxis* to be alienated. Capitalism was the tragedy of man who lived in a foreign world that had been constructed by his own expropriated labor, it was man-made but not made in the image of man.[53]

The concepts of surplus value and labor, as understood by Marx, are not present in Engels. These ideas did not exist in Engels, because he lacked an understanding of the idea of alienation. Unless Engels had been prepared to see the world as entirely constructed and composed of human *praxis*, he could not have arrived at a Marxian theory of value, or surplus value. The anthropological center was missing in Engels. Marx had that anthropological center. He was prepared to see man as the primary agent of change, the source of social creation. Because Marx was prepared to do this, he could invent the theory of surplus value, as well as the labor theory of value. He could invent a new economics. Because Engels was not prepared to take this step, he followed (at this stage of his life) the English economists, he followed his metaphysical predisposition and believed that value was determined by forces external to man.

The divergence between the two men becomes more apparent through an analysis of their definitions of property and class. By "property," Engels meant possession. By "property," Marx meant the conditions of labor. That is, for Marx, property was land, tolls, material, anything upon which men could labor, could objectify themselves. Private property, for Marx, was thus the removal of the conditions of labor from the free accessibility of all. In other words, under a system of private property all people could not freely objectify themselves, because the conditions of labor were not accessible to them.

Lastly, "class" for Engels meant wealth. A class was determined by the amount of property, that is, wealth, it possessed. Engels talked in terms of three classes. "Class," for Marx, meant function. In brief, a class was defined by its economic role, the social function it fulfilled. For Marx as well, there were three classes in nineteenth-century society.

Nothing in this chapter is intended to deny that Engels's socioeconomic views changed during his lifetime. Engels fell under the influence of Marx, and they did collaborate on the *Communist Manifesto, The German Ideology,* and *The Holy Family.* In point of fact, the influence was reciprocal. It was Engels who conclusively showed Marx the importance of economics, and Marx indeed acknowledged his indebtedness to Engels in this area. But to say Engels drew Marx's attention to this field is not the same thing as saying they both defined or understood economics in exactly the same way. Marx's understanding of economics from the 1844 manuscripts until the *Grundrisse* and *Kapital* was based on the theme of dehumanization, and in the *Grundrisse* and *Kapital* was heavily influenced by Hegelian logic. Engels's socioeconomic thinking enlarged in his lifetime, was augmented by Marx, but there always existed a predisposition in his mind to give greater weight, to see the balance of importance shifted to technological factors, to deterministic factors, to material factors simply in the sense of physicalness and tangibility. When Marx wrote about economics, he did so in terms of alienation, but also in terms of form and content, inherent contradiction, and relationship. When Engels wrote about economics, he did so in terms of pauperism, of economic egalitarianism, of bourgeois reification; that is, he accepted the English classical economists' categories of competition, rent, exchange. This predisposition made up the uniqueness, the inherent subjectivity of Engels's mind.

Regardless of these differences between Marx and Engels, there can be no doubt of Engels's own intellectual growth from 1842 until 1847. The years of his rationalistic pantheism, of his liberal nationalism, were years of his youth. The years of his conversion to materialism, of his communism, were the years of his maturation. Not only was there maturity, but also a keener scientific vision. The presumptions, the hyperbolic qualities of youth, were replaced by a more precise, more acute understanding of social processes. Nevertheless, the central ideas of alienation and objectification were absent from his economics. Even though Engels wished to use his economics to illustrate the need for socialism and a more humane society, the internal structure of his economics, the inner principles were not derived from a naturalistic humanism. Nowhere does Engels explain value, surplus value, production as expressions of species activity. Nowhere does he try to explain the constitution of the socioeconomic world as ultimately derivative from human species being. The dedication to the anthropological foundation of the social sciences simply was not present in Engels. Conversely, Engels was a metaphysician. That is, he always placed the agency of change or activity outside the human being. Engels was metaphysical as compared to Marx's being anthropological, because Engels always located the activating principle of the social cosmos in sources external to man, in material forces.

In the period from 1842 through 1847, Engels had moved beyond the rationalistic pantheism of his Hegelian period. The spiritual in all its forms no longer existed for him. But characteristically for Engels, although the spiritual had been transcended in content, its function had been simply replaced. Materialism became the dominant principle of his philosophy. What Engels meant by materialism was essentially science and technology. Engels had not surrendered the idea of finding a single principle by which to explain the entire universe. That single principle was no longer Mind or God. Rather, that single principle was now material science, and in its applied form, machinery. Engels remained bound to metaphysics, but his metaphysics was now a metaphysics of matter. Engels made the connection between communism and natural science.[54]

Footnotes

1. Friedrich Engels, "Fortschritte der Sozialreform auf dem Kontinent," *Marx-Engels Werke* (Berlin: Dietz Verlag, 1970), I, p. 494.
2. Moses Hess, *Philosophische und Sozialistische Schriften*, ed. A. Cornu and W. Mönke (Berlin: Academie-Verlag, 1961), p. 312.
3. *Ibid.*, p. 313.
4. *Ibid.*, pp. 200–204.

5. Heinrich Heine, *Religion and Philosophy in Germany*, trans. John Snodgrass (Boston: Beacon Press, 1959).
6. Engels, "Fortschritte der Sozialreform auf dem Kontinent," *Marx-Engels Werke*, I, p. 490.
7. Wilhelm Weitling, *Garantieen der Harmonie und Freiheit* (Hamburg: M. H. T. Christen, 1849).
8. P. Buonarroti, *Babeuf Conspiracy for Equality*, (London: H. Hetherington, 1936).
9. Engels, "Fortschritte der Sozialreform auf dem Kontinent," *Marx-Engels Werke*, I, p. 481.
10. *Ibid.*, pp. 482–484.
11. Frank Manuel, *Prophets of Paris* (New York: Harper & Row, 1965), pp. 103–194.
12. Engels, "Die Lage Englands: Das Achtzehnte Jahrhundert," *Marx-Engels Werke*, I, p. 555.
13. Engels, "Die Lage Englands: Das Achtzehnte Jahrhundert," *Ibid.*, p. 550.
14. Engels, "Briefe aus London," *Ibid.*, p. 468.
15. Engels, "Die Lage Englands: Das Achtzehnte Jahrhundert," *Ibid.*, p. 577.
16. Engels, "Stellung der Politischen Partei," *Ibid.*, p. 461.
17. *Ibid.*, p. 462.
18. *Ibid.*, pp. 462–463. On this same point see Engels, "Die Innern Krisen," *Ibid.*, pp. 456–460.
19. Engels, "Die Lage Englands. Die Englische Konstitution," *Ibid.*, p. 577.
20. Engels, "Englische Ansicht über die Innern Krisen," *Ibid.*, p. 454.
21. Engels, "Stellung der Politischen Partei," *Ibid.*, p. 461.
22. Engels, "Briefe aus London," *Ibid.*, p. 468.
23. Engels, "Die Innern Krisen," *Ibid.*, p. 460.
24. *Ibid.*
25. Engels, "Die Lage Englands: Das Achtzehnte Jahrhundert," *Ibid.*, p. 556.
26. *Ibid.*, pp. 550–556.
27. *Ibid.*, p. 564.
28. *Ibid.*, p. 566.
29. *Ibid.*, p. 568.
30. Engels, *The Principles of Communism*, trans. Paul M. Sweezy (New York: International Publishers, 1969), pp. 12–13.
31. Engels, "Outline of a Critique of Political Economy," *Marx's Early Manuscripts*, trans. Ed. Mulligan (Moscow: Foreign Languages Publishing House, 1966), p. 193.
32. *Ibid.*, pp. 192–193.
33. *Ibid.*, p. 180.
34. Engels, *The Principles of Communism*, p. 14.
35. Engels, *The Condition of the Working Class in England*, trans. W. O. Henderson and W. H. Chaloner (Stanford, Cal.: Stanford University Press, 1968), p. 88.
36. Engels, "Outline of a Critique of Political Economy," *Marx's Early Manuscripts*, p. 180.
37. Engels, *The Condition of the Working Class in England*, p. 91.
38. Engels, "Outline of a Critique of Political Economy," *Marx's Early Manuscripts*, p. 206.
39. *Ibid.*, p. 195.
40. Engels, *The Condition of the Working Class in England*, p. 88.
41. Engels, *The Principles of Communism*, p. 5–6.
42. Engels, "Die Lage Englands: Das Achtzehnte Jahrhundert," *Marx-Engels Werke*, I, p. 566.

43. Engels, "Outline of a Critique of Political Economy," *Marx's Early Manuscripts,* p. 204.
44. *Ibid.*
45. *Ibid.*
46. Engels, *The Condition of the Working Class in England,* p. 199.
47. Engels, "Outline of a Critique of Political Economy," *Marx's Early Manuscripts,* p. 186.
48. Engels, *The Principles of Communism,* pp. 7–8.
49. Engels, *The Condition of the Working Class in England,* pp. 246–313.
50. *Ibid.,* p. 97.
51. Engels, *The Principles of Communism,* pp. 9–10.
52. *Ibid.,* p. 14.
53. For a discussion of the early economic theory of Engels see Ernst Mandel, *The Formation of the Economic Thought of Karl Marx* (London: New Left Edition, 1971). Mandel is sound on Marx, but only offers a brief and not too penetrating analysis of Engels. Communist writers continue to misinterpret Engels, and their commentary on him is marked by veneration and little objectivity. A prime example of this *a priori* approach to Engels is in I. Rosenberg, *Oekonomischen Lehre von Marx und Engels* (Berlin: Dietz Verlag, 1966).
54. For an analysis of the role that religion played in Engels's early life and later thought see the following two works: Karl Kupisch, *Vom Pietismus Zum Kommunismus* (Berlin: Lettner-Verlag, 1953); Reinhart Seeger, *Friedrich Engels: Die Religiöse Entwicklung des Spatpietisten und Fruhsozialisten* (Halle: Akademisch-Verlag, 1935). For an East German interpretation of Engels, one that incorporates much humanistic atmosphere but is uncritical and hagiographic, see Horst Ullrich, *Der Junge Engels* (Berlin: Deutscher Verlag der Wissenschaften, 1961).

Nine

The Foundation of Engels's Metaphysics

DURING HIS LIFETIME, Engels passed through four phases of development. (1) The years from 1839 until 1848 were the years of formation; Engels became a communist, began his collaboration with Marx, and laid the foundations of his metaphysical materialism. (2) From 1849 until 1878 Engels dedicated himself to military and political affairs. He was not only an active participant in the Baden uprising of 1849, but also made a study of military history, wrote extensively on the military aspects of the Crimean War, the Franco-Austrian War of 1859, the Austro-Prussian War of 1866, and the Franco-Prussian War of 1870. In addition, he wrote a large part of the journalism that appeared in the *New York Daily Tribune* under Marx's name, for which Marx was paid, and also wrote numerous articles on military subjects for the *New American Encyclopedia.* From 1850 through 1870, Engels ran the cotton manufacturing firm of Erman and Engels, of which his father was a partner, in Manchester, England, and regularly used the financial resources of the business to support Marx and his family during these years of their deepest poverty. (3) The third period of Engels's career, from 1878 until 1890, was the most self-expressive of his life. After acquainting himself with the contemporary state of natural and biological sciences, Engels attempted to apply what he conceived to be the laws of dialectics to the physical universe. In his *Anti-Dühring, Socialism: Utopian and Scientific,* but more specifically in the *Dialectics of Nature* and "Ludwig Feuerbach and the End of Classical German Philosophy," Engels outlined what he thought to be the materialist dialectics of the universe. (4) The last period of Engels's life, from 1890 until his death in 1895, was the apogee of his labors and fame. Engels assumed the position of executor of Marx's work and thought; he was the true disciple with the true word, and had become master of the sacred dogma. Continuing to respond to the newer cultural trends of the late nineteenth-century Europe, Engels during these last five years sought to distinguish Marxism from the encroachments of extreme positivism and idealism. As the Pope of Marxism, Engels, basically in his letters to the leaders of the various European socialist parties, also sketched the tactical options and the strategic opportunities of the Marxist movement, but ended by hardening his form of Marxism into the rigidities of economic determinism.

The focus of this chapter, however, falls upon the continuities rather than upon the discontinuities of Engels's thought. It is seeking permanence, seeking to isolate those features of Engels's thought pattern that remained constant throughout his life. The criteria applied to Marx is also valid for Engels: there existed in both men a hard and unchanging substructure of thought, an inherent inclination of mind, that stamped their thought with its essential and unique qualities, that made it distinctive regardless of the phases that this thought inevitably traversed. It is these essential and unique qualities of mind, the logical presuppositions, that this book is attempting to isolate and categorize in the work of Engels.

As part of this exercise in categorization, the role of nature in Engels's thought holds a crucial position. Engels's serious study of nature dated from 1858.[1] Engels distinguished three broad periods in the history of natural science: classical, eighteenth-century, and modern. The Greek view of the universe, although fundamentally correct in its conception of the world, failed to explain the details of nature, lacked specific and empirical documentation. Nevertheless, Heraclitus had penetrated to the core of scientific insight, according to Engels, when he described the universe as flux.[2] Aristotle also rejected the attempt to divide nature into fixed, rigid categories. Rather, he thought of nature in terms of fluid, interpenetrating categories, and thought of motion as the primary force in the universe.[3] To the Greeks, then, nature was everlasting change, and Engels thought their somewhat primitive and naive insights correct in their basic and underlying assumptions.

The eighteenth-century view of the world, which had originated in the scientific discoveries of the late sixteenth century, was totally mechanistic. In the eighteenth century the level of development attained by the natural sciences had taken these sciences to a mastery of mechanics, "indeed only the mechanics of solid bodies."[4] Because of the success of the mechanical model in Newtonian physics, the same model was applied to every branch of science. Chemistry and biology were interpreted mechanistically, and man was what the animal had been to Descartes: a machine. Thus, eighteenth-century materialism was imprisoned within a static view of nature. Change and process, the laws of motion, were not part of the conceptual armory of eighteenth-century mechanistic materialism.

Empirical investigations in the modern period had revolutionized the understanding of the physical universe. Engels felt that three great discoveries had overturned the static, eighteenth-century conception of nature, resurrecting the ancient Greek view of nature as flux. The discovery of the cell had shown that the highest plant and animal organisms developed from the multiplication and differentiation of the simple cell, and also suggested that by means of this same process of multiplication and differentiation organisms could change their species. Thus, modern biology had proven that there were no fixed and unchangeable species, but rather that species were interconnected, that one species could be transformed into another. The discovery of the transformation of energy in physics had shown that all forms of motion and force in the universe were derivable from one form of universal motion. Energy, heat, radiation, electricity, magnetism, and chemical energy were but different forms of one universal force, and thus the whole process of nature was reducible to the unceasing transformation of this one universal force into its various manifestations. Lastly, Darwin's theory of evolution had proven that man himself was the end result of a long process of development. The highest form of organic life itself had a history, which originated as a few unicellular germs, but which culminated in time as human consciousness.[5] Because of these three great discoveries, Engels concluded, nature in the nineteenth century must be interpreted as being itself historical.

The contribution that Engels wished to make to the natural sciences was to apply dialectics, which Marx restricted to an explanation of economic and historical events, to the physical universe. Marx had taken the idealist dialectic of Hegel and transformed it into a materialist dialectic. Society, according to Marx, functioned in accordance with dialectical processes. Engels wished to move beyond the realm of human history. He wanted to encompass all of nature, wanted to demonstrate that the operational laws of nature itself were dialectical. Engels was seeking a grand system in the style of the older metaphysicians, like Spinoza, Leibnitz, Kant, and even Hegel himself. Engels was a totalist. He felt he had completed Marx.

Although Engels rejected the idealism of Hegel, he admired the Hegel who talked of incessant process and movement. Engels recognized that Hegel had left an inescapable impress upon the mind of his century and succeeding centuries. Hegel had shown that process, evolution, and development were the laws of logic, of mind, of human history. The time had come to complete the work begun by Marx, to remove the idealist obfuscation of Hegel, to demythologize him. The time had come to show that process, evolution, and development were also part of the metaphysical being of nature. To this task, Engels dedicated himself.

According to Engels, the fundamental dialectical laws of the universe were reducible to three: (1) the law of the transformation of quantity into quality; (2) the law of the interpenetration of opposites; (3) the law of the negation of the negation.[6] Engels noted that all three had been developed by Hegel but "as mere laws of thought."[7] The first law, quantity into quality, was discussed by Hegel in the first part of his *Logic,* the Doctrine of Being. The second law, interpenetration of opposites, was discussed by Hegel in Part Two of the *Logic,* the Doctrine of Essence. The third law, negation of the negation, formed the basis of the whole system.

The law of the transformation of quantity into quality was most applicable to the realm of chemistry. All qualitative changes could only occur by the quantitative addition or subtraction of matter or motion. Engels illustrated this point by imagining a nonliving body successively cut up into smaller and smaller sections. Eventually, we would penetrate to the molecule, and then even the molecule would be decomposed into its separate atoms. Clearly, the properties of the atom were different from the properties of the molecule. Molecules were qualitatively different from their constituent parts. Quantitative addition or subtraction of matter or motion caused qualitative uniqueness.

The law of the interpenetration of opposites was best illustrated, however, in the realm of mechanical motion, in the forms of motion of nonliving nature. All motion, according to Engels, was related to change of place. Nature was a system of bodies, from large bodies down to atomic particles. These bodies were constantly changing their place, were constantly reacting upon each other, and it was exactly this mutual reaction that constituted motion. All motion, furthermore, consisted of the interplay between attraction and repulsion. Bodies either moved closer to one another, were attracted, or bodies moved further from each other, were repulsed. Thus, mechanical motion assumed two forms, two polar opposites, attraction and repulsion, and from the subforms of attraction and repulsion all the various forms of heat, electricity, and magnetism in the universe were derived.

Influenced by Helmholtz, Engels believed that matter was unthinkable without motion. In addition, since matter was an eternal given, it was equally uncreatable as well as indestructible. Engels was also an adherent of the idea of the "conservation of energy," first established by V. R. Mayer in 1842, and later perfected by Helmholtz. Motion can neither be destroyed nor created. Since continued motion was only possible when each individual attraction was compensated by a corresponding repulsion, the sum of all attractions in the universe must be equal to the sum of all repulsions. Therefore, the pool of motion available to the universe must be fixed.[8]

Mechanical motion need not only manifest itself as attraction or repulsion. Mechanical motion could be transformed; it could assume other qualities, acquire different properties. In this change, not of the form, but of the quality of mechanical motion, there were again manifest the dialectical laws of the transformation of quantity into quality, of the interpenetration of opposites. Engels was asserting that only one primordial and indestructible substance existed in the universe: motion. Engels thus reduced all materiality in the universe to one phenomenon: motion. This uniforce and unisubstance appeared in different forms, as attraction or repulsion, or in qualitatively different modes, as heat or electricity, as light or magnetism.

Underlying the entire dialectical structure of the universe, Engels maintained, was the law of the negation of the negation, or "the fundamental law for the construction of the whole system."[9] Engels understood the law of the negation of the negation to mean the absolute certainty that an object, or thought, or condition will turn into its opposite. In the realm of mathematics, Engels saw the law operative in the multiplication of $-a$ by $-a$, which resulted in $+a^2$. By negating the negation we had moved to a higher degree raised to its second power.[10] In the organic world the law of the negation of the negation was manifest by a seed, which under the proper conditions of heat and moisture, would germinate into a plant. The plant had negated the seed. Or when a butterfly emerged from an egg, the butterfly had negated that egg.[11] In the realm of history, the realm in which Marx held undisputed mastery, Engels argued that the law of the negation of the negation was shown in the transcendence of original, primitive communal property by private property. On a universal basis, men in their primitive stage of development shared property, but this stage had been or was being universally transcended by private property.[12] On the level of pure thought, in philosophy itself, the law of the negation of the negation was the principle of motion. The philosophy of the Greeks was naturalistic materialism, and as such was incapable of solving the relationship between thought and matter. Ancient naturalistic materialism, according to Engels, had to be negated. It had been negated, and what emerged was its opposite, idealism.[13] In summary, Engels maintained that the negation of the negation was the "law of development of nature, history and thought."[14] Engels assumed that he had discovered the energizing principle of the universe; in Aristotelian terms, the prime mover.

Life, too, was an expression of the dialectical laws of motion. Life was "the mode of existence of albuminous substances."[15] For Engels, to talk about albuminous substances was to talk of the realm of chemistry, to analyze protein substances. Albuminous organisms possessed, as their peculiar quality, the ability to appropriate substances from their environment, assimilate these, use them in their own renewal, and excrete older parts of their bodies. According to Engels, the fundamental condition of existence for albuminous substances was the carrying on of an uninterrupted metamorphosis between the organism and its environment. If no such interaction took place, the organism died. Consistent in his application of the dialectical model, Engels therefore saw that life consisted "primarily in the part that at each moment it is itself and at the same time something else."[16] Because of the exchange of matter that took place through nutrition and excretion, life itself was process.

In man, thought had developed as a function of life. But, argued Engels, before thought could come into existence, a brain had to come into existence. In short, brain was a precondition for mind, or an organ of thought was necessary before thought could take place. Brain, also, for

Engels was motion. "But the motion of matter is not merely crude mechanical motion, mere change of place, it is heat and light, electric and magnetic stress, chemical combination and dissociation, life and finally, consciousness."[17] The agency of thought itself, brain, as consciousness, was itself merely a "mode of energy,"[18] a form and reflection of the primary ontological substance, motion.

In several books, Engels continuously affirmed the copy theory of knowledge. If brain was motion, then thought itself was simply a picture of the internal world. "We comprehended the concepts in our heads once more materialistically as images (Abbilder) of real things instead of regarding the real things as images of this or that stage of the absolute concept."[19] Engels maintained that there was absolutely no variance, no difference between our comprehension of the external world and the external world itself.[20]

Furthermore, Engels argued that thought itself was dialectical. Men could only think dialectically, because their ideas were merely exact copies of the actual dialectical processes of the external world. "In reality it is the reverse: the dialectics of the brain is only the reflection of the forms of motion of the real world, both of nature and of history."[21] Engels believed that he had also stood Hegel on his head. True thinking was inherently a dialectical process, but it was so because nature functioned dialectically and our ideas were perfect images of these natural processes.

Engels's materialism was thus intended to be a total metaphysical system. It was intended to describe and account for existence from its origins in motion, to its organic forms as albuminous substance, to its final expression as idea. It was a cold, unremitting, and remorseless system. Men had little impact on fashioning the course of development of history and nature. Rather than being the subject of history, men were basically the passive objects of unrelenting external forces. Causation originated and flowed from the physical. The same laws that governed the physical universe also governed the social universe. Life existed in this solar system because the energy forces were sufficient to maintain it. But it was probable that this solar system would burn out, and life too on this solar system would burn out. A different solar system would have sufficient energy resources to sustain life, and life would spring up there. Engels was talking about continuous creation, but a continuous creation that was totally governed by the physical laws of motion. Engels's system was an eternal cycle of death and creation, but it was a cycle in which human death and rebirth were solely dependent upon the blind mechanics of nature.

Engels's philosophy of nature was a materialist monism. His basic assertion can be reduced to the claim that everything that was, was matter and its motion.[22] Furthermore, Engels's metaphysical materialism was mechanistic. He conceived of the universe as a vast machine, operating directly in terms of quantitative shifts of matter and motion. Mechanistic models were also deterministic models, and Engels's account of that functioning in quantities of matter and motion led him to embrace a cosmological determinism.

The view of the natural universe that had come to fruition in Engels's mind after 1858 had existed in embryo in the mind of the young Engels. There were present in Engels's mind throughout his lifetime certain predispositions of thought and attitude that gave shape, that served as the ground of his more concrete and specific meditations. In short, given Engels's mental predispositions as a young man, the intellectual assumptions that had taken root in his mind before he met Marx, it was predictable that his mature view of nature would take the shape that it did in his mature years.

Engels began his life as a Pietist. After his conversion to Hegelianism, the God of his youth was transformed into the pantheism of Reason. After 1858 matter and motion were to take the place of Reason. Engels was a man in search of an absolute. He was seeking ontology. In successive stages, he was to find the metaphysical origin of the universe in God, Reason, and matter. His reductivist tendency of thought was manifested when he approached the problem of history, in the naive positivism of his view of social change. His simplistic acceptance of mechanist determinism in relation to nature was to become a simplistic acceptance of economic determinism in relation to history.

The preceding paragraphs described and categorized Engels's philosophy of nature. That philosophy, as we have seen, was predicated upon the attempt to take the dialectic from its Hegelian format and make matter itself behave dialectically. At this point it would be extremely productive to compare Hegel and Engels in terms of their views of nature and their views of dialectics. Several enlightening results will emerge from this comparison. First, it will be interesting to see how well Engels understood Hegel, that is, to test Engels's philosophic and analytic acuity. Second, we will see whether there was any logical justification, to see whether there was any sense left to the idea of dialectics when nature itself was interpreted dialectically. Third, after determining Engels's understanding of Hegel, we will then compare Engels to Marx in terms of their understanding of Hegel. In this way, we will examine not only their respective insights into Hegel, but also what each took from Hegel, and thus again expose their basic and distinctive aptitudes and intellectual predispositions.

Hegel defined nature "as the idea in the form of otherness."[23] Nature was the notion of nature in its external form. The specific character of nature was externality. Nature could not exist at all if it did not exist as externality.

Drawing upon Christian theology, Hegel allegorically alluded to nature as "the son of God."[24] Just as Christ stood outside of God, just as Christ existed as otherness, Nature stood outside of Spirit, existed as contradiction. Christ must be resurrected, must unite with God, and in parallel fashion, Hegel maintained, Nature must reunite with Spirit. Nature as estranged Spirit must become Spirit again. It did this by sublating itself as contradiction, by transcending itself as otherness.

Externality, however, did not act. Nature itself did not rejoin Spirit. Rather Spirit used Nature to become absolute Freedom. Spirit overcame externality, Spirit in transcending otherness became conscious of itself as absolute Freedom. Spirit was the motivating force; Nature was passive. In fact, the various grades of Nature, the separate hierarchies of Nature, were not brought into being through any emergent quality of Nature itself. For Hegel, Nature did not evolve, did not transform itself, but rather it was Spirit that placed Nature in its distinctive grades. Spirit pulled Nature into unity with itself. But Nature gave Spirit the opportunity to become absolute Freedom by just existing as pure externality, and as estrangement.

Hegel conceived of Nature as a system of three stages: mechanics, physics, and organics. One stage arose necessarily from the previous stage, but this did not mean that one stage generated naturally out of the other. Externality would not generate from itself a different form of externality. Metamorphosis pertained only to Spirit, that is, only Spirit had the power to produce development or generation. Mechanics was the realm of "infinite separatedness," "of asunderness," or of "mutual outsideness."[25] There was no unity in this realm, no formal connectedness, but this was the ideal state of matter, that is, disjointedness. Unity must be imposed from the outside. The realm of physics was the realm of "natural individuality."[26] Here nature was posited as a determinate form. Physics was hung-within-itself in its external form. True subjectivity belonged to organics. The organic entity, regardless of differences of form, had found a unity in itself and was for itself; it was therefore subjectivity.

Clearly, Hegel and Engels had two entirely different conceptions of the structure of nature. Hegel thought in terms of three distinct stages, of hierarchy. Engels, on the other hand, as a mechanistic materialist, thought of nature as a continuum, without separate hierarchies. Beginning with motion, Engels believed that quantitative changes of motion could produce qualitative changes, and thus all nature, from mechanics to conscious life, was a mere serial extension of this primitive, ontological substance. Engels's perversion of Hegel's *Philosophy of Nature* stemmed from the fact that Engels completely disregarded Hegel's own wishes; that is, he interpreted Hegel in a way that Hegel himself specifically did not want to be interpreted.

For instance, Hegel directly asserted that it was impossible to account for qualitative change in terms of quantitative increase or decrease.[27] Hegel directly refuted the idea of Engels that quantitative change only made for qualitative change in the organic world. It does not, Hegel argued, because to do so would be to surrender the idea of identity. It would be impossible to distinguish difference, to isolate and separate one thing from another. Thus, the very law that Engels claimed to be one of three general laws of the universe, the law of the transformation of quantity into quality, which

Engels said was developed by Hegel in the Doctrine of Being of the *Logic,* was, in fact, rejected by Hegel in terms of the organic world as inadequate to properly explain qualitative change. Furthermore, Hegel was convinced that qualitative change could only be brought about by Idea or Spirit. Idea displayed itself in the finitude of each grade, but it was Idea, through the dialectic, that broke through the limitation of each grade to move to a higher stage. For Hegel, quality was always a function of Idea, and therefore real metamorphosis could only be understood as a product or result of Idea.

Furthermore, Hegel, in specific and concrete terms, also categorically rejected Engels's idea of nature as a continuum, as a serial extension of matter and motion. It is necessary at this point to extract a rather long passage from Hegel's *Philosophy of Nature.*

> The two forms under which the serial progression of Nature is conceived are evolution and emanation. The way of evolution, which starts from the imperfect and formless, is as follows: at first there was the liquid element and aqueous forms of life, and from the water there evolved plants, polyps, molluscs, and finally fishes; then from the fishes were evolved the land animals, and finally from the land animals came man. This gradual alteration is called an explanation and understanding; it is a conception which comes from the Philosophy of Nature, and it still flourishes. But though this quantitative difference is of all theories the easiest to understand, it does not really explain anything at all. The way of emanation is peculiar to the oriental world. It involves a series of degradations of being, starting from the perfect being, the absolute totality, God. Emanation thus ends with the absence of all form. Both ways are one-sided and superficial, and postulate an indeterminate goal.[28]

The preceding paragraph sounds like a short summary of Engels's whole philosophy of nature. In fact, Hegel almost appeared to be offering a parody of the model of explanation based upon evolution or serial extension. Concretely, however, Hegel rejected all serial explanation because it blurred difference, and because it blurred difference it also blurred identity. All individuality, all determinate forms, tended to be lost in amorphous primal substance. Thus, the end result of serial explanation, even though it was the easiest to understand, was that "it does not really explain anything at all."

Not only was the method of explanation used by Engels a method specifically rejected by Hegel himself, but Engels also demonstrated a fundamental inability to comprehend the basic principles of Hegel's more inclusive system. Engels completely distorted this system; in fact, he destroyed it. Motion, for Engels, became the energizing principle of the universe. Hegel would have branded such an idea pure nonsense. Only Spirit had the power of motivation, according to Hegel. Spirit was motion because only Spirit desired Freedom. Spirit wished to be self-determining, wished to be self-dependent, and therefore it embarked upon a journey to conquer that self-determination. It was impossible, according to Hegel, to ascribe the desire for Freedom to motion, and therefore impossible to ascribe to motion the power to produce quality. In short, Engels assigned to motion the potential that Hegel categorically and exclusively assigned to spirit.

Engels also did not understand what Hegel meant by subjectivity. The subjective for Hegel was purposeful activity. The subjective was activity for itself, it was self-relation and self-containment. Therefore, subject could only be Spirit, because only Spirit was capable of self-determination. For Hegel, the subjective was that which moved toward self-determination.[29]

In his philosophy of nature, Engels made matter subject. In so doing he completely destroyed any meaning that Hegel had assigned to the notion of subjectivity. Matter could not indulge in purposive activity. Matter could not be self-determinate, nor could it be self-dependent and for itself. By distorting Hegel, by making matter subject, Engels in addition lost all contact with the Hegelian ideas of individuality, freedom, self-objectification, and *praxis*. The subject, the individual, acted for Hegel, while for Engels only nature was subject, therefore only nature acted.

The fact that Engels did not understand the idea of the subjective in Hegel meant that he did not understand what Hegel meant by the dialectic. When Engels referred to nature as functioning by dialectical laws, he absolutely misconstrued what Hegel meant by the dialectic, and therefore Engels used the term in a meaningless fashion. Engels used the term dialectic as being synonymous with process, with change. The central model with which Engels dealt was the image of two molecules colliding and thus producing heat or electricity. From two solid objects a form of energy was produced. Solidness had been changed into nonsolidness. When Engels said dialectics, he meant process. He was a Heraclitian.

What Hegel meant by dialectic was something fundamentally different:

> It [Spirit] is the inner being of the world, that which essentially is, and is per se; it assumes objective, determinate form, and enters into relations with itself—it is externality [otherness], and exists for self; yet, in the determination, and in its otherness, it is still one with itself—it is self-contained and self-complete in itself and for itself at once. This self-containedness, however, is first something known by us, it is implicit in its nature (an sich); it is substance spiritual. It has become self-contained for itself, on its own account; it must be knowledge of spirit, and must be consciousness of itself as spirit. This means, it must be presented to itself as an object, but at the same time straightway annul and transcend this objective form; it must be its own object in which it finds itself reflected.[30]

For Hegel, the dialectical process was not itself synonymous with motion. Development, movement, was a result, a consequence of this dialectical process, but was not the process itself. According to Hegel, development was a result of certain structures of existence. There were certain formal contents of existence, certain given determinations within reality, which clashed and were in opposition. The consequence of this clash, the result of this collision, was motion.

Inherent in the Hegelian notion of dialectic was the idea of negativity, or opposition. The basic structure of existence, for Hegel, counterposed a Subject (Spirit) to Negativity (Objectivity or Materiality). In order for Spirit, for Individuality, to become free to become self-determining, it must be confronted with Otherness. Only in this way could Subject transcend Otherness, Externality, and acquire greater self-determination and self-relatedness. Hegel's world was a world of struggle, of combat, of tragedy. Two entities were indispensable: a Subject seeking to function solely in terms of its own desires, and the Negative, the Not-Self, which hindered the Subject's attainment of absolute self-relatedness. A resolution of this duality was required; this resolution was motion. That is, the opposition of Self and Negation must be transcended, and this transcendence this canceling took the form of development, of change.

Hegel's dialectic required concrete determinations: Subject and Negativity. It was inherently a dualistic system, composed of determinate oppositions. It also required activity. It required that the Subject have a purpose: freedom. The notion of *praxis* was central to the Hegelian dialectic. The Subject must desire to engage in combat, must desire to cancel the Negative, must find its purpose in absolute self-relatedness, otherwise the system would remain static and have no meaning.

Engels's use of the term dialectic thus had little meaning, and bore not the slightest resemblance to the Hegelian notion. Engels did not think in terms of opposition, of Negativity. There was no drama, no resolution of inherent conflict. Hegel pitted two concrete determinations against each other: Individuality and the Objective. For Engels, there was emanation; there was the continuity of motion and process. For Engels, there was no conflict, no resolution of that conflict on a higher and qualitatively different stage; but rather a stream of motion, and the different forms that motion could assume.

Marx bore a much closer relationship to Hegel than did Engels. Marx revised Hegel, whereas Engels completely distorted him. The uniqueness of the Marxian system derived in large measure from what it retained of Hegel. The uniqueness of Engels's thought arises in part from what it rejected and lost of Hegel.[31]

Marx turned the Hegelian dialectic on its head, but he kept its basic structure. The notion of subjectivity was retained by Marx. A conscious, active, modifying agent existed in the Hegelian dialectic. For Hegel, that agent was Spirit. For Marx, that agent was social man as he modified his natural environment to produce his sustenance. Both Spirit and social man were active, purposeful, and causal agents; the difference was that the Hegelian Spirit was nonmaterial, while social man for Marx was a natural creature.

Marx also retained the Hegelian notion of *praxis.* For both, man was a being who labored, who was change-enduring and changing-creating. Man was the subject of history, the causal agent. For Marx, man interpenetrated with nature, fashioned from its brute materiality objects necessary for his existence. The Marxian man humanized nature, molded and controlled nature in accordance with his own needs. For Hegel, man was a being who brought forth Idea, and in so doing altered the conceptual world in which he lived. Again, Hegel thought in nonmaterial terms, and Marx in material terms. But essential to both their systems was the idea of man as *praxis,* as conscious purposive activity.

Marx also was true to the Hegelian notion of Negativity, or Externality. For both, Externality was passive. It could be acted upon, but could itself not be an active force. For Hegel, the External as opposition was transcended by Idea, was incorporated by Idea, was refashioned by Idea in Idea's march to its own freedom. For Marx, Negativity was overcome when man in the act of *praxis* created tools or sustenance or shelter.

Indeed, the Marx of the *Grundrisse* and *Kapital* was far more of a Hegelian than the Marx of the Paris manuscripts. In the early writings Marx, attempting to escape the deadening idealism of Hegel, was predominately working in the Feuerbachian mold. But when he came to explain the inner dynamics of capitalist society in 1857, Marx returned to the structure of Hegelian logic. The language of the *Grundrisse* was thickly and self-consciously Hegelian. In fact, Marx attempted to explain the working of capitalist society, and of all societies, according to the logical principles contained in the second volume of Hegel's *Logic.* When Marx wrote *Kapital,* the Hegelian structure was still there but the density of the Hegelian terminology had been replaced by statistical and mathematical data. A rebaptized Hegelian, Marx sought to explain capitalism in terms of the Hegelian notions of inherent contradiction, moment, determination, negation, and totality and essential relationships.

Marx and Engels thus had completely dissimilar views of Hegel. Marx perpetuated the Hegelian notions of subjectivity, human *praxis,* and conscious purposeful activity. Engels, on the other hand, made nature the subject, that is, imparted to externality all activity, all causality in the universe. Engels overlooked the role of human *praxis,* rather seeing in quantitative alteration of matter and motion that which produced change in the universe. Lastly, Engels found no place for purposeful activity, for consciousness, in his interpretation of Hegel. Rather, for Engels consciousness itself was a product of motion, and it was only due to the activity of matter that direction or movement was imparted to the universe.

Marx and Engels had openly conflicting views of Hegel and the universe. Marx's universe was anthropocentric. Engels's universe was cosmopocentric. Marx was a left-wing Hegelian who made man the center of his world, the laboring Prometheus. Engels was a right-wing Hegelian who made man the victim of universal motion, who saw in man something that did not act, but rather who was acted upon and shaped by forces totally external to him and totally beyond his control. Engels's proclivity to right-wing Hegelianism has already been noted.[32] As a young man, when Engels first came across Hegel, he interpreted Hegel as saying that the only thing that moved in the universe was Absolute Spirit; everything else in the universe, including man, was a mere appendage to Absolute Spirit. As a mature man, Engels was to say, in perfect consistency with his youthful frame of mind, that everything that moved in the universe, that which brought forth particulars and life, was matter and motion. Everything else, including man, was merely reflexes, reactions of this absolute motion.

The differences that divided Marx and Engels in their interpretation of Hegel also divided Marx and Engels in their interpretation of nature. In making the laws of nature themselves dialectical, Engels attempted something that Marx himself never attempted. For Marx, the dialectic was not in nature itself, but in the interaction between man and nature. The dialectical process for Marx was the motion of form and content; species being was the content for which nature was the form. Engelsism totally erased the subjectivist element. For Engels, the being of nature was dialectical, and all other existence proceeded from these laws.

The central idea that distinguished the Marxian from the Engelsian interpretation of nature was the notion of *praxis.* Whereas Marx spoke of a pregiven natural and social environment in which men coexisted and interpenetrated with the physical environment, Engels described a macrocosmic determinism in which thought was merely the epiphenomenon of physical forces. Marx referred to humanistic and dialectical naturalism, the belief that man modified the inorganic world, while Engels referred to a metaphysical monism, the belief that organic and inorganic existence were both reducible to a universal monosubstance. The Marxian vision was always on man who acted, while the Engelsian vision was on cosmological determinism. Marx was an immanist; Engels was an emanationist.

Epistemologically, also, wide differences existed between Marx and Engels. Characteristically, Engels approached the problem of knowledge in a basically simplistic fashion. He drew an absolute distinction between mind and matter. Those who asserted the primacy of matter were, according to Engels, materialistic. Those who asserted the primacy of mind or spirit were idealists.[33] Engels, then, created an absolutely polarized epistemological world. Consciousness and matter were dichotomous entities. There was no mixture, no interpenetration, no fusion of these two forces.

In "Ludwig Feuerbach and the End of Classical German Philosophy," Engels defined materialism as the belief that matter was not mind, but rather mind the product of matter.[34] It is not surprising, then, that Engels expounded a "copy theory" of the truth. Our ideas were mere replicas of external objects. Mind was essentially photographic film upon which the external world imprinted pictures of itself. Such an interpretation of knowledge was a direct consequence of the model from which Engels started. If man and nature were distinctive, the only way to obtain ideas of the external world was to have the external world imprint them onto man's consciousness.

Epistemologically, Marx came from an entirely different tradition from Engels. Again, Marx was a Hegelian. In short, he, like Hegel, tried to overcome the absolute separation of subject from object. Hegel transcended the Kantian and Lockean position that consciousness and the thing-in-itself were totally divorced. Knowledge, for Marx, was something created or attained through the practico-critical activity of man. Species being meant to be in a state of constant interchange between oneself and one's environment. Species being meant to interpenetrate with the world, to modify it, to fuse with it and therefore to humanize it.[35]

In effect, Engels did away with philosophy. He replaced philosophy with positive science. Because mind was simply a mirror image of the dialectical process of the external world, mind was a passive agent. What could affect the external world was not practico-critical activity, but rather empirical data. Knowledge of how the world functioned was more important than man's own approach to the world. Positive science took the place of critical consciousness.

This discussion of Engels's philosophy of nature has revealed weaknesses in his intellectual armory. Engels did not have an acute, analytic, precise mind. As a young man and as a student, Engels never received formal academic training in philosophy or any other discipline. He was not a trained scholar. His lack of ability to apply rigid and exacting standards of judgment was clearly demonstrated in his views of the physical universe. Engels misunderstood Hegel. He assumed he was applying the Hegelian dialectic to nature when in fact he was completely destroying that dialectic. Such misconceptions, such gross errors of interpretation reveal a mind not trained to rigors of philosophic thought, a mind unable to arrive at precise definitions, a mind unable to see distinctions. Engels had a tendency to see the similarity of things rather than their distinctiveness. He blurred difference, and thus tended to confuse ideas.

Engels's talent lay in the field of narrative and description. His writings on nature were not an analysis or critical examination of recent scientific discoveries, but rather an explication of these discoveries. Engels was a talented and sophisticated popularizer who, because of a lucid and clear style, could express complex ideas in a straightforward and comprehensible fashion. However, it was because of his talent for description, because of his talent for narrative, that Engels confused and misinterpreted more speculative ideas. He believed in similarity, rather than in surgery. He tended to synthesize, rather than to separate. Thus he was led into inexact formulation, hazy definition, and a lack of precise categorization.

Within his time, to his contemporaries Engels had performed a valuable service for the socialist movement. The late nineteenth century was a period of rapid scientific advancement, and Engels assumed the responsibility as well as the mission of offering a left interpretation of the burgeoning empirical data. Here again Engels's gift for popularization, for description proved of value to him. He summarized and evaluated; from a left perspective, he made available to the socialist movement the most important scientific discoveries of the nineteenth century. Engels thus buttressed socialist ideology. He imparted to the socialism of his day the theoretical and conceptual tools with which to interpret the plethora of scientific experimentation.

On the one hand, Engels had to respond to revival of idealism, Eügene Dühring, for example. This threat from the right was the lesser of two evils. There was enough scientific data to destroy any notions of Spirit, of eternal verities. The force theory of Dühring, even Treitschke could be negated by the class interpretation of society. The assigning of an independent and autonomous existence to the state, in the fashion of Burckhardt, could be dispelled through economic analysis.

Conversely, Engels had to respond to positivism. Engels's grasp of the science of his day was sound. He abandoned the corpuscular theory of matter. He saw electromagnetic fields the basic building blocks of the universe. He made Darwinism an accepted tenet of socialist philosophy. In these respects, he was ahead of his time. However, although he was aware of the rigidities of positivist thought, he ultimately failed to avoid them. In his letters of the 1890s to C. Schmidt and J. Bloch, Engels attempted to avoid the positivist simplification of the historical process. He drew attention to the role of ideas in history. He drew attention to the importance of social, as distinct from economic, forces in history. However, the inclusion of ideas and of the social amplified the picture but did not decide it. Indeed, Engels took note of the ideational but always concluded that in the last analysis economic and technological causality was primary. The sufficient conditions were always economic; the necessary conditions were both economic and ideational. Thus, although he made room for value, something other, more shortsighted positivists would not have done, Engels nevertheless ended as a positivist himself.

In the same way that Engels misinterpreted Hegel, so he misinterpreted Marx. His inability to exactly categorize, to make distinctions, led him to assume that his ideas and Marx's ideas ran parallel to each other. His penchant to seek out similarity led him to assume that he and Marx spoke in one voice. It is easy to understand why Engels never disclaimed or challenged any of Marx's ideas or writings. The real problem is to determine why Marx never disclaimed any of Engels's ideas, even when Engels misinterpreted his friend, as he had misinterpreted Hegel, and also Feuerbach.

Footnotes

1. Karl Marx and Friedrich Engels, *Selected Correspondence* (New York: International Publishers, 1942), pp. 113–114.
2. Friedrich Engels, *Anti-Dühring*, trans. Emile Burns (New York: International Publishers, 1966), p. 27.
3. Engels, *Dialectics of Nature*, trans. Clemens Dutt (New York: International Publishers, 1940), pp. 243–246.
4. Engels, "Ludwig Feuerbach and the End of Classical German Philosophy," *Karl Marx and Friedrich Engels: Selected Works* (New York: International Publishers, 1968), p. 607.
5. *Ibid.*, p. 621.
6. Engels, *Dialectics of Nature*, p. 26.
7. *Ibid.*
8. *Ibid.*, pp. 38–39.
9. *Ibid.*, p. 26.
10. Engels, *Anti-Dühring*, p. 150.
11. *Ibid.*, p. 149.
12. *Ibid.*, pp. 144–145.
13. *Ibid.*, p. 152.
14. *Ibid.*, p. 154.
15. *Ibid.*, p. 91.
16. *Ibid.*, p. 92.
17. Engels, *Dialectics of Nature*, p. 21.
18. Engels, "Socialism: Scientific and Utopian," *Karl Marx and Friedrich Engels: Selected Works*, p. 386.
19. Engels, "Ludwig Feuerbach and the End of Classical German Philosophy," *Karl Marx and Friedrich Engels: Selected Works*, p. 619.
20. Engels, "Socialism: Scientific and Utopian," *Ibid.*, p. 385.
21. Engels, *Dialectics of Nature*, p. 153.
22. Zbigniew Jordan, *The Evolution of Dialectical Materialism* (New York: St. Martins Press, 1967), p. 153.
23. G. W. F. Hegel, *The Philosophy of Mind*, trans. William Wallace (Oxford: Oxford University Press, 1970), p. 13.
24. *Ibid.*, p. 14.
25. *Ibid.*, p. 25.
26. *Ibid.*, p. 25.
27. *Ibid.*, p. 22.
28. *Ibid.*, p. 21.
29. Hegel, *The Phenomenology of Mind*, trans. J. B. Baillie (New York: Harper & Row, 1967), p. 85–86.
30. *Ibid.*, p. 86.
31. On the relationship between Marx and Hegel see the following works: Gunther Hillman, *Hegel und Marx* (Frankfurt: Suhrkamp Verlag, 1970); Paul Kaegi, *Genesis des historischen Materialismus* (Vienna: Europa-Verlag, 1965); Gottfried Stiehler, *Dialektik und Praxis* (Berlin: Akademie-Verlag, 1968). A book that does not concentrate on the epistemological relationship between Marx and Hegel, but which nevertheless offers illuminating insights into their connectedness, is Jean Hyppolite, *Studies on Marx and Hegel* (New York: Basic Books, 1969).
32. Refer to Chapter Eight for the fuller analysis of Engels's right-wing Hegelianism.

33. Engels, "Ludwig Feuerbach and the End of Classical German Philosophy," *Karl Marx and Friedrich Engels: Selected Works, p. 604.*
34. *Ibid.*, p. 607.
35. There is a growing body of work that focuses upon the epistemological problem in Marxism. The more outstanding are: Ernst Bloch, *Über Karl Marx* (Frankfurt: Suhrkamp Verlag, 1968); Nicholas Lobkowicz, *Theory and Practice* (Notre Dame, Indiana: University of Notre Dame Press, 1967); Karl Löwith, *Die Hegelische Linke* (Stuttgart: Europäische Verlag, 1962); Alfred Schmidt, *Beitrage Zur Marxistischen Erkenntnistheorie* (Frankfurt: Suhrkamp Verlag, 1969); Nathan Rotenstreich, *Basic Problems of Marx's Philosophy* (Indianapolis: World Books, 1965).

Ten

The Origins of Economic Determinism

BASED UPON THE preceding discussion of Engels's philosophy of nature, it is logical to expect his philosophy of history to be equally deterministic. Such was indeed the case. The internal rationality of Engels's thought moved from a mechanistic materialist view of the universe to a deterministic view of human history. This chapter will demonstrate that it was Engels, not Marx, who was the originator of economic determinism. It will also demonstrate that what Engels meant by economics was really invention, machinery, tools.

Human history, for Engels, had moved on a global scale through a fixed series of evolutionary stages. All societies, regardless of location, must evolve in a four-stage sequence: from primitive communism to feudalism to capitalism to communism. Engels recognized that there could be local variations to this pattern. Although the general law would always predominate at the end, there could be specific modifications during this inevitable development. Engels was a unilinear evolutionist.

In *The Origin of the Family, Private Property and the State,* Engels attempted to solve two interrelated problems, the rise of monogamy and the rise of the state.[1] Engels received most of his factual data on these matters from the notes that Marx took on the book *Ancient Society* by the famous American anthropologist Lewis Henry Morgan. From both the Marx notes and some other reading Engels did on the primitive condition of mankind, Engels learned that before monogamous society had come into being, gentile society had existed. The gentile organization of society was based on mother-right; descent was traced through the matriarchal line. The *gens* was composed of all those children who could claim descent from a common mother. Within the *gens,* property was owned communally. Furthermore, political life within the *gens* was highly democratic, with decisions arrived at by an entire assemblage of the *gens.* In effect the *gens* was a primitive form of communism, where private property did not exist, where direct participatory democracy was practiced, and where both practices were direct consequences of the matriarchal constitution, kinship through the female.

The problem that Engels tried to resolve was the mechanisms by which gentile society had been overthrown. He sought to account for the destruction of matriarchal society, and the coming into being of a monogamous society based on the rights of the father. The origin of patriarchic monogamy was solely due, in Engels's eyes, to the acquisition of private property.[2] As soon as the male won exclusive possession over property, possession of the herds (arising out of the division of labor where women did agricultural work and men pastured the herd), the male had to invent a form of marriage that would insure that his inheritance would pass to his sons alone, father-right, partriarchic monogamy. The causal factor in the destruction of the gentile constitution, according to Engels, was economic. The revolutionizing force was property, or a material, productive social agent.

Engels used the same line of argument when he tried to solve his second problem, the origin of the state. The determining factor in the rise of the state was also economic. Engels accounted for the rise of the Athenian and Roman states as a two–stage development. Patriarchic monogamy arose from the basis of private property, and the state arose from the basis of patriarchic monogamy. The state and male domination, two kinds of authoritarianism, were coexistent. The state developed because the gentile constitution could no longer reconcile the differences that had developed within itself. Economic conditions had compelled the *gens* to split into rich and poor. A third force was needed to suppress the open conflict between propertied and propertyless classes.[3] This third force was the state, an organ of repression to be used in the interest of the wealthy.[4]

Engels, however, did not limit his investigations to the overthrow of the gentile order, or the birth of the state in Greece. He was seeking a more universal law. He was attempting to discover a general principle for the development of the family on a worldwide basis. In *The Origin of the Family, Private Property and the State,* Engels outlined an anthropological parallelism. He attempted to show how the "three principal forms of marriage" perfectly corresponded "to the three principal stages of human development."[5] In the period of savagery man lived a basically tribal and nomadic existence, and in this stage group marriage was practiced. In the period of barbarism man learned to domesticate animals and undertake agriculture, and in this stage the gentile constitution was in practice. Lastly, in the period of civilization man developed some technological and industrial skills, and in this stage the monogamous family came to be the norm. At all times, however, the form of the family, the most nuclear human social relationship, was dependent upon a definite stage of human productivity.

In *The Origin*, then, Engels outlined a three-stage developmental pattern for the human family that was applicable on a universal scale. Engels thus demonstrated that he was a unilinear evolutionist. He maintained that it was a universal law that a certain stage of economic development would produce a certain form of family structure. The following passage from *The Origin* clearly illustrates this point:

> But chance is only the one pole of a relation whose other pole is named "necessity". In the world of nature, where chance also seems to rule, we have long since demonstrated in each separate field the inner necessity and law asserting itself in this chance. But what is true of the natural world is true also of society. The more a social activity, a series of social processes, becomes too powerful for men's conscious control and grows above their heads, and the more it appears a matter of pure chance, then all the more surely within this chance the laws peculiar to it and inherent in it assert themselves as if by natural necessity. Such laws also govern the changes of commodity production and exchange to the individuals producing or exchanging, they appear as alien and at first often unrecognized powers, whose nature must first be laboriously investigated and established. These economic laws of commodity production are modified with the various stages of this form of production; but in general the whole period of civilization is dominated by them.[6]

When Engels wrote of the economic, the center of gravity of that definition was always the technological. Machinery, social productivity were the most important forces in all societies. Therefore, as the tools and industrial infrastructure of society changed, so the form of the family of necessity changed. As technology and economic productivity moved through various stages of development, so social forms and customs evolved through corresponding unilinear stages.

Engels manifested the same group of principles when he speculated on the nature of history in *Anti-Dühring.* In this book he interpreted the human past from the perspective of six principles to which he was unalterably bound: (1) The necessary causal agent for economic and social evolution was technological change; (2) technological change proceeded in a deterministic and necessary fashion; (3) economic and social change paralleled, conformed to, and was dependent upon technological change; (4) since technological change was deterministic and necessary, so social change must be deterministic and necessary; (5) all societies must conform to a general line of evolution, a unilinear path of development; (6) these rules of historical development are natural laws of the physical universe. These six principles taken together constitute what Engels understood as Marxism.

In Part Two, Chapter III, of *Anti-Dühring,* Engels briefly sketched some of the more important military events of western Europe from the fourteenth century until the Franco-Prussian War of 1870–1871. In the fourteenth century gunpowder was introduced by the Arabs to western

Europe. With gunpowder came cannon and firearms, and the political relations of domination and subjection in the feudal world were completely altered. The thick castle walls of the nobility were no longer impregnable, and the armor-clad cavalry of the feudal barons could be pierced. Armed with cannon and musket, the bourgeoisie could support their political claims with military power. In the early nineteenth century the column replaced the rigid, mathematical line formations of the eighteenth century. The column imparted speed and maneuverability to military strategy, both tactics being exploited to the fullest by Napoleon Bonaparte. But before the column could become a reality, two technological inventions were necessary. Gribeauval invented lighter carriages for field guns, and this increased their capacity for rapid movement; and the slanting of the butt on rifles greatly increased their accuracy. Prussia was the next country to make a military breakthrough. The breech-loading rifle, which it perfected between 1830 and 1860, enormously increased the firepower and the accuracy of the infantry.[7]

In describing some of the military turning points in the history of Europe since the eleventh century, Engels clearly made technological change the most important agent of this development. He wrote that nothing was "more dependent on economic pre-conditions than precisely the army and navy."[8] But here Engels showed that he was prone to use terms inaccurately. He showed that he often used terms without defining them with perfect distinction, and thereby confused and muddled his argument. It was not economics that formed the precondition of the army or navy; it was, rather, invention, mechanics. The history of warfare was the history of "instruments, the more perfect of which vanquish the less perfect."[9] Later on in the same chapter Engels affirmed that in case after case "advances in technique . . . produced changes in the methods of warfare."[10] Indeed, force could not be force without machinery, because it was the "instruments of force which help 'force' to victory."[11] Lastly, the late nineteenth-century warship was itself an offshoot of the industrial revolution, "a specimen of modern large-scale industry."[12]

Just as invention had determined the evolution of warfare, so invention had determined the evolution of private property. In the *Anti-Dühring*, Engels offered an account of the evolution of property throughout the world. "All civilized peoples begin with the common ownership of the land."[13] Engels had alluded to this primitive stage of human development in *The Origin*. In that work he had characterized this primitive stage as one in which men learned to domesticate animals and to undertake agriculture in settled communities. It was the period of the gentile constitution, the period of familial communism. When "all peoples"[14] passed through this primitive stage, common ownership of land proved to be a hindrance to increased production. Common ownership was consequently negated and transformed into private property. In *The Origin* Engels had also referred to this second stage of development, characterizing it as the period of civilization. Men in this period had developed some basic technological and industrial skills. Men, because of the divisions of labor that sent them out of the household, won exclusive control over productive property, that is, herds and lands. Once the male had gained domination over property, he also brought partriarchic monogamy into existence. The third stage in the history of property was the period of the communist revolution. Capitalist private property, in its turn, now proved a deterrent to increased productivity and therefore would have to be abolished and transcended into a higher form of communal ownership.[15]

The laws of the social universe were similar in invariability and predictability to the laws that functioned in the physical universe. "But this distinction important as it is for historical investigation, particularly of single epochs and events, cannot alter the fact that the course of history is governed by inner general laws."[16] In fact, Engels maintained that the transformation of primitive communal property into private property was an illustration of the law of the negation of the negation, one of the primary dialectical laws of the cosmos. Thus Engels paralleled the physical universe to the social universe. Just as it had been possible to discover the three basic laws of the natural world, so it would be possible to discover the basic laws of history. Just as it could be shown that the three basic laws of nature functioned mechanistically, so it could be shown that the laws of history necessitated a unilinear evolutionary pattern of growth. Engels's metaphysics of nature had concluded in a metaphysics of history.

Even into the 1890s, in the years just before his death, Engels continued to affirm that technology was the most important agent in history. In a famous letter to H. Starkenburg, written on January 25, 1894, Engels sought to explain his view of history:

> What we understand by the economic conditions which we regard as the determining basis of the history of society are the methods by which human beings in a given society produce their means of subsistence and exchange the products among themselves (in so far as division of labor exists). Thus the *entire technique* of production and transport is here included. According to our conception this technique also determines the method of exchange and further, the division of products, and with it, after the dissolution of tribal society, the division into classes also and hence the relations of lordship and servitude and with them the state, politics, law, etc."[17]

In the paragraph above Engels affirmed that productive technology was the root influence upon society. The underlying forces of societal change were the "methods" by which individuals provided for their sustenance, and Engels also found "*technique*" to be the determining agent for legal relations and politics, the societal superstructure. Society, for Engels, was an inclusive term encompassing ideas, institutions, economics. Nevertheless, in the last analysis when Engels was seeking the final denominator for economic movement, his vision always fell upon the tools, the instruments and the machinery of a given society. The "method of exchange," "the division of products," "the relation of lordship and servitude" were always derivative from technique, from instruments.

A similar note was struck by Engels in his September 22, 1892, letter to Danielson. In this letter Engels was speculating upon the course of development of Russian history. Engels wrote:

> Now I maintain, that industrial production nowadays means *grande industrie,* steam, electricity, self-acting mules, powerlooms, finally machines that produce machinery. From the day Russia introduced railways, the introduction of these modern means of production was a foregone conclusion. . . . if Russia required after the Crimean War a *grande industrie* of her own, she could have it in one form only: the capitalist form and along with that form she was obliged to take over all the consequences which accompany capitalistic *grande industrie* in all other countries.[18]

In the above paragraph Engels clearly showed that by industry he did not mean a social relationship, but simply machinery. It is clear that Engels understood society to be a complex and multifaced entity. Men's ideas and legal arrangements, political factors must always be recognized and accounted for when explaining the movement of history. Nevertheless, for Engels, industry was "steam, electricity, self-acting mules, powerlooms, finally machines that produce machinery." The introduction into a country of one such industrial instrument, i.e., the railroad, made it a "foregone conclusion" that the whole plethora of industrial tools would be introduced into that country. In terms of Russia, *grande industrie* required a capitalist form. The introduction of machinery in Russia must produce capitalism. With capitalism and with industry, a proletariat and social misery must also come to Russia. The process was an inevitable one: technology produced capitalism; technology produced a proletariat; and capitalist technology produced mass pauperization.

Having uncovered the basic principles of Engels's view of social development, we can now apply them to two case studies: the history of Germany and the history of Russia. If the foregoing analysis has been correct, if Engels was indeed a social determinist, then we would expect to find that Engels felt both Germany and Russia must follow a unilinear path of evolution, must follow the classical pattern of growth as illustrated by England. It would be expected that Engels saw Germany as having been an underdeveloped country—a country to which the Industrial Revolution came late, but a country that at the end of the nineteenth century had risen to the leadership of the European socialist movement because the industrialization and capitalization of Germany had been so thorough and deep. In fact, these were exactly Engels's beliefs. It would be expected that Engels saw Russia as another illustration of a backward country, a country that must follow the path of development of England and western Europe generally, a country that must expect that its ancient agrarian commune, the *mir,* would of necessity be destroyed. Such, in fact, was exactly Engels's belief. In short, Engels's interpretation of German and Russian history conformed perfectly to his social positivism.

At the dawn of the modern era, economic conditions in Germany were not as advanced as those of England, France, and Low Countries. By the beginning of the sixteenth century, western Europe had already assumed the productive and industrial leadership of European civilization generally. German agriculture lagged behind English and Dutch output. German industry trailed that of the English, the Flemish, and the French. The German population was very sparse. In England and France, commercial and industrial growth had worked to socially and politically centralize these countries. Germany, on the other hand, because of its retarded economic development, remained decentralized. Civilization in Germany existed in isolated areas, in scattered centers of industry and commerce. The economic backwardness of Germany strengthened the provincial and local regions, and thus acted as the social foundation for the political power of the German princes. Engels maintained, in brief, that the origin of German particularism, its developmental stagnation at the level of feudalism, derived from Germany's aborted and delayed economic advancement.[19]

The class structure of sixteenth-century Germany mirrored the economic underdevelopment of central Europe. Nobility and clergy were still the dominant classes. The new sixteenth-century princes had emerged directly out of the old medieval baronry. The new princes had evolved from, had taken the place of, and had adopted the same social and political attitudes as the old baronry. They were simply up-to-date replicas of the bygone feudal lords.

In the cities, the dominant class stemmed from the great patrician families, the richest of the town dwellers. They held all the city offices and arbitrarily administered all the revenues of the city. They formed, in fact, a financial and commercial autocracy. The opposition to domination came from a "middle class opposition,"[20] came from the commercial and financial class of moderate means. This middle class opposition wanted to participate in the urban legislative process, wanted to share control over the finances of the city. "This moderate, law-abiding, well-off and intelligent opposition"[21] fulfilled the same historic role as the constitutional party during the revolutionary movement of 1848–1849. Indeed, the constitutional party of 1848 was the direct "heir" of the "middle class opposition" of the sixteenth century. Similar to the case of the princes, Engels believed that the constitutional opposition of 1848 had evolved from, taken the place of, and adopted the same political role as the "middle class opposition" of the sixteenth century. Again, Engels had simply paralleled the middle class dissidents of 1848 to those of 1525 and assumed that the nineteenth-century version had evolved from its sixteenth-century precursor, and that both had demanded the same political reforms.

The plebeian opposition to the patrician oligarchy came from the members of former feudal organizations. Cast-off masters from broken guild societies helped make up the plebeian opposition. Journeymen and apprentices were another source of recruitment. Financially ruined members of the middle classes were a third source of supply. It was this plebeian opposition, basically from the broken remnants of guild organizations, that Engels saw as the precursor of the modern proletariat. In the context of the peasant wars of the sixteenth century, this plebeian opposition followed the political leadership of the "middle class opposition." In doing this, it played a similar role to the petite bourgeoisie of 1848. In that revolutionary epoch the petite bourgeoisie had also supported the moderate middle classes. Even though the modern industrial proletariat, according to Engels, emerged from the destroyed guild institutions, the bourgeoisie of 1848 and the plebeians of 1525 both allied themselves with the bourgeoisie, thus following an ultimately reactionary policy and thus separating themselves from the revolutionary peasantry as well as from the revolutionary proletariat. Engels again drew an exact parallel between lower middle class activity in 1525 and 1848.[22]

This discussion of Engels's analysis of German class structure in the sixteenth century is important for two reasons. First, it illustrated Engels's method of social analysis. This method can best be described as a search for parallelism, as a search for recurrence. Engels was obviously struck by the fact that opposition to the existing aristocratic order both in 1848 and in 1525 seemingly sprang from middle class groups and also from plebeian or petty bourgeois groups. By paralleling these two events, by juxtaposing one picture of a historical event against another picture of a historical event and by noticing a class that appeared to be similar in both pictures, Engels was too easily led to conclude that the modern bourgeoisie evolved directly from the Reformation bourgeoisie and that both historic middle classes had made exactly parallel political and social demands. From the purely logical point of view, both conclusions are wrong or at least unfounded. From the empirical point of view, Engels did not support either conclusion with persuasive or incontestable historical documentation.

The search for recurrence formed the basis for Engels's interpretation of class warfare. In every historical period there were movements of dissent. Given the fact that from Roman times down to the nineteenth century some form of aristocratic order had prevailed in Europe, it was not surprising that the middle layers of society wished to increase their political and economic privileges. It was also not surprising that throughout this long span of Western history and alongside the demands of the middle layers, there also developed more extreme demands, demands that were expressive of the interests of the less fortunate in society. However, because of Engels's tendency to think in terms of absolute recurrence, he was led to the invalid assumption that the reformist demands of the middle layers of society were always illustrations of middle class opposition and that the more extreme demands of the less fortunate in society were always illustrations of proletarian opposition. In other words, Engels's search for absolute parallelism forced him to impose a middle class–proletarian pattern on history. Class struggle in history, seen from the perspective of Engels's parallelism, must always conform to the aristocratic–middle class–proletarian pattern. It was a triadic vision of European dissent.

Engels's style of composition confirms the impression that Engels in an *a priori* fashion tried to subsume all social dissent under the aristocratic–middle class–proletarian model. Engels's work in history was never based upon original research. The factual data for his *The Peasant War in Germany* was derived entirely from one secondary source, Wilhelm Zimmermann's *The History of the Great Peasant War*, published in 1841. The anthropological data for his *The Origin of the Family, Private Property and the State* was taken almost completely from Marx's notes on Lewis Morgan's *Ancient Society*. His *Revolution and Counter-Revolution* was merely a compendium of newspaper articles he wrote for the *New York Daily Tribune*, and was inspired predominantly by his personal experiences during the 1848–1849 revolutions. Engels did not write history from documents. He was not an empirical historian, sifting through a welter of evidence in order to arrive at a scientific and private synthesis. Engels's talent lay in exposition. Fortified with a lucid style, Engels was an excellent narrator. He did not present a new vision but rather offered a readable exposition of complex events. It was, in essence, superior journalism.

Engels also saw his mission in life to be and his abilities best expressed in the application of the Marxian dialectical method as he understood that method. In the realm of the natural sciences Engels sought to apply dialectics to physics, chemistry, and biology. In the same way, Engels sought to apply the dialectical method to past epochs of history. What resulted from this application was merely the superimposition of the aristocratic-bourgeois-proletarian model on all past history. His history, then, did not expose the unique. We are not confronted with nuances. We are not shown the differences between the late feudal middle classes and the modern capitalistic middle classes. We are not shown the different mechanisms of social domination, of exploitation in the sixteenth and nineteenth centuries, and thus we are left uninformed as to the differences in social relationship, in social meaning, in the comparative sociology of master-slave interrelations. Engels did not submit proof, but rather a formula. He accepted the Marxian triadic model, which Marx reserved for and restricted to the nineteenth century, and which Engels sought to universalize that formula.

For example, Engels's method of parallelism, the juxtaposing of an unemployed journeyman beside a factory worker, predisposed him to see the modern proletarian as a direct outgrowth of the sixteenth-century workingman. Engels's history of the rise of the modern working class was different from Marx's analysis.

Marx never equated capitalism with materiality. "Money and commodities are not, from the first, capital,"[23] he wrote in *Das Kapital.* Tools, factories, the entire technique of production, rates of interest, the credit system, were not in themselves sufficient to produce a capitalist system. Capitalism was not a thing, an object, it was a social relationship. The peculiar meaning, according to Marx, of capitalist social relationships was domination due to the purchase of labor. Capitalism was the commodization of labor and therefore the subjection of the individual laborer.

In order, then, for a full capitalist society to come into existence, the great mass of the population must be separated from the opportunity to produce their own sustenance. They must be divorced from the tools of production and be driven to sell their labor, thus life, on the marketplace: be proletarianized. In Marx's account, recruitment into the ranks of the proletariat followed an "agricultural revolution."[24] Capitalism in the West developed only after the massive and forcible migrations of the "agricultural revolution." The peasant, the serf, must be separated from the soil and come to the city in the guise of a commodity. For Marx the industrial proletariat was recruited from the displaced agricultural worker. For Engels, the industrial proletariat evolved directly out of ruined guild members.

Furthermore, Marx never argued by parallelism. In the *Grundrisse,* Marx devoted many pages to a discussion of Asiatic, primitive Russian, or slave societies. He did so not only to discover the immanent economic relationships of these societies, but also the essential economic relationship, by comparison, of capitalist society. Economic relationships differed greatly from society to society, and the people who were caught in those economic relationships also differed. Marx was not simply concerned with the general category of underprivileged, the pauper. He was more concerned with the uniqueness, the separateness of the poor under the economic relationship of feudalism as compared to the poor under a totally different economic relationship known as capitalism. It would never have occurred to Marx that the feudal poor would act in the same way, or think in the same terms as the capitalist poor.

From the perspective of Engels's vision of German history, the coming of the Reformation into an economically backward Germany, into a Germany with its singular class and political structure, culminated in the further decentralization of the country. Ultimately, according to Engels, the princes were the chief victors of the Reformation and after the peasant wars in Germany the *Kleinstaaterei* took a three-hundred-year hold on the country. Engels's hero in the peasant wars was Thomas Muenzer. He was not only the religious radical, but the revolutionary leader. The man who symbolized compromise, who allowed himself to be co-opted by the princes, was Martin Luther. When Luther turned his back on the peasantry in 1525, his treachery worked only to strengthen the domination of the feudal aristocracy.[25]

Engels maintained that the "parallel between the German Revolutions of 1525 and of 1848–9 was too obvious to be left entirely without attention."[26] In both instances the upper and middle bourgeoisie joined with the nobility to suppress the revolutionaries. The long history of bourgeois reaction, of bourgeois opposition to the proletariat was thus established. Both in 1848 and 1525 the petty bourgeoisie proved an untrustworthy ally of the revolutionary elements. Engels said of the petty bourgeoisie that "this class is entirely unreliable"[27] and more often than not would join with the enemies of the revolution. Similarly, the proletariat and the peasantry were disunified in 1848 and 1525, and Engels wrote *The Peasant War in Germany* as a plea for the unity of peasant and worker in the next German revolution.

Just as Germany was not ripe for revolution in 1525, so she was not ripe for revolution in 1848. Again, the cause was industrial backwardness. Indeed, industry had grown rapidly in Germany after 1815, and the *Zollverein* helped the spread of manufacture. Nevertheless, German manufacture still trailed that of England and France. Consequently, the bourgeoisie was also less advanced and powerful in Germany than either in England or in France. In England, the middle classes had conquered political power in 1688, while in France they had conquered power in 1789. In Germany the middle classes were still excluded from the exercise of political power.

The industrial backwardness of Germany not only retarded the development of the German manufacturing and commercial classes, but also that of the German proletariat. Again the German proletariat was far behind that of England and France. But the spread of the working class movement could never be complete until after the conquest of power by the bourgeoisie. The future success of the proletariat was dependent upon the present success of the bourgeoisie. It was only after the more progressive wing of the bourgeoisie, the large manufacturers, took political power and fashioned the state in accordance with their own needs that a large working class would develop and the "inevitable conflict" between employer and employee become "imminent."[28]

The chief culprits in the defeat of the 1848–1849 revolution were the middle classes and the petty bourgeoisie. The middle classes, frightened by the thunder from the left, allied themselves to the aristocracy. Thereby, they succeeded in destroying the proletarian revolution, but they also succeeded in destroying their own chances for power. The aristocracy again emerged in 1848 as it had in 1525 as the chief victors of the revolution, and the German bourgeoisie was to continue as before, a politically powerless class, a class that would fulfill its role as an addendum to the feudality. Because of this bourgeois failure, Germany would never experience a liberal revolution.

The chief victims of the debacle of 1848 were, of course, the German proletarian and, of equal importance, German nationalism. Since the bourgeoisie in England and France had been the driving force of English and French nationalism, and since the German bourgeoisie remained an appendage of the Teutonic nobility, it was not surprising that Germany itself remained divided along the lines of princely *Kleinstaaterei.* In 1848, the revolutionary proletariat was perhaps the main driving force for national unity, but its defeat was also the defeat of national unification. Thus, the cause of German nationalism did not reach fulfillment in either its bourgeois form or its proletarian form. The cause of nationalism in Germany must wait therefore for Junkerdom to co-opt it for the purpose of monarchical preservation.[29]

Just as the force of Italian nationalism could not be stopped in 1859, so the force of German nationalism was not completely destroyed by the defeat of 1848. Rather, its principal agent changed from the German bourgeoisie to the Prussian aristocracy. The war of 1866, a civil war, witnessed the end of the German Confederation and the beginning of the end of German *Kleinstaaterei*—"1866 was a complete revolution."[30] German dualism was destroyed and Prussian hegemony established in central Europe. Bismarck had usurped but nevertheless fulfilled the historic task of the bourgeoisie.

In terms of political realism, however, it was only Prussia who could play Savoy, it was only Prussia that possessed the needed military power and national coherence to achieve unification. The liberal-democratic road had proven to be a failure. "German unity under Austria's wing was a romantic dream,"[31] as Austria was both bound to the petty princes as well as too deeply involved in the Balkans. Only the third way remained—unification under Prussia. This position had been advocated by Engels as early as 1842.[32] In 1866 he was to see its political realization. His excellent sense of political realism was confirmed. Engels's basic criticism of the accomplishment of 1866 was that Bismarck had not been revolutionary enough. Since the revolution had come from the top it had only been half a revolution, and Bismarck's creation had not destroyed the aristocracy but rather subsumed them under the Prussian Empire.[33]

Not only had the German bourgeoisie seen its mission preempted by its aristocratic enemy, but it had also witnessed its constitutional mission destroyed by that same enemy. Force had made the North German Confederation, and force had also made the Bismarckian constitution of 1866. What emerged from all these events was not the old Prussian Frederickian state, nor the Manchester state of England. What emerged was something else, the Bonapartist state, which first took historical form under Napoleon III.

According to Engels, the Bonapartist state was Bismarck's gift to Germany after the Revolution of 1871. Ever the political realist, Engels, although he understood the reactionary nature of the Bismarckian settlement, nevertheless felt that the Hohenzollern denouncement was a progressive step within the politico-social conditions of central Europe.

The victory of 1871 was merely the logical outcome of a process that had begun in 1848. The incapacity of the German bourgeoisie simply meant that Bismarck had completed their historic mission for them. The Prussian Empire had uprooted the relics of feudalism in central Europe. National unity had been achieved. It was Engels's belief that no widespread workers' movement, no true proletarian revolutionary movement, could make headway in Germany without the existence of a national state. Bismarck, for Engels, was both victor and dupe. He was victor because he had preempted the mission of the bourgeoisie; he was dupe because he unwittingly created the fundamental prerequisites for a proletariat movement.

Although national unity had been achieved, the Revolution of 1871 had not been a national revolution. It had proceeded on the basis of monarchical imperialism. After 1866 Germany had become a protectorate of Prussia. In 1871, Prussia had simply annexed the remaining portions of Germany. The Prussian Crown had militarily imposed unity, and through that military imposition had Prussianized Germany.

From the diplomatic point of view, it was Engels's belief that the basic flaw in the new Prussian Empire had been the incorporation of Alsace-Lorraine. By means of that acquisition, Bismarck had sown the seeds of future war. French animosity toward Germany was now a given. France must seek an ally. German annexation of Alsace-Lorraine had driven France into the arms of Russia. Furthermore, a Franco-Russian alliance made Russia the arbiter of Europe. Because of her military potential, in possession of an ally in western Europe, Russia would emerge as the dominant power on the continent. Russian dominance on the continent also meant the dominance of the forces of conservatism. The Prussian conquest of Germany had brought unity to Germany, but not diplomatic stability to Europe.

In Engels's eyes, the Franco-Prussian War had another important consequence. The center of the European labor movement had shifted to Germany. The defeat of the Paris Commune, the lack of real trade union militance in England, the rapid industrialization of Germany, meant that the center of European socialism lay in Germany. The German workers had demonstrated their proletarian idealism by forthrightly denouncing the annexation of Alsace-Lorraine. They had wanted peace without annexation, although defending Germany and recognizing Napoleon III as the aggressor in the war of 1870. For all these reasons, plus the fact that the German working class was rapidly increasing numerically, Germany after 1871 had become the vanguard of the European proletarian movement.[34]

Engels's description of the course of German history was determinist. It was deterministic because the lateness of the liberal revolution in Germany derived from the retarded economic growth of Germany. The weakness of the German bourgeoisie derived from the weakness, in the first half of the century, of German industry. The failures of the German bourgeoisie in 1848 and 1866 were therefore deducible from the thinness and paucity of German technological development. The constitutional debacle of the liberals in 1870–1871 was also predicated upon the technological backwardness of Germany. But after 1870 industrial growth mushroomed through Germany. It mushroomed from the cities to the countryside, and therefore surpassed in thoroughness and intensity the industrialization of England and France; consequently there were more German workers, and the German labor movement assumed the leadership of the West.[35]

Germany had imitated the pattern of development of France and England. Of course, there was a certain uniqueness to German history. Germany developed later than England and France. Because of this late development, German unification differed from that of England and France. Certain specific laws of development could coexist inside the unilinear pattern. But the general line of development recapitulated the French and English experience. Technology had required Germany to have a liberal revolution, even though a belated one. Technology required Germany to achieve national unity, even though belated. Technology required Germany to experience the conflict between proletariat and bourgeoisie; even though the bourgeois elements had amalgamated with aristocratic elements, Germany had copied the pattern of the west European countries.[36]

The ideas and attitudes Engels applied to the study of German history he also applied to the analysis of Russian society. Just as Engels concluded that Germany must follow the path of Western development, so Engels believed that Russia too must copy the developmental pattern of the West.

After defeat in the Crimean War, even the Czar realized that Russia must be modernized. In 1861, the emancipation of the serfs opened the dikes to social reform. Expectantly, western European as well as Russian socialists began to speculate on when and how revolution would come to Imperial Russia. However, the Russian populists felt that the *mir*, a village commune, could serve as the basis for an immediate transition to communism after the Czar had been overthrown. Maintaining that it was not necessary for Russia to move from feudalism to capitalism to communism, the *narodniks* were considered by Engels to be anti-Marxists since they did not understand dialectical materialism, since Russia would indeed necessarily have to pass from feudalism to capitalism to communism. The path to communism could only move in a monodevelopmental line.

The *mir* for Engels did not possess unqualified virtue. In fact, Engels assumed that it represented a lower stage in the development of civilization.[37] Similar thoughts were expressed by Engels as late as 1894[38] in his concluding remarks to *Sociales aus Russland*, where Engels indicated that the Russian village commune was merely a vestige of the ancient gentile constitution. But the gentile system had either already been overthrown, or was in the process of decay all over the world. For instance, the *gens* had been eradicated in Europe. Its place had been taken by the capitalist order. Just as in *The Origin of the Family, Private Property and the State*, Engels could say that the "gentile constitution was absolutely irreconcilable with money economy," so he could argue that the *mir* would be inevitably destroyed by industrial capitalism.[39]

The Russian *narodniks* were wrong, and Engels never tired of making this point. But one detects in Engels's assault upon the populists not merely a squabble over socialist theory and dogma. This was not a Marxian internecine struggle. Rather, one hears overtones of Engels anti-Slavism. Engels accused the *narodniks* of being Pan-Slavist. Engels hated Pan-Slavism, seeing it as a tool of Czarist imperialism. But he also hated Pan-Slavism because it was a form of Slavic imperial nationalism. There is, then, in this struggle between the German Engels and Slavic *narodniks*, the ancient antipathy between Teuton and Slav badly disguised in the form of dialectical materialism.

Not only was it necessary to have capitalism before communism, but for Engels it was also just as indispensable for a bourgeois and proletarian class to exist before communism became a realistic possibility.

> This requires not only a proletariat that carries out this revolution, but also a bourgeoisie in whose hands the productive forces of society have developed so far that they allow of the final destruction of class distinctions. . . . The bourgeoisie, therefore, in this respect also is just as necessary a condition of the socialist revolution as the proletariat itself. Hence a man who will say that this revolution can be more easily carried out in a country, because, although it has no proletariat, it has not bourgeoisie either, only proves that he has still to learn the ABC of socialism.[40]

Only the industrial proletariat could produce communism. Only the industrial proletariat, because of the wage slavery it had suffered, had attained a communist consciousness. That is, because of capitalist exploitation, only a proletarian revolution could be a communist revolution. However, the proletariat itself was a product of large-scale industry. The existence, then, of the bourgeoisie was a necessary precondition for the existence of the proletariat. It was the historic task of the bourgeoisie to develop the factory system to a high capacity, and thus create those conditions that gave rise to the industrial working class. Engels's monodevelopmentalism was thus composed of three stages. On the historic level, all societies must pass from private communism to feudalism to capitalism. From the perspective of social classes, and corresponding exactly with the three prior historic stages, all societies must undergo the class rule of the *gens*, the aristocracy, and the bourgeoisie. Only after this third stage had been completed, only after capitalism and the bourgeoisie-proletariat class conflict existed, was it possible to advance to the fourth stage, the stage of communism and a classless society.

Engels was aware, of course, that in the nineteenth century, Russia was ready for revolution. The Crimean War had been a turning point. It had forced Russia to seek to overcome her backwardness by capitalist industrialization and compelled her to free the serfs. Both events were severely straining the traditional structure of Russia, and were indeed bringing the Czarist system to the point of collapse. The revolution in Russia, according to Engels, would not be a communist revolution. Russia did not possess a fully developed capitalist system nor a large proletariat and thus could not progress to the fourth stage of evolution. But a Russian revolution in the East would spark a proletarian revolution in the West. Although Russia was not ready for communism, a Russian revolution would precipitate a communist revolution in the West where conditions were ripe for a proletarian uprising.[41]

Only after a successful communist revolution in the West could the Russian revolution advance to communism. A Western communist revolution was a necessary precondition for a Russian communist revolution. The technological skills, the industrial power, the proletarian consciousness of the West were needed in order to direct, to help support Russia on its path to communism. In this sense, a communist society must be imported to Russia. While the beginning of revolution in Russia would be indigenous, the creation of a communist society in Russia would come from outside. In his thinking on the possibilities of revolution in Russia, Engels also worked within a unilinear framework. Backward countries must follow the path of the West, must imitate the stages of development already traversed by the more advanced, the higher civilization of western Europe.

By using Germany and Russia as case studies, Engels's understanding of the historic process has been clarified. Engels viewed history as a deterministic, unilinear evolutionary process. The basic, primary motivating force in all societies was technological growth. Using technological growth as a measure, societies could be ranked on the evolutionary scale from lower to higher. Because the logic of technological invention was additive, sequential, there existed in history a necessary order of development of technology and therefore a necessary order for societies as well. As technology advanced, societies would deterministically move up the evolutionary ladder from primitive communism to feudalism to capitalism to communism. The part of the world to first embark upon this necessary order of development was western Europe.

This was, of course, the general march of world history. But Engels was aware that local, specific variations could exist. Clearly, the specific histories and destinies of Russia and Germany varied. Thus Engels's theory allowed for temporary, local differentiation. In terms of the concrete historical moment, societal uniqueness and distinctiveness were present. Marxism, Engels asserted, was not a formula. The point at issue here, however, is the overall movement and progress of history. Engels believed Russia and Germany would inevitably become communist: each in its own way. The general pattern of history, then, was given, and in broad terms it was a system of inevitable stages of evolution.

By the 1890s Engels's major work lay behind him. His creative energies were spent. Yet he had reached the apogee of his fame. He carried on a voluminous correspondence, responding to people who had requested further clarification of his ideas, people who assumed that Engels's ideas were exactly similar to Marx's ideas. The letters of the 1890s were the letters of an old man who was reviewing a lifetime of work and effort. They might be seen as reminiscences, as a summary or introduction to fifty years of arduous intellectual labor. They were distillations, crystals of what Engels conceived to be the essentials of his work, and are therefore vitally important.

Primarily, Engels sought to defend Marx and himself against the charge that their doctrine completely eliminated the role of ideas in history.[42] Above all, Engels did not wish to advocate a form of positivism that completely negated the determining agency of human thought. Engels did not wish to eradicate mind in favor of physiology. Even though Engels accepted the copy theory of knowledge, once ideas had been placed into mind then mind responded to these ideas rather than solely to instinct or learned behavior. Engels believed in human rationality: he defined one aspect of communist society as the rational and conscious control of the forces of production. Ideas, for Engels, thus played an important role in history, and any description of a society must take them into account, but the question is the degree of the causal determinacy of ideas. Since Engels did advocate a determining agency for ideas in history, some have interpreted this as proof that Engels was never a positivist.[43] Such a conclusion appears to be unwarranted. In fact, the letters of 1890 demonstrate the endurance of his positivism.

Engels worked within the framework of the substructure-superstructure dichotomy. Law, art, politics, culture belonged to the realm of the superstructure. It was possible, once this realm of ideas had originated in the substructure, once they had taken on an existence independent of the substructure, to react back on that substructure. It was possible for ideas to have a determining impact on the realm of the economic. Engels had not changed or altered his position in the 1890s; he had merely clarified beliefs that he had always maintained.[44]

However, the realm of ideas was a determining agent only on a secondary level for Engels. "And if this man has not yet discovered that while the material mode of existence is the premium agins (primary agent, prime cause) this does not preclude the ideological spheres from reacting upon it in their turn, though with a secondary effect."[45] In the passage of history, Engels believed, substructure and superstructure interacted, the ideological and the economic interpenetrated. But in the last analysis, the substructure assumed primary causal power. The economic realm possessed causal priority, a predominance of determination. "There is an interaction of all these elements in which, amid all the endless host of accident (that is, of things and events whose inner interconnection is so remote or so impossible of proof that we can regard it as non-existent, as negligible) the economic movement finally asserts itself as necessary."[46] Although ideas did influence history, although one must be aware of this and watch for the impact of ideas, the fundamental determining agent in history was still the economic. It was here that we must look for the ultimate causality, for the ultimate meaning of history. Far from removing us from the imprisoning clutches of the economic, Engels's letters of 1890 reaffirm the preeminence of the techno-economic realm. By making economics the primary causal agent, by seeing ideas themselves as being caused by the techno-economic substructure, Engels remained in the camp of positivism.

> Men make their history themselves, but not as yet with a collective will or according to a collective plan or even in a definitely defined given society. Their efforts clash, and for that very reason all such societies are governed by necessity, which is supplemented by and appears under the forms of accident. The necessity which here asserts itself amidst all accident is again ultimately economic necessity.[47]

The notion of human *praxis* was absent from Engels's historical speculations. Marx's view of history was an anthropocentric view of history, with man as the activating principle, who interacted with reality in order to modify, in order to construct. Engels lacked this anthropocentric vision of man. The subject of history for Engels was nature, or technological forces, or some larger agency external to man. That which acted, that which predicated, was always some abstract economic or natural power outside of man. A parallel existed between Engels's view of nature and his view of history. Matter and motion, forces far beyond the control of the human being, exercised dominion in the physical universe. Technology and economics, potencies also beyond the control of the human agent, assumed causal priority in the social universe. In both instances, man was primarily object, primarily respondent.

As we have seen, Engels understood neither the Hegelian left nor the naturalistic basis of Feuerbachian philosophy. Lacking the Hegelian notion of thought as an active, critical agent, lacking the Feuerbachian notion of a world created from alienated human essence, Engels could never develop the idea of *praxis.* Without the notion of *praxis,* Engels saw history as unfolding according to laws extrinsic to man, while Marx saw history as unfolding according to powers intrinsic in human labor. Marx believed in immanence; Engels in emanation.

Engels's concentration on the extrinsic, on forces that emanated from outside of man, led him to judge causal factors solely in terms of materiality. For Engels, social relations, like kinship grouping, social customs and mores, were never productive forces, did not determine history. Productive forces were always concrete materiality, like machines, money, herds, population. Engels always reduced cause to physicality, to concrete presence, and never to the complex web of human interrelationships. As a correlate of his general positivism, only an object had reality, and his view of historical causality corresponded perfectly with the positivist nineteenth-century interpretation of causality.

Marx, on the other hand, had a completely different notion of historical causality. He did not think in terms of linear progression. Rather, he thought in terms of the inherent structure of a given society. Every society was a unique composite, a totality. Marx's vision was a holistic vision, which was founded on the assumption that every social organism was composed of different formal content. Therefore, every social totality would function in accordance with its own inherent structure. Rather than look for sequence, Marx looked for mutation. He looked for the indigenous structure of a social organism, the conflict between form and content in that structure, and the splitting of that totality because of its inherent faults. Causality for Marx did not mean linear accumulation. Causality for Marx meant the kind of movement, the kind of growth that was open to a social structure with a particular kind of constitution. Like Hegel, Marx thought of causality as relation.

Marx's view of social development was anatomical. The view of Engels was modeled upon physics. Engels accepted the model of the predominate science of his day. Marx made the statement that "human anatomy contains a key to the anatomy of the ape."[48] Marx looked upon societies as organisms, as totalities. Of course, organisms were transformed. One societal totality followed another societal totality. But the transformation of a social organism depended on its internal structure and the relation of that structure to the surrounding world. The relation of that organism to its own internal content and to its historical environment was unique, was singular. Marx's multilinear view of history did not mean there was no development in history. Rather it meant that the development was not inevitable, that each pattern of evolution must be worked out in its own terms. On the other hand, Engels was a linear necessitarian: all societies must pass through successive stages. Progress was defined by Engels as the successful passage through these stages.

Engels was wedded to a traditional nineteenth-century view of causality. For Engels, causality meant necessary succession. His view was linear and additive. If the necessary cause of B was A, then the necessary cause of C must be B. Engels thought in terms of a string of beads, where it was impossible to add any bead without the necessary prior bead's being present. Explanation for Engels meant the linear juxtaposition of sequential events. Causality for Engels meant additive sequence. It was not surprising that Engels adopted a unilinear view of history. If explanation meant necessary succession, then the way to explain in history was by means of necessary succession. Engels saw history as additive and cumulative sequence, capitalism following feudalism and communism following capitalism.

The Marxian notion of causality, then, when superimposed upon the historical process, meant that Marx was a multilinearist. Because causality for Marx meant movement relative to the internal structure of a social totality, the developmental path of most societies would differ because the internal structure of most societies would. Unilinearism was foreign to the very spirit of Marx. Correctly understood, the Marxian view of history did not maintain that all societies had to follow the path of feudalism-capitalism-communism. Western Europe had, indeed, followed such a path, but Western society was only one social totality.

Furthermore, causality to Marx was not synonymous with materiality. Marx believed that social forces could be productive forces, that social forces could help shape the structure of society. By a social force, Marx understood not materiality, but relationships. Marx meant the relationships between man and man, or the relationships between man and the means of productivity. A particular mode of interhuman relationship could be a productive force, that is, could modify and shape the structure of a society. This is not to deny that Marx ascribed causal priority when accounting for social change to the means of production. The argument presented here is solely intended to refute the claim that Marx thought the means of production and only the means of production were sufficient to induce social movement.

Marx's concern for social forces and interhuman relationships as productive influences again illustrates his anthropocentric view of history. Because of his concern for man as an active, critical agent, Marx could never assert that human interrelationships were nonproductive. If man is his *praxis,* if history is the autogenesis of man, then the social forms he creates, the customs and mores he lives under, must contribute to his self-creation. The Marxian theme of historic immanence focused his attention not only on individual *praxis,* but social *praxis.* In short, social *praxis* was a part of historical autogenesis.

Conversely, Engels developed a metaphysics of history. Engels thought of historical change as an epiphenomenon of economic development. His major concern was with factors of causality extrinsic to human labor. Engels had not participated in the Marxian anthropocentric revolution of the social sciences. He was guilty of idealizing materiality. His metaphysical materialism led him to see history as ruled by deterministic material forces. Engels's materialism became essentially a form of idealism. By claiming that only the physical had reality, Engels slipped into dogmatism.

In the last chapter we noted how Engels did away with philosophy. Because Engels did not understand the critico-creative aspect of thought, he simply replaced active consciousness with positivist science. Mind, for Engels, was what science had empirically verified. In the same way, Engels did away with history. He replaced history through the study of economics and technology. In the hands of Engels, history was no longer the study of the unique, the multifarious, but rather the compilation of economic data. History was not the story of human deeds, but rather the quantitative description of technological inventions.

Engels's tendency to view technological growth as the basic determining factor in history has been discussed in earlier sections of this work. In

Chapter Nine we saw how Engels explained the use of capitalism, the rise of a proletariat as a consequence of the rise of large industry. The thought patterns that he manifested as a mature man were already present in the young man who first attempted to interpret English society and history. The continuity of his thought is clear. It was not that Engels was unaware of the ideational. It was not that Engels was unaware of the social. Engels took account of these factors and weighed these factors. But there was in Engels a predisposition of mind. There were mental presuppositions. Thus, after weighing all the factors, Engels invariably stressed, focused upon, found the center of gravity in materiality and industrial growth. This predisposition formed the foundation of what is referred to in these pages as Engelsism.

Footnotes

1. Two articles that I have written deal with the question of primitive society in the thought of Marx and Engels: "Anthropology in the Thought of Marx and Engels," *Studies in Comparative Communism* (Jan. 1974), pp. 3–21; and "Dialectical Materialism and the Mir," *Berkeley Journal of Sociology* (1973–1974), pp. 87–104.
2. Friedrich Engels, *The Origin of the Family, Private Property and the State* (New York: International Publishers, 1942), p. 67.
3. *Ibid.*, p. 154.
4. *Ibid.*, pp. 101–102.
5. *Ibid.*, p. 66.
6. *Ibid.*, pp. 159–160.
7. Engels, *Anti-Dühring,* trans. Emile Burns (New York: International Publishers, 1966), pp. 188–192.
8. *Ibid.*, p. 185.
9. *Ibid.*, p. 184.
10. *Ibid.*, p. 190.
11. *Ibid.*
12. *Ibid.*, p. 191.
13. *Ibid.*, p. 151.
14. *Ibid.*
15. *Ibid.*, pp. 151–152.
16. Friedrich Engels, "Ludwig Feuerbach and the End of Classical German Philosophy," *Karl Marx and Friedrich Engels: Selected Works* (New York: International Publishers, 1968), pp. 622–632. For further clarification of Engels's philosophy of history see Zbigniew Jordan, *The Evolution of Dialectical Materialism* (New York: St. Martins Press, (1960), pp. 160–165.
17. Engels to H. Starkenburg, January 25, 1894, in Karl Marx and Friedrich Engels, *Selected Correspondence* (New York: International Publishers, 1942), p. 516.
18. Engels to S. Danielson, September 22, 1892, in Marx and Engels, *Selected Correspondence,* pp. 498–499. For further commentary on primitive societies see Engels, "Die Mark," *Marx-Engels Werke* (Berlin: Dietz Verlag, 1969), XIX,

p. 320. For a similar argument on the early history of the Germanic tribes see Engels, "Zur Urgeschichte der Deutschen," *Marx-Engels Werke,* XIX, pp. 425–518.

19. Engels, *The Peasant War in Germany* (New York: International Publishers, 1966), pp. 35–37.
20. *Ibid.*, p. 44.
21. *Ibid.*
22. *Ibid.*, pp. 42–49.
23. Marx, *Das Kapital,* trans. Samuel Moore and Edward Aneling (New York: International Publishers, 1967), I, p. 714.
24. *Ibid.*, p. 718.
25. Engels, *The Peasant War in Germany,* pp. 147–153.
26. *Ibid.*, p. 12.
27. *Ibid.*, p. 18.
28. Engels, "Germany: Revolution and Counter-Revolution," in *The German Revolutions,* ed. Leonard Krieger (Chicago: University of Chicago Press, 1967), p. 129.
29. *Ibid.*, pp. 125–147.
30. Engels to Bebel, November 18, 1884, in Marx and Engels, *Selected Correspondence,* p. 427.
31. Engels, *The Role of Force in History,* trans. Jack Cohen (New York: International Publishers, 1968), p. 46.
32. For further clarification of Engels's attitude toward Prussia and its role in German unification see Chapter Nine of this book. Also see the following essays: "Po und Rhein," *Marx-Engels Werke,* XIII, 1971, pp. 229–267; and "Savoyen, Nizza und der Rhein," *Ibid.*, XIII, pp. 573–611.
33. Engels, *The Role of Force in History,* pp. 65–69.
34. *Ibid.*, pp. 66–87.
35. Engels, *The Housing Question,* ed. by C. P. Dutt (New York International Publishers, 1950), pp. 10–17.
36. Engels, *The Role of Force in History,* pp. 88–110.
37. Engels to Danielson, October 17, 1893, in Marx and Engels, *Selected Correspondence,* p. 515.
38. Engels, "Fluchtlings Literator," *Marx-Engels Werke,* XVIII, 1969, pp. 521–567. Additional views of Engels on the *mir* in Russia can be found in his "Nachwort (1894) Zu Soziales aus Russland," *Ibid.*, pp. 663–674.
39. Engels, "Russia and the Social Revolution Reconsidered," in *The Russian Menace to Europe,* ed. Paul W. Blackstock and Bert F. Hoselitz (Glencoe, Ill.: The Free Press, 1952), pp. 233–234.
40. Engels, "On Social Relations in Russia," Marx-Engels, *Selected Works,* (Moscow: Foreign Languages Publishing House, 1955), II, pp. 46–47.
41. Engels, "Russia and the Social Revolution Reconsidered," *The Russian Menace to Europe,* pp. 239–241.
42. Engels to C. Schmidt, October 27, 1890, in Marx-Engels, *Selected Works,* (New York: International Publishers, 1968) pp. 696–697.
43. A very insightful discussion of Engels's philosophy of history is Leonard Krieger's "Introduction," in *The German Revolutions.* Other insights into Engels's mentality are suggested by Ernest Mandel, *The Formation of the Economic Thought of Karl Marx,* trans. Brian Pearce (New York: Monthly Review Press, 1971. In addition, the differences between Marx and Engels over the question of the evolution of Russia are ably discussed by A. Walicki, *Controversy Over Capitalism* (Oxford: Clarendon Press, 1969).

44. Engels to V. Bloch, September 21, 1890, in Marx-Engels, *Selected Works,* pp. 692–693.
45. Engels to C. Schmidt, August 5, 1890, in Marx-Engels, *Selected Works,* p. 688.
46. Engels to V. Bloch, September 21, 1890, in Marx-Engels, *Selected Works,* p. 692.
47. Engels to Starkenburg, January 25, 1894, in Marx-Engels, *Selected Works,* p. 518.
48. Marx, *Grundrisse,* trans. Martin Nicolaus (New York: Vintage Press, 1974), p. 105.

Eleven

Scientific Socialism as National Messianism

ON THE PHILOSOPHIC level the distinctions between Marx and Engels were pronounced. Not only were they major, but the distinctions were readily observable. Engels's mechanistic materialism stood in clear contrast to Marx's naturalistic humanism and his concept of *praxis.* On the philosophical level, a Marxian center of gravity and an Engelsian center of gravity can be delineated. On the practical level, the realm of party and political tactics, the distinctions remained hidden. There seemed to be unanimity of viewpoint. Closer examination will reveal, however, that Engels interpreted the strategy and development of the proletarian movement in Europe and Asia in a fashion radically different from the intent and the spirit of Marx. An attempt will be made to explain why on the tactical level the appearance of unanimity was given, when in fact, in the more subtle and theoretic ranges of tactical thinking, major disparity was the case.

In discussing this question, the concept of tactics must be divided into applied and theoretic. The term "applied tactics" is meant to incorporate everyday questions of strategy, decision making within realistic political configurations. The term "theoretic tactics" is meant to incorporate the goal and end of the proletarian movement, the consummation of victories of applied tactics. Marx and Engels were in general agreement on the question of applied tactics. They were not in general agreement on the theoretic level of tactics. It is my opinion that the differences over theoretic tactics between Marx and Engels corresponded exactly to the larger philosophical differences between the two men.

In terms of applied tactics, Marx and Engels both agreed that a separate proletarian party was a political necessity if the workers were to emancipate themselves. They both felt that the leadership of the proletarian party should be drawn from the workers themselves. Neither Marx nor Engels was a Leninist, since neither wanted a nonproletarian, professional, elitist intelligentsia leading the working classes. Both men believed in the cataclysmic theory of revolution, that is, that capitalism would collapse because of its inherent tendency to bring about industrial anarchy, to overproduce. Both men thought that the bourgeois classes must be violently overthrown. They believed that only force or compulsion, power in the hands of the industrial workers, could effect and institute the radical changes the proletariat demanded. A revolution, the forceful execution of proletarian wishes, was needed to usher in communism. Throughout their lives, Marx and Engels continued to believe in, to extol, the revolutionary nature of the working masses. Throughout their lives, Marx and Engels continued to see Czarist Russia as the bulwark of European reaction, while at the same time feeling that Imperial Russia was ripe for social revolution. Both men had a sound grasp of European imperialism and understood that European colonialism was engendering a social revolution in Asia.

The list is not exhaustive. There were other areas of agreement between Marx and Engels. But this list tells us a great deal. It tells us that the agreement on applied tactics was the real basis for the assumption that Marx and Engels were in agreement generally.

In addition, in the 1880s and 1890s, Engels responded almost intuitively to the needs of the various Marxist parties in Germany, France, and Italy. He carried on a voluminous correspondence with the leadership of these parties. Some of the correspondence was personal; most of it was pedagogical, intended to instruct and to guide in questions of strategy and political options. Furthermore, a large part of Engels's writing during this period was not done as an objective or disinterested theoretic pursuit. He wrote in response to the political requirements of the European Marxist movement; he made attempts to offer clarification and elucidation of Marxist thought, as well as polemic attempts to defend the Marxist movement from critics and detractors. *Anti-Dühring,* for instance, was written to defend Marxian materialism, as Engels understood it, from the late nineteenth-century revival of idealism. *Socialism: Scientific and Utopian* was written as a high-level political pamphlet. It was a popular venture composed for the express purpose of explaining Marxism to the French working classes. In these works, Engels tended to stress the unanimity between himself and Marx. Thus, the foundation was laid for the belief that Marx and Engels spoke with one voice.

Nevertheless, this surface appearance of unanimity was not only deceiving, but can be dispelled. Even though there was general agreement between Marx and Engels on applied tactics, on the theoretic level, Engels's tactics complemented his unilinear view of history, while Marx's tactics complemented his multilinear view of history. Engels's strategy for revolution in the nineteenth century was influenced by his macrocosmic, deterministic scheme of historical development. Although Marx and Engels agreed on specific points, on the level of the theory of tactics Engels was confined to the concept of the inevitability of the communist revolution in Europe, to the loss of revolutionary *praxis*, to the loss of revolutionary *élan*, to the idealistic expectation that the hard laws of social evolution would produce the communist revolution. In other words, Engels's tactics corroborated his economic determinism. On the other hand, on the level of the theory of tactics, Marx's viewpoint corroborated his multilinear view of history.

For Engels, the communist revolution would produce itself rather than be fashioned by conscious men.[1] The revolution would start during an economic depression. The capitalist order had created a world market. The class struggle had been globalized, between proprietor and worker, or between capitalist nation and proletarian nation. In both its national and global dimensions, the capitalist mode of production was planless, unorganized, anarchic. The inherent anarchy of capitalist production led inevitably to overproduction. The economic depression, the economic cataclysm that would free the socialist revolution would arise from overproduction.[2]

Pauperization would make the workers rebel. Misery was the cause of political insurrection. The inevitable economic crisis of the capitalist order would lead to the pauperization of the working class, the polarization of the stricken society between the few rich and the many poor, the irreconcilability of class warfare.[3] Throughout his life, Engels maintained a profound faith in the industrial masses. He saw in them the indispensable as well as committed cadres of social revolution. Engels tended to romanticize the pauper. He remained wedded to Moses Hess's idolization of the impoverished, of the ancient struggle of poor against rich. The communist revolution, for Engels, was a revolution of the pauperized. Proletariat, for Engels, meant the poor.

Because of socioeconomic conditions, the communist revolution must be violent. Embittered and polarized class warfare meant that the wealthy would not willingly surrender their class privileges, i.e., the ownership of productive property. Therefore, force must be used. Productive property must be forcibly taken from the possessing classes. Class compulsion, a proletarian state, would not only be used to expropriate property from the capitalists, but a proletarian state would be necessary to repress the remnants of the bourgeoisie during the communist revolution. A working class state, or an instrument of political coercion controlled by the proletariat, was as much a necessity for Engels as the use of violence to initially topple the bourgeois class at the beginning of the pauper revolution.[4] Only after private ownership of the means of production was ended, only after the class enemies of the proletariat were stilled, would the state "wither away."[5]

Nevertheless, even though philosophically and theoretically Engels continuously affirmed the theme of political revolution and class struggle, after 1871 what he did and advised not only was nonrevolutionary, but also led to the loss of revolutionary *élan* in the western European working classes. Basing our judgments upon what Engels wanted done instead of what he literally affirmed, the tactics of Engels led to the replacement of the revolution by mechanistic determinism, to the replacement of conscious *praxis* by the faith in inevitabilism, to the replacement of class warfare by parliamentarianism. Engels was directly responsible for the evolutionism and accommodationism of the Second International.

In the area of tactics, as in the area of philosophy and ideology, Engels attempted to steer a middle course between two extremes. On his left stood the anarchists. To his credit, with a greater grasp of political reality, Engels kept the separation between socialism and anarchism. He successfully fought against the extreme voluntarism of the anarchists, their easy resort to terror, their mythic conception of the immediate overthrow of the state. On his right stood the Fabians and Possibilists and Lassalleans, all those who adopted a policy of social reformism. Against these forces, Engels continued to talk in terms of revolution, of fundamental social structural change, of proletarian insurrection. In this sense Engels protected the integrity and independence of the Marxist socialist movement. But he laid the foundation for Kautsky and Bebel. The sum total of his political writing produced a heritage that supported and encouraged the gradualism and nonrevolutionary policies of the Second International.

The images that Engels had in mind as he calculated the revolutionary situation after 1871 were the revolutions of 1848 and 1871. But Engels faced a unique revolutionary situation after 1871. Above all, the errors of the past must be avoided. Both in 1848 and in 1871 the proletarian movement had suffered severe setbacks. Toward the end of the century Engels grew cautious. The socialist movement had come back to life, and Engels was primarily concerned with avoiding any action that would jeopardize what he felt was the assured continued growth of the proletarian movement. Specifically, as Engels faced the reality of the post-1871 world, he accepted a series of political perimeters. In short, he accepted a horizon of historical givens, and the applied tactics he advocated after 1871 conformed to these, as he saw them, historical givens. There were six political perimeters: (1) Armed insurrections were a thing of the past; (2) wars should be avoided; (3) a bourgeois republic was the most favorable political environment in which a revolution could move progressively leftward; (4) a separate proletarian party was a necessity; (5) the territorial structure of a national state was an indispensable factor for the outbreak of proletarian revolution; (6) the revolutionary as well as reactionary potential of Russia must be taken into account.

The new method of proletarian struggle was through parliamentarian elections. In his 1895 introduction to Marx's *The Class Struggles in France: 1848–1850,* Engels affirmed that rebellion in the old style, the street fight with barricades, which up to 1848 gave everywhere the final decision, was to a considerable extent obsolete.[6] Engels was aware of the growth of military power at the disposal of the state. As long as the army remained loyal to the state, the state would have preponderate military power over any attempted insurrection from the street. In addition, Engels was also opposed to external wars. Because the bourgeois states of western Europe and the feudal-aristocratic states of eastern Europe controlled the balance of military power, armed insurrection and revolutionary warfare could easily be put down, the progressive forces destroyed, and consequently capitalist and feudal conservatism strengthened. In short, Engels believed that two revolutionary instruments used by the proletarian movement in the past, armed urban insurrection and revolutionary warfare, were no longer applicable to the conditions of the late nineteenth century. But the ending of the usefulness of armed insurrection and warfare did not mean the ending of proletarian struggle in itself. Fortunately, the spread of suffrage rights had opened up a new arena of proletarian struggle. Class struggle would continue, but only in a new mode.[7]

The replacement of the heroism of the street by the heroism of the ballot box required that socialist parties throughout Europe have two levels to their party programs. On the philosophical level, these socialist parties must affirm the need of a structural revolution. They must affirm that only a proletarian seizure of power, even though it entailed violence, could place in the hands of the proletariat the needed power to carry out their social goals. On the other hand, Engels stated, it was necessary for these socialist parties to also have immediate demands. The battle of the ballot box required socialist parties to win votes. Immediate demands, the redress of specific sources of proletarian or other underprivileged class distress, would act as a vote-getting device. On the basis of immediate demands, socialist parties must take part in the parliamentarian struggle between classes. They must form temporary alliances with parliamentarian groups and in this way try to insure victory for the demands of these groups with the full understanding that such a victory would enhance the possibilities of a final proletarian takeover.[8]

Engels's program called for a series of temporary tactical alliances, but it was alliance politics without illusion. Within the framework of the battle of the ballot box, these tactical alliances would be understood as merely temporary. It would also be understood that as soon as the purpose of a tactical coalition had been attained, the socialists would immediately break the alliance and form another opposition.[9] Finally, a revolutionary situation would come into existence.

The model that Engels had in mind when he thought of revolution was France in 1789. Like Marx, Engels assumed that the events of 1789 was the archetypal pattern of all revolutions. For Engels, revolutions moved to the left. They began moderately, but were increasingly radicalized as different classes in society, consistently moving toward the poorer strata, took political power. The proletarian revolution of the future would assume the same pattern. At the final moment, Engels believed, a society in a revolutionary condition would be completely polarized. "In any case our sole adversary on the day of the crisis and on the day after the crisis will be the whole collective reaction which will group itself around pure democracy, and this, I think, should not be lost sight of."[10] Such an absolute duality was the hallmark of a revolutionary crisis for Engels, but it could only be reached after the intermediary classes had been destroyed or forced to one or the other of the extreme sides.[11] Engels's concept of revolution was the permanent revolution, the revolution that continued until it came to rest in the most unfortunate class in all society, the class that would liberate society generally from all oppression, the proletariat.

The revolution that moved to the left would more readily unfold within a bourgeois republic, according to Engels. A parliamentarian form of government, based upon wide suffrage rights, had contributed to the radicalization of the French revolutions of 1789 and 1848. Toward the end of the nineteenth century, Engels adamantly maintained that a bourgeois republic would not only facilitate the outbreak of revolution, but would also facilitate the movement of that revolution to its proletarian culmination. For these reasons, Engels argued until his death in 1895 that socialists must support representative republics. They must follow this tactic not out of dedication to the principles of representative government, but out of knowledge that republican systems provided more opportunity for the proletarian conquest of power.

Even though Engels favored temporary alliances, he never wished to compromise the political independence or the doctrinal purity of a separate and autonomous socialist party. When August Bebel and Ferdinand Lassalle opened negotiations for the possible fusion of their two parties, Engels was at first very cool to this eventuality. He wrote to Bebel that the Social-Democratic Workers' Party had "absolutely nothing to learn from the Lassalleans in the theoretical sphere and therefore in what is decisive for the programme."[12] Engels's position called for the continued separate existence of the Social-Democratic Workers' Party rather than tamper with or dilute the doctrinal purity of the party. Both Marx and Engels were to reiterate this same view approximately four years later. In the famous "Circular Letter" to Bebel, Wilhelm Liebknecht, and W. Bracke of September 17–18, 1879, Marx and Engels again opposed any compromise with the Lassalleans and stated that it was impossible for them and should be impossible for the Social-Democratic Workers' Party "to cooperate with people who wish to expunge this class struggle from the movement."[13] Marx and Engels were in agreement on all these points, which were essentially a continuation of the ideas expressed in Marx's "Address of the Central Committee to the Communist League" (1850), in which he asserted that the working classes must carry out their own emancipation.

In his voluminous correspondence with Edward Bernstein, Karl Kautsky, August Bebel, and Paul and Laura Lafargue, Engels stressed repeatedly that a workers' party must lead the socialist movement. When Engels talked of the working class, he meant those who labored in large industrial plants. Proletariat, for Engels, meant industrial workers, or those who labored "in the great industrial cities."[14] There was a difference, according to Engels, between the industrial worker and the handweavers of Saxony. "These people [Saxon handweavers] find themselves in an economically reactionary situation, representatives of a decaying level of production. Therefore, they are not to the same degree born representatives of revolutionary socialism as the worker in great industry."[15]

Labor unions were the natural organizations for an industrial proletariat. The backbone of a workingmen's party would be formed by labor unions.[16] Engels, and Marx as well, tended to overestimate the revolutionary nature of the industrial proletariat. They both manifested a failure of realism, a tendency to romanticize the revolutionary virtues of the industrial workers.[17]

Engels glorified the masses. He tended to see them as possessing an "instinctive drive"[18] for socialism. He recognized that they were not as incisive in their thinking as the individual leaders of the party or labor unions. Nevertheless, the working masses were still "much better than all the leaders put together."[19] Even though they were slower to learn, their consciousness would rise to a proletarian consciousness eventually. Only patience was needed. Then, the acquired communist consciousness of the industrial workers, plus his inherent heroism, and his inherent uncorruptibility, would make the communist revolution a certainty.

From this point of view, Engels affirmed again and again that bourgeois and petty bourgeois intellectuals should be eliminated from the workers' party. Property owning elements could not understand the interests of the proletariat. Generally, they were less militant. They were given to compromise. They were prone to think in legalistic and institutional terms rather than in terms of class struggle. Engels displayed a profound distrust not of intelligence, but of the bourgeois intellectual.[20] The preservation of the idea of class struggle, the preservation of the proletarian core of the socialist movement, entailed for Engels and for Marx the exclusion of bourgeois elements from the socialist party. What Engels feared, as well as Marx, was the embourgeoisment of the proletariat.

Capitalist economy seemed to have found in the national state the best political form for its most expansive growth. The best chance of success for the communist revolution was to unfold within a national territorial unit, and then spread from one country to the next. For instance, both Marx and Engels, beginning in the 1870s, thought it likely that a revolution would begin first inside the Russian state and then subsequently spread to the German state. In addition, the First International Workingmen's Association, according to Marx, was never meant to co-opt the independence of national socialist parties. Rather, the International was intended to coordinate and to guide the sovereign acts of the national socialist parties. Engels agreed and after Marx's death continued to perpetuate the policy of autonomous national parties. Engels's own opinions on this matter were clearly stated in his March 18–22, 1875, letter to Bebel, in which he said that

> . . . although the German workers party is operating first of all within the state boundaries laid down for it (it has no right to speak in the name of the European proletariat and especially no right to say something false), it is conscious of its solidarity with the workers of all countries and will always be ready hereafter, as it has been hitherto, to fulfill the obligation imposed upon it by this solidarity.[21]

On no point were Marx and Engels more insistent than on the preservation of the idea of class struggle within the doctrine and policies of the separate national proletarian parties. Only the idea of the class struggle, of the irreconcilability of interests of the proletariat and the bourgeoisie, could produce a revolution, and only a revolution could give to the proletariat the political power necessary to carry out its reforms. In their "Circular Letter" to Bebel, Liebknecht, and Bracke, Marx and Engels wrote that for "almost forty years we have stressed the class struggle as the immediate driving power of history and in particular the class struggle between bourgeoisie and proletariat as the great lever of the modern social revolution."[22] Engels held this position from 1842 onward, and articulated it again in his October 28, 1882, letter to Bebel.[23]

However, the prospects for revolution in Europe could not be adequately weighed without an analysis of the role of Russia. Engels believed that a continental war must be avoided. Russia was the bulwark of aristocratic conservatism. Pan-Slavism was a strong element within the circles around the Czar. A Russian victory in Europe would thus enlarge the Czarist imperium. The smaller and weaker Slavic states of eastern Europe would be absorbed by the great Slavic motherland. Secondly, a German defeat would entail the destruction of the German socialist movement. Russian conservation would resort to the same, or even harsher, repressive measures as Bismarck had attempted in his antisocialist crusade. In either case, a Russian victory would be another setback for the European revolutionary movement. On the other hand, Engels believed that Russia was ripe for revolution. Peace, then, was what Europe needed, according to Engels. Peace to allow the revolution to come to the surface in Russia. Peace to allow the German socialist party to grow to the largest in western Europe; so it could powerfully join and lead the revolutionary movement as it flowed out of the east. Engels's main concern was the preservation of the gains made by socialism in western Europe since 1871. His was an essentially nonadventurist policy. It was distinctly conservative.

Engels's applied tactics were not meant to be rigid and inflexible. Although he had definite ideas about the broad pattern of the revolutionary movement, from the economic breakup of capitalism to the installation of a proletarian state, he never assumed that the proletarian movement in every nation must imitate exactly the same specific pattern of growth. On December 28, 1886, Engels wrote to Florence Wischnewetsky that "our theory is not a dogma but the exposition of a process of evolution, and that process involves successive phases."[24] About a month later, he again expressed similar sentiments to Florence Wischnewetsky when he wrote that our "theory is a theory of evolution, not a dogma to be learned by heart and to be repeated mechanically."[25] To Bebel, he wrote on November 19, 1892, that it was "nonsense to expect the movement in varying countries to conform to one pattern."[26]

On the level of his theory of tactics, on the level of his philosophy of history, Engels was a dogmatist. The general pattern of historical development must be unilinear. The general pattern of historical development was governed by the laws of economic determinism. On the level of applied tactics, in terms of temporary political strategy, Engels proved to be flexible. There could be specific variations to the general law of growth. Because of these specific variations, applied tactical flexibility was required.

Engels used his applied theory of revolution as a criterion by which to judge the French, English, Russian, and German socialist movements. The revival of the socialist movements in the 1880s made Engels's assessment of them assume climactic historical importance. Engels died only nineteen years before the outbreak of World War One. His evaluation of these socialist parties, of their role and importance, thus had extremely weighty bearing on the policies of the Second International in the years and days immediately preceding the outbreak of the War. In particular, Engels's attitude toward the German socialist party, his close contacts with Kautsky, Bebel, and Liebknecht, formed the framework in which the German socialist party operated from 1895 until 1914. What Engels thought about Germany, what Engels thought about Russia, was an unchallenged heritage that Kautsky, Bebel, and Liebknecht voluntarily accepted. The principles upon which these men acted in August 1914 were the principles first enunciated and defended by Engels.

In his letters to Paul and Laura Lafargue, Engels commented extensively on the French socialist movement. The great enemy in France was the Possibilists, led by Paul Brousse. Even though critical of the erratic personality of Paul Lafargue (Marx's son-in-law, husband of Laura Marx) Engels supported the French Workers' Party of Jules Guesde and Lafargue. The French Workers' Party was a true Marxist party, while the Possibilists were merely bourgeois reformers masquerading as socialists. The Possibilists were the classic example of a socialist party composed mostly of bourgeois intellectuals. In condemning the Possibilists, Engels not only reaffirmed his opposition to the embourgeoisment of the socialist movement, but also editorially rejected evolutionism as a theoretical or applied possibility for the socialist movement. In short, Engels did not think evolutionism was a valid Marxian concept. Engels, in terms of rhetoric, remained bound to revolutionism.

In 1889, however, the Possibilists had gained the position of representing the socialist movement in France. On March 27 of that year, Engels wrote to Lafargue severely admonishing him for the tactical blunders that had permitted the Possibilists to be "in sole possession of the field" and urging him to accept the German offer of an international congress at which the Possibilists would be read out and the Lafargue-Guesde party read in as the true representative of socialism in France.[27] Lafargue conceded to Engels's advice, and in 1889 the Second International met in Paris under the leadership of the German Social Democratic Party. The Brousse groups, however, did not sit with the Second International, but met in a separate hall as a show of opposition to the International and the Lafargue-Guesde faction. Engels was opposed to any mediation between the International and Brousse, and as Engels wished, the Paris International conferred upon the French Workers' Party the mantle of representing the socialist forces in France.

Interestingly, Paul Brousse had received the support of Henry Hyndman and the English Social Democratic Federation. The struggle against Brousse, as well as the struggle against Hyndman and the Fabians, was a struggle, for Engels, against reformism.[28] According to Engels, Brousse, Hyndman, the Fabians were really cut from the same cloth as Ferdinand Lassalle; all were revisionists.

The Paris victory was a great one for Engels, because it affirmed the idea of class struggle and revolution in all socialist programs. However, another obstacle remained in France, which prevented "the formation of an independent working men's party."[29] That obstacle was Boulangerism. Engels defined Boulangerism in the following terms:

> But it is the third time that such an aberration occurs since 1789—the first time Napoleon No. 1, the second time Napoleon No. 3 was carried to the top by that wave of aberration, and now it's a worse creature than either—but fortunately the force of the wave, too, is broken. Anyhow we must apparently come to the conclusion that the negative side of the Parisian revolutionary character—chauvinistic Bonapartism—is as essential to it as the positive side, and that after every great revolutionary effort, we may have a recrudescence of Bonapartism, of an appeal to a savior . . ."[30]

Boulangerism was one of the enemies on the right against which Engels fought. Many working class people in Paris supported Boulanger, and Engels proclaimed the need of socialists to expose Boulanger and thus win these working class people back into the fold of socialism. Paul Lafargue himself had shown some sympathy for the Boulangerist movement. Lafargue was aware of the appeal that Boulanger had for the proletariat, and wished to exploit Boulanger in the interests of the socialist movement. Engels's attitude was unmitigated opposition, and he accused Lafargue of hurting the cause of socialism in France by his public display of sympathy for Boulanger.[31]

Boulanger stood for French chauvinism, for *revanche,* for "Alsace reconquered."[32] The collapse of Boulanger had created the conditions for a sound proletarian movement inside France. In fact, "the monarchist attack on the Republic, has failed."[33] The bourgeois republic had been stabilized. According to Engels's theory of revolution, the bourgeois republic was the most conducive environment for the growth and development of a proletarian movement. Engels looked upon the parliamentarian republic as the last defense of the bourgeoisie in general.

Indeed, Engels's letters to Lafargue after the fall of Boulanger reflect this optimism. He anticipated the gradual but steady polarization of the various parties within the bourgeois republic. He anticipated that the bourgeois republic would be increasingly radicalized, that this would be continuous and permanent movement to the left until a position of unreconcilable confrontation had been reached: a revolutionary situation.

When Engels described the future development of the republic in France, the model that he had in mind was the great French Revolution of 1789.[34] Engels envisioned the increasing polarization and radicalization of the Third Republic. Like the revolution of 1789, the Third Republic would move to the left. Monarchist rule would give way to conservative rule, and conservative would be replaced by bourgeois rule. When the workers confronted the bourgeoisie with implacable resolve, the petty bourgeoisie would join the entire bourgeoisie camp. Thus two great armed camps would face each other: the camp of the status quo, and the revolutionary camp of workers and peasants. This state of categorical opposition was the revolutionary condition.

When looking at the proletarian movement in England from the vantage point of 1892, Engels had reason to be hopeful. In thirteen years, from 1879 until 1892, there had been considerable growth. Three years before his death, Engels saw an independent workingmen's party in England that had begun to win electoral victories. Engels had every expectation that Keir Hardie's Independent Labor Party would continue to win at the polls and through their electoral triumphs emerge as a serious political threat to the Tories and Liberals. However, in 1879 Engels wrote to Edward Bernstein that a "workers' movement in the continental sense does not exist in England."[35]

Engels understood that the English working class had been co-opted by the prosperity stemming from British imperialism and on September 12, 1882, said so in a letter to Kautsky.[36] British domination of the world market had kept English industry flourishing, had kept employment high, and consequently had kept the industrial proletariat satisfied. Prosperity, then, was one reason why the English worker had not formed an independent workers' party, but preferred to remain a tail of the Liberal Party. Engels anticipated that the collapse of British domination of the world market would bring unemployment, proletarian distress, and renewed proletarian vigor and independence.

In the 1882 period, before a true proletarian party developed, the representative of English socialism was Henry Hyndman's Social Democratic Federation, and later the Fabians. Engels had nothing but scorn for the Social Democratic Federation and the Fabians. To Engels they represented the worst of middle class socialism. They did not understand the suffering of the workers, and therefore could not adequately represent the political interests of the workers. Furthermore, the political programs of the Social Democratic Federation and the Fabians were both un-Marxian. Hyndman, Engels maintained, was in actuality an ex-Conservative Party member, as well as being a chauvinist. The Social Democratic Federation, according to Engels, was not a party at all but merely an amalgam of confused sects, the remains of the great movement of the 1840s.[37] The Fabians, too, were composed of bourgeois intellectuals and were dedicated to evolutionist thought. Engels in 1892 was severely critical of Edward Bernstein's interest in the Fabians. He referred to Bernstein's "Fabian romanticism"[38] and indicated that Bernstein's interest in the Fabians was probably an expression of Bernstein's "sickness."[39] The evolutionary thought of the Fabians was irreconcilable to the Marxist revolutionary message.

In 1888 unemployment had come to England. Out of the poverty of the worker, proletarian militancy began to grow. The trade union movement was resuscitated. In 1890 the London dock strike was won. Engels called the London dock strike the "greatest event in England since both previous reform bills."[40] On May 4, 1890, there were mass worker demonstrations in Hyde Park. To Engels it seemed clear that the old bourgeois socialist sects had been bypassed, and that newer and greater layers of workers were being drawn into the socialist movement. On May 9, 1890, Engels wrote to Bebel that in England "on May 4th there had begun a real socialist mass movement."[41]

Out of this mass discontent, an independent workers' party had developed, the party of Keir Hardie and John Burns. In 1892 Hardie and Burns won seats in the House of Commons as Labor representatives.[42] Thus the battle of the ballot box had worked to the advantage of the socialists. Engels could only anticipate that the use of his electoral strategy would bring continued victories to the working class. Although Engels philosophized about revolution, although Engels would never compromise a socialist program by dropping the idea, the call for revolution, in point of fact, the class war for Engels would develop on the basis of electoral victories. The ideas that he himself condemned in the revisionists were the ideas that he, in fact, advocated in actuality.

Russia occupied a rather ambiguous place in Engels's thought. On the one hand, Russia was the bulwark of European reaction. As the major conservative power on the continent, its presence meant that no proletarian victory was possible in western Europe.[43] Engels remembered the Russian intervention in the 1848–1849 revolution, and how her aid in suppressing the Hungarian rebellion was instrumental in preserving the Hapsburg dynasty. Engels assumed that a conservative, Czarist Russia would take similar action if a proletarian revolution were to break out in western Europe at the end of the nineteenth century.

On the other hand, Engels was aware that Russia was ripe for revolution. The two decisive turning points in nineteenth-century Russian history were the Crimean War and the emancipation of the serf in 1861. The defeat in the Crimean War showed the decadence of the Czarist system, and the liberation of the serfs prepared the social foundation for a future revolution. "This great act of emancipation, which was so universally acclaimed and praised by the liberal press of Europe, has created nothing but the foundations and the absolute necessity of a future revolution."[44]

Like Marx, Engels was certain that a revolution was coming to Russia. The problem that perplexed Engels, was what kind of revolution this would be. Engels had a vehement dislike of Pan-Slavism. He saw it as a tool of Czarist reaction. The *mir*, the Russian communal village, was a favored social institution of the Pan-Slav populists. They saw in the preservation of the *mir* an opportunity to prevent the horrors of capitalism from coming to Russia, an opportunity to build a communal society in general starting from the communal nature of the *mir*. To Engels's mind, the *mir* was simply a figment of Pan-Slav romantic conservative ideology. Just as Pan-Slavism was the creed of conservative bourgeois intellectuals, so the *mir* as a social institution was not only conservative, but outdated.[45]

To Engels's mind, the *mir* was a vestige of ancient, precapitalist society. The communal village was a typical form of socioeconomic organization in ancient civilizations like India, Java, and western Europe, as well as Russia. Engels was quick to point out, however, that capitalism had destroyed the communal village in western Europe. He further pointed out that capitalist imperialism was in the process of destroying the village community in India and Java as well. Therefore, he concluded that capitalist development would destroy the *mir* in Russia. There was no historically documented reason to argue that Russia differed from all the other sectors of the globe, that it alone could escape the ravages of capitalism and preserve the village commune.[46]

Secondly, the *mir*, in Engels's eyes, represented a low stage of historical development. Engels believed in necessitarian stages of development: history moved from lower to higher. Capitalism, for Engels, represented the highest state of productive capacity yet attained by man. Thus, the law of monodevelop-growth required that a lower stage of historical development be replaced by a higher stage of historical development. That had been the course taken by western Europe. If historical laws had any validity, and they did according to Engels, Russia must follow the path of western Europe. Russia must move from primitive society to capitalist society, and the *mir* must be destroyed.[47]

Consequently, the revolution that was immanent in Russia was not the proletarian revolution. Rather, it was the bourgeois revolution. Autocracy must first be overthrown. A constitutional democratic order must be established. An electoral system must be established. Capitalism must create the class war in the countryside. Only after a representative national life had been created, could a proletarian movement begin.[48] "And it signifies the beginning of an active, internal national life for the Russian people and simultaneously the beginning of a real workers' movement in Russia."[49]

Even though the bourgeois revolution would rid Russia of Czarist autocracy it would not necessarily release the revolutionary movement in western Europe. Engels was well aware of bourgeois hatred of the proletarian class. Just as the Czar would intervene to repress working class revolution in the West, so the western capitalists would intervene in Russia to support a bourgeois capitalist government. The subsequent proletarian revolution in Russia would, however, release the revolutionary potential of western Europe. With Czarist and then capitalist conservatism removed, the working classes of western Europe would rebel. A workers' insurrection in Russia would thus be the signal for a workers' insurrection in the West.

A workers' insurrection in Russia, if Russia were still a relatively undeveloped capitalist state, could not alone lead directly to communism in Russia. Following a workers' revolution in Russia, a workers' revolution in more technologically advanced and more capitalized western Europe (with its eastern border secured) could lead directly to communism. Not only could the western workers build communism in their own countries, but they could extend assistance to the Russian worker. With the help of the West, with the guidance of the West, but not alone, the Russian worker could build communism. Engels again reaffirmed the leadership, the higher stage of evolutionary development, of western Europe.

If Russia was the most problematical state in Europe as far as the socialist movement was concerned, Germany, in Engels's eyes, was the most well-defined. The fate of German socialism and the fate of international socialism were one, according to Engels. In 1883 he wrote to Eduard Bernstein that the German Social Democratic Party must preserve its "unique position as representative of international socialism."[50] Thus German socialism assumed a messianic mission. Its success entailed the success of the socialist movement around the world.

Until the Franco-Prussian War of 1870, France had been the center of the European socialist movement. The defeat of the Paris Commune ended that revolutionary tradition. When the socialist movement revived again, Germany became the center of energy. In his famous introduction to the 1895 edition of Marx's *Class Struggles in France: 1848–1850,* Engels wrote that the "war of 1870–71 and the defeat of the Commune had transferred the center of gravity of the European workers movement for the time being from France to Germany, as Marx foretold."[51] The center of gravity of world socialism was to remain in Germany.

One reason why German socialism would retain its messianic mission was because of the rapid proletarianization of the German laboring masses. The Industrial Revolution, the production of a downtrodden industrial working class, was proceeding with greater thoroughness and depth in Germany than had been the case in either England or France. To begin with, Germany had a larger population than either England or France. Secondly, Germany had retained its small peasant proprietary class into the 1880s, as well as its hand weavers and other artisans. The rigorous and complete capitalization of Germany meant, therefore, the destruction of the small peasant proprietor and the artisans. Of great number, the former peasants and artisans would find their economic functions destroyed, would find themselves forced to join the industrial laboring force. This experience would serve to radicalize this new German proletariat. Thirdly, by the 1880s England's monopoly on the world market had been broken by the United States and Germany. The penetration of Germany into the world market meant greater economic opportunity, and thus further industrialization inside Germany to meet these new markets.[52]

An additional reason why Germany would hold onto its leadership role in world socialism was the test of strength and hardening it had endured under Bismarck's antisocialist laws. From 1878 until 1890, Bismarck, short of absolute prohibition, attempted to legislate the German Social Democratic Party out of existence. The Social Democrats weathered this storm, whereas other national parties might have been broken, and Engels thought this a testament to the will, dedication, discipline, and militancy of the German proletariat. The German socialist party was a stronger party because it had overcome the oppression of the antisocialist laws. Engels's optimism, his faith in the ultimate triumph of German socialism, was manifested by his belief that Bismarck was inadvertently doing the work of the German socialists. That is, Engels believed that Bismarck's policies were exacerbating the class struggle in Germany, demonstrating the repressive nature of the monarchy and bourgeoisie, demonstrating through state socialism some of the attractive points of socialism to the working class, and thus enhancing the objective conditions that would eventually lead to proletarian socialism.[53]

But the most important reason why the German socialists would continue to be the leading revolutionary class in Europe was due to their excellent grasp of theory.[54] The theoretic superiority of the Germans meant that only the Germans were truly capable of understanding Marx, and thus only the Germans were capable of writing a socialist program that embodied the ideas of Marx. Presumably, the theoretic excellence of the German workers also meant that the tactics of the German workers would adhere more faithfully to the tactics of Marx. For instance, the German workers would not be as indifferent or as uninspired as the English workers were in the late 1870s. The German workers would not fall prey to other misguided creeds that promised to redress their ills as the French workers had fallen prey to Proudhonism.[55] What Engels was suggesting was that the leadership of international socialism did, in fact, belong in Germany because only Germans had the intellectual background necessary to properly exercise this leadership.

Engels, then, watched the growth of the German Social Democratic Party with joy and anticipation. The extension of the suffrage had given the workers a new weapon, a new field of battle. As Engels watched the electoral growth of the socialist party, he considered this tantamount to the coming of the proletarian revolution. Electoral victories took the place of actual revolutionary tactics. Even though Engels would have denied it, he contributed immensely to the derevolutionizing of Marxism.

The real electoral growth of the German Social Democratic Party began in the election of 1884. The gains of the socialists signified a breakthrough for them as a political force. Engels wrote to Bernstein that the "election of 1884 was for us what the 1866 was for the German philistine."[56] But the election of 1890 was the real turning point. Not only did it witness the end of the antisocialist laws, but it also produced a resounding victory at the polls for the party. Engels called it the beginning of the German revolution.

Since Engels felt assured of the steady and uninterrupted electoral growth of the German socialist party, his major tactical concern then was one of preservation and conservation. Only a catastrophe could halt the inevitable popular growth of the party, could halt the ultimate electoral victory. Thus the tactics of the German Social Democrat must aim at the preservation of the party. Above all Germany must avoid a war. Engels was explicit on these points:

> But whatever may happen in other countries, German Social-Democracy has a special situation and therewith, at least in the first instance, a special task. The two million voters, whom it sends to the ballot box, together with the young men and women, who stand behind them as non-voters, form the most numerous most compact mass, the decisive "shock force" of the international proletarian army. This mass already supplies over a fourth of the recorded votes; and as the by-election to the Reichstag, the direct election in individual states, the municipal council and industrial court election demonstrate, it increases uninterruptedly. . . . And there is only one means by which the steady rise of the socialist fighting forces in Germany could be momentarily halted, and even thrown back for some time: a clash on a big scale with the military, a blood-bath like that of 1871 in Paris. In the long run that would also be overcome. To shoot out the world a party which numbers millions—all the magazine rifles of Europe and America are not enough for this.[57]

Engels remained wedded to a policy of parliamentarianism. The enormous electoral growth of the party begged the preservation of the party.

There were only two ways in which the party could be destroyed: premature revolution and the loss of an external war. To conserve the electoral power of the party required a continuation of the policy of parliamentarianism. When Engels did this, he opened wide the door to revisionism, which he himself was to pass through.

Engels had worked himself into a tactical box. He had closed off most other tactical options. When Engels refused to investigate the revolutionary utility of other forms of violence (e.g., the general strike), when he refused to consider the revolutionary potential of the peasantry, he left himself with no tactical option other than electoral politics. Engels was, in fact, the founder of the policy of gradualism, the policy of the German Social Democratic Party and the policy of the Second International.

The roots of Engels's gradualism lay in his devotion to the proletariat as the only true revolutionary force. When Engels said proletariat, he meant exclusively the hard-core industrial working classes. Engels tended to overestimate, to exaggerate the revolutionary *élan* of the industrial laborers. He was guilty of romanticizing the pauper. He remained bound throughout his life to Moses Hess's concept of class struggle as constituted of the warfare between rich and poor. But Engels also made the logical error of assuming that the pauper was always the rebel, always the incendiary.

Most importantly, Engels failed to properly evaluate the revolutionary potential of the peasants. It was not, however, that Engels was entirely closed-minded on the question of the peasantry. It was rather his belief that before the peasantry could become revolutionary they must first be transformed into a rural proletariat. The class struggle must be brought to the countryside, polarization must take place between the landless, wage-earning peasant and the rich middle class landowning peasant. In short, only when the peasant was pauperized would he become a revolutionary.

Engels wrote his book, *The Peasant War in Germany,* not only as an illustration of historical materialism, but also for frankly political reasons. *The Peasant War in Germany* was written in 1850, two years after the failure of the 1848 revolution. It was clear to Engels, as it was clear to Marx, that the revolution of 1848 failed in part because the rural peasants turned against the urban proletariat. Thus, Engels wrote *The Peasant War in Germany* in an attempt not only to lift the sagging revolutionary spirit inside Germany but also to stress and illustrate the revolutionary tradition, and therefore, revolutionary potential of the peasants themselves.[58]

In his 1870 preface to the second edition of *The Peasant War in Germany,* Engels called for a worker-peasant alliance.[59] Based on previous experience, Engels understood that an urban insurrection would not succeed unless it was supported by the rural countryside. Here, again, Engels used the revolutionary models of 1789, 1848, and 1871. Furthermore, Engels clearly foresaw that electoral majorities for the European social democratic parties would not come into being unless the great rural reservoir of peasant votes was won for the socialist parties. These peasant votes must be stripped from the feudal, aristocratic parties.

A worker-peasant alliance was the correct formula, but Engels then espoused a policy that made a worker-peasant alliance an impossibility. Land nationalization remained an uncompromisable principle in Engels's socialist platform. He would not deviate from the principle of land nationalization, even to capture the votes of the landless peasants.[60]

Tactically, the implementation of a worker-peasant alliance required a temporary retreat from the policy of land nationalization. If the European peasants were to join the workers either in the battle of the ballot box or in actual insurrection, they must be promised what they wanted the most: land. But Engels indicated that the socialists could not promise to give land to the peasants, but must rather staunchly affirm the need for land nationalization: the policy that the peasants wanted least.

Engels remained prisoner of the proletarian, urban model of class struggle. He saw the necessity of bringing the class struggle to the countryside. But the class struggle he saw was the class struggle of the great industrial centers, propertyless against capitalist wage-laborer against proprietor. This model must be duplicated in the countryside. Therefore, just as the urban, industrial working class called out for nationalization of the means of production, so the rural proletariat must call out for the nationalization of land. Consequently, Engels ultimately failed to appreciate the uniqueness of the peasant problem. In the last analysis, he failed to find the correct way to release the revolutionary nature of the peasantry.

Because of his philosophy of history, Engels remained tied to the proletarian-urban model of revolution. Because all societies must pass through capitalism in order to reach communism, Engels's eyes were focused on the development of large factories, on the development of an industrial working class near urban areas. Thus, Engels's unilinear view of history, by making capitalism a necessary precondition for communism, enslaved Engels to a proletarian-urban formula of revolution.

Furthermore, because of his social positivism Engels was led to identify the fate of world socialism with the destiny of the German Social Democratic Party. Germany was the most industrialized country in Europe; Germany had the largest number of proletarians in Europe; and Germany had the strongest and most militant socialist party in Europe. It stood at the head of the European socialist movement. Since Europe was the most advanced section of the globe, the German proletariat was the vanguard of the world socialist movement. Engels's view of history supported his deep sense of German nationalism. Germany was to be the salvation of the world.

Footnotes

1. For a description of the origins and onset on the communist revolution, see the following two works: Friedrich Engels, *Anti-Dühring,* trans. Emile Burns (New York: International Publishers, 1966), pp. 299–310; and Engels, *Socialism: Utopian and Scientific,* Marx-Engels, *Selected Works* (New York: International Publishers, 1968) pp. 420–429.
2. Engels to J. P. Becker, June 15, 1885, in Karl Marx and Friedrich Engels, *Selected Correspondence,* trans. Dona Torr (New York: International Publishers, 1942), p. 439.
3. Engels to Florence Kelley Wischnewetsky, January 7, 1886, *Ibid.,* p. 443.
4. Engels to Turati, January 26, 1894, *Ibid.,* p. 521. For further clarification of this point, see Engels's comments on the Erfurt Program which accompanied his letter to K. Kautsky, June 29, 1891, *Ibid.,* pp. 485–486.
5. Engels, *Anti-Dühring,* p. 307.
6. Engels, "Introduction, 1895," to Marx, *The Class Struggles in France, 1848–1850* (New York: International Publishers, 1964), p. 21.
7. *Ibid.*
8. Engels to Turati, January 26, 1894, in Marx and Engels, *Selected Correspondence,* pp. 521–522.
9. *Ibid.,* p. 523.
10. Engels to A. Bebel, October 28, 1882, *Ibid.,* p. 434.
11. Engels to A. Bebel, October 28, 1882, *Ibid.,* p. 401.
12. Engels to A. Bebel, March 18–28, 1875, *Karl Marx and Friedrich Engels: Selected Works* (New York: International Publishers, 1968), p. 336.
13. Marx and Engels, "Circular Letter," Marx-Engels, *Selected Works* (Moscow: Foreign Languages Publishing House, 1955), II, p. 440.
14. Engels, *Briefwechsel mit E. Bernstein* (The Hague: Mouton & Co., 1969), p. 59.
15. *Ibid.,* pp. 59–60.
16. Engels to Sorge, February 8, 1890, in Marx and Engels, *Selected Correspondence,* p. 467.
17. Engels to Sorge, April 19, 1890, *Ibid.,* p. 468.
18. Engels, *Briefwechsel mit K. Kautsky* (Vienna: Europäische Verlag, 1928), p. 420.
19. *Ibid.*
20. Engels, *Briefwechsel mit A. Bebel* (The Hague: Mouton & Co., 1968), pp. 599–600.
21. Engels to A. Bebel, March 18–22, 1875, *Karl Marx and Friedrich Engels: Selected Works* (New York), p. 337.
22. Marx and Engels, "Circular Letter," Marx-Engels, *Selected Works* (Moscow), II, p. 440.
23. Engels to A. Bebel, October 28, 1882, in Marx and Engels, *Selected Correspondence,* p. 402.
24. Engels to Florence Kelley Wischnewetsky, December 28, 1886, *Ibid.,* p. 453.
25. Engels to Florence Kelley Wischnewetsky, January 27, 1887, *Ibid.,* p. 454.
26. Engels, *Briefwechsel mit A. Bebel,* p. 618.
27. Engels to Paul Lafargue, March 27, 1889, *Engels-Lafargue Correspondence* (Moscow: Foreign Languages Publishing House, 1968), II, pp. 211–213.
28. George Lichtheim, *A Short History of Socialism* (New York: Praeger, 1970), pp. 225–230.
29. Engels to P. Lafargue, October 8, 1889, *Engels-Lafargue Correspondence,* II, p. 325.

30. Engels to Laura Lafargue, April 16, 1890, *Ibid.*, p. 371.
31. Engels to P. Lafargue, October 30, 1889, *Ibid.*, p. 333.
32. Engels to Laura Lafargue, April 16, 1890, *Ibid.*, p. 370.
33. Engels to P. Lafargue, October 8, 1889, *Ibid.*, p. 325.
34. *Ibid.*, pp. 325–326.
35. Engels *Briefwechsel mit Bernstein,* p. 5.
36. Engels, *Briefwechsel mit K. Kautsky,* p. 63.
37. Engels, *Briefwechsel mit A. Bebel,* pp. 165–166.
38. *Ibid.*, p. 576.
39. *Ibid.*
40. Engels, *Briefwechsel mit K. Kautsky,* p. 248.
41. Engels, *Briefwechsel mit A. Bebel,* p. 391.
42. *Ibid.*, pp. 558–559.
43. Engels, "Vorbemerkung Zu der Broschüre Soziales Aus Russland," *Marx-Engels Werke* (Berlin: Dietz Verlag, 1969), XVIII, p. 585.
44. Engels, "Die Europäischen Arbeiter im Jahre 1877," *Ibid.*, XIX, p. 134.
45. Engels, "Nachwort (1894) zu Soziales Aus Russland," *Ibid.*, XVIII, p. 663.
46. *Ibid.*, XVIII, p. 666.
47. Engels, "Flüchtlingsliteratur," *Ibid.*, XVIII, p. 563.
48. Engels, "Die Europäischen Arbeiter im Jahre 1877," *Ibid.*, XIX, p. 136.
49. *Ibid.*, p. 137.
50. Engels, *Briefwechsel mit E. Bernstein,* p. 194.
51. Engels "Introduction, 1895," to Marx, *The Class Struggles in France: 1848–1850,* p. 19.
52. Engels *Briefwechsel mit K. Kautsky,* pp. 154–155. For additional documentation of this point, see Engels, *Briefwechsel mit E. Bernstein,* p. 60.
53. Engels, *Briefwechsel mit E. Bernstein,* pp. 214–215.
54. Engels, *The Peasant War in Germany* (New York: International Publishers, 1966), p. 27.
55. *Ibid.*, p. 28.
56. Engels, *Briefwechsel mit E. Bernstein,* p. 307.
57. Engels, "Introduction, 1895," to Marx, *The Class Struggles in France: 1848–1850,* pp. 26–27.
58. Engels, *The Peasant War in Germany,* p. 33.
59. *Ibid.*, pp. 20–21.
60. Engels, "The Peasant Question in France and Germany," Marx-Engels, *Selected Works* (Moscow), II, p. 395.

Twelve

Scientific Socialism as German Ethnocentrism

ENGELS'S UNILINEAR VIEW of history also shaped his attitude toward imperialism. Living until 1895, Engels experienced the first stage of Europe's great expansion overseas. His attitude toward the non-Western world was one of cultural superiority. Technologically and economically, western Europe was the most advanced portion of the globe; it was further advanced along the necessitarian line of development (feudalism-capitalism-communism) than any other area of the world. Engels was guilty of European ethnocentrism. He was tainted by European, more particularly, German nationalism, and this sense of cultural superiority was buttressed and confirmed by his unilinear view of history.

Like Marx, Engels was aware that imperialism was bringing about a social revolution in Asia. Western imperialism, because it was supported by superior technology, because it was supported by a higher economic formation like capitalism, was breaking down traditional and outmoded socio-economic formations in the non-Western world. Engels, but not Marx, felt that Western imperialism was a revolutionary force because it represented a higher and more advanced stage of eco-technological development. Engels, but not Marx, believed that Asia, after the revolution caused by capitalist imperialism, must imitate the path of Western evolution.

Like Marx, Engels was aware of a unique mode of Asiatic production. The central feature of this Asiatic mode of production, Engels wrote to Marx in 1853, was that the "absence of property in land is indeed the key to the whole of the East."[1] Engels attributed the lack of private property in the Orient to climatic conditions and the nature of the soil. The desert that stretched from the Sahara across Arabia and Persia to India required artificial irrigation if agriculture was to be undertaken. Engels indicated that construction and maintenance of an irrigation system was "a matter either for the communes, the provinces or the central government."[2] Engels was thus in basic agreement with Marx on the nature and characteristics of the Asiatic mode of production: communal ownership of land, despotic government, control of the irrigation system by the despotic government.

Nevertheless, Engels both consistently and adamantly affirmed the superiority of Western society. It was both higher and better than non-Western society. Marx never made a value judgment as to the relationship between Western and non-Western societies. Engels did, and penned the following words on this matter:

> The struggle of the Bedouins was a hopeless one, and though the manner in which brutal soldiers, like Bugeaud, have carried on the war is highly blameable, the conquest of Algeria is an important and fortunate fact for the progress of civilization.... And after all, the modern bourgeois with civilization, industry, and at least relative enlightenment following him, is preferable to the feudal lord or to the marauding robber with the barbarian state of society to which they belong.[3]

Furthermore, Engels was strongly opposed to any romanticization of underdeveloped or primitive peoples. While he overestimated the revolutionary potential of the proletariat, he urged that European socialists not glorify and idealize people in peasant societies. On August 9, 1882, Engels wrote to Bernstein that western European socialists should be very guarded in their appraisal of oriental revolutions. "And yet, no sooner does a riot break out somewhere than the entire Romance revolutionary world is uncritically in raptures over it."[4] Engels preferred a more realistic and tough-minded understanding that peasants were slow to change, and readily accepted autocracy in whatever form.

In fact, by his constant juxtaposition of the word "civilized" with western Europe and the word "barbarian" with the Asian and noncapitalistic world, Engels made Western society synonymous with civilization. Conversely, he made oriental society synonymous with primitive or backward, retrograde societies.

Engels's ingrained sense of Western superiority was manifested still further in his military writing on Asia. As we have seen, in terms of European events, Engels tended to specialize in military matters, leaving the commentary on politics and economics to Marx. The same division of labor, military versus political, was adhered to in relation to contemporary events in Asia.

Engels simply assumed that in regular battle Asian armies were no match for armies led and equipped by Europeans. The tactics and strategy, the discipline and organization, the military technology of the Europeans were simply superior to regular Asian armies. In writing on the Sepoy Mutiny, Engels commented that "the vast superiority of the English troops for such operations gave them every advantage."[5] Not only were regular

English troops inherently better than regular Asian troops, but because of their better schooling English troops had a better grasp of science and therefore scientific warfare. Asians, because of their weak grasp of science, would require a long time before they could master scientific warfare. "This requires a long time, and is sure to meet with the most obstinate opposition from Oriental ignorance, impatience, prejudice, and the vicissitudes of fortune and favor inherent to Eastern courts."[6] Furthermore, the English troops were better organized, accepted the leadership of their officers; the Asians fought as clans, rather than having any sense of national cohesiveness.[7] Engels asserted that the intelligence, heroism, and cooperativeness of the regular European army were superior and therefore must prove victorious over the Asian. In fact, his general attitude toward the Asian was disparaging and condescending. Scientific warfare, in regular battles, was invincible, and Engels had come to associate scientific technology with Western civilization.

This is not to say that Engels was not acquainted with guerrilla warfare. He recognized how the Sepoy Mutiny changed, after the defeats of the Indian regular armies, into guerrilla warfare. He saw how the Chinese people during the Second Opium War had moved toward guerrilla warfare. Above all, he was aware that regular European military strategy was either impotent or seriously challenged by guerrilla activities. But Engels did not feel that guerrilla warfare could lead to the military exhaustion and total political defeat of European forces in Asia. Although Engels favored liberation of the underdeveloped world from Europe, he nowhere indicated that guerrilla warfare would be the chief military means to that end.

Engels was, of course, in favor of Asian national liberation movements. On September 12, 1882, he wrote to Kautsky that in

> . . . my opinion the colonies proper, i.e., the countries occupied by a European population—Canada, the Cape, Australia—will all become independent; on the other hand, the countries inhabited by a native population which are simply subjugated . . . must be taken over for the time being by the proletariat and led as rapidly as possible towards independence.[8]

It is interesting to note that Engels did not select the peasantry as the class that would achieve national liberation for the colonies. Rather, as in the case of Europe, the proletariat, as the only true revolutionary class, must lead the movement toward independence. Indeed, then, Asia must pass through capitalism, because capitalism was the only form of society that had produced a proletariat from within itself.[9]

Like Marx, Engels was aware that Western imperialism was revolutionizing China. In 1857, Engels wrote that "before many years pass away we shall have to witness the death struggle of the oldest empire in the world and the opening day of a new era for all Asia."[10] The Asiatic mode of production was not only disappearing in China, but it was also being replaced by capitalism. In his letters to Danielson, Engels noted how big industry and railroads were beginning to make inroads in Chinese society. Engels assumed that wherever modern industry penetrated, capitalism would follow in its wake. Thus, China, because it was industrializing, would also be capitalized.[11] Engels expressed similar views to Kautsky, when he said that "the capitalist mode of production only remains to conquer China."[12] Thus, according to Engels, China must pass from feudalism to capitalism and then to communism. It must also follow the same path of evolution as the West.

Engels was tainted by the sense of cultural dominance that the great age of European imperialism bred throughout Europe. Engels accepted this superiority. Europe had a world mission. The salvation of the world was in the hands of Europe. Engels's sense of superiority was cultural rather than racist. He used economic determinism to substantiate his cultural elitism.

Engels's cultural ethnocentrism was demonstrated most clearly in his attitude toward the South Slavs. When Engels talked of the South Slavs he meant the Czechs, Slovaks, Slovenes, Croats, Serbians, Ukrainians, Rumanians, and Bulgars.[13] From 1848 until his death, he did not think these various nationalities were ready for national independence. In fact, he talked in terms of the unique cultural mission the Germans had to these lesser nationalities. The same kind of cultural ethnocentrism, of cultural elitism, that Engels manifested toward the Asians, he manifested, but with greater articulateness, toward the South Slavs. However, in the case of the South Slavs his cultural nationalism was narrower; that is, it was centered on Germany. It was Germany in particular, and not Western society in general, which carried the mission to civilize these people of a lower societal order.

Engels was no stranger to nationalism. He was an ardent German nationalist. In the cases of Ireland, Poland, Italy, he supported the nationality movements. His condescending attitude toward the Slavs had nothing to do with proletarian internationalism, but was rather a case in which he thought the South Slavs were unfit for national independence. That is, he thought them incapable of building and preserving states. Only the great nations of Europe, those nations that were highly civilized like the French, English, Italians, Germans, and Poles had proven themselves historically capable of founding states.[14]

Engels spoke in extraordinarily disparaging terms about the South Slavs. He referred to them as "geschichtlosen" (historyless), "Raübergesindel" (a pack of thieves), "Zwergstämme" (dwarf peoples), and "Trümmerstücke" (pieces of wreckage). He sought to disassociate himself from the liberal and radical attitude toward the South Slavs. The liberals and radicals expressed great sympathy for the "suppressed nationalities," but Engels himself had no such sympathies.[15] Furthermore, Engels did not want to romanticize the South Slavs. Dreamers and idealists could sympathize and glorify these "nature people," but Engels judged—and he advised Bernstein and Bebel to judge also—on the basis of brutal realism.[16] Scientific socialism showed these "dwarf nations," this "pack of thieves," to be historically unprepared to achieve national independence.

For instance, in 1882 Engels maintained that a greater Serbia was still "two to four generations" from being realized.[17] In 1882 the elements that would be needed to create a greater Serbia were still not in existence. In 1886 Engels said the same thing about the Bulgars. In the case of the Bulgars, however, it would take them "sixty years of bourgeois development" before they were ready to achieve national independence.[18] Engels felt the same way about the other "historyless" people in the Balkans. Regardless of their quaint customs, regardless of their primitive appeal, regardless of their reputed purity, the South Slavs were not ready to attain political sovereignty.

European national liberation movements, according to Engels, should be supported as long as they were at the same time socially progressive. German unification was acceptable and was necessary because it helped to bring about the ascendancy of the bourgeoisie. Polish liberation was acceptable because a free Poland would act as a buffer against Czarist aristocratic expressionism. Chinese independence should be supported because it would shrink the European mastery of the world market, and thus hasten the collapse of European capitalism. Irish independence was needed because it would help destroy the British Empire.

The case of the South Slavs was different, however, because these national liberation movements were not socially progressive. Engels desperately feared their Pan-Slavist tendencies. Pan-Slavism, in Engels's eyes, was the most reactionary force in Europe. It was simply a tool, an instrument of Czarist imperialism. For these South Slav peoples to win their independence as satellites of Czarist expansionism would allow reactionary Russia to move to the heart of central Europe. Such an extension of Czarist influence would be a major setback for the revolutionary forces of western Europe. It was better, then, for these "suppressed nationalities," even if they were ready for independence, not to achieve independence. It was better for these "suppressed nationalities" to remain suppressed, because then the doorway to central Europe and Constantinople would be barred to Czarism.

From this perspective, Engels was an Austrophile.[19] If the South Slavs must remain suppressed, it was best that they remain colonized within an Austro-Hungarian Empire. Austro-Hungary then had a two-fold purpose in the Balkans. By dominating the Slavs, it was a dam against Russian expansion in the Balkans. Secondly, in relation to Austro-Hungary, Engels believed that "one could speak of it as having a certain cultural, international mission."[20] That is, the Germans had a cultural mission to perform in the Balkans. It was their duty to raise the Slavs to a higher level of civilization, to prepare them for eventual liberation.

The liberation of the South Slav would come in either of two ways. First, if Russia had a revolution. A revolution in Russia would not only rid Russia of Czardom, but also of Pan-Slavism. With the threat of Czarist Pan-Slavism removed, the "suppressed nationalities" in the Balkans could achieve independence. A revolutionized Russia would mean that the nationalities in the Balkans would again unite with social progressivism. Second, if the proletariat came to power in the West. The "suppressed nationalities" of the Balkans would be allied with a progressive proletarian revolution in the West, and therefore South Slav independence would also carry with it a socially reformist program. Once more, however, in Engels's opinion, it was the proletariat who must lead, who were the only carriers of revolution. A proletarian revolution in Russia or the West was a necessary precondition for South Slav independence.

Allied to Engels's notion of the mission of the proletariat was Engels's notion of the mission of German culture. A part of the advanced culture of the West, German civilization had a salvationist purpose: to prepare the Slav for statism. In short, the German proletariat was the hope of civilization. German culture must civilize the Slavs, but the German proletariat must lead them to independence. Engels had not only identified Germany as having a messianic purpose, but in particular it was the German socialist party that specifically carried the messianic goal of communism. The unilinear view of history had imparted to the German proletariat a global salvationist function.

Engels's identification of the German proletariat with the fate of the global socialist revolution received greater confirmation when he turned to the problems of war and peace at the end of the nineteenth century. The identification of the worldwide proletarian revolution with German socialism was hardened when Engels pondered the relationship between Germany and Russia in the European balance of power. Engels's view of Russia contained two levels. First, there was Russia as a social entity: the Russia to which capitalism was coming, the Russia that was pregnant with social revolution. Second, there was the diplomatic Russia: the Russia that was under the actual guidance of the Czar, the present Russia that intervened in the affairs of Europe in terms of her imperial conservatism. When Engels talked of the messianic mission of the German proletariat, he did so in relation to the second Russia, the present Russia of imperial conservatism.

The Franco-Prussian War, according to Engels, was one of the decisive turning points of the nineteenth century. Because of the German acquisition of Alsace and Lorraine, Engels, like Marx, believed that Russia had become the arbiter of Europe. France would desire the return of the lost provinces, and would seek an alliance with Russia in her next war with Germany, and thus Russia held the European balance of power. Bismarck, wishing to conserve the aristocratic structure of Imperial Germany, also needed the support of reactionary Russia. The social structure of a Prussianized Germany would be consolidated through an alliance with an inherently conservative Czardom. Thus, the German aristocracy needed the social alliance of the Russian aristocracy, and in this manner also Russia was the arbiter of Europe. In fact, Russia was the bulwark of the conservative order in Europe.[21] Furthermore, the defeat of France and the subsequent defeat of the Paris Commune fundamentally shifted the center of gravity of the European workers' movement. Germany had become that center. In the preunification days, Engels could call for a war against Russia as a means of unifying Germany. In the postunification period, after Germany had become the leader of the European proletarian movement, Engels thought not of war, but of peace as a means of preserving the German socialist movement.

Peace was the policy Engels advocated after 1871. Peace would allow the industrialization, and thus the capitalization of the remainder of Europe to proceed in an uninterrupted fashion. The further industrialization of Germany and Russia would inevitably occasion the proletarian revolution. When Engels related to Russia on the first level, on the level of socioeconomic development, he was of the opinion that the maintenance of peace would enhance the possibilities of the Russian revolutionary movement's coming to power. On September 29, 1891, he wrote to Bebel that "internal contradictions must of necessity dissolve Russia."[22] War, however, would check and delay this necessity. War would unleash the emotions of nationalism and chauvinism, and this would only repress the workers' movement in Russia. "The entire work of the revolutionaries in Russia, which stands for the dawning of victory, would be needlessly destroyed" by war,[23] Engels wrote to Bebel on an earlier occasion after 1871. Engels was committed to the idea that war was a tool of the reactionaries.

Similarly, peace was the ally of revolution in Germany. Another date of major significance in the history of nineteenth-century Europe, according to Engels, was 1890. In February of that year the German Social Democratic Party won their largest electoral victory. Engels was ecstatic and on March 7, 1890, wrote to Paul Lafargue:

> February 20th is the date of the beginning of the revolution in Germany; that is why we must not let ourselves be smashed up before our time.. . . That is why we must come out for the time being for legal action and not react to the provocation which will be lavished upon us. For short of a bloodletting, and a pretty severe one at that, Bismarck and Wilhelm are doomed.[24]

In the above paragraph Engels made two equally vital statements. First, he affirmed his dedication to a nonrevolutionary proletarian policy. The forces of history were on the side of the proletariat, and thus peace would allow these forces to come to fruition. This statement, coupled with Engels's remarks in his "Introduction" of 1895 to Marx's *Class Struggles in France,* in which he surrendered the idea of urban insurrection and violence, marked Engels as one of the chief spokesmen for the socialist policy of social peace. In effect, Engels surrendered the instrument of violence as a revolutionary instrument; he, in effect, surrendered the idea of irreconcilable class warfare as a revolutionary instrument. In short, even though Engels philosophically and theoretically denied it, he, in actuality, had given up the idea of proletarian revolution, had given up the essence of the concept of class warfare and espoused a policy of nonrevolutionary evolutionism and gradualism. Second, Engels affirmed his dedication to the idea of the inevitability of the socialist revolution. For him "Bismarck and Wilhelm are doomed." Nothing could save them. The laws of history had decreed their demise.

Engels's commitment to the inevitability of the proletarian revolution was further evidenced by a letter he sent to Bebel on October 24, 1891. In that letter he wrote:

> In the report you [Bebel] indicated that I affirmed that the collapse of bourgeois society would occur in 1898. That is a small error. I have only said that there exists the possibility that we can come to power in 1898. The old bourgeois society can, in case this does not happen, still vegetate for some time, so long as an external attack does not crack the decadent exterior. So foul an old corpse can be preserved for two more decades, if the surroundings remain calm.[25]

Engels assumed that the German socialists would come to power by 1898. If not, then bourgeois society could not last any longer than twenty more years. Furthermore, Engels's inevitabilism directly strengthened his policy of social peace. If the revolution were sure to come, there was no reason to pursue a policy of irreconcilable class struggle and violence.

On the other hand, war would strengthen the reactionary forces both in Russia and in Germany. In the Germany of Wilhelm II, war would be a serious setback for the socialist movement. On September 13, 1886, Engels wrote to Bebel that "war would be a setback for our movement throughout Europe, in many lands it would be totally destroyed, chauvinism and national hate would be unleashed."[26] In Germany itself, the movement would revive after the war, but there was no guarantee that conditions would be as favorable for its growth as they were now.

In the diplomatic Russia of the Czar, war was an instrument of conservative expansionism. The chief ideological expression of Czarist imperialism was Pan-Slavism. The chief reason for the Russian autocrat to expand was to forestall social revolution at home.[27] Germany thus displayed an ambivalent attitude toward Russia. On the one hand, Germany needed Czarist Russia as a support for the essentially artistocratic nature of Germany's social structure. On the other hand, Russia's expansionism under the aegis of Pan-Slavism was a mortal enemy to Germany. A victory for Pan-Slavism in central Europe, Engels wrote to Kautsky, would virtually end the revolutionary movement in Germany.[28] If Germany unstintingly supported existent Czarist diplomatic ambitions, she ran the risk of being engulfed under the Pan-Slavic horde. If Germany resisted Russia, she ran the risk of unleashing social revolution in Russia, not only a disaster for Russia but a serious threat to conservative Germany as well. The ambivalence of Germany's attitude toward Russia was acutely expressed by Engels in a letter to Paul Lafargue: "This is the situation. To avoid a revolution in Russia, the Czar must have Constantinople. Bismarck hesitates, he would like to find a way of avoiding either contingency."[29]

Engels had a good grasp of the balance of social and diplomatic forces in Europe at the end of the century. He understood that the conservative order in Europe rested upon the continuation of Czardom. He also understood that the fall of Czardom to a social revolution would mean the end of the conservative order in Europe generally, and the spreading of the social revolution in Europe. However, in Engels's eyes, peace would inevitably bring the social revolution to Russia. War would only strengthen Czarism because of its concomitant chauvinism. Engels failed to see that war could be a revolutionary device. He failed to see that a Czarist defeat in a war could unleash the social revolution in Russia. Again he was caught in a tactical box. By not seeing the revolutionary implications of war, Engels could only turn back to the ballot box, to parliamentarianism.[30]

As we have seen, the year 1890 was a crucial one for Engels. It was a high-water mark in the growth of a German socialist movement. It was crucial also because in 1890 Germany ended its Russian connection. What Engels had feared when he wrote about the consequences of the annexation of Alsace-Lorraine had come to pass. France and Russia would be allies. Engels's diplomatic speculations changed after 1890. Germany now was confronted with a two-front war, a war in which Germany would face on its eastern front the armies of Pan-Slavist Czarism.

Essentially, Engels still favored a policy of peace. But if war did come, Germany must fight an all-out war against Russia. The German socialists must support this war. The German socialists must "demand the universal arming of the people."[31] They also must see that this war be carried on against Russia with all "revolutionary means."[32] Engels was more specific in a letter he wrote to Bebel on October 24, 1891:

> We German socialists who, if peace were to be maintained would come to power in ten years, have the duty to preserve our unconquered position as the avant garde of the workers' movement, not only against internal enemies, but also against external opponents. If Russia wins we are suppressed. If Russia begins the war, we must attack not only Russia, but Russia's allies, no matter who they are. We must be concerned to carry out this war with every revolutionary means. . . . We have not forgotten the glorious example of the French of 1793, and if we are pressed, we can show that we will celebrate the unilineal jubilee of 1793, in which we will demonstrate that the German workers of 1893 are not unworthy of the sans-culotter of one hundred years ago.[33]

What Engels did was to identify the fate of the German Social Democratic Party with the European and, therefore, the world revolution. At the end of his life, Engels called upon the German socialists to support imperial spending for armaments and national defense. Engels asked the German proletariat to enter the imperial army in order to directly defend the feudal conservative order of Germany on the assumption that the proletariat would also be indirectly defending German socialism. There had taken place in Engels's mind a fusion between his German nationalism and the messianic mission of the German proletariat. A victory for Germany, in terms of Engels's own logic, was a concomitant victory for the world socialist revolution.

Thus, Engels laid the basis for the policy of the German Social Democratic Party and the entire Second International in the crisis of 1914. By not opposing war at all costs, by not thinking of war as a revolutionary tool, Engels encouraged the Second International to think in terms of a policy of national defensism. Engels's own nationalism proved to be endemic. It spread to the socialist movements in other European countries.

Engels believed that the laws by which society evolved were as firm, as unalterable, as necessitarian as the laws of the physical universe. Essentially, society evolved in accordance with the laws of economic determinism; that is, the laws of technological innovation finally determined the general line of historical growth. Propelled by technological advances, society had moved from primitive communism to feudalism to capitalism. It would next move to communism.

Western civilization was the first area of the globe to have passed through the stages from primitive communism to capitalism. Because the West had advanced already to this state, the technological forces of society would make it the first portion of the globe to move upward to communism. Asia, and all other areas of the globe, must also follow this four-stage pattern of growth. Global history was a unilinear process for Engels. Europe had reached the highest stage. Asia must imitate Europe. The communist revolution must first break out in Europe.

Western civilization led the world. The proletarian party in Germany led Western civilization. Therefore, the German proletarian party led the world. Engels's view of history supported his German nationalism. His conception that the laws of economic growth necessitated societies passing through fixed stages, his conception that Europe stood at the stage just below communism prepared him to see the German proletarian party as the messianic party of the world communist revolution.

Engels's view of history meant that inevitabilism replaced consciousness. Because Engels was so certain that the communist revolution would come to Germany within two decades, it was enough for the German socialists to wait. Vulgar Marxism replaced vital, creative Marxism. Social determinism replaced consciousness.

Footnotes

1. Engels to Marx, June 6, 1853, *Karl Marx on Colonialism and Modernization,* ed. Shlomo Avineri (New York: Doubleday & Co., 1969), p. 451.
2. *Ibid.,* p. 452.
3. Friedrich Engels, "French Rule in Algeria," *Karl Marx on Colonialism and Modernization,* pp. 47–48.
4. Engels to Bernstein, August 9, 1882, *Karl Marx on Colonialism and Modernization,* p. 472.
5. Engels, "Military Aftermath of the Capture of Lucknow," *Karl Marx on Colonialism and Modernization,* p. 317.
6. Engels, "Persia—China," *Karl Marx on Colonialism and Modernization,* p. 186.
7. Engels to Marx, December 31, 1857, *Karl Marx on Colonialism and Modernization,* p. 462.
8. Engels to K. Kautsky, September 12, 1882, *Karl Marx and Friedrich Engels: Selected Works* (New York: International Publishers, 1968), p. 688.
9. *Ibid.*
10. Engels, "Persia—China," *Karl Marx on Colonialism and Modernization,* p. 190.
11. Engels to Danielson, September 22, 1892, in Marx and Engels, *Selected Correspondence,* trans. Dona Torr (New York: International Publishers, 1942), pp. 497–501.
12. Engels, *Briefwechsel mit K. Kautsky* (Vienna: Europäische Verlag, 1928), p. 411.
13. Roman Rosdolsky, "Friedrich Engels und Das Problem Der Geschichtslosen Völker," *Archiv für Sozialgeschichte,* Band IV (1964), pp. 87–88.
14. *Ibid.*
15. Engels, *Briefwechsel mit E. Bernstein* (The Hague: Mouton & Co., 1969), p. 80.
16. *Ibid.,* p. 83.
17. *Ibid.,* p. 82.
18. *Ibid.,* p. 343.
19. *Ibid.,* pp. 80–83.
20. *Ibid., p. 77.*
21. Engels, "Introduction, 1891," to Marx, *Civil War in France* (New York: International Publishers, 1940), p. 10.
22. Engels, *Briefwechsel mit A. Bebel* (The Hague: Mouton & Co., 1968), p. 438.
23. *Ibid.,* p. 143.
24. Engels, *Engels-Lafargue Correspondence,* ed. Emile Bottigelli, trans. Yvonne Kapp (Moscow: Foreign Languages Publishing House, 1968), II, pp. 366–367.
25. Engels, *Briefwechsel mit A. Bebel,* p. 465.
26. *Ibid.,* p. 286.
27. Engels, *Engels-Lafargue Correspondence,* I, p. 386.
28. Engels, *Briefwechsel mit K. Kautsky,* p. 52.
29. Engels, *Engels-Lafargue Correspondence,* I, p. 388.
30. *Ibid.,* pp. 390–391.
31. Engels, *Briefwechsel mit A. Bebel,* p. 439.
32. *Ibid.,* p. 440.
33. *Ibid., p. 464.*

Thirteen

Communism as Industrial Puritanism

IN CHAPTER FOUR, "Toward a Philosophical Anthropology," an attempt was made to define the Marxian idea of communism. In this chapter an attempt will be made to accurately characterize Engels's conception of communism. The divergence of thought between the two men was nowhere more clearly manifest than in their conflicting interpretation of the future communist society. This was entirely logical. Their vision of socialism was the culmination of their basic thought patterns. The divergence between their philosophies of man, nature, and history thus exploded into sharp polarity on the issue in which these philosophies were to achieve their fullest crystalization. It was at that point where both men tried to suggest the consequences and results of their theories that their irreconcilable differences became most apparent.

Primarily, the divergent views of Marx and Engels over communism derived from a different interpretation of the anthropological nature of man. To put it more succinctly, the two men learned different things from Ludwig Feuerbach. Although critical of Feuerbach, Marx was greatly influenced by his anthropological humanism.[1] Marx was to incorporate this anthropological center, the centrality of species being, into his view of history and into his view of communism. Engels did no such thing. The Feuerbachian notion of species being was entirely overlooked by Engels. In fact, Engels seemed unaware of the naturalism that was at the base of Feuerbach's philosophy. Therefore, when Engels came to define a communist society, he did so without reference to anthropological humanism, but rather from a Victorian, Calvinist idolization of work and productivity. One could speculate that Engels's childhood Pietism finally triumphed over his thought in later life.

Written in 1886,[2] nine years before his death, "Ludwig Feuerbach and the End of Classical German Philosophy" contained Engels's mature and final evaluation of this pivotal German philosopher. As a young man in 1846, after his initial acquaintance with the work of Feuerbach, Engels had written several letters to Marx in which he was critical and hostile to the author of the *Essence of Christianity.*[3] The Engels of 1886 held the same opinion of Feuerbach as he had forty years earlier. The same confusion and misunderstanding toward this man were manifest by Engels throughout his life.

According to Engels, the *Essence of Christianity* revolutionized classical German philosophy. It brought an end to the idealism of Fichte, Kant, and Hegel. "The great basic question of all philosophy,"[4] Engels believed, was the relationship between thinking and being. German idealism assumed the priority of thinking to being. Feuerbach reintroduced materialism to German philosophy. Engels defined materialism as the belief that nature took priority over thinking. Feuerbach educated a generation of German scholars to the causal predominance of nature over idea, according to Engels.[5]

Engels's definition of materialism was both unsophisticated and naive. Materialism for Engels meant that the explanations for events must always be located in external and physical objects. Materialism for Engels was synonymous with things. Furthermore, Engels could not discern the distinction between materialism and naturalism. Feuerbach was really a naturalist, but Engels never referred to him by this nomenclature. The failure to distinguish between materialism and naturalism meant that Engels remained unaware of the serious difference between physics and anthropology. Rather than interpret human nature as a universal being of the species, Engels interpreted human nature from the perspective of a chemist or physicist. Engels began, not with the emotional and psychological nature of man, but rather with physical nature. For Engels, the world did not proceed from man, but rather man proceeded out of nature; man was reduced to molecular and atomic constituents.

Furthermore, in "Ludwig Feuerbach and the End of Classical German Philosophy," Engels credited Hegel, even though at the same time condemning him for his idealism, with one of the greatest discoveries of the nineteenth century. It was Hegel who had proclaimed that history, philosophy, man, were all process and change. Feuerbach was also responsible for one of the great discoveries of the nineteenth century: he proclaimed the primacy of nature. But Feuerbach's materialism was defective, according to Engels. It was a static materialism; it was a materialism that lacked the notions of process and change. Engels referred to him as a mechanistic materialist.[6] For Engels, mechanistic materialism meant a view of nature that was static. There were other features of mechanistic materialism, but Engels preferred to limit his judgment to the notion of a fixed, finite, and stable universe. Engels was clearly critical of such a view and felt that any interpretation of nature that was not predicated on the notion of process was, ipso facto, a defective interpretation of nature. Engels joined materialism to the idea of process, but Engels defined materialism as nature in its appearance as chemistry or physics.

In the same book, Engels also criticized Feuerbach for his static view of man. According to Engels, the Feuerbachian man "remains always the same abstract man who occupied the field in the philosophy of religion." In other words, the attempt of Feuerbach to abstract an unchanging essence of the species was labeled by Engels as "real idealism."[7] On the other hand, Engels criticized Feuerbach because Feuerbach's abstraction of man abstracted man from society. Feuerbach dealt with man as man would always exist. He had not taken into account the social or political influences on the species, or how the species had changed throughout history. On this score, Engels was on solid ground. Marx had criticized Feuerbach for much the same reasons in his "Theses on Feuerbach." Engels, however, had failed to make an important distinction. He had failed to separate the attempt to abstract a being of man from the attempt to abstract man entirely from history. Marx was able to see man both as historicity and as anthropological essence. Marx combined process with naturalistic ontology. Engels, conversely, completely overlooked the naturalistic core, and fell to the other extreme of viewing human nature itself as totally historical. Essence, for Engels, was completely absorbed in flux.

In addition, Engels also accused Feuerbach of making a religion out of his theory of human needs and human sentiments. For example, Engels wrote that "with Feuerbach, sex love becomes one of the highest forms, if not the highest form, of the practice of his new religion."[8] However, far from creating a new religion, Feuerbach wished to show the source of religion in human sentiments. Feuerbach was creating not a religion of God but a religion of man. Supernatural religion, a religion totally divorced from its origins in human anthropology, was, according to Feuerbach, the highest proof of the process of species alienation. By attacking Feuerbach so totally, Engels illustrated that he understood neither the idea of alienation nor its implications.[9]

When Engels wished to study anthropology, he did not, like Marx, turn to Feuerbach, but turned instead to Darwin. Engels's predisposition to positivism was again revealed by his trying to explain man solely on the basis of evolutionary biology. According to Engels, man must be process, he must evolve. Engels denied the Feuerbachian abstraction of man, and maintained that human nature itself was an evolutionary product. This evolutionary process was still continuing. It was Engels who wed socialism to Darwinism.

In "The Part Played by Labour in the Transition from Ape to Man," Engels acknowledged his debt to Darwin and claimed "that labour created man himself."[10] From Engels's understanding of Darwinian theory, "the decisive step in the transition from ape to man"[11] was the achievement of erect posture by homo sapiens. Man was a descendant of the anthropoid apes, and his erect gait allowed him to use his hands with ever increasing freedom and dexterity. With the development of the hand, with man's increased productivity, members of society could work with greater cooperation. Production increased the need for social harmony, and social harmony produced the need for speech. The brain was also stimulated to grow in capacity as speech became a human trait. Speech had encouraged the growth of mental powers, and increased mental powers also encouraged the development of the different senses. The freeing of the hand as an instrument for labor was the necessary first step in the evolution of the vocal, mental, and sensory constitution of man.

Engels sought to reduce all evolutionary activity and economic activity to one source, labor. In so doing, he completely distorted the meaning of the term "labor." When Engels referred to labor in his evolutionary picture of human nature, he really meant adaptation. In the Darwinian sense, he meant the ability of the organism to adapt, adjust to the natural environment. This definition of labor was not what political economists, including Marx, meant by labor. Labor for the political economists implied an outpouring of activity, human *praxis* that modified and thus added something to the world. Labor for the economist referred to the additive quality, the capacity to enhance and increase beyond an object's natural properties, which was lodged in human practice. Adaptation referred to a selective process that was carried on by the natural environment. It was the environment that either destroyed or else preserved specific properties of the organism. The difference between destruction or preservation rested on the mutual correspondence between the properties of the organism and the properties of the environment. Conversely, labor implied that the human or animal was active; adaptation implied that the environment was active, or selective, that the preservation of species properties was the function of the natural or social surroundings.

When Engels confused labor with adaptability, he again demonstrated that imprecision of thought which blurred his thinking throughout his life. Engels's inability to arrive at precise definition of terms, to distinctly categorize concepts, led him to confuse one idea with another, led to gross logical errors. Engels made the mistake of confusing labor with adaptability because he was looking for a material reason to explain human physical development. Material reason, for Engels, meant external object, meant a "thing." The hand was such a thing. The hand was active, it labored. Therefore, labor must be the cause of human physical evolution.[12]

Engels's cosmological determinism found its correlate in an evolutionary determinism. The physiological development of man proceeded with the same iron-bound linear necessity as the functioning of the universe. Engels again affirmed that the more scientific knowledge increased "the more men will not only feel but also know their oneness with nature, and the more impossible will become the senseless and unnatural idea of a contrast between mind and matter, man and nature, soul and body."[13] Mind and man were products of materialistic laws, the growth of brain capacity being a necessary consequence of the greater demands of a more developed larynx. The mechanistic laws of the universe were the same mechanistic laws of human biological evolution. In the hands of Engels, anthropology became synonymous with evolutionary positivism. It was impossible for Engels to develop a philosophic anthropology of man, because anthropology for Engels meant linear and mechanistic evolutionism.

In the 1890s Engels began to refer to his theories (feeling that they were also Marx's) as "historical materialism." The exact meaning that Engels gave to this term is now clear. By historical materialism, Engels meant a view of nature, understood as physics and chemistry, that was based on change. On another level, Engels defined historical materialism as the belief that technical and industrial changes were the central causative factors in history, and as they inevitably changed so must society inevitably change. Historical materialism meant economic determinism.

The Marxian view of social change was at variance with this Engelsian conception on two counts. First, when Marx spoke of nature he meant the anthropological nature of man. Marx did not speculate about the ultimate constitution of the universe. That was Engels. When Marx meditated about nature he pondered the naturalistic being of the species man. Materialism did not imply chemistry for Marx, but rather naturalism. Furthermore, it was a constitutive naturalism, rather than a reductive materialism as in the case of Engels. That is, Marx's naturalism presupposed that one element of the species being of man was the need of man to objectify himself and that this objectification of the essence of man was a constitutive and genetic cause of the social universe.

Secondly, when investigating society Marx did not, like Engels, begin with the notion of process. Rather, Marx began with the notion of structure. Marx did not presume flux, but he presumed structures that were imbalanced and because of this imbalance must alter their internal organization. Marxism was an analytical tool, a device to investigate the internal structure of social organisms from the point of view of conflict, from the point of view of clash between form and content. Change was a consequence of this clash, rather than a cause. Process was a result of this conflict and imbalance rather than its source. For Marx what was given was structure; for Engels what was given was flux.

For these reasons, the theories of Engels could be referred to as "historical materialism," but not the theories of Marx. The best term to not only epitomize Marxism, but also distinguish it from Engelsism, is "dialectical naturalism." Marxism was dialectical because it presumed a societal structure in conflict, imbalanced between form and content. Marxism was naturalistic because it presumed that both the form and content of a given societal structure were in part constituted by the anthropological being of man.

The lack of a philosophical anthropology had clear implications for Engels's definition of communism. Engels did not, like Marx, develop a philosophy of culture. Rather, Engels developed a philosophy of production, or a philosophy of the distribution of goods. For Engels, communism was synonymous with the mathematical apportionment of labor, and the mathematical apportionment of distribution. It was a social calculus for the equality of work and the equality of possession. Engels and Marx disagreed over the definition of communism because Engels's intellectual lexicon lacked such concepts as objectification, alienation, reappropriation and self-affirmation.[14]

FOR MARX, MEN were compelled to *objectify* themselves. Therefore, they were active. Labor was one mode of their activity. Labor was the form of mediation between the objective natural essence of man and the objective external object made by man. The object made by man corresponded to the species being of man. For Marx, man humanized nature, because something of himself was implanted in the dumb material that physical nature offered to him.

Without a concept of species being, Engels could not arrive at a concept of objectification. Since Engels did not recognize an anthropological human essence, he could not see that an external object fashioned by man must correspond to the internal objective essence of man. Labor for Engels was not a form of mediation between an active human nature and an inactive external nature. Labor, for Engels, meant the manipulation of matter. It meant understanding the laws of matter in order to control matter, to make matter work for human interests. The difference between Marx and Engels was the difference between the mutual interpenetration between man and nature, and the control of nature by man. Marx again talked of immanence, Engels talked of a scientifically precocious factory manager.

FOR MARX, *ALIENATION* meant the separation between the object made and the objective essence of man. That is, once the object was made it was not returned to its maker, it was not used to confirm or to complement the anthropological core. The object made was divorced from man, was expropriated from him by an alien power. Communism, for Marx, meant the end of alienation, meant that the objectification of man would be returned to him and therefore corroborate his objective power. Communist society would be the sociological affirmation of species being.

Engels had no theory of alienation. He had no theory of alienation because he had no theory of species being. Therefore, Engels simply assumed that under communism the administration of the economy, which would replace the state, would be the ground of freedom. Only the state was oppressive: economic administration would liberate.

Engels was blind to the fact that the administration of products itself could lead to human alienation. Because Engels did not see that the state and also every social product was an objectification of the human essence, Engels did not see that the administration of economic life could be just as exploitative, just as alienating as capitalist society. For instance, the administration of economic life through a great extension of the working day would be just as exploitative under Engels's communism as it would be under capitalism. Engels failed to see that economic decisions must be made on the criteria of anthropological eudaemonism.

THE NOTION OF *reappropriation* played an immensely important role in Marx's definition of communism. In communist society man would reappropriate his own objectification. Reappropriation in this sense meant direct return or a total absence of mediation. What would be returned to man would not be materiality, not merely the formal aspects of the object made, but instead the content. That is, that part of the external objectification which carried the talents, abilities, dispositions, and drives of man would be immediately present for man to experience. This experience, either mental or sensual, of the internal objective content of man in the external objectifications of man confirmed man to himself; that is, communist society was a self-confirming society.

Engels had no notion of reappropriation. When Engels talked about return, he meant simply materiality. What was returned to man in Engels's communist society was merely an equal quantity of labor embodied as a physical object. Human talents, abilities, dispositions, drives were not returned, but only a thing, a possession was returned. Engels equated communism with materiality; Marx equated communism with the human essence.

Engels's stress was really upon acquisition of things. Engel's communist man was still an acquisitive man. What he acquired was food, clothing, shelter, education, leisure. Again, communism for Engels was an additive process. The continued augmentation of productive power would mean a corresponding decrease of necessary labor time. A lessening of socially necessary labor time would mean an expansion of leisure time, and thus man would have more time to do the things he liked.

THE NOTION OF *self-affirmation* was another vital concept for Marx. The confirmation of internal objective essence by external objectifications affirmed the human self. The talents of the self, the abilities of the self, the drives of the self were positively affirmed by the appearance and power of these talents, abilities, and drives in an external object. To experience self as expression, as power, as a generative force, was to experience contentment with self. Communist society, by making reappropriation immediate, made self-affirmation immediate. Marx was concerned with the inner man, and communism for him was allied with eudaemonism.

Engels possessed no idea of self-affirmation. Engels was not dealing with a self that found its complement in society, but instead a self that was concerned and committed to industrial productivity. His concern was not with a being who was content with itself because it was self-expressive but a being who was diligent and responsible in his work, in his labor to produce an abundance in the Faustian theme of domination over nature. The Marxian vision derived from the classical ideal of an organic, harmonius society. Behind Marx stood the Greek ideal of the polis. Behind Engels stood the Renaissance theme of the magician-alchemist.

Ironically, Engels's vision of communism was heavily overlaid with many bourgeois elements. Engels talked of economic abundance. He talked of control over nature. He also talked about social control and rational socioeconomic centralized planning. He talked of acquisitiveness. The communist society he described was the epitome of Weberian and middle class entrepreneurial economic rationality. Engels manifested the bourgeois belief in unending progress based upon scientific gadgetry, scientific alchemy. Engels seemed to be saying that a communist society, one without private property and the state, could do everything bourgeois society tried to do, only better. Thus Engels's communist society perpetuated bourgeois ideals, values, and ethics. Engels's socialism would not breed a new socialist man. Rather, Engels's socialism would allow the bourgeois man to continue to exist, only within the framework of a rationalized economy.

Engels's Pietism triumphed at the end. His vision of communism combined a superabundant scientific utopia with Calvinist morality. He began with the grey discipline of work. He ended with the Calvinist commandment to make provision on this earth and to materially prosper on this earth. Geneva, rather than Athens, was the image in Engels's mind. In his hands, communism assumed a puritanical stamp.

SO FAR THIS chapter has focused on what communism did not mean for Engels. We must now describe with accuracy what communism did mean for Engels. We shall do so under the following categories: (1) the technological base for communism, (2) the state, (3) the end of classes, (4) production, (5) distribution, (6) centralized planning and worker control, (7) freedom and necessity.

1. The Technological Base for Communism

Communism came into existence, for Engels, when the means of production stood at a high productive level.[15] In short, communism was a function of a certain level of technological development. Conversely, communism could not have existed during the Renaissance or the feudal period, or the age of Greece or Rome. In periods of underproductivity, classes developed as a consequence of the struggle to possess the few or scanty material objects produced. However, in a period of sufficient productivity or abundant productivity, the age that dawned at the end of the nineteenth century, there would be no need for classes, no need for the struggle of possession, because there would be enough for everyone.

Communism for Engels was not a static society; it was not a fixed, eternally formed, perfect society. It was a cardinal feature of Engels's *Weltanschauung* that process and flux were primary. Communism, therefore, would undergo transformation. The victory of communism over capitalism, for Engels, meant the abolition of the state, the destruction of classes and the division of labor, and the transcendence of the dichotomy between production as a social activity and distribution carried out in terms of private appropriation. Once the communist revolution had eradicated these forms of capitalist expropriation, communist society would evolve; however, always within the perimeters of what had been destroyed. In short, the lack of a state, the lack of classes and a division of labor, the lack of a tension between social production and private appropriation would be the conditions, the ground of future communist evolution.

2. The State

Engels had a decidedly mechanistic view of the state. In Engels's understanding of the origin of the state, there first came property, then classes to contend the ownership of this property, and then the state as a form of oppression to keep the propertyless from asserting themselves. The state, for Engels, was simply power. It was simply a political tool of domination. In Engels's eyes the state was solely a machine, operating in the interests of those who wished to preserve their monopolization of possession.

Unlike Marx, Engels did not see the state as a form of alienation. Furthermore, Engels did not see the difference between state and society. For Marx, society was the activity and behavior of man that grew out of his species being. Society was the practice of man's anthropological core. The state, for Marx, came into existence because there was a defect in society. The defect was the division of labor, out of which classes grew, out of which the struggle for property grew, out of which the state grew. In Marx's vision the state and society were counterposed against each other, the state representing alienated human existence, society representing the naturalistic core of human existence. The communist revolution, for Marx, meant the destruction of the state, but it also meant the reemergence of society. Or as Marx put it, social life in fact became political life.

What was abolished for Engels after the communist revolution was solely political power:[17] the domination of one person by another based on property. Political life as such, within Engels's terminology, came to an end.[18] But social regulation continued. There would still be the "administration of things." There would still be "the conduct of the processes of production." In his essay "On Authority," Engels strongly upheld the need for social regulation in the factory and society; that is, "the conduct of the processes of production" must dictate or organize many areas of social activity.[19] What Engels did not see was that the "administration of things," "the conduct of the processes of production" could be just as dominating as the state. Because Engels defined oppression simply in political terms, he could not see that economic administration could be oppressive and alienating.[16]

Communism, for Engels, meant the end of political existence. Such was not the case with Marx. For Marx, communism meant the triumph of society. Thus, political life was possible for Marx under communism as long as it was expressive, or as long as it was subordinate to human social life, or species being. What Marx did not want was that the state should act "as an independent entity that possesses its own intellectual, moral and free basis."[20] What he did want was that the state should be converted "from an organ standing above society into one completely subordinated to it."[21] That is, for Marx communism meant species and anthropological life becoming political life—the unanimity and harmony of natural and political man.

It was because Engels allowed administrative legislation to become an "independent entity that possesses its own intellectual, moral and free basis" that he inadvertently allowed administrative legislation to develop into another state. Engels's version was not inconsonant with the Saint-Simonian managerial society.

3. The End of Classes

Under communism, not only the state, but also social classes would cease to exist. But social classes, according to Engels, were merely a function of property and the division of labor. Property, when introduced into a society in which the division of labor existed, caused a struggle between different branches within the division of labor for its possession. The branch that won possession of property thereby formed itself into a class. But the fundamental cause for the development of social classes was the social division of labor.

In a communist society, therefore, the division of labor must be abolished. Engels proposed to do this by increasing job mobility. By means of better education, better job training, an individual could be trained to perform many jobs within his vocational lifetime. The rotation, the circulation, of the laboring force would end the division of labor and end social classes.

The rotation of jobs would democratize the vocational structure of communist society. The democratization of the occupational hierarchy would prevent eco-administrative power from being monopolized by people in a specific set of occupational groups. Engels was again primarily concerned with questions of power and oppression. The use of the democratic rotation system in occupational placement would prevent power from accruing to a certain set of occupational groups, and their present eco-administrative expropriation.

Just as Engels was opposed to the monopolization of property, so he was opposed to the monopolization of economic functions. Exclusivity in terms of socioeconomic function would lead to excessive privilege and control. Under communism, for Engels, there could be no monopoly of function because such exclusivity entailed possession and control.

Engels was opposed to occupational elitism because it implied the same kind of domination as property elitism. For instance, Engels was opposed to an independent intellectual group. In other words, Engels was opposed to a group that simply specialized in evaluating and producing culture. He was against it because such an intellectual group would then have an autonomous existence; that is, its occupational function would be totally divorced from the social and productive needs of society. The culture produced would not be representative of society generally but only representative of a small group of people.[22]

4. Production

Production for Engels meant mastery. It meant the control and domination of both technology and nature that would insure economic abundance. Under communism, man would no longer be subject to the laws of the factory or the laws of the physical universe. Rather, under communism the laws of the factory and the laws of the physical universe would be under the control of man and thus be enormously productive. Man would be master.[23]

Production in Engels's communist society would be organized on the basis of centralized plan. Mastery involved control and control involved rationalization, according to Engels. He also apparently believed that productivity increased when it was organized from and by one center. In *Anti-Dühring* he wrote: "Only a society which makes possible the harmonious cooperation of its productive forces on the basis of one single vast plan"[24] could properly manage the economic development of a country.

Engels was aware, however, that a communist society would never be a society of complete equality. Even though the enormous differences between rural life and urban life would be destroyed, some disparity of living style would remain. Likewise, the end of the division of labor would bring an end to classes, but not total equality of occupational power.[25] Socioeconomic egalitarianism was the end toward which communist society moved, it was the principle of communist society, but it was not an end easily realized. Even in a communist society, deviations from the ideal would occur. But Engels throughout his life was an adherent of the Babeuvist notion that communism meant economic egalitarianism.[26]

Certainly Engels believed in labor egalitarianism. When he wrote that under communism "no individual can put on to other persons his share in productive labor," he obviously meant that every person must labor in equal shares. Babeuf's notion of egalitarianism was extended by Engels to productive egalitarianism. Everyone must labor in accordance with equal quotas of labor-duration. Again, Engels the materialist was apparent. Equality for Engels came to mean like measure, like quantities. Equality of labor meant for Engels equal quantities of time duration spent in labor.

Even though the mechanistic side, the quantifiable side of Engels did predominate, he was not exclusively mechanistic. In other words, he also believed that labor under communism would "become a pleasure instead of a burden." Because people would not be fixed into classes, would not become hard specialists solely performing one repetitive task, labor would become less monotonous. In fact, based upon the principle of democratization of function where people would perform several tasks, labor would become enjoyable because their full abilities and talents would be free to be expressed. The mere absence of specialization would encourage the positive expression of the vanity of human abilities. The laborer would not be a cog, but a full, expressive person.

5. Distribution

In Engels's mind economics could be reduced to mathematics.[27] The model that Engels kept before his eyes when he thought of a communist economic science was borrowed from mathematical chemistry and mathematical physics. Here again, Engels sought to reduce economics to a quantifiable natural science. His latent sense of positivism drove his economic thinking in the direction of a productive and distributive calculus. Engels's communism was merely a society in which the function of production and distribution could be carried on with a rationalized, mathematical certainty and apportionment.

In his *Anti-Dühring,* Engels indicated that commodity production would cease under communism. That arch-commodity, money, would also cease to exist, because it would be possible to quantify all objects made by the amount of labor placed into them. "The quantity of social labor contained in a product has then no need to be established in a roundabout way; daily experience shows in a direct way how much of it is required on the average."[28] Engels felt it possible to quantifiably determine the exact amount of labor necessary to produce the objects society needed. He also felt it possible to quantifiably calculate the amount of labor available in society. The possession of such data would make economic planning merely a matter of mathematical calculation. Planning could be conducted with the accuracy of an algebraic formula. "Society can calculate simply how many hours are contained in a steam engine, a bushel of wheat of the last harvest, or a hundred square yards of cloth of a certain quality."[29] For instance, the formula used to calculate productive egalitarianism might be expressed as labor necessary divided by *labor available.* The division of available labor into necessary labor would inform us as to the quantity of labor each person must perform in order for society to produce the objects required for its sustenance. The calculus of economics would be a certain guide as to the distribution of equal shares of labor.

Similarly, the calculus of economics would be a certain guide to the egalitarianism of distribution. Again in his *Anti-Dühring,* Engels made the following statement:

> It is true that even then it will still be necessary for society to know how much labor each article of consumption requires for its production. It will have to arrange its plan of production in accordance with its means of production, which include, in particular, its labor forces. The useful effects of the various articles of consumption, compared with each other and with the quantity of labor required for their production, will in the last analysis determine the plan.[30]

The central production plan was an expression of the ratio of available labor to necessary labor. The distribution of goods could proceed in terms of the same ratio. By knowing what society needed, we could then calculate the quantity of goods each person must receive in order for each person to receive equally. In short, the formula for distributive egalitarianism might be: *labor expended* divided by *labor in goods produced.* This is a simple inversion of the formula for productive egalitarianism. The communist society, for Engels, did not mean that each person had returned to him an amount of labor-in-goods equivalent to the amount of labor-time he had expended. It meant, however, that each person received an equal portion of the total labor-in-goods produced by society. The ideal of distributive egalitarianism was applied to the total product of society.

Engels's vision of a communist society was thus an amalgam of Saint-Simonian technocracy and Babeuvist economic egalitarianism. It was a mathematically rationalized society. It was Engels's belief that advances in physics and chemistry had made communist economic egalitarianism a practical possibility. By quantifying labor, it would then be possible to distribute productive labor-time equally and distribute labor-in-goods equally. The absolute standard for Engels was not value, but labor. An economic calculus could apportion the pool of labor-in-goods on an egalitarian basis. This would prevent an unbalanced apportionment of labor-in-goods to any particular person or social group. In short, equality of possession meant equality of social power, social privilege, and social rights.

Marx had offered a different description of communism. In his *Critique of the Gotha Programme* Marx referred to production and distribution under communism in the following words: "from each according to his ability, to each according to his needs."[31] The standard Marx set up for production and distribution was not the quantification of labor. The standard Marx set up related to abilities, talents, and needs.

According to Marx, what one produced corresponded to his abilities. Conversely, what one consumed corresponded to his needs. The standard of judgment was the species being of man. Communist society, according to Marx, was a society in which the processes of production and distribution were carried on in accordance with the naturalistic needs and abilities of man. Marx's economics was anthropocentric; that is, the naturalistic core of man determined the procedure and balance of production and distribution. According to Engels, production and distribution under communism were carried on by means of mathematical formulae. The standard judgment was not the species being of man but the need for algebraic balance. Engels's economics was not anthropocentric, but rather mathematical.

6. Centralized Planning and Worker Control

Engels was a centralist. Economic planning should be carried on by one central organization. Industrial production should be carried on in large, manufacturing units. Agriculture, too, should be centralized.[32] Small farms would be eliminated under communism. Large agrarian units, what amounted to agricultural industrial units, would take the place of the small farm.[33] Engels was primarily concerned about productivity. The most productive units for him, both in industry and agriculture, were large and centrally organized.

The workers themselves could be trained to run these manufacturing and agricultural combines. Primarily, the skills needed were technical and managerial skills. The educational system under communism would train workers to function also as engineers and industrial bureaucrats. Engels believed that the workers themselves, with proper training, could be taught to administer the industrial bureaucracy. Then it would be possible to rotate and circulate a worker through many levels and functions of the agricultural and manufacturing combines.[34]

The end of centralized planning and worker control was increased output. The fundamental criterion for Engels was always quantity. In discussing the communist method of distribution, Engels wrote to C. Schmidt on August 5, 1890, that "after all the method of distribution essentially depends on how much there is to distribute."[35] The quest for the "how much" determined the "how."

7. Freedom and Necessity

Engels felt that he had solved the riddle between freedom and necessity. By necessity Engels meant natural law that was uncontrolled by human consciousness. Capitalism, for instance, was still the realm of necessity. Natural and economic law operated in capitalist society but without human guidance. Therefore, capitalism was unorganized, uncontrolled, anachronistic, and blind necessity would lead to its destruction.[36]

Natural and economic laws still operated in communist society. But in a communist society these laws would be subject to conscious, human control. Communism was therefore the realm of human freedom. It was the realm of human freedom because necessity was guided, was directed by a human plan. Man was not subject to necessity. Necessity was subject to man.[37]

Engels still defined freedom as freedom *from.* According to Engels man was free when he was not controlled by external forces, when he was not mastered by external forces. To be free, for Engels, was to have control over. Not to be free, for Engels, was to be dependent upon forces outside of one.

Marx had defined freedom in a totally different way. Marx had not defined freedom as either freedom from or as freedom over. Rather, Marx had defined freedom as freedom *to.* Freedom for Marx meant the ability of the human being to function in accordance with the laws of its nature.[38] Marx was talking about individual and social harmony; whereas Engels was talking about Faustian control over nature. Marx was talking about happiness. Engels was talking about output. For Marx, communism would make man at home in nature; for Engels, communism would allow man to exercise control over nature.

Engels's ideal of communism combined the Saint-Simonian dream of technological and managerial efficiency with the economic egalitarianism of Gracchus Babeuf. Its central image was the conception of nature and society as a gigantic industrial unit, with man standing augustly atop it, controlling its laws and thereby controlling its output. Its essential moral component was the ethic of work, Puritanism in the guise of industrial productivity. Engels was primarily concerned with man who worked, still the bourgeois Pietistic dream, and he joined the man who labored to the scientific and industrial utopianism that seemed to be dawning at the end of the nineteenth century.

Engels's conclusions at the end of his life need not surprise us. They were there at the beginning of his life. In his "*Outline of a Critique of Political Economy*" and in his *Principles of Communism,* he had already made communism synonymous with productivity, had already made communism synonymous with work and equal distribution. His basic ideas of communism were continuous and persistent throughout his life. He did not change. Rather, it was the death of Marx that freed him, both in the psychological sense and in the time he could devote to his own work, to express his own unique ideas, his own system of thought. It was at that time that he could give voice to his own intellectual predispositions, to his own inclinations of mind. Dialectics as understood by Marx meant dialectical naturalism. Conversely, it was Engels who used the phrase "scientific socialism." In the hands of Engels, socialism was the methodology of industrial and scientific inevitability. Socialism became the study of economic law. Socialism therefore meant predictability. Socialism became then a mechanistic science. It had been rigidified and dogmatized.

Footnotes

1. Ludwig Feuerbach, *Principles of the Philosophy of the Future,* trans. Manfred Vogel (New York: Bobbs-Merrill Co., 1966), p. 70.
2. "Ludwig Feuerbach and the End of Classical German Philosophy" was originally published in the fourth and fifth numbers of the *Neue Zeit* in 1886. In 1888 these two articles were combined and published as a book.
3. These letters and Engels's comments on Feuerbach contained in them have already been discussed in Chapter Eight.
4. Friedrich Engels, "Ludwig Feuerbach and the End of Classical German Philosophy," in *Karl Marx and Friedrich Engels: Selected Works* (New York: International Publishers, 1968), p. 603.
5. *Ibid.*, p. 602.
6. *Ibid.*, pp. 607–608.
7. *Ibid.*, p. 611.
8. *Ibid.*, p. 612.
9. *Ibid.*
10. Engels, "The Part Played by Labour in the Transition from Ape to Man," in *Karl Marx and Friedrich Engels: Selected Works,* p. 358.
11. *Ibid.*
12. *Ibid.*, p. 360.
13. *Ibid.*, p. 366.
14. For a full discussion of Marx's definition of communism see Chapter Four. Marx's approach to all these ideas is described in detail in that chapter. Marx's anthropological thought has become the subject of several books: Ernest Mandel, *The Formation of the Economic Thought of Karl Marx* (New York: Monthly Review Press, 1971); Istvan Meszaros, *Marx's Theory of Alienation* (London: Oxford University Press, 1971); Bertell Ollman, *Marx's Conception of Man in Capitalist Society* (London: Cambridge University Press, 1971). For a completely opposite view, one that denies the relevance of anthropological thought in Marx, see Louis Althusser, *For Marx,* trans. Ben Brewster (New York: Vintage Press, 1971).
15. Engels, "Socialism: Scientific and Utopian," in *Karl Marx and Friedrich Engels: Selected Works,* p. 431.
16. Engels, *Anti-Dühring,* trans. Emile Burns (New York: International Publishers, 1939), pp. 306–307.
17. Engels to T. Cuno, Jan. 24, 1872, Marx-Engels, *Selected Works* (Moscow: Foreign Languages Publishing House, 1955, II, pp. 424–425.

18. Engels, "Socialism: Utopian and Scientific," in *Karl Marx and Friedrich Engels: Selected Works* (New York), p. 430.
19. Engels, "On Authority," Marx-Engels, *Selected Works* (Moscow), II, pp. 635–638.
20. Marx, *Critique of the Gotha Programme* (New York: International Publishers, 1940), p. 17.
21. *Ibid.*
22. Engels, *Anti-Dühring,* p. 118.
23. *Ibid.*, p. 320.
24. *Ibid.*, p. 323.
25. Engels to Bebel, March 18, 1875, in Marx-Engels, *Selected Correspondence,* trans. Dona Torr (New York: International Publishers, 1942), p. 337.
26. For a fuller discussion of Engels and his relation to Babeuf, see Chapter Nine.
27. Engels, *Anti-Dühring,* pp. 336–337.
28. *Ibid.*, p. 337.
29. *Ibid.*
30. *Ibid.*, p. 338.
31. Marx, *Critique of the Gotha Programme,* p. 10.
32. Engels to Otto Von Boenigk, August 21, 1890, in *Karl Marx and Friedrich Engels: Selected Works* (New York), p. 691.
33. Engels, "The Housing Question," *in Marx-Engels, Selected Works* (Moscow), II, p. 631.
34. Engels, "On Authority," *Ibid.*, II, pp. 635–636.
35. Engels to Conrad Schmidt, August 5, 1890, *Ibid.*, II, p. 689.
36. Engels, *Anti-Dühring,* p. 125.
37. Engels, "The Part Played by Labor in the Evolution of Man from Ape," in Marx-Engels, *Selected Works,* pp. 358–368.
38. For a fuller discussion on this whole matter, see Chapter Four.

Fourteen

The Dutiful Disciple and the Exploitative Master

THE CENTRAL THESIS of this book is that major differences of thought existed between Marx and Engels. These differences of thought arose because of the psychological predispositions and logical presuppositions inherent in each mind. Marx and Engels were subjective entities. They responded to common stimuli in unique terms, in accordance with the innate proclivities that were the definition of their subjectivity.[1]

What this book has described and analyzed is the case study of two men who observe and speculate upon a common body of knowledge. The fact that Marx was primarily the originator of this body of knowledge can be laid aside at this point, because it is not germane to the present argument. Because of the laws of their own inwardness, each of the two men interpreted this body of knowledge differently. Marx gave to this theory a certain focus, a certain emphasis, a certain center of gravity; this was Marxism. Engels gave to this theory a different focus, emphasis, and center of gravity; this was Engelsism.

Engelsian subjectivity thus made of Engels the first revisionist. Engels was really the founder of the view that Marxism was predestinarian economic determinism. He originated the school of positivist, dogmatic, necessitarian Marxism, which was the dominant school of Marxism for the Second International and subsequently for Soviet Stalinists. In essence, Engels was the first "vulgar Marxist."

These significant differences between Marx and Engels were not merely expressions of the distinction between theory and practice.[2] To see Engels as the person who was designated to implement, to carry out the abstract and speculative ideas of Marx is to distort and misconceive the personality and talents of Engels. It is also to distort and misjudge the intelligence and character of Marx. The speculative genius of Marx is unchallenged. But Marx always sought to involve himself in the activist and practical aspects of the European socialist movement. He was a political journalist in 1842 and 1848. He was a political exile in 1843 and again in 1849. One of the founders of the First International in 1864, he was secretary for the International until its demise in 1872, all this at the same time that his scholarly pursuits involved him deeply in the writing of *Das Kapital.* Furthermore, major portions of his writings were intended to be involved, committed, activist, and politically oriented. The *Communist Manifesto* is the most obvious illustration. In addition, his *Critique of the Gotha Programme,* his *Civil War in France,* his *Class Struggles in France, 1848–1850,* and *Eighteenth Brumaire of Louis Bonaparte* were all written with the intent of being politically efficacious. Marx wished to be a great philosopher, but he also just as ardently wished to be the leader of a powerful political movement. His years at the British Museum were intended to make him an economic philosopher of the first order. His years of political squabbling, of jealousy, of bickering, of catcalls and prestige mongering, were intended to make him the leader of European socialist dissent. To infer that Marx was nonactivist, was nonpractical, is to overlook a significant position of his biography as well as his own definition and understanding of himself.

The same type of argument holds true for Engels. To see Engels simply as an activist, a practitioner, a convenient political troubleshooter, is also to distort not only Engels's character but also Engels's own self-evaluation and self-definition. Engels not only enjoyed the study of philosophy in itself, but he also enjoyed philosophic disputation. This is not to say that Engels had a skilled or adept speculative mind. Rather, he possessed a second-rate philosophical ability. In his early years he studied Hegel and Schelling. He indicated as a young man his desire to give up his career in journalism for a year in order to devote time to a serious study of philosophy. Later in life, particularly in *Anti-Dühring* and *Dialectics of Nature,* Engels demonstrated that he had not only kept in touch with the history of modern philosophy, but that he had also made a study of physics, chemistry, and biology. Regardless of the quality of Engels's philosophic efforts, Engels was not merely all practice, all practical criticism. There was present in Engels a mind that sought a philosophical understanding of and penetration into the world around him.

Furthermore, differences between Marx and Engels cannot be attributed to the division of labor that was consciously cultivated between the two men. Marx and Engels specialized, with each other's consent and encouragement, in different aspects of the social universe. Engels, due to inherent interest and Marx's prodding, specialized in military history and natural science. Conversely, Marx, because of inherent interests and Engels's encouragement, specialized in socioeconomic philosophy. This division of labor was illustrative of the meaning of the relationship between the two men. Marx was the acknowledged leader of the two. His was the seminal mind; his socioeconomic philosophy would sketch the basic construction of the social universe. Engels would be his resource person. Engels, in peripheral areas where Marx had little interest or had no time to penetrate, would find supportive evidence and documentation for Marx's more general theories. Again, the division of labor was expressive of their deepest character and their interrelationship. On the intellectual level, Engels was content with a secondary, supportive, dependent role.

Marxism and Engelsism cannot be explained as the difference between theory and practice. They cannot be explained as a consequence of the division of labor that existed between the two men. Marxism and Engelsism can only be explained as arising from philosophical differences between Marx and Engels. Of necessity, then, the basic tone of this book has been to separate, to draw distinctions. It has consciously and tactically stressed and investigated those areas where Marx and Engels disagreed. However, it has never been assumed that Marx and Engels disagreed on everything. It was taken as a given, based upon the lifelong association between the two men, that large areas of agreement did in fact exist. It would simply be impossible to account for the relationship at all if the two men had no areas of commonality. The real question, the essential intellectual exercise, comes in trying to separate the areas of disagreement from the areas of agreement, and then in trying to evaluate and weigh these two areas.

The themes, the ideas, about which Marx and Engels agreed were numerous. The listing that follows is not meant to be exhaustive. It is meant to select the themes of agreement that were intellectually the most important, those ideas that had the widest ramifications and influence.

Both Marx and Engels were nationalists, German nationalists in particular. They both felt that a separate national state was a necessary precondition, a necessary environment for a successful communist revolution. Although defining economics in totally different ways, both believed that economics determined the course of history. Both believed in the class struggle, and both thought that the working class must be revolutionary. Marx and Engels argued all their lives for a separate workers' party, a workers' party that drew its support from the masses, that was not elitist. Based on labor unions, the leadership of a separate workers' party must not be totally divorced from the masses. Both suffered from an overestimation of the masses, from romanticizing the revolutionary potential of the working classes. Although their understanding of the economics of capitalist society differed, both assumed that industrial anarchy and overproduction would eventually cause the collapse of capitalist society. Depression due to overproduction would bring about the communist revolution, and capitalist society would perish in a breakdown, in a cataclysm. Both held somewhat ambivalent views on Russia. On the one hand, Russia was ripe for revolution. On the other hand, it was the center of European reaction. A Russian revolution could spread to the West. Furthermore, both saw the positive and negative features of European imperialism. The imperialism of Western civilization enslaved the dark-skinned inhabitants of underdeveloped areas. But the imperialism of Western civilization was also the reason for the destruction of ancient and outmoded social orders in these same areas. Thus, imperialism was a progressive force but a progressive force that enslaved, even if the enslavement was only temporary, for a social revolution was also coming to Asia. Both were humanitarians and prophets. Both dreamed of the future society, communism, which would replace the horrors of capitalism. Both believed they had discovered the way this transformation was going to take place.

The areas of agreement between Marx and Engels were on the applied level. They were agreements over description and of a practical, strategic kind. It was because of these descriptive agreements that the impression was cast that Marx and Engels were always in agreement. The contrary was true.

The areas of differing interpretation were on the philosophical and speculative level. It was on this level that Engelsism and Marxism emerged. It was on this level that Engels's mechanistic materialism, his economic predestinarianism and Marx's dialectic naturalism became apparent. This book was essentially written about this philosophical level. The basic question which must be answered is this: If there was Marxism and Engelsism, and there was, why did Marx and Engels not articulate these differing interpretations to each other? There is little evidence of any major intellectual dispute between the two men. If they each had a unique focus and emphasis why weren't these shadings expressed?

The answer to these questions may be found in the personal relationship between the two men. It is necessary to discover the meaning of their relationship, the needs the relationship fulfilled for each of them. In short, in order to understand why basic intellectual differences between the two men did not come to the surface as tangible and real, articulated and acknowledged dispute, it is necessary to examine the psychological meaning the friendship had for each.[3] Indeed, the relationship between Marx and Engels was symbiotic, like a relationship between twin brothers. Each served as the other's alter ego. Each complemented the other.

In the realm of ideas, in terms of philosophic leadership, Marx played the role of exploitative master. In this area, Engels willingly accepted Marx's strength and primacy. Engels needed someone like Marx in order to establish his own self-esteem. Engels found his individuality in other people. Engels borrowed his personal and historic identity from Marx.

In his early life Engels rebelled against the Pietist fundamentalism of his parental home.[4] As an artillery officer in the Prussian army stationed in Berlin, he eagerly entered into the Bohemian life of the capital. That life gave him the liberality in terms of personal habit and thought he had always wanted and contact with the progressive historical forces in his epoch. Engels was young, idealistic, searching for a cause to which to dedicate his energies; his involvement with the political and intellectual radicalism of Berlin offered him an entrance into the life style he wished to pursue for himself. His letters to his friend, Graebner, demonstrate this transition clearly.[5] He left his home. He rejected the way of his father. He sought identification with confirmation of a new mode of being. History and his personal search for identity united to offer Engels the highest level of meaning by means of his commitment to political radicalism.

The role that Marx played in Engels's life was therefore climactic. Marx fulfilled every aspect of Engels's search for personal identity. His association with Marx was therefore a part of his own being and self-definition. It must never be shattered. Engels recognized Marx's genius. He recognized Marx as the intellectual leader, the man who would make history. Engels chose to tie himself to this epoch-making individual because that active and shaping individual would also build a place of fame and renown in time for him.

On the other hand, Marx was also dependent on Engels. In the areas of financial and emotional support, Engels was the person upon whom Marx leaned. He was the one true friend Marx had during his life. Unthreatened by him, Marx felt free to show warmth and friendship to Engels. On several occasions in their correspondence, Marx acknowledges his human indebtedness to Engels.[6] Marx did not find the emotional and professional support he needed from his wife. Basically, he thought of her as a mother, a housekeeper. For his professional confirmation he turned elsewhere. He turned to Engels. The friendship then became crucial.

In order to substantiate the above conclusions about Marx and Engels, particular areas of their association will be investigated. In addition, it will also be shown how the deserving master and the supportive disciple, the core of their relationship, was replicated by both Marx and Engels in their other associations. In other words, the central structure of their personalities, the dutiful disciple and the exploitative master, was not only self-images, but also the form by which they interrelated, as well as the style by which they related to the world around themselves.

Engels's financial support of Marx during their long exile in England is well known. Their correspondence was repeatedly punctuated by Marx's asking for financial help from Engels and Engels's offering financial help to Marx. This help was not limited to monetary stipends, but included gift giving, such as Engels's sending caskets of wine to Marx.[7] This financial relationship not only illustrated what Marx expected from Engels, but what Engels was prepared to give to Marx. Monetary support from Engels to Marx began soon after the 1848–1849 revolution, when, after the failure of these revolutions, Engels fled from Baden to Switzerland, and from Switzerland to Manchester. Marx came to England in 1849, with his wife, and financially destitute. Rather than seek gainful employment, Marx plunged into his economic studies at the British Museum, into the preliminary stages for his composition of *Das Kapital.* Marx thus played the typical German professor of the nineteenth century, a cultural elitist who was totally dedicated to his craft and who sought economic support from a patron. Engels was willing to be the patron. Engels financially adopted Marx. This financial support not only indicated the freedom with which Marx could ask Engels to sacrifice himself, but also the willingness, the voluntary consent by which Engels did sacrifice himself. Engels ran his family's business in Manchester for many years until he finally jettisoned this onus in 1870. But the toll, the burden upon Engels was clear. From 1850 until 1870, for twenty years, while Marx studied and wrote, Engels for most of his day was occupied with entrepreneurial matters. Engels's study, his own intellectual development was limited to the evening hours. Thus his self-denial was not only financial, but cultural as well as professional. He lost in terms of study and self-development, and in terms of professional advancement and literary renown.

In actuality, there is no indication that Engels managed his Manchester factory with anything but good capitalist efficiency. He was visited by relatives from Germany to see whether sufficient profit was being produced. Engels embarked upon no designs, like Owen, to improve or ameliorate the conditions of the working class in his factories. Neither Marx nor Engels were perplexed by this contradiction between their socialist theory and Engels's capitalist practice. Their attitude appeared to have been that the capitalist system must be exploited in this way so that both Marx and Engels could survive. Marx never suggested to Engels that he sell the factory, and although Engels complained about the work he understood this burden as a necessary one to support Marx. Since their lives depended upon the Manchester factory they decided to live with this hypocrisy, and to rationalize their inconsistency in terms of exploiting the capitalist system, as well as Engels's family, for their own subversive purposes.

It is understandable, therefore, that Engels came into his own after Marx's death. Only after Engels was freed from the need to service the exploitative master did he enjoy the openness and latitude to express his own talents. The height of Engels's career corresponded with the termination of Marx's life. It is, therefore, entirely consistent that five of Engels's major works were published in the years closely preceding Marx's death, or after the termination of Marx's life. *Anti-Dühring* appeared in 1878, *Socialism: Scientific and Utopian* in 1882, *The Origin of the Family, Private Property and the State* in 1884, and "Ludwig Feuerbach and the End of Classical German Philosophy" in 1888. *The Dialectics of Nature* was first published in 1927 by Riazanov, although the manuscript itself appears to have been completed by 1882.

This is not to say that Engels, after Marx's death, was entirely freed of the burdens he felt toward Marx, or the burdens he assumed on behalf of other European socialists. It is to say that many of the burdens were relieved and that Engels could develop his own talents to a greater extent than he had in the past. In truth, Engels was a very late bloomer. During

Marx's life Engels's own ideas, his own intellectual character were held in check. His financial support was simply the material side of his deeper intellectual borrowing from Marx. But after death had removed the brother through whom he had gained personal identity, Engels had greater latitude to express his own style. The years from 1883 until his own death in 1895 were probably the most rewarding years of Engels's life. Not only did he shine like a moon in the posthumous sunlight of Marx, but Engels could talk for the first time in his own voice. Not only was he bequeathed the leadership of the European socialist movement because of his prior association with Marx, but he also found that he had something of merit to say in his own right. It was during the years from 1883 to 1895 that Engelsism fully emerged. Although the differences between the two men were always present, the differences were suppressed during the years of the brother's primacy. When the emotional and financial expropriation ended, Engelsism was articulated. The differences between the two men moved from a conscious, misunderstood, unexpressed stage, to a conscious, misunderstood, expressed stage.

The death of Marx gave Engels latitude but not total freedom. Engels was never totally free of the charisma of Marx, of the need not only to serve the man, but the man's image even after death. Marx, of course, never finished *Das Kapital.* He bequeathed all his manuscripts to Engels, and Engels assumed the responsibility of preparing them for publication. The major literary effort of Engels after Marx's death was the editing and publishing of the last two volumes of *Kapital.* Engels asserted more of his own intellectual independence after Marx's death and he had more time for himself after Marx died. But again, Engels's self-expression was subservient to his major activity, which was the bringing to public knowledge of the great opus of Marx. Engels had to give this one last gift to Marx. He had sustained Marx in life, now he must preserve and maintain the fame and work of Marx after death. In essence, the trajectory of Engels's life moved from being Marx's literary agent to being Marx's literary executor.

Marx, when alive, also used Engels as a literary assistant and as a literary collaborator. The two men collaborated on several important works. The *Communist Manifesto* is the best known; but there were also *The German Ideology, The Holy Family,* and the *Great Men of the Exile.* What is of interest here, however, is not the collaboration of the two men, but those instances where Engels acted as Marx's literary assistant—in other words, those literary instances where Engels supplied the supportive work, where Engels did some secondary tasks in order to free Marx to work on the higher planes of theory.

In 1851 Marx began to write editorials for the *New York Daily Tribune.* His journalistic output was quite voluminous and very interesting. He wrote for the *Tribune* during the years of the Crimean War, the Sepoy Mutiny in India, and the Second Opium War in China. It is in Marx's journalism that we find ample and penetrating comments on the new

Eastern question, the Russian situation, the role of imperialism in Asia, and the role of Asia in the worldwide socialist revolution. In a very real sense, Marx's intellectual interests were stimulated by and in fact followed the current events of the day. His economics studies took precedence, of course. But with that exception, Marx began to read heavily in Russian history and society during the Crimean crisis. He began to read widely in Indian and Asian history and social structure during the Sepoy Mutiny.[8] One gets the impression of an inherently academic mind, of an essentially scholarly personality, who simply had to know, who was driven to uncover the informational core of events. The results of such study would take two forms. During the 1850s he wrote insightful and perspicacious journalism for the *Tribune.* Secondly, his reading in Asian society, his reading in primitive agrarian structures of Russia acquainted him with the whole problem of the Asiatic mode of production and was fed into his general theory of economic development. The *Grundrisse* and *Kapital* refer repeatedly to the Asiatic mode of production. Marx never wasted any scholarship. Everything he learned was to play a part in his overall theory of historical evolution.

Journalism, although enjoyable, was nevertheless peripheral to Marx's major areas of concern. The money that he received from Charles Dana, editor of the *Tribune,* was helpful, but the time spent in the preparation of the articles was expensive. Marx turned to Engels and used him as a literary second. On numerous occasions, Marx asked Engels to write the articles for him. Engels complied, and the articles were sent to New York as Marx's own. In addition, Marx received the payment for them. Engels not only sent direct monetary stipends to Marx from the family business in Manchester, but also worked as an editorial assistant for Marx and allowed Marx to expropriate his remuneration.[9]

Even though Marx took Engels for granted, he nevertheless appreciated Engels's help. When he liked an article by Engels, he would make his approval known. Basically, Marx agreed with the opinions expressed by Engels. Occasionally, Marx disagreed. At these moments, Marx took it upon himself to arbitrarily change Engels's manuscript. In short, Marx exercised intellectual leadership. Without consulting Engels, he would unilaterally amend an article by Engels and send it off to the *Tribune.* Engels never protested this practice.[10]

Marx's assertion of intellectual leadership was never duplicated by Engels. Whereas Marx felt free to willfully change an Engels manuscript, Engels never exercised that same freedom toward a Marx manuscript. In fact, Engels recognized that he must never do this because he was not always certain or clear about what Marx was saying. For instance, in relation to *Das Kapital,* Engels recognized in 1858 that it was very abstract, and that he must slowly and arduously study its dialectical movement.[11] On another occasion, in 1862, Engels again admitted that he was experiencing difficulty in comprehending what Marx was attempting in *Kapital.* At this time, he indicated that Marx's theory of rent was "really too abstract" and that he must "meditate upon the matter if I am to have any peace."[12] The awareness of the speculative nature of Marx's thought, and of his own difficulty in comprehending such abstractness, deterred Engels from editorial arbitrariness in relation to Marx's work. On the other hand, Marx encountered no such difficulty in comprehending Engels's ideas, and thus took it upon himself to change a manuscript when he saw fit.

Marx had a perceptive understanding of the content of his relationship to Engels. He understood himself to be the theoretic leader, the philosophical originator. He saw Engels as more of the laboratory assistant, as someone who was going to supply the supportive evidence. In 1866 he wrote to Engels saying that a second edition of Engels's *The Situation of the Working Class in England* was now both "necessary and comparatively easy."[13] This was true because Marx's *Kapital* had already provided the basic theoretic understanding of capitalist society. Engels's book, almost as an appendix to *Kapital,* would provide the requisite documentation and empirical evidence.[14] Engels's book would really act as a footnote to the master's philosophic investigation and analysis. Engels did not protest this categorization of roles.

This same intellectual exploitation can also be seen in the division of labor that was cultivated by the two friends. To put the idea in other terms, the core relationship of the dutiful disciple and the exploitative master was also the reason that a division of labor developed between Marx and Engels. It freed Marx to develop the higher levels of his philosophical sociology. Engels was asked to work in those areas where Marx had little interest. Again, Marx laid down the basic principles. Engels provided the peripheral documentation.

As we have seen, Marx began to write for the *Daily Tribune* in 1851, and his journalism for the *Tribune* spanned the years of the Crimean War, the Sepoy Mutiny, and the Second Opium War. When dealing with these events, Marx concentrated on their political and economic ramifications. He defined their inherent meaning. But all these events contained a military dimension to them. Engels's specialty thus became military affairs. Engels willingly yielded the larger field to Marx and worked in an area in which Marx had no interest. Beginning in 1851 until the end of his life, Engels became quite competent as a military commentator and analyst.[15]

Furthermore, Marx had little interest in natural science. In this area as well he was happy to have Engels become the expert.[16] It was a period of the rapid growth of natural science. It was the period of Darwinism, and dialectics must be related to these developments. The interest Engels developed in science, beginning in 1858, any expertise he was to acquire, was to be an interest and expertise that lasted throughout his remaining life. The empirical data, the scientific knowledge that Engels used to construct his mechanistic and positivistic materialism, he began to acquire in his studies of the late 1850s.

The quality of mind of the two men was revealed by the areas of knowledge in which they chose to specialize. Marx's concentration was on the human, the made social world. His eyes were always fixed upon the man who labored, and he made it his life's study to understand the social context of that labor and the products of that labor. Activity was paramount for Marx, and he investigated the construction and the potentiality of that activity. When Marx did become involved in science, it was always in terms of applied science. That is, the science that drew any attention from Marx was the science that could be used to improve and enhance human productivity. For instance, Marx became interested in chemistry and geology. He read some standard texts in each of these fields.[17] But he read chemistry to discover a better way to improve the fertility of the soil. In addition, he read geology to find out how to increase food production. The science of primary interest to him was the science that would enlarge the productive powers of man.[18]

Engels had a different character of mind. He was drawn to more material and more technical studies. His commitment to military history and natural science documents this point. The world for Engels was the reality of things. He concentrated upon the functioning of physical objects external to man. The quality of his mind was not anthropologically oriented, but rather mechanistically oriented. As we have seen, in his view of historical evolution, it was mechanical invention that acted as the driving force, the dynamics.

This division of labor and Marx's own relative disinterest in natural science had enormous implications for the full emergence of Engelsism in the 1880s and thereafter. It was in the area of the philosophy of nature that Marxism and Engelsism were most clearly opposed. It was Engels's mechanistic materialism that also turned him into a social positivist. It was Marx's anthropological view of the social universe that turned him into a dialectic naturalist. Thus, the philosophy of nature was the crucial dividing point between these two polar systems. Portentously, it was in the area of the philosophy of the physical universe that Marx had little interest, and it was in the area of the philosophy of the physical universe in which Engels specialized. Thus, Engels could pursue his studies in this field generally unsupervised by his friend. Marx's own involvement in *Das Kapital* and Engels's own involvement in natural science presented them with a hiatus in communication.

This psychological interpretation of the relationship between Marx and Engels would be less convincing if the mode of disciple and master were limited to just the two men. But it was not. Engels replicated this mode in all his relationships. He always played the role of the provider, of the one who sustained. He seemed to adopt people in order to help them. He was a disciple to all. On the other hand, there was strength in Engels. He was a congenial and compassionate man to whom people turned for help. Furthermore, he was a wealthy man, who used his wealth to support a socialist movement from which he had gained so much. Engels's relationship to the socialist movement was also complementary. Engels needed the socialist movement for his identity. For many reasons, the socialist movement needed Engels.

Engels's relationship to Bebel, Berstein, Kautsky, and Lafargue replicated his relationship to Marx. He helped to financially support Lafargue.[19] At times he also sent money to Bernstein, Kautsky, and Bebel.[20] He also gave these men intellectual and emotional sustenance. Just as he wrote articles for Marx to the *Daily Tribune*, so he wrote articles for the socialist journals of these men in order to sustain these publications, to give them prestige and prominence.

Engels personally sacrificed himself for the European socialist movement. Marx's health and vigor began to decline after 1871, and he was no longer able to carry on his extensive correspondence. Engels became his secretary. It was during the period of the 1870s, when Engels relieved Marx of the burden of a politically efficacious but physically fatiguing correspondence, that Engels assumed the role of Marx's spokesman. The view that there was essential unanimity of viewpoint between Marx and Engels was constructed by confusing political agreement with philosophical agreement. Engels again assumed Marx's drudgery. By assuming Marx's correspondence he again acted as Marx's public relations agent, as the person who guarded and enhanced Marx's prestige and position in the socialist movement of the various European countries.

Engels's self-sacrifice for the European socialist movement was really of major proportions. After 1883, his correspondence was vast. He advised, encouraged, admonished, befriended practically every socialist leader of the end of the nineteenth century. He also turned himself into a literary second for these men, as he had for Marx. When they needed an article for a journal, when they sent him manuscripts for his editorial comments, when they needed his political prestige in an internecine party struggle, Engels always put aside his own work and responded to their requests. The services, the functions he fulfilled for Marx he also replicated for Bernstein, Bebel, Kautsky, Lafargue, and others. He continued to play the strong, helpful disciple. In fact, Engels's own literary career clearly suffered because of the responsibilities and duties he took on himself. From 1883 until 1895, Engels's major efforts were in preparing the second and third volumes of *Das Kapital* for publication and in sustaining Marx's name and position within the European socialist movement through his continental and transcontinental letter writing. Even after Marx's death, he was Marx's second. Not only was he Marx's second, but he was also the second of Bebel, Bernstein, Kautsky, and Lafargue.

Engels's self-sacrifice for the European socialist movement was extraordinary. Engels took severe personal losses due to his political involvement. Although Engels wrote more, the quality and intellectual depth of his writing suffered. *The Dialectics of Nature* was not published during his lifetime. *Anti-Dühring* was a composite of articles written for socialist journals. "Socialism: Scientific and Utopian" was written at the request of Paul Lafargue and was essentially a propaganda tract intended to explain Marxism to the French working class. *The Origin of the Family, Private Property and the State* was written from the scantiest documentation and research. Thus, because of the extra burdens Engels took upon himself, his own work containing his own perceptions was incomplete, poorly researched, and done on demand as high-class journalism. But Engels willingly assumed the role. Nevertheless, even within the confines of his continued self-sacrifice, Engels was undoubtedly a more self-expressive person after the death of Marx than during the lifetime of the exploitative master.

Furthermore, the role of the dutiful disciple was replicated by Engels toward the Marx family. After Marx's death Engels essentially adopted the Marx family. He looked after the three daughters, gave them advice, and sent them money. They, in fact, became the children that he never had naturally. Like someone who does adopt children, his role toward the Marx daughters was that of sustainer, of provider. In his will, Engels bequeathed a quarter of his estate to each of the Marx daughters.

From the point of view of Marx, his relationship to Engels fulfilled his primitive, basic, human need for friendship. Engels was one of the few men with whom Marx did not fight and undergo a fundamental break. This happened not only because Engels was Marx's alter ego, but also because Marx needed someone he could trust and talk to in an unguarded and open fashion. Engels offered him human companionship. Engels offered him this human companionship through extraordinarily difficult times for Marx: through isolation, through the death of some of Marx's children, through Marx's own illnesses.[21] But it was basically from Marx's human isolation that he reached out for Engels's friendship. Marx did not confide to his wife. His references to her in his letters to Engels paint her as a harried, overburdened woman who was often physically ill. Furthermore, he talked disparagingly of her, referring to her as a "silly."[22] Certainly, he did not turn to her for intellectual companionship. He showed more affection for his daughters. Engels supplied emotional companionship to Marx. In the psychological and emotional areas, Marx's dependency on Engels was profound. Engels refused to fight Marx like Bakunin, Proudhon, Lassalle, Mazzini, Ledru Rollin, Louis Blanc, and a plethora of other political or philosophical opponents who contested with Marx.[23]

The fact that Marx received emotional support from Engels does not mean, of course, that Marx returned emotional support to Engels. He decidedly did not. The master emotionally, as well as in other areas, expropriated the disciple. The perfect illustration of the emotional exploitation was Marx's callousness to the news that Mary Burns had died. Engels had warmly commiserated with Marx's suffering upon the death of his two younger children. But when Engels wrote to Marx that Mary Burns had died, Marx insensitively took note of her passing in the first line of his letter of reply to Engels and then proceeded to list the reasons for his own discontent and anxiety. This was one of the rare occasions when Engels complained of Marx's lack of awareness of others' needs and pain.[24]

Marx also replicated this master role in every one of his human contacts. He sought dominance everywhere. In his political and scholarly life, he clearly sought dominance and control over others. Those who could not give this obedience toward Marx were chased away from him. Marx's life is strewn with broken and severed political and scholarly associations. He was arrogant and a difficult person.

Marx replicated his master-dominant role not only in his political and scholarly life but also in his private life. Marx's family was a Victorian family. But more than that, Marx also turned his daughters into disciples. He turned his daughters into literary assistants. He turned his daughters into political agitators and advocates. Marx's offspring were not only loving children, but also admirers.

This chapter has attempted to answer the question why, if different emphasis and intellectual centers of gravity existed between Marx and Engels, the two men never articulated or acknowledged the presence of these differences. The two men were aware of their differences, as they were aware of their unique personalities, as they were aware of their particular character of thought. However, because their symbiotic relationship was so vital to them, because it had so great and climactic a meaning for both Marx and Engels, they chose not to allow these differences to interfere with or destroy their friendship. Marx did not fear Engels's intellectual abilities. He understood Engels to have an essentially dilettantish, although sensitive, receptive, and quick mind. Engels did not think his differences with Marx would lead to the distortion of the master's theory. He did not think his own writing would essentially revise the meaning of Marx. Their brotherlike relationship, then, was threatened neither by jealousy nor by ambition. It stood above Marx's fear of competition and challenge, and above any self-seeking aggrandizement by Engels. Thus it was left intact. The two men agreed for the sake of their symbiotic relationship not to openly disagree.[25]

Succeeding generations also helped in the creation of Engelsism. They made the fundamental mistake of assuming that agreement on politics implied agreement on philosophy. They made the crucial mistake of thinking that the close association of the two men both during and after Marx's death meant that Marx and Engels shared common ideas about everything. Therefore, when they read Marx through the eyes of Engels, they thought they were reading Marx. In truth, they were reading Engelsism. Thus, Engelsism was represented as Marxism.

Unintentionally, but nevertheless obeying a law of life that people will read into a doctrine what they themselves wish to see in it, Engels became the first revisionist. Without a conscious plan, Engels revised and fundamentally altered Marxism because he interpreted Marxism from the frame of reference of his own philosophical mind set and presuppositions. Lenin took it for granted that Marx and Engels had one voice. Stalin took it for granted that Marx and Engels had one voice. Western scholars also perpetrated the same confusion. Thus, it came to pass that Bolshevik tradition and Western tradition accepted Engelsism as Marxism. In effect, they both accepted revisionism as the true philosophy of Marx. The career of Engelsism, although a distortion, was of long duration and of uncalculated importance.

The career of Marxism was less fortunate. It was essentially lost. It was lost because some important documents of Marx were lost, not to be recovered until the 1930s. Marxism, in short, became a hidden and relatively unknown tradition. A few men intuitively and with great genius could nevertheless penetrate to its core. A Lukács, a Gramsci, a Korsch, could see past Engelsism. The Marxist core was recaptured in the great period of reevaluation, which was sparked by the publication of the 1844 manuscripts and the *Grundrisse.* Only then could the work of dissecting Marx and Engels begin. Only after knowing what Marx himself said was it possible to disentangle Marx from the subsequent distortion of Engels.

Marx and Engels practiced a tragic deception on each other and themselves. They assumed that the differences of which they were aware would remain suppressed, as they were in life, and would therefore pass in history unnoticed. Herein they were deceived. They did not foresee that their differences would become categorical and structural. Herein history was deceived. Protagonists and historians mistakenly interpreted the silence of Marx and Engels as implying essential unanimity of viewpoint and thus unknowingly misinformed succeeding generations. History has paid for this folly.

Footnotes

1. The biographies of Marx are extensive in number. The following list is not meant to be exhaustive, but to suggest those biographies of Marx and those of Engels that are the most informative and helpful to the student. The Marx biographies include: Isaiah Berlin, *Karl Marx* (London: Oxford University Press, 1970); Werner Blumenber, *Portrait of Marx* (New York: Herder and Herder, 1972); August Cornu, *Karl Marx et Friedrich Engels,* 4 vols. (Paris: Gallimard, 1955), Oscar V. Hammen, *The Red '48ers* (New York: Charles Scribner's Sons, 1969); O. Maenchen-Helfen and B. Nicolaevsky, *Karl Marx: Man and Fighter* (London: Oxford University Press, 1936); Franz Mehring, *Karl Marx* (Ann Arbor: University of Michigan Press, 1962); D. Riazanov, *Karl Marx, Man, Thinker, and Revolutionist* (London: Oxford University Press, 1927). The standard work on Engels is Gustav Mayer, *Friedrich Engels,* 2 vols. (The Hague: Mouton & Co., 1934). Another biography of Engels, which

borders on hagiography, is E. A. Stepanowa, *Friedrich Engels: Sein Leben und Werk* (Berlin: Dietz Verlag, 1958).

The author acknowledges his indebtedness to the Seminar on Psychohistory of the Washington School of Psychiatrists. This last chapter was read at the Seminar and the comments from the psychiatrist present were helpful in arriving at a justifiable interpretation of the relationship between Marx and Engels. In particular, the author would like to thank Gerald Perman, Robert Cohen, and Edith Weigert for their sound psychiatric opinions.

2. Prof. Lawrence Krader, Chairman, Department of Anthropology, the University of Waterloo, Ontario, Canada, is of the opinion that the differences between Marx and Engels can be traced to differences between theory and practice. Dr. Krader's opinions are located in the "Introduction" to his manuscript *The Works of Marx and Engels in Ethnology Compared* (The Hague: Mouton & Co., 1973). The author would like to thank Dr. Krader for allowing him to see the "Introduction" before it was actually published. Nevertheless, the author cannot agree with Prof. Krader that only theory and practice separated Marx and Engels. The best place to study the character and relationship of the two men is in their correspondence. Even though their *Briefwechsel* is largely dull, it does expose the core and essence of their intersubjectivity.
3. As far as I know, only one other person has attempted to judge the Marx-Engels *Briefwechsel* on its own terms and merits. That person is Prof. Oscar Hammen; see his article "The Marx-Engels Briefwechsel," *The Journal of the History of Ideas* (March–April 1972), pp. 172–190. Although I disagree with Prof. Hammen's conclusions, I do agree with Prof. Hammen that the correspondence is disappointing.
4. For a more detailed description of Engels's early years and growth, and the meaning of Marx to his life, see Chapters Eight and Nine.
5. Also refer to the relevant sections of Chapters Eight and Nine.
6. Marx to Engels, *Marx-Engels Werke* (Berlin: Dietz Verlag, 1969), XXVIII, p. 42.
7. It is not necessary to footnote every occasion upon which Marx sought financial support from Engels. Any general perusal of their correspondence will reveal the multitude of instances where Marx asked Engels for help. For just a few illustrations of this financial support, see *Ibid.*, XXVIII, pp. 64, 78; XXX, p. 215. These are only a tiny sampling. The correspondence is studded with such requests and donations.
8. For insight into the manner and form of Marx's and Engels's work habits and procedure of composition, the Marx-Engels *exzerpte* are extraordinarily helpful. In addition, the depth of Marx's study of Asia will become apparent. In order to compare capitalist society with noncapitalist society, in order by way of this comparison to arrive at the essential relationship of capitalism, Marx read voluminously into the history of Asia.
9. See the *Marx-Engels Werke,* XXVIII, 1963, pp. 12, 54, 59, 251, 298, 315, 354, 367; XXIX, 1967, pp. 208, 214, 371, 383, 505, 508, 687.
10. *Ibid.*, XXIX, 1967, pp. 383, 428, 463.
11. *Ibid.*, XXIX, 1967, p. 319.
12. *Ibid.*, XXX, 1964, p. 284.
13. *Ibid.*, XXXI, 1965, p. 174.
14. *Ibid.*
15. *Ibid.*, XXVIII, 1963, pp. 71–72, 365, 672. This is only one reference. The correspondence is profusely studded with Engels's references to military matters.

16. *Ibid.*, XXVII, 1965, p. 190; XXII 1970, pp. 286–287. Again, this is only one reference. The correspondence contains extensive comments from Engels on the natural sciences—they are too numerous, and it would serve no constructive purpose, to list them all here.
17. For Marx's reading and study into the area of chemistry and geology, see the *exzerpte.* It should surprise one to see the arduous and detailed notes that Marx took when reading textbooks on geology and agricultural chemistry.
18. *Marx-Engels Werke,* XXVII, pp. 245–246, 252–253, 257.
19. For one example see the letter from Paul Lafargue to Engels, February 5, 1888, in *Engels-Lafargue Correspondence,* ed. Emile Bottigelli, trans. Yvonne Kapp (Moscow: Foreign Languages Publishing House, 1968), II, p. 91.
20. Engels's correspondence with Bernstein, Kautsky, and Bebel is punctuated with such requests.
21. *Marx-Engels Werke,* XXVII, pp. 184, 190–191; XXVIII, pp. 205, 206, 443, 444.
22. *Ibid.*, XXXI, p. 306.
23. *Ibid.*, XXVII, pp. 28, 78–79, 242, 693; XXXII, p. 95.
24. *Ibid.*, XXX, pp. 309, 310, 317.
25. Psychological studies of Marx are beginning to appear. See Arnold Kunzli, *Karl Marx: Eine Psychographie* (Vienna: Europäische Verlag, 1966). Also see the article by J. E. Siegel, "Marx's Early Development: Vocation, Rebellion, and Realism," *The Journal of Interdisciplinary History* (Winter 1973), pp. 475–508.

Index

Activity.
Engels on, 120
Human, 3, 5-7, 11
Marx on, 120
Practical-Critical Activity, 6, 10, 57-58, 153
"Address of the Central Committee to the Communist League," 50, 52-53, 64, 71
Afghanistan.
Marx on, 75
Agrarianism.
Engels on, Asian Agrarian Communalism, 201
Engels on, Russian Agrarian Communalism, 162-63, 170-71
Marx on Agrarian Communalism, 86, 91-92
Marx on Russian Agrarian Communalism, 94-101
Revolution, 166
Society, 87
Alsace-Lorraine, 169, 205, 208
Alienation.
Marx on, 2, 4, 31-32, 34-35, 90, 136, 216
Engels on, 118-19, 135-36, 216, 219
Althusser, Louis, xv
America.
Engels on, 133
American Civil War.
Marx on, 54, 67, 73
Amsterdam Speech (1872), 48, 61
Anarchism, 19
Ancient Society, 157, 165
Anthropology.
Engels on, 118-19, 136-37, 157-59, 211-16
Marx on, 3-7, 9, 26, 30-41, 90-94, 136-37, 211, 237
Anti-Duhring, 116, 140, 159-60, 181, 221-23, 229, 233, 239
Aristocracy.
Engels on, 164-67, 169, 204-208
Marx on, 61-62, 65-66, 68-71
Aristotle, 141, 144
Armed Insurrection.
Engels on, 183-84, 208
Asia.
Engels on, 200-202
Marx on, 75-80, 91-92, 94, 133
Asiatic Mode of Production.
Engels on, 200-201
Marx on, 75-76, 78, 85, 91-93, 96, 166
Athens, 158
Atomism.
Ancient, 5

Austria.
Engels on, 168, 204-205
Marx on, 49, 61-62, 66-71
Austro-Prussian War (1866), 140, 168
Autogenesis.
Marx on, 34, 84, 176

Babeuf, Gracchus, 14-16, 18, 43-45, 50, 52, 125-26, 134, 222-23, 225
Bakunin, Michael, 48, 239
Balkan Question.
Engels on, 203-205
Marx on, 66, 68-71
Bauer, Bruno, 10
Bebel, August, 183, 185, 187-88, 191, 203, 206, 208, 238
Becker, J. P., 66
Berlin, Isaiah, xiv
Bernstein, Edward, 185, 190-91, 194, 201, 203, 238
Bismarch, Otto V.
Engels on, 168-69, 187, 194
Marx on, 67-68
Blanquism.
Lenin on, xvi
Marx on, 47-48, 57
Bloch, J., 154
Bolshevism. xvi-xvii, 241
Bonaparte, Louis.
Engels on, 168
Marx on, 52, 55, 57, 66
Börne, Ludwig, 111-12, 126
Boulangerism, 189-90
Bourgeois.
Engels on, 164-65, 167-70, 218
Bourgeois Republic, 185
On Petit Bourgeois, 167
Marx on Class, 17
Conservatism, 61
Dictatorship, 52, 57
English, 64
French, 63-64
German, 63
Idea of Freedom, 24-25
Notion of Equality, 17
Peasants and, 75
Revolution, xvii, 16, 45-46, 61-63
Society, 15, 90
State, 54
Bourgeoisie.
Marx on, 45-46
Brousse, Paul, 188-89
Bulgars.
Engels on, 203-204
Burckhardt, Jaco B., 154
Bureaucracy.
Engels on, 220, 222-25
Marx on, xv
Burns, John, 191
Burns, Mary, 239

Calvinism, xvi
Engels on, 211, 218
Camphausen, Ludolf, 50
Capital.
Engels on, 132
Capitalism.
Engels on, 128-34, 162, 170-71, 182, 191-94, 203, 209
Marx on, 61-62, 74-79, 89-91, 93, 98-101, 166
Causality.
Engels on, 149, 152-54, 161-62, 174-75, 215
Marx on, 152-53, 174-75
Cavour, Camillo de.
Marx on, 66
Celts, 93
Chartists.
Engels on, 126-28, 133
China.
Engels on, 133-34, 202-204

Marx on, xvii, 78-79
National Liberation, 79
Christianity.
Engels on, 128
Marx on, 44
"Circular Letter to Bebel, Wilhelm Liebknecht, and W. Bracke," 185, 187
Civil War in France, 229
Civilization.
Marx on, 26, 37
Class Struggles in France (1850), 50, 183, 193, 206, 229
Classes.
Engels on, 127, 132, 136, 163-66, 218-19
Marx on, xvii, 15-17, 24-25, 44-46, 50-52, 54, 57, 61-64, 71, 75, 136
Class Warfare.
Engels on, 182, 187, 196
Marx on, 187
Cole, C.D.H., xv
Committee of Public Safety, 15
Communism.
Marx on Communist
Consciousness, 74
Communist Revolution, 61-64, 98-99
Communist Society, xv
Philosophic Basis of, 8, 35-41, 43
Peasants and, 74
Soviet, xvi
Engels on Communist Revolution, 119, 123-37, 171-72, 182, 197
Communist Society, 211-26
Competition.
Engels on, 129-32
Consciousness.
Engels on, 209
Marx on, 2-3, 5, 10-11
Conservatism.
Engels on, 187, 191, 204-208
Marx on, 61-62, 65-66, 68-71
Contradiction.
Marx on, 87, 99-101, 136, 175-77
Corn Laws.
Engels on, 126-27
Counter Revolution.
Marx on, 57
Crimean War, 47, 68-71, 140, 170, 191, 234-36
Criticism.
Engels on, 120
Marx on, 120, 153
Critique of Political Economy, 92
"Critique of Hegel's Dialectic and General Philosophy," 29
Critique of the Gotha Program, 17, 224, 229
Croats.
Engels on, 203
Culture.
Asian, 201-203
European, 201-203
German, 203-209
Czechs.
Engels on, 203
Marx on, 49

Dana, Charles, 235
Danielson, N. F., 162, 203
Darwin, Charles, 142, 154, 213, 236
Democracy.
Bourgeois, 14-15
Marx on, 22
Democritus, 5, 120
Descartes, Rene, 8, 141
Determinism.
Cosmological, xv, 146, 214
Engels on, 135, 141-54, 157-77, 183, 209, 214
Marx on, 85, 95-101
Deutsche JahrBucher, 123

Dialectic, xiv-xv
 Engels on, 119, 142-46, 149-52, 159-62, 165, 174-77, 215, 226
 Law of the Transformation of Quantity into Quality, 142-43
 Law of the Interpenetration of Opposites, 142-43
 Law of the Negation of the Negation, 142-44
 Marx on Dialectical Naturalism, 11, 84-101, 150-54, 215, 226, 237
Dialectics of Nature, 116, 140, 229, 233, 238
"Dictatorship of the Proletariat."
 Lenin on, xvi
 Marx on, 52
Distribution.
 Engels on, 222-23
Domila–Nieumenhuis, F., 56
Duhring, Eugene, 154

East India Company, 176-77
Economics.
 Classical, 90
 Economic Determinism, 141, 154, 157-77, 228
 Economic Egalitarianism, 222-23
 Economic Mode, 86-87, 99-101
 Engels on, 135-37, 157, 159, 222-23
 Marx on, 7, 26, 85, 135-37
 Theory, 95
Egalitarianism, 15, 125-26, 134, 136, 221-23, 225
Elitism.
 Engels on, 200-209, 221
 Lenin on, xvi
Emancipation.
 Marx on, 44-45, 58, 63
Engels, Friedrich.
 Dilettantism, 114, 153-54, 165
 Life, 109-115, 123-27, 137, 140-41, 172-73, 181-82, 231-34, 238-39
 Lack of Philosophical Training, 110, 116
 Literary Criticism, 109-115
 Relation to Hegel, 146-54
 Relation to Marx, 107-108, 134-37, 141, 150-54, 164-66, 174-77, 180-81, 185, 187, 197, 211, 213-18, 224-26, 228-41
Engelsism, xiv-xv, xvii-xviii, 134-37, 141, 164-66, 169-70, 174-77, 197, 209, 211, 213-18, 224-26, 228-41
England.
 Engels on, 124, 126, 129-33, 162-63, 167-68, 170, 203
 Marx on, 54, 61-62, 65-66, 68-72, 76-79, 86, 99
 Socialist Party, 188-91
English Constitution.
 Engels on, 126
English Revolution.
 Engels on, 126
Enrages, 46
Epicurus, 5, 120
Epiphenomenology, 9
Epistemology.
 Engels on, 145, 152-54
 Marx on, 152-53
Equality.
 Political, 14-18
 Proudhon on, 18-19
 Social, 14-18
Essence.
 Engels on, 119, 126-27, 211, 213, 215-16
 Human, 20
 Marx on, 24, 30, 33-34, 37-40, 90, 211
Essence of Christianity, 212
Estrangement, 2, 4
Ethics.
 Marx on, 22, 25
 Social, 21

Ethnocentricism.
  Engels Inclination, 171, 197, 200-209
Eudamonism.
  Engels on, 217
  Marx on, 21-22, 24, 37
Europe.
  Engels on, 162-64, 187, 197, 200-204, 209
  Marx on, 61-62, 65-74, 76-80, 91-92, 94
Expropriation.
  Marx on, 31

Fabians, 183, 189, 191
Fenians.
  Marx on, 65
Feudalism.
  Engels on, 163, 204-208
  Marx on, 61-62, 65-66, 68-71
Feuerbach, Ludwig, xv, 6, 8-10, 20, 90
  Engels on, 116-18, 154, 174, 211-13
Fichte, J. G., 10, 212
"First Address of the General Council on the Franco-Prussian War," 55
First International, Working Men's Association, 53-55, 64-66, 186, 229
"Fortschritte der Sozialreform auf dem Kontinent," 125
Fourier, Charles, 117-18
France.
  Engels on, 126, 133, 163, 167-68, 170, 203
  Marx on, 54, 61-62, 66, 68-71, 99
  Socialist Party, 188-90
Franco-Austrian War (1859), 140
Franco-Russian Alliance, 169, 208
Franco-Prussian War.
  Engels on, 169-70, 193, 205
  Marx on, 55, 68, 140, 159
"Free Human Production," 2
Freedom.
  Engels on, 225-26
  Hess's idea of, 22
  Marx's idea of, 24-25
  Stirner's idea of, 20-21
French Revolution (1789), 14, 16-18, 43-47, 49, 61, 184-85
French Revolution (1848-50), 50-53, 185
Friedrich Engels.
  Meyer, Gustav, xiv

G*arantien der Harmonie und Freiheit,* 21, 125
Garibaldi, Giuseppi.
  Marx on, 66
General Strike, 196
Gens, 157-58, 170
German Social Democratic Party.
  Engels on, 185, 188-89, 193-95, 197, 206-209
  Marx on, 48
Germanic Mode of Production, 85, 91, 93-94, 96
Germany.
  Engels on, 126, 133, 162-70, 187, 197, 200, 203-209
  Marx on, 48-50, 54, 63-68, 99
Graeber, Friedrich, 112-14, 232
Gramsci Antonio, xiv-xv, 241
Great Men of the Exile, 234
Greco-Roman Mode of Production, 85, 93-94
Greeks.
  Marx on, 68-71
Grundriss, 6-7, 25-26, 33-34, 37, 45, 84, 86-89, 92-94, 136, 151, 166, 235, 241
Guerrilla Warfare.
  Engels on, 202
  Lenin on, xvi
  Marx on, 75
Guesde, Jules, 188-89

Hansemann, David, 50
Hardie, Keir, 190-91
Hegel, G. W. F., 2, 4, 6, 8-10, 20, 29-33, 36, 111-13, 118-20, 135-37, 142-43, 145, 212, 229
  Engels and, 146-54, 174
  Engels and Hegelian Right, 114-16
  Relation to Marx, 150-54
Heine, Heinrich, 112, 124-25
Heraclitus, 141, 149
Helmholtz, Hermann, 143
Hess, Moses, 21-22, 182
  Engels and, 123-24, 126, 196
  Idea of Communism, 22
  Idea of Freedom, 22-24
  Idea of Individualism, 23
Historical Inevitability.
  Engels on, 157-59, 161-62, 169-72, 174-77, 200, 209
  Marx on, xvi, 95-101
History.
  Engels on, 157-59, 161-62, 165, 197
  Engels and Unilinear View, 157-62, 169-72, 174-77, 181-82, 197, 200, 209
  Evolution of, xv
  History and Development, 86-101
  Laws of, 95
  Marx and Multilinear View, 85-87, 90, 92, 94-101, 175-77, 181-82
  Marx and Unilinear View, 87, 94, 95-101
History and Class Consciousness, 40
History of Philosophy, 114
Hobbes, Thomas, 8, 10
Humanism, xiii, 11
  Marx on, 25-26, 43, 58, 84-85, 90
  Engels on, 118, 211
Hungarian Revolution, 47, 67
Hutchinson, Thomas, 38
Hyndman, Henry, 189-90

Idea.
  Engels on, 119-20
Idealism, 2-3
  Engels on, 212-13
Imperialism.
  Engels on, 133, 191, 200-209
  Lenin on, xvi
  Marx on, 175-79
Independent Labor Party, 190
India.
  Engels on, 133-34, 191, 202
  Indian Village, 91-92, 96
  Marx on, 75-78
  Mode of Production, 85
  National Revolution, 76
Individualism.
  Marx's idea of, 20-21, 23
  Proudhon's idea of, 19
  Stirner's idea of, 20-21
Industrial Revolution.
  Engels on, 132
Industry.
  Engels on, 131-32, 135, 157, 159-62, 169-70, 200, 203, 218-19, 225
Ireland.
  Engels on, 203-204
  Marx on, 54, 65-66, 72-73
Italy.
  Engels on, 203
  Marx on, 49, 66-67, 72, 86, 168

Jacobin, 15-16, 18, 45, 47-48, 50, 53, 56, 58, 71, 73
Java, 191
Jew, 44
Jung, Herman, 67

Kant, I., 9, 111, 142, 153, 212
Kapital, 7, 25-26, 33-35, 73-74, 84, 86, 89, 94-95, 136, 151, 166, 229, 232, 234-38
Karl Marx.
  Berlin, Isaiah, xiv
  Mehring, Franz, xiv
Kautsky, Karl, xv, 183, 185, 188, 190, 202-203, 207, 238
Kleinstaaterei, 166, 168
Korsch, Karl, xiv-xv, 241
Kossuth, Louis, 47, 67
Kugelmann, Ludwig, 57, 67

Labor, 6-7, 87-89
  Engels on, 129, 135, 214, 216, 220-25
  Labor Movement, (Marx on), 67-68
  Marx on, 216
  Serf, 88
  Slave, 88
Lafargue, Paul & Laura, 185, 188-89, 206, 208, 238-39
Lamettrie, J. O., 10
Lassalle, Ferdinand, 66-67, 185
  Lassalleans, 183, 189, 239
Leibnitz, G. W., 142
Lenin, Nicolai, xiv-xv, 9, 54
  Communism of, xvi
"Letters from Wuppertal," 109, 112
Liberal Party, 190
Liberal Supernaturalism.
  Engels on, 113, 116
Liberation.
  Marx on, 45
Lincoln, Abraham, 67, 73
Locke, John, 8, 153
Logic (Hegel), 143, 151
London Dock Strike (1890), 191
Low Countries, 163
"Ludwig Feuerbach and the End of Classical German Philosophy," 9, 140, 152, 212
Lukács, György, xiv-xv, 40-41, 241
Luther, Martin, 166

Machinery.
  Engels on, 13, 157, 159-62
  Marx on, 35
Malthus, Robert, 90, 131
Manuscripts of 1844, 241
Mao, Tse-Tung, xiv
Marx, Karl.
  Career, 228-29, 234-36, 238, 240
  Doctoral Dissertation, 5
  Grundrisse, 6
  Relation to Engels, 107-108, 134-37, 141, 150-54, 164-66, 174-77, 180-81, 185, 187, 211, 213-18, 224-26, 228-41
  Relation to Hegel, 150-54
Marxism, xiv-xv, xvii-xviii, 141, 165-66, 174-77, 211, 213-18, 224-26, 228-41
Materialism.
  Ancient, 5, 144
  Engels on, 141, 145, 212, 215
  Marx's Form of, 8-11
  Mechanistic Materialism, 142, 145-46
  Monism, 145-46
Materialism and Empirico-Criticism, xvi, 9
Mazzini, Giuseppe.
  Marx on, 66, 72, 239
Mechanistic Materialism.
  Engels on, 159-62, 174-77, 183, 200, 209, 212, 215, 219, 222, 226, 237
  Marx on, xiii-xiv, 8
Mediation, 3
Medieval Society.
  Engels on, 129
  Marx on, 88-89, 93

Mehring, Franz, xiv
Messianism, 194, 197, 209
Metaphysical Materialism.
  Engels on, 116, 136-37, 140-54, 160-62, 174-77, 200
Metaphysics.
  Engels on, 115, 140-54
Mexico, 93-94
Meyer, Gustav, xiv
Middle Classes.
  German, 63
Military.
  Engels on, 159-60, 201-202, 236
Mir, 94-101, 163, 170-71, 191
Monogamy.
  Engels on, 157-59, 161
Morgan, Lewis Henry, 157
Motion.
  Engels on, 116, 143-45
  Mechanical, 143
Muenzer, Thomas, 166

Nationalism.
  Engels on, 112, 123, 204
  Lenin on, xvi
  Marx on, 49, 61-80
  National Liberation.
    Marx on, 50, 61-80
  National Revolution.
    Marx on, 61-62, 65, 72, 77, 79
    National State, 63-64
  Slavonic Nationalism.
    Engels on, 204
    Marx on, 62, 66
Nationalization.
  Engels on, 197
  Land, (Marx on), 71
Naturalism.
  Engels on, 117-18, 137, 211-13, 215
  Marx on, xiv-xv, 4, 11, 30, 38, 84-85, 90, 215, 237
Natural Rights, 14-18
Nature.
  Engels on, 116-17, 128, 141-54
  Hegel on, 146-48
  Human Nature, 2, 4
  Insensate Nature, 3-4
  Marx on, 1-11
  Nature as History, 4, 30
  Philosophy of, xiv-xv, 7-11, 145-46
  Sensate Nature, 1-2, 4
Necessity.
  Engels on, 118, 158-59, 161-62, 169-72, 174-77, 200, 209, 225-26
Need, 3
Negation.
  Engels on, 119-20
  Marx on, xvii, 120
Neve Rheinische Zeitung, 46-48, 51, 53, 63, 123
New American Encyclopedia, 140
New York Daily Tribune, 47, 75, 140, 165, 234-36, 238
North German Confederation, 168
North German Liberalism.
  Engels on, 111

Objectification.
  Marx on, 3-5, 30-31, 39, 216
  Engels on, 118, 216
Objective Spirit.
  Engels on, 114-15
Ontology.
  Marx on, 4-5
"On Authority," 220
"On the Jewish Question," 44-45, 90
Opium Wars.
  Engels on, 202
  Marx on, 75, 79, 234, 236

Ottoman Empire, 47, 61-62, 66, 68-71
"Outline of a Critique of Political Economy," 130, 225

Pan-Slavism.
Engels on, 187, 191, 204-205, 207-208
Marx on, 70, 171
Pantheism.
Engels on, 113, 137
Palmerston, Lord, 71
Paris Commune.
Engels on, 168, 170, 183, 193, 208
Marx on, 55-57, 73
Parliamentarianism.
Engels on, 183-85, 194-97, 208
Pauperism.
Engels on, 126, 136, 182, 196
Peasants.
Engels on, 167, 170-71, 194, 196-97
Lenin on, xvi
Marx on, xvii, 71-80
Peasant Revolution.
Marx on, 61-62, 72-73
Peasants and Guerrilla Warfare, 75
Persia.
Marx on, 75
Peru, 93-94
Petit Bourgeois.
Marx on, xvii
Phenomenology of Mind, 120
Philosophical Anthropology.
Engels on, 118-19, 211, 215-16
Marx on, xv, 7, 29-35, 43, 84-85, 90
Philosophical Notebooks, xvi
Philosophy.
Engels on, 120, 145, 153-54, 176, 237
Marx on, 120, 237
Philosophy of Culture, 29-35
Philosophy of History, 120
Philosophy of Nature (Hegel), 147-48
Philosophy of Science.
Engels on, 116, 137, 145-46, 153, 237
Marx on, 237
Physiocrats, 89
Pietism, 110, 112, 116, 146, 211, 218, 225, 231
Planning.
Engels on, 224-25
Poland.
Engels on, 203-204
Marx on, 49, 54, 65
Politics.
Political Life, 220
Proletarian, 185-87
Populists.
Engels on, 170-71
Positivism.
Engels on, 154, 163, 165, 173-77, 228, 237
Marx on, 85, 95-101
Social, xiii-xv, 163
Possibilists, 183, 188-90
Power.
Engels on, 218-19
Marx on, 25, 45-46, 53, 55, 64
Praxis.
Engels on, 119-20, 149, 183, 214
Marx on, xii, xvii, 1-2, 4-7, 39-40, 48, 58, 84, 88, 90, 135-36, 151-52, 174, 176, 182, 214
Principles of Communism, 225
Production.
Engels on, 134, 221-22
Proletarian.
Engels on Proletarian Revolution, 167-69, 171
Marx on Proletarian Revolution, 44, 51-52, 55, 61-64
Proletarian-Peasant Alliance, 71

Proletariat.
Engels on, 128, 130, 132-33, 164-71, 186, 194, 196-97, 205, 207, 209
Marx on, xvii, 44-46, 50-51, 54
Proletariat and Peasants, 71
Property.
Communal, 91-92
Engels on, 124, 128-30, 136, 157-59
Marx on, 15, 18, 20, 25, 136
Polis, 93
Private, 91-92
Proudhon, Pierre, 18-19, 36, 68, 194, 239
Prussia.
Engels on, 111, 167-69
Marx on, 49-50, 61-62, 65, 67-68
Puritanism, xiv-xvi
Engels on, 211, 225-26

Rationalism.
Engels on, 113, 115-16, 137
Reappropriation.
Engels on, 217
Marx on, 32-33, 39, 217
Reformation.
Engels on, 128
Marx on, 166-67
Reign of Terror, 15, 45-46, 50, 52
Religion and Philosophy in Germany, 124
Rent.
Engels on, 132
"Rent of Land," 73
"Retrograde Zeichen der Zeit," 110
Revisionism, xiv-xv
Engels on, 12, 183, 191, 195-97, 228, 240-41
Revolution.
Bourgeois, 14, 16
Engels on, 133-34, 182-85, 205-209, 218-19
Lenin on, xvi-xvii
Marx on, xvi-xvii, 43-58, 61-80
Proletarian, 14, 16
Russian, 98, 193, 205-206
Revolution and Counter-Revolution, 165
"Revolution in Permanence."
Engels on, 185
Marx on, 46, 50, 52-53
Revolution of 1848.
Marx on, xvii, 46-50
Engels on, 140, 183, 185
Ricardo, David, 36, 90
Robespierre, Maximilien, 14-17, 44-46, 49-50
Rome, 158
Rousseau, J. J., 38
Ruge, Arnold, 110, 123
Rumanian Village Communities, 93-94
Rumanians.
Engels on, 203
Russia.
Engels on, 162, 169-72, 187, 204-209
Marx on, xvii, 47-48, 54, 62-63, 65-66, 68-71, 90, 93-101, 166
Socialist Party, 188, 191-93
Russian Intelligentsia, xvii
Russo-Turkish War (1876), 71
Ryot.
Marx on, 76-77

Saint- Just, 17, 46
Saint-Simon, C. H., 125-26, 223, 225
Schelling, F. W. J.,
Engels on, 126, 229
"Schelling und die Offenbarung," 114-15
Schleiermacher, F. E. D., 113
Schmidt, C., 154, 224
Science.
Engels on, 128, 131, 137, 140-54, 237
Marx on, 237

"Second Address of the General Council on the Franco-Prussian War," 55-56
Second International Workingmen's Association.
Engels on, 183, 188-89, 196, 209
Self-Affirmation.
Engels on, 217
Marx on, 3-4, 33-34, 217
SePoy Mutiny.
Engels on, 202
Marx on, 75-76, 234-36
Serbians.
Engels on, 203-204
Marx on, 68-71
Slavic Mode of Production, 85, 91, 93-101
Slavonic Nationalities.
Engels on, 203-205
Marx on, 62, 66, 68-71
Village Community, 93-94
Slovaks.
Engels on, 203
Slovenes.
Engels on, 203
Smith, Adam, 36, 38, 90
Social Democratic Federation, 191
Sociales aus Rusland, 170
Socialism.
History, xv
Movement, 169, 193-94
Philosophic Basis of, 8, 154
Scientific, 200, 209, 226
Socialist Parties, 184, 193-94
Socialism: Utopian and Scientific, 140, 181, 233, 239
Society.
Engels on, 119, 126-27, 161, 174-77, 211, 220
Marx on, 23, 85, 94, 175-77
Society of Equals, 14
South German Liberalism.
Engels on, 111
Spain.
Marx on, 72-73, 75
Species Being.
Engels on, 116-19, 126-27, 137, 211-13, 215-16
Marx on, 3, 20, 23-24, 30, 33-34, 37-40, 58, 84, 90, 153, 211, 216
Spinoza, Baruch, 142
Stalin, Joseph, xiv-xvi, 228, 241
Starkenburg, H., 161
State.
Engels on, 118-19, 126-27, 157-58, 183-84, 186, 217, 219-20
Marx on, xv, 61, 63-64
Stirner, Max, 19-21
Strauss, D. F., 113
Structuralism.
Marx on, xv, 85-90, 94-95, 99-101, 166, 175-77, 215
Structural Relations, 85, 100-101
Subjectivity.
Philosophy of, 149, 152-53, 174-75, 215
Psychology of, 14-15, 228-41
Surplus Value.
Engels on, 136
Marx on, 136
Szemere, Bertalan, 67

Tactics.
Applied, 180-83, 185, 187
Theoretical, 180-82
Taiping Rebellion.
Marx on, 75
Technology.
Engels on, 125-26, 128-31, 134-35, 137, 154, 157, 159-62, 169-70, 172, 174, 176-77, 200, 203, 218-19, 225
Telegraph Fur Deutschland, 110
The Communist Manifesto, 136, 229, 234
The Condition of the Working Class in England, 109, 133, 236
The Ego and His Own, 20

The Eighteenth Brumaire of Louis Bonaparte (1852), 50, 52-53, 57, 229
The German Ideology, 9, 19, 39, 116-17, 136, 234
The History of Socialist Thought.
  Cole, G. D. H., xv
The Holy Family, 8-9, 38, 40, 136, 234
The Origin of the Family, Private Property and the State, 119, 157-60, 165, 170, 233, 239
"The Part Played by Labour in The Transition from Ape to Man," 213
The Peasant War in Germany, 165, 167, 196
The Secret Diplomatic History of The Eighteenth Century, 70
The Tragic Deception: Marx Contra Engels, xv
Theories of Surplus Value, 36, 89
"Theses on Feuerbach," 6, 10, 43, 213
Thiers, Adolphe, 56
"Third Address of the General Council in the Franco–Prussian War," 55-56
To the Finland Station.
  Wilson, Edmund, xv
Tories.
  Engels on, 127, 190
Totalitarianism, xvi
Totality.
  Marx on, 85-90, 94-95, 99-101, 166, 175-77, 215
"Toward the Critique of Hegel's Philosophy of Law," 44-45, 63, 90, 99
Trade.
  Engels on, 129
Trade Unions.
  Engels on, 133
  Marx on, 54
Transcendence.
  Marx on, xvii
Treitschke, Heinrich, 154
Tribalism.
  Marx on, 86
Trotsky, Leon, xiv

Ukrainians.
  Engels on, 203
Utility.
  Engels on, 132

Value.
  Engels on, 132, 136
  Marx on, 89, 136
Victor Emmanuel.
  Marx on, 66
Voluntarism.
  Lenin on, xvi
  Marx on, 47, 57

Wages.
  Engels on, 132
Wage Labor.
  Engels on, 130
  Marx on, 89
Wallachians.
  Marx on, 68-71
Weydemeyer, George, 72
Weitling, Wilhelm, 21-22, 124-25, 134
  Idea of Individualism, 23-24
  Idea of Freedom, 23-24
What Is Property? 18
Whigs.
  Engels on, 127
Wilson, Edmund, xv
Wischnewetsky, Florence, 188
Working Day.
  Marx on, 35

Young German Movement.
Engels on, 110, 112
Young Hegelians, 123

Zasoulich, Vera, 95, 99
Zemindar.
Marx on, 76
Zollverein, 167